# A Critical Introduction to Social Research

# A Critical Introduction to Social Research

## Second Edition

Matt Henn, Mark Weinstein and Nick Foard

Reprint 2023



First published 2006

Originally published in 2009

This South Asia edition published in 2010

**Sage Publications India Pvt Ltd**
Unit No. 323-333, Third Floor, F-Block
International Trade Tower
Nehru Place
New Delhi - 110 019, India

*Exclusively Distributed in South Asia by*

7/22, Ansari Road, Darya Ganj, New Delhi
Tel.: +91-11-4077 5252, 2327 3880
E-mail: orders@atlanticbooks.com
Web: www.atlanticbooks.com

Published by Sonia Kumar for Sage Publications India Pvt Ltd.

**ISBN:** 978-81-321-0578-7 (PB)

# CONTENTS

# PREFACE

This is the second edition of our book, and although there are certain features that we have added or updated, we still have the same particular audience in mind – those lone researchers who are specifically charged with conducting small-scale research and who have access to a very limited budget with which to carry it out. Such lone researchers might be students or new researchers. It seems to us that whether you are enrolled on an undergraduate or Masters course, starting out on your doctoral programme, or are asked to design and execute a one-off research project at work, there is a need for a book that sensitises you to the essentials of social research, and which helps you to design projects that are realistic, viable, and above all manageable. If you are someone who finds yourself in this position, may we first offer you our sympathies! Conducting a small-scale research project is a very demanding and challenging endeavour, and it can be extremely unnerving. But it can also be immensely rewarding to take ownership of such a project, to identify a research question that no one else has considered, and to design and execute a project that has your hallmark stamped all over it – regardless of all the angst that it may create for you along the way. Whatever your experience, we hope our book sheds some light into what's involved in the art and practice of research, and that it offers some insight into how to approach your research project.

The book is based on one of the modules taken from a Masters course in research methods that the three of us have taught for over a decade at Nottingham Trent University in the UK. The module has undergone significant change over this period, and we would like to thank all our students past and present for their (sometimes very frank) views and observations about its content and about our teaching approach. It was initially taught in a traditional classroom setting to Masters and PhD students from different academic disciplines as well as to non-academics in the research practitioner community, and then subsequently rewritten as a distance learning module. In doing so, we have spent considerable time reflecting upon how to engage students through the written word without the benefit of their having face-to-face discussions with tutors about research methods issues and their own research plans. Having invested such effort in the development of this distance learning course, we took little persuasion from colleagues at Sage to take the next step and try our hand at writing it up as a book. We hope that the book that you have in your hands is one that is accessible and instructive in equal measures.

Essentially, this book aims to assist you in becoming a more effective social researcher through a heightening of your research awareness. This contrasts with many other undergraduate research methods books which we feel tend to over-prioritise the design and application of specific techniques. Our book sets out to explore the principles of constructing research projects, the ethical and political issues in the design and conduct of the research process, and the relationship between qualitative and quantitative methods. It also offers a critical assessment of a range of different research techniques and their applications. The intention is to enable readers to explore the circumstances in which a method is most appropriately used, and to allow them to practise and apply the relevant techniques through a series of exercises and tasks.

Our experiences of teaching research methods to university students across numerous disciplines, and to non-academics from diverse backgrounds, has led us to write a book that places a specific emphasis on catering for readers with a variety of different aptitude levels. Given that this is the case, we have adopted an approach that will stretch and challenge the more experienced of you, while at the same time engaging others who are less familiar with some of the themes and concepts so that you can design and conduct projects in an informed and confident way. To this end we have tried to employ an interactive and participative style that we hope will appeal to all readers in a very practical manner. Thus the book contains numerous practical examples from our own research as well as from the research of others – this should help to contextualise the research issues discussed. Definition boxes are included to help you grapple with key concepts and themes, and with different research approaches and styles. And at the end of each chapter we have included a short research task which should give you an opportunity to practise a particular research approach or method, and reflect upon your experience in doing so. The only exception is Chapter 10 which does not include such a task but several activities, the outcomes to which will form the basis of a research proposal.

## The revised edition

We were delighted when colleagues at Sage asked us to revise the book only a year after the first edition appeared on the bookshelves. For us, it meant of course that students and researchers were finding value in our ideas, and this in itself was very satisfying. But to be completely honest, we also enjoyed the buzz that academics get from knowing that people like your work enough to go and seek it out!

Anyone who has seen the previous version of our book will notice that we have changed the title to, *A Critical Introduction to Social Research*. This is to reflect the critical focus of the text. We hope that it will continue to serve the needs of a variety of readers including postgraduate taught and PhD research students who are particularly interested in the appropriateness, reliability and validity of approaches and methods before deploying them in research projects. Although the title has changed, the broad thrust of the book remains the same – to provide guidance to those intending to become more effective social researchers through a heightening of research awareness.

All chapters of our book have been generally revised and expanded. However, we have also made a series of particular and major revisions, which are as follow:

- In Chapter 2 we have updated the sections on 'Feminism', and in doing so have taken into account recent debates and developments in this area. But we have also expanded this chapter to look at other areas of contention for critical social researchers, and we have included a dedicated section on emancipatory disability research.
- We have expanded the discussion of research designs open to the researcher in Chapter 3, and include substantial overviews of comparative design, experimental research design, cross-sectional design, longitudinal design, case study design, action research design, evaluation research design.
- Chapter 5 now includes a section on the secondary analysis of survey data, to reflect the increasing ease with which large survey data sets can be accessed by academic researchers and submitted to scrutiny in order to tackle new research problems.
- We have carried out a major reorganisation of Chapter 8, which considers the analysis of data, in particular to the section on qualitative data. Here we have made a distinction between three types of qualitative research: (1) theory-generating, exploratory research, (2) theory-driven, confirmatory research, and (3) research that is concerned with the latent meanings to be found in textual and visual data. The existing section on discourse analysis has been extended, including an overview of the work of Foucault. The discussion of the approaches open to researchers for the analysis of quantitative data now includes an extended section on the principles of multivariate analysis; while specific techniques are not described in detail, we provide an introduction to the concepts of statistical modelling, variance and prediction.
- We have incorporated online research methods and issues into existing chapters throughout the book. By adopting this approach, readers will be introduced to methodological issues which are specific to online research, while being reminded that many of the existing issues that are already discussed throughout the book remain relevant.
- In addition to the particular revisions and additions noted above, we have now provided a comprehensive glossary of key terms.

# ACKNOWLEDGEMENTS

We'd really like to thank colleagues at Sage for their continued faith in our work. And of course, the thoughtful comments from the reviewers were of immense value and very reassuring. We'd also like to extend a big thank you to all our past and present students for the very constructive feedback that they have offered to us over the years.

Matt would like to dedicate his contributions to the book to his Mum, to Jacob and Oliver, and to the memory of his Dad, for his love, his wisdom, and his gentleness.

Mark would like to thank Ann for her love, support, and encouragement.

Nick would like to thank Suzie for all the love and happiness she has brought him, and for her undying support. He would also like to thank his family for always being there for him, and to dedicate this book to the memory of his wonderful, loving mum, Maggie Foard.

**Matt Henn**
**Mark Weinstein**
**Nick Foard**

**Nottingham Trent University**

# INTRODUCTION

This book is concerned with introducing students and researchers to the ideas and issues that are associated with research practice. It assumes that the primary motivating force driving such people is the pursuit of knowledge – asking questions about some aspect of the social world that we are interested in, and collecting empirical evidence in an attempt to further our understanding of the matter.

But where do such questions come from? The questions may be theoretically informed. Put another way, they may be the result of our desire to test out – or challenge – existing explanations for issues that we are interested in. Alternatively, and at a more immediate level, the issues that may preoccupy the student or researcher may be policy oriented. They may originate in a concern that we have in our own day-to-day life. This may, perhaps, be a problem at work or in our local community.

Irrespective of where the questions come from, our task as researchers is to seek evidence to answer them. If we are to conclude that an existing theory is a credible one or that it is lacking in some respect, then we shall need to demonstrate that our conclusions are supported by evidence. Not to do so would lead others to dispute our claims about the explanatory power of the theory that we are examining. In the same way, an initiative that has been proposed to resolve an issue at work is likely only to be sanctioned if it can be demonstrated that it is likely to achieve the desired effect. Without evidence to indicate the feasibility and predicted impact of the plan, such support is not likely to be forthcoming.

So, what are the approaches that are available to the researcher to answer such questions? Social research is diverse. There is no unanimity on which methods best serve the purpose of answering questions about the social world. Indeed, there is significant disagreement among social researchers as to what should count as knowledge about a particular issue in the first place. In this book we shall address such issues – and others – by asking the questions:

- What is social research, and why do we conduct it?
- What are the different general positions that are taken concerning what is and what is not acceptable knowledge about the social world?
- What are the different general positions that are taken concerning what are and what are not acceptable methods for acquiring such knowledge? The primary

debate concerns the relative merits and weaknesses of quantitative and qualitative research styles. But to what extent is it possible to combine methods in a single research study?

- Can – and should – social research ever be objective and value-free?
- How can we ensure that our research methods are reliable?
- How do we attain validity in our research?
- How can we be assured that our research is ethically sound?
- What are the constraints that we face in carrying out our research study, and to what extent do these serve to shape the course of our research, and impact upon our findings?
- What are the possible consequences of our research project, and how might it affect the world around us – in particular the individuals, group, culture or organisation that we are studying?

It is the intention of this book to prepare people for their research, whether this is for a Masters dissertation or an academic or practitioner research project. By considering these and related questions, you will be in a much stronger position to reflect critically upon your intended research and, in doing so, to develop strategies for conducting your project that are more feasible, manageable and appropriate than if you had not read our book.

## Approach

The focus of the book involves examining the alleged dichotomy of research 'styles' (quantitative and qualitative) which permeates and tends to guide research practice. These research styles are set within their philosophical, political and practical contexts. The book considers different models through which research is conceptualised and operationalised, and covers problem formulation and the 'design' or 'logic' that underlies research studies. There is then a consideration of a range of methods for collecting and analysing different forms of data. Finally, there is a focus on issues in developing research proposals for dissertation approval and for applying to external funding bodies.

Throughout the book, there is an emphasis on the need to adopt a critical and reflexive approach to research. This is one in which the researcher is involved in a process of constant renegotiation of strategy, pays particular attention to the social, political and ethical contexts and consequences of the research, and is aware of the cultural assumptions that she or he brings to the research.

At the end of each chapter there is a research task for you to carry out. There are two key related objectives to these exercises. First, they should assist you in gaining a full appreciation of the ideas and issues covered in each chapter. Secondly, the awareness and sensitivity to methodological issues that you acquire should help you to develop research projects that are sophisticated, critical and reflexive.

The first chapter is concerned with introducing students and researchers to the ideas and issues that are associated with research practice. It assumes that the primary motivating force driving such people is the pursuit of knowledge – asking questions about some aspect of the social world that we are interested in, and collecting empirical evidence in an attempt to further our understanding of the matter. Yet there is little agreement about the status of different sources and forms of evidence, or of how to acquire it. As we shall see, the chief protagonists here are, on the one hand, social researchers who follow a broadly positivist approach in their work, claiming that the social world can be studied 'scientifically', where the aim is to uncover laws which explain human behaviour. On the other hand, a second interpretivist tradition suggests that we can only account for human behaviour if we are able to understand the motives and intentions that underpin human action. For some, the position that is taken here will largely determine the approach taken in the conduct of a research project. However, the chapter also considers the possibilities for combining different approaches and methods in the same research project through a process commonly referred to as 'triangulation'. Advocates of this multi-methods strategy would argue that this is helpful for researchers in seeking to reduce the impact of personal bias and maximise validity in research.

While positivism and interpretivism represent the two dominant research perspectives, there is also a third approach to social research that is broadly called critical social research. In Chapter 2 we shall look at the characteristics of a critical approach to social research by focusing on two significant contributions: those that come under the banners of *feminist methodology* and *emancipatory disability research*. We shall start by locating the case for critical social research within the tradition of critical research as developed by the Frankfurt School, before going on to examine the main features that distinguish both radical feminist and disability research approaches. Some of these, such as the appropriateness of emancipatory research goals and debates around objectivity and subjectivity, are common to both feminist and disability research. However, where debates among feminist researchers have tended to focus predominately on the appropriateness of particular methods and epistemological issues around the status of knowledge claims, emancipatory disability researchers have given greater attention to the distinction between emancipatory and participatory research approaches and issues of control within the research process. We shall also address some of the criticisms that have been levelled at emancipatory and critical social researchers and consider the general methodological implications that can be drawn from this debate.

In Chapter 3 we shall focus upon what is often considered to be a relatively practical aspect in research – *research design*. Typically, this is associated with the notion that there are various stages that research goes through, from taking a theory, focusing upon different aspects of it, devising clearly formulated and expressed research problems, designing appropriate research tools for collecting data, and then, having analysed the findings, drawing conclusions which are written up in a research report or academic paper. But readers are introduced to the notion that research design is much more than this. It is not a linear process, but rather it is cyclical and ongoing, or *iterative*. Furthermore, in designing a research project, researchers should consider the various constraints that may impinge upon social science investigations, and the role of values, politics and power in research.

All research raises ethical issues that have the potential to impact at *every* stage of the research process and within any research project. In Chapter 4 we shall consider the ways in which major ethical issues impinge upon research using quantitative methods such as survey and experimental research, as well as observation, ethnography and documentary research. We shall identify the principles that help to differentiate ethical research from unethical research, and consider some of the important debates that have taken place in recent years, such as that between the supporters and opponents of 'covert' research. In reviewing the ethical 'ground rules' that frame research inquiry, we shall also consider the new *Research Governance* paradigm introduced by the UK government in recent years. The use of information published in various formats on the Internet forms the basis of a discussion around ethical issues in online research, focusing in particular on the blurred distinction between categorisation of online and offline data. We shall also seek to address the key question that is posed when carrying out social research – do the ends (research findings) always justify the means? It is intended that the chapter will encourage readers to think about some of the problems that are inherent in studying human behaviour, to assess critically the ways in which other researchers have carried out their research, and to prepare them for any possible criticism of their own research in the future.

In Chapter 5 we shall examine what constitutes a document and how social researchers classify the different types of document that are used in the research process. We shall also look at the way in which different epistemologies impact on the use to which documents are put in the research process. This will be followed by a discussion of the general merits of documentary research before taking a more detailed look at the main documentary sources that are used. Attention will be brought to some general problems that arise when conducting documentary research. Within this chapter, official statistics are given special attention because of their wide but often controversial usage within the social sciences. The very substantial benefits of official statistics are discussed while drawing attention to a consideration of their weaknesses. Most importantly, we shall examine the claim that official statistics often employ unexamined assumptions about social life which social science researchers may inherit and reproduce in their studies if they do not guard against them. Finally, we look at other sources of quantitative data available for secondary analysis. We shall consider how data quality and validity must be evaluated, with particular attention to the issues which arise from using data created by others.

We focus on the main quantitative methods that are used in research – sample surveys and experiments – in Chapter 6. There is an explicit connection with many of the issues that are raised in Chapter 1, where the quantitative–qualitative debate is first encountered. The logic of quantitative research is set out – to *explain* social phenomena (why people behave in the way they do, or hold certain views and values) by reference to underlying *causes*. This emphasis on the search for causal connections between different phenomena (or variables) tends to steer researchers working within this tradition towards favouring highly structured research approaches and techniques such as experiments and questionnaire-based sample surveys. The chapter examines the use of both methods, some of their advantages and disadvantages, and the issues that arise by their use. Design issues and techniques in experiments and sample surveys are reviewed (types of method used, differing sampling strategies, and so on), together with an overview of the debate concerning the legitimacy of these quantitative methods within the social sciences. Taking account of the rapidly increasing use of Internet surveys, we consider some of the techniques available for conducting survey research online, paying attention to the advantages and limitations of this relatively new medium. Finally, there is a focus on the opinion polling method as an example of an application of the general sample survey method designed for uncovering peoples' political values and orientations. In particular, the chapter considers the role and effectiveness of political opinion polls at previous British electoral contests, in order to develop insights into the value of the sample survey method for researchers.

In Chapter 7 we shall look at the logic of qualitative research – to explore the meanings that people have of the world around them. This is a research approach that favours small-scale but detailed and intensive study of the lives of people as they are really lived. As a consequence, the researchers' objective in using this style of research is to construct an understanding of the social world from the point of view of those whom they are examining. This approach will be contrasted with the logic of quantitative research. The chapter will examine the use of different types of approach and method that are favoured by qualitative researchers to offer an overview of the defining characteristics of the qualitative approach – these include ethnography and participant observation as well as in-depth personal or group interviews. Special attention will also be given to the issues that researchers must consider when using a broadly qualitative research approach. Chiefly, these concern issues to do with validity, access, ethics and reflexivity. The chapter also offers a discussion of issues of identity, anonymity and communication in relation to conducting interviews and observation online.

Having conducted a research project and gathered the data, the researcher is left with the question: 'What do I do with this information to make sense of it, and how can I use it to address my research question?' We attempt to deal with this question in Chapter 8. The strategies and techniques that are used in the process of analysing data will be somewhat different, depending on whether one is dealing with information that is broadly quantitative or qualitative in nature. Nonetheless, two broad objectives must be met if the researcher is fully to exploit the data irrespective of whether it is quantitative or qualitative in nature – that of *data preparation* (to format the data, and reduce its scope and size) and *data analysis* (to abstract from it and draw attention to what is important). In this chapter, we will consider what approaches, strategies and techniques are available to the researcher in order to make best use of the research data. We introduce a range of techniques for tackling various research problems, using different types of data. We will identify a range of quantitative techniques used for the description and explanation of variables, and their relationships with one another, before addressing techniques for analysing textual, visual and discursive data using a qualitative approach. This chapter aims to introduce readers to the *essentials* of a variety of data analysis methods, and to enable readers to become familiar with the core principles of those methods. It is intended that readers will have a sufficient understanding of the most commonly adopted analytical techniques which will provide the foundation for further reading, and a selection of guided readings is provided at the end of the chapter. We also recognise that, particularly in small-scale projects, researchers will often make use of a *variety* of different types of data (both qualitative and quantitative) in the course of conducting a single research project, and that this requires them to analyse such data in tandem. In this chapter, we therefore consider strategies for integrating different approaches and techniques for analysing different types of data in order to generate meaningful, credible and insightful results.

A research report should present the outcome of your endeavours, demonstrate the validity of your research and its conclusions, and show why the research was worth doing. It should also make interesting reading. Research reports can be distinguished from other types of report which aim only to relay findings to readers – research reports seek to link these findings to a theoretical model, or to one or more empirically testable hypotheses. Chapter 9 will examine the way in which research findings can be used to address the research question under investigation within the chosen theoretical framework. Given that the presentation of such data is not something that comes naturally to most people, this chapter will look at a variety of writing strategies that are aimed at managing the process of writing, and also facilitate the development of a writing style that is concise and confident. Chapter 9 will also emphasise the importance of writing for your audience, whether that be an academic tutor, a funding body or an employer. While there is no single model of report writing that academics and practitioners would agree to follow, there is a conventionally agreed set of sections that researchers should always include and this will be examined in turn, paying particular attention to the importance of report structure and style. This chapter will also include clear guidance on the correct citation of references and discuss the various reasons for doing so.

Having considered the variety of approaches to research, their strengths, weaknesses and limits, the final chapter is concerned with how to get support for one's research plans – how to write a research proposal to gain a place on a PhD programme, get a research grant from an external research funding agency, or convince an employer to support a particular research project. Readers are introduced to the idea that a research proposal is not just a statement about the purposes of the research, how it is to be carried out, the resource implications of the proposed investigation, and a timescale for completion. It is also an *argument*. Through the proposal, the researcher is presenting a case, in which the intention is to convince others of the general merits and feasibility of the proposed study. In this chapter there is an overview of the criteria that are commonly used to assess the merits of research proposals. They need to provide a clear understanding for the reader of how to approach the development of the proposal, and how to persuade both specialist and non-specialist members of any review committee that the proposed activity is sound and worthy of support under their criteria on the selection of projects. Finally, there is a step-by-step guide on how to write a research proposal. This draws upon examples from a successful application that won a grant from an external research funding agency. Throughout, attention is paid to the similarities and differences of research proposals that are developed for broadly qualitative and quantitative research studies.

# ONE

# What is Social Research?

- To introduce readers to alternative definitions of social research and key terms
- To place social research within the context of a pursuit of knowledge
- To introduce readers to two traditionally opposed approaches to the pursuit of knowledge: positivism and interpretivism
- To introduce readers to the main features of qualitative and quantitative approaches to research
- To highlight the distinctions between qualitative and quantitative approaches
- To discuss the potential for combining qualitative and quantitative approaches

- **Introduction**
- **Problems of knowledge**
- **Combining methods**
- **Reflection**
- **Summary**
- **Chapter research task**
- **Recommended reading**

## Introduction

Social research may be carried out for a variety of reasons. For students and university academics, social research is conducted in order to extend our knowledge about some aspect of social life that we are interested in – whether our field is in business studies, humanities or one of the social sciences. Typically, we are interested in either testing the appropriateness of existing theories which seek to account for the behaviour we are studying, or in developing new insights – constructing new theories – to help build up our understanding of the processes behind this behaviour. We may, for instance, ask why certain people become addicted to gambling, in order to contribute to our more general understanding about psychological compulsion. Or, as part of a study into the broader phenomenon of New Politics, we might examine why it is that anti-roads protestors take part in direct action to pursue their environmental concerns, rather than in more conventional forms of political activity, such as writing to a member of parliament.

For research practitioners, social research is usually carried out in order to inform decisions about which policies or initiatives might be most usefully implemented to solve everyday issues and problems, or to evaluate the effectiveness of such policies in meeting the objectives of those who originally instigated them. An example of such applied research may include an investigation into the feasibility of introducing CCTV (closed-circuit television) cameras into a shoppers' car-parking area in which there has recently been a spate of car break-ins and thefts. What do the police think about the proposed measures as a means of tackling crime? How much confidence do users of the car park have in the initiative for improving general security and safety? How much demand is there for such an initiative from local shopkeepers and traders? And how will local residents, who may have concerns about the invasion of their privacy that the surveillance equipment represents, view the introduction of CCTV? And what about the effectiveness of the introduction of CCTV? Research can be conducted to evaluate the impact of the surveillance system on car crime, to measure changes in car park users' 'fear of crime', and to assess the impact on the financial well-being of the local shopkeepers.

For action researchers, social research studies are likely to be initiated in order to solve an ongoing problem within an organisational setting or a particular workplace. For example, what can account for persistently high levels of absenteeism within a particular organisation? To what extent is occupational stress associated with the issue (and, indeed, what might be the source(s) of this problem)? And what measures might be introduced to alleviate the problem? Or the research may be based at a particular school in which there have been high rates of indiscipline and exclusions – what steps might the school leadership take to overcome these problems?

All of these styles of research have something that binds them together – they are all based upon the pursuit of information-gathering to answer questions about some aspect of social life.

## Defining social research

But what does social research actually entail? This is not an easy question to answer. At one level, it is social, and as such the focus of the research is upon human behaviour. Whether we are investigating juvenile crime, why men choose to father children, the political loyalties of first-time voters, an organisation's decision to pursue a particular marketing strategy, or the experiences of the 'old–elderly' in residential care, we are examining human behaviour and the relationships with other human beings, groups, (sub)cultures and organisations.

As such, social research can be contrasted with the natural sciences – physics, chemistry and biology. The distinction is not always obvious, however, and it is possible to find areas of research that straddle both the social world and the natural sciences. For instance, much *experimental psychology* that is concerned with animal behaviour is also *biological* in nature. Nonetheless, it is generally accepted that when it comes to the focus of research, the activities of social researchers differ from those working within the natural sciences.

However, the difference between the social sciences and the natural sciences is not so clear when it comes to the question of how we actually conduct our research. This is the subject of considerable debate, and some of this centres on the question of methodology (see Definition 1.1). On the one hand, there are social researchers who would argue that when undertaking research projects, we should borrow approaches, designs and methods that are commonly used within the natural sciences – such as experiments and measurement. Others would argue that the social world is different from the natural world, and if it is to be investigated effectively social research needs to design its own approaches, designs and methods, which are more relevant and fit for purpose. This is a debate that we shall return to presently in this chapter.

## Definition 1.1 Method and methodology

It is important to note the distinction between method and methodology. *Method* refers to the range of techniques that are available to us to collect evidence about the social world. *Methodology*, however, concerns the research strategy as a whole, including, as Seale (1998, p.3) notes, 'the political, theoretical and philosophical implications of making choices of method when doing research'. To this we might add the need to consider the ethical implications and consequences of our research, negotiating access to the field, and the role of values – both those of the author and those who have the power to impose some control over the research agenda, such as sponsors of research.

While it is difficult to define precisely what social research actually is, there are certain aspects of the notion 'research' upon which we can largely agree. The first of these is that research is not an arbitrary activity, but follows certain rules and procedures. There are many types of research method available; some of those in common usage include, for instance, social surveys, experiments, observations and in-depth interviews. Furthermore, we are interested in generating information of sorts, either to develop further insights into an area – to explain or explore a particular phenomenon – or to solve a problem, perhaps at work or in our local community. Research therefore consists of a means – method – and an end – knowledge.

Two important aspects of research that are not so readily agreed upon, however, are:

- what counts as *valid* knowledge; and
- how should we acquire that knowledge?

## Problems of knowledge

There are two broadly divergent views about the nature of knowledge, or what we call competing paradigms (see Definition 1.2), which we can group as:

- a positivist paradigm (most often associated with quantitative research strategies); and
- an interpretive paradigm (usually associated with qualitative research strategies).

The distinction between positivism and interpretivism as two polar opposites is somewhat artificial, and you will come across a great many other '-isms' which fall somewhere within the spectrum which spans the two: empiricism, realism, relativism, social constructionism, idealism, postmodernism – the list is extensive. The positivist and interpretivist paradigms can, however, be said to have been enormously influential in the development of quantitative and qualitative approaches to social research.

### Definition 1.2 Paradigm

According to Bryman (1988, p.4), a paradigm is 'a cluster of beliefs and dictates which for scientists in a particular discipline influence what should be studied, how research should be done, how results should be interpreted, and so on'. Essentially, then, a paradigm is a set of assumptions about how the issue of concern to the researcher should be studied.

There are different styles of research (which are linked to different philosophical or world views that we hold) as well as different actual methods and techniques for collecting information (or data). For some of us, the method(s) and technique(s) we choose will largely be determined by our understanding of what constitutes acceptable knowledge, or what is termed our epistemological position (Definition 1.3). As Bryman (1989, p.248) states, the study of society:

> exhibits contrasting paradigms about the nature of social reality and about what is acceptable knowledge concerning that reality. In this way, the distinction between quantitative and qualitative research is not simply a matter of different approaches to the research process, each with its own cluster of research methods ... but it concerns antagonistic views about more fundamental issues to do with the nature of one's subject matter.

## Definition 1.3 Epistemology

Epistemology is a crucial philosophical concept for social scientists, which considers questions to do with the theory of knowledge. Essentially, the two positions of positivism and interpretivism that are outlined here and in the following pages hold contrasting epistemologies. They differ in terms of their views about the status of different claims to knowledge and about how to judge knowledge claims.

### The positivist approach

Very broadly speaking, there is one particular view of how research should be conducted that suggests that we should carry out research in the social sciences in ways that are similar to the methods within the natural sciences (physics, chemistry and biology). This is often called the positivist or 'scientific' approach. A consideration of the historical roots of positivism takes us back to the Enlightenment period of the eighteenth century. Up to this point, faith in God had provided the generally accepted reasoning behind our existence and the way the world was. The world in which we lived was a matter of divine creation, and many explanations rested on a notion that things occurred because of God's will. Industrial development led to a shift in the relative position between humans and the natural world: industrialisation gave us the means to exert control over the natural world. This gave rise to the emergence of science, which challenged previous, theologically based explanations of the social order. Rather, science sought to explain the world by developing general laws. The natural world came to be understood by studying what could be observed as facts. As such, metaphysical notions of explanation were disregarded. This idea, as applied to the social world, can be traced back to the work of nineteenth-century philosopher August Comte (1798–1857), in his work *The Positive Philosophy* (Comte 1974). While the development of positivism has travelled a long and winding path, much of its essence can still be found in Comte's original writings.

Comte was very much concerned with progress in terms of finding the 'truth' about the social world. He regarded the scientific world as having achieved this goal in its application of natural laws based on observable facts. Such an approach to knowledge had superseded previous theological and metaphysical attempts at explanation: science was not concerned with divine or abstract explanations, but concrete facts based on empirical observations. These ideas were developed in the early part of the twentieth century, in particular through the work of a group of philosophers known as the Vienna Circle, in what was to become known as *logical positivism*.

Logical positivism took a stance which entirely rejected the metaphysical. Indeed, metaphysics should be:

> written off as nonsense. The term 'nonsense' was used here not merely to express strong disagreement or disapproval, but as an exact description of metaphysical statements, something that followed from a 'logical analysis of language'. It was thought that all genuine questions must be capable of scientific treatment, and all genuine knowledge part of a single system of science. (Hanfling 1981, p.2)

This suggestion that questions should be open to investigation through scientific treatment necessitated the development of demarcation criteria. These criteria enabled science and non-science (i.e. metaphysics) to be distinguished, thereby laying down rules as to what could and what could not contribute to valid knowledge. Phenomena that could be directly observed, and articulated, would lead to the advancement of social knowledge; abstract phenomena, such as inner-meanings, had no place in a scientific treatment of the social world. Logical positivism also took on an inductive approach – that is, phenomena are first observed, and from these observations, theories are developed. Logical positivism, then, continues by a process of verification: more observations are made of similar phenomena in order to develop the theory further so it eventually becomes a law which can be applied to all similar social phenomena.

This approach found its critics, most notably Karl Popper (1902–94). For Popper (1959, 1972), the inductive, verificationalist approach of logical positivism was fundamentally flawed, since in seeking to continually verify established theories, he felt that knowledge would not progress. He also saw the possibility that there would always be another situation, yet to be witnessed, that does not work according to the corresponding law, and so laws based on induction are based on assumptions. For example, if we wanted to develop a theory about why some workers perform better in their jobs than others, we may make a number of observations in the workplace that suggest that job satisfaction is linked to performance. Repeated observations in ten different workplaces would then concentrate on whether people who are satisfied in their jobs are outperforming those who are not. The question is, at what point do we stop trying to verify our theory? After ten observations, or 20 or 50? Whenever we stop, there will always be the possibility that we could have continued and found an example of people who were not satisfied outperforming those who were. Also, in pursuing this line of investigation, we are not exploring other possibilities, such as pay or desire to get promoted, and so forth. In Popper's view, a solution to both of these problems lies not in attempting to verify what we already know, but in trying to falsify it. By adopting this approach, theories are put to the test against newly collected data. If the data refute the theory, then we have reason to doubt the theory's usefulness in general application. In doing this, we continually challenge established theory, and inevitably make progress in our pursuit of knowledge. This idea lays the groundwork for many of the characteristics of Popper's approach, and what is often regarded as the foundation for the contemporary positivist paradigm.

The first characteristic of positivism, which has been a central element of the paradigm throughout its many manifestations, is that social phenomena can be explained by observing cause and effect. This is something which has been borrowed directly from the natural sciences, for example in the famous story of Newton's discovery of gravity: the cause of gravity leads to the effect of an apple, when unsupported, falling to the ground. In positivist social research, we seek to identify similar causal relationships, for example what causes some workers to perform better in their jobs than others.

Typically, this approach aims to test an existing theory by establishing a hypothesis (employee satisfaction at work and performance are positively related), and then collecting data to assess how appropriate the initial theory (as expressed in the hypothesis) actually is. Popper called this research approach the hypothetico-deductive method. It is a *theory-then-research* approach, meaning that our research question and strategy is guided by an *a priori* theoretical proposition. Data are collected so that the initial theory can be tested. This suggests that at the outset of the project, the researcher knows what the issues are that need to be examined, and what questions or hypotheses need to be addressed through the research. This theory-then-research approach is discussed in more detail in Chapter 3.

Shifting from an inductive to the hypothetico-deductive method also leads to two other characteristics of the positivist approach, as presented by Popper. First, it is concerned with applying the general (theory) to the specific (case). Secondly, the demarcation criteria become refined so that valid inquiry is no longer governed simply by what can be observed, but by what is testable So, in looking at employee performance at work, we should focus on issues such as pay, skill levels, training opportunities, degree of democracy in the workplace, whether trades are unionised, local unemployment rates, and so on. All these phenomena are tangible and can be 'scientifically' measured. They can also be framed in terms of hypotheses: for example, those with more training opportunities will perform better in their jobs. Attempting to look beyond these measurable phenomena, at things like people's motivations, their belief systems, their consciousness, and so on, amounts to no more than meaningless speculation because these are things that cannot be easily (let alone precisely!) measured, or therefore tested.

In this search for precision, this approach favours quantitative measuring instruments, including experiments, questionnaire surveys and content analysis. The research will be highly structured, typically large-scale and statistically based.

The logic of a positivist research design, then, is that:

- we seek to identify processes of cause and effect to explain phenomena, and to test theory;
- knowledge should be based on what can be tested by observation of tangible evidence; and
- researchers should use the scientific method, which emphasises control, standardisation and objectivity.

The implications are that:

- the research design should be highly structured;
- methods should be reliable; and
- the research design will aim to generate large-scale, statistically based studies.

## Interpretivism

Throughout this book we shall come across many examples of instances where social researchers disagree on important aspects of methodology and methods. Many of these can be traced back to a difference of opinion on epistemology. For some, positivism offers a useful approach to the pursuit of knowledge in that it is considered to be scientific, a characteristic which is often associated with rigour, precision and reliability. Positivists' empirical and objective techniques of inquiry enable them to support their claims to knowledge as reliable facts. To others, however, the complexities of the social world demand an altogether different approach, which acknowledges those qualities peculiar to the human consciousness:

> Because sociologists are human too, we can put ourselves in the place of others, appreciate the structural circumstances in which they find themselves, take account of their goals, and thereby *understand* their actions. This is what distinguishes a social science from a natural science. Daffodils don't *choose* to open their leaves and apples don't *decide* to fall from trees. Natural scientists therefore don't have to be like daffodils or apples to explain their behaviour. (Jones 1993, pp.67–8, original emphases)

This notion of understanding is often referred to as *Verstehen* (literally 'to understand'). It is based on a tradition that has its roots in the writings of figures such as Max Weber (1864–1930), who argued that in order to increase our knowledge of the social world, we must seek to understand it from the points of view of the people we are studying, rather than explaining human action by means of cause and effect (Weber 1949). From this perspective, understanding human behaviour and the intentions behind it demands a degree of empathy with our subjects, whereas explaining their behaviour as the result of some external cause does not (von Wright 1993).

Interpretivist researchers are keen to reinforce this distinction between the natural and social sciences, suggesting that unlike, say, the molecular structure of ice, which changes when heat is applied to it, we human beings do not passively respond to what is going on around us. Instead, we have the capacity to think through different courses of action, and respond (or not, as the case may be) on the basis of our interpretations and ideas. So, human action can only be understood by relating it to the conscious intentions, motives and purposes, and ultimately the values of the agent who performs it.

This interpretive paradigm is associated with unstructured qualitative methods, including *participant observation* studies and *in-depth interviews*.

The *a priori* approach of positivism suits quantitative methods since their use of predetermined measures can easily reflect the specific hypotheses of the researcher. The desire to understand human action from the perspective of our participants in an interpretivist approach, however, makes such predetermined measures unsuitable. Emphasis is placed on allowing the participants to provide an account of their world in their own words. Language is considered a tool with which we make meanings, and so in order to empathise with participants, it is important to allow their meanings to be expressed in the way they normally would be through their language.

Through piecing together an understanding, we eventually build (not test) theory. This analytic–inductive method is therefore a *research-then-theory* approach, in which we start with a relatively broad research question (rather than a prespecified hypothesis), and in the course of collecting our data, gradually develop our understanding of the issue. The research-then-theory approach and analytic induction are discussed in more detail in Chapter 3.

Unlike positivism, the interpretivist approach assumes that human behaviour is not determined by external factors and processes that researchers can measure, but instead is shaped by the meanings people have of the world. So employees, for instance, will not automatically improve their performance at work when offered a pay rise, and they will certainly not all respond in a uniform way. Instead, they will carefully consider the pay rise, and a whole host of other issues and what these mean to them, before deciding how to respond. Such specific and unique issues might include their personal and collective relations with the employers, the history of industrial relations in their workplace, whether in their experience the manager is trying to bribe them, and so on.

These meanings and interpretations are difficult to measure in a precise and scientific way, and they will certainly differ from one firm to another. So the researcher must use more qualitative methods and personal involvement to gain an understanding of how people interpret the world around them, and how this informs their action. The research will therefore tend to be small-scale and intensive. It will also usually be flexible and relatively unstructured, and based upon detailed descriptions (rather than statistics) of what is seen and heard.

The logic of such an interpretive research design is not to explain why something happens, but to explore or build up an understanding of something of which we have little or no knowledge. Through piecing together such an understanding, we eventually build up a theory.

The implications are therefore that:

- the research design should be flexible and unstructured;
- methods should be valid; and
- the research design will generate small-scale and intensive data, using insider accounts and based on descriptions of what is seen and what is heard.

The key contrasting features of the two epistemological positions described so far are set out in Table 1.1.

Table 1.1 The positivist/interpretivist divide

| *Positivism* | *Interpretivism* |
|---|---|
| 1. Knowledge is based on phenomena that are directly observable (phenomenalism) | 1. Knowledge is based on understanding interpretations and meanings that are not directly observable |
| 2. The social world should be researched using the principles of natural science (such as experiments). Such a shared approach is often referred to as the unity of scientific method | 2. The social world should be studied in its natural state (using participant observation and in-depth interviews) to understand naturally occurring behaviour |
| 3. There is a stress on reliability and generalisability | 3. There is a stress on validity |
| 4. Explanation is achieved through the formulation of causal laws or law-like generalisations (nomothetic approach) | 4. Explanation is achieved through descriptions of social meanings/reasons and other dispositions to action (idiographic approach) |
| 5. There is use of the hypothetico-deductive method, in which there is an emphasis on testing given theory | 5. There is use of the analytic–inductive method, in which theory is generated from the data |
| 6. Methods imply researcher/respondent detachment in the objective collection of data | 6. Methods imply insider approach – participation in life and culture of respondent/closeness of respondent and researcher in the joint construction of subjective data |
| 7. Analysis is based on the statistical testing of given theories | 7. Analysis is based on the verbal description and observation of actions and situations from which theory evolves |

## Critical social research

A third critical-emancipatory position can be identified within the social sciences which suggests that to know the social world, researchers need to take account of the historical, social and political contexts which constrain human thought and human action. Such researchers are concerned with understanding how underlying social structures have historically served to oppress particularly the working class, women and ethnic minority groups.

Ultimately, such an approach has emancipatory goals and claims empowerment for specific oppressed groups. The purposes of the research therefore are:

- to expose inequalities, malpractices, injustices, and exploitation;
- to give a voice to these excluded and marginalised groups; and
- to help explain generalised oppression in order to precipitate social change.

As Fay (1993, p.34) explains: 'To have the practical force it requires, critical theory must become an enabling, motivating resource for its audience – it must, in short, empower them. This empowerment has emancipation as its goal.'

As we shall see, critical social researchers are likely to adopt a flexible approach in their use of research methods, although they are likely to use these methods in particular ways that they consider to be appropriate for realising the emancipatory aims of their research. Indeed, some researchers have argued for a specifically feminist methodology, which approaches the research process in a way that is very different from conventional styles of social research.

There is a debate between those who advocate a model of social science research whereby the aim is to generate *knowledge*, and those who conduct politically committed research in order to pursue a political agenda. For instance, Hammersley (1995, p.x) has stated that: 'I believe their [critical social researchers'] proposals that research should serve political goals directly represents an abandonment of the obligations of the researcher.'

In response, Humphries (1997, 2.6) claims that 'all research is inevitably political, since it represents the interests of particular (usually powerful, usually white male) groups'.

According to such a view, no research can ever be entirely objective or value-free. Such researchers seek to promote agendas that are at best 'masked' by conventional research and are often suppressed in various ways. This epistemological position will not be developed further in this chapter, but will be referred to throughout the book as a whole, and in particular in Chapter 2.

## The relationship between epistemology, methodology and methods

We have already seen that there exist different epistemological perspectives, and that these reflect a number of assumptions about the social world. These assumptions are often referred to as ontology, so, for example, a positivist researcher might view the social world as an objective reality which exists regardless of how we interpret it. This ontological perspective informs an epistemological perspective that suggests that in order to know something of this world, we merely have to observe it from an objective point of view. An interpretivist might view the world as a subjective reality which is an accumulation of our experiences and the meanings we associate with them. In order to know something of *this* world, we must adopt an epistemological perspective which allows us to understand these subjective meanings.

So ontology is a set of assumptions about what the world *is*, and epistemology is a way of knowing about that world which reflects these assumptions. The way in which our ontological perspective feeds into our epistemological perspective is further reflected in our methodological approach. As noted in Definition 1.1, methodology concerns a wide-ranging number of considerations based upon our philosophical perspective as well as practical issues. Based upon this argument, it follows that epistemology should inform methodology, which in turn would inform methods. This relationship sees our ontological perspective at the foundation of our approach to research, with our methods being arrived at after a process of consideration of our epistemological position and our chosen methodology. This relationship is illustrated in Figure 1.1.

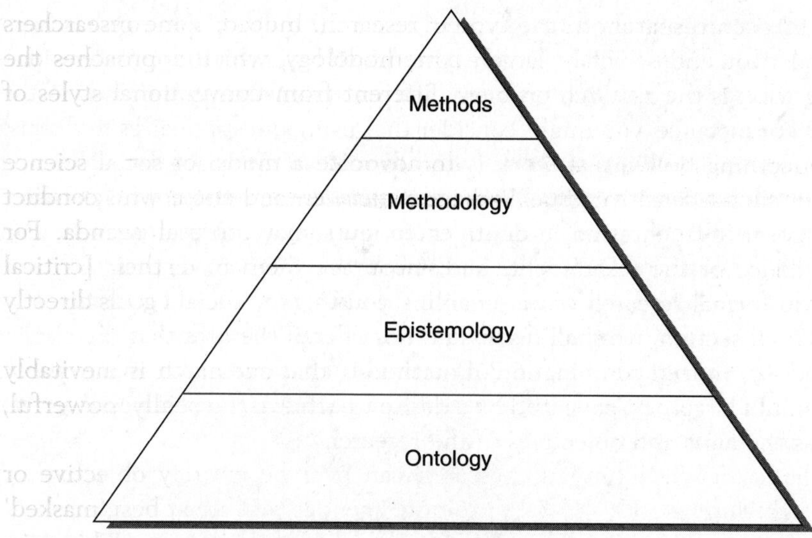


Figure 1.1 The relationship between theory and method

This suggests that our choice of methods will ultimately be determined by our philosophical perspective, therefore meaning that compromise on methods reflects a shift in our philosophical outlook on the world. As we shall see in the next section, though, this view can be challenged, and the rewards for doing so can be highly advantageous.

## Combining methods

So, we have seen that for some, the type of method to be used for research is largely determined by one's commitment to a particular epistemological position. This, then, 'assumes a correspondence between epistemological position and research method' (Bryman 1988, p.118). Most commonly, this will involve adherence either to a positivist–quantitative style or to an interpretivist–qualitative style of research, or, as we have seen, a critical social research approach.

This approach to the use of methods in research is not without its critics, however. Increasingly, social researchers are inclined to adopt more flexible approaches to research methods in their studies. As Bryman (1989, p.255) states:

> Each design and method should be taken on its merits as a means of facilitating (or obscuring) the understanding of particular research problems, and that a fetishistic espousal of favoured designs or methods and an excessive preoccupation with their epistemological underpinnings can only stand in the way of developing such an understanding.

For such chosen researchers, the type of research method (or combination of methods) you choose will be largely determined by pragmatic considerations, including what is the research problem, and what constraints are faced in the research? For instance, you might consider that using questionnaires to discuss issues concerning bullying at work is too formal an approach for collecting data about such a sensitive issue. Perhaps a more empathetic approach, using personal contact (such as an in-depth interview), may more effectively gain the confidence of the respondents and encourage them to discuss the issue frankly – in formal research terms, enabling you to gain 'social access'.

In this final section, we shall discuss in more detail the idea that the choice of method – or indeed combination of methods – that one makes in a research project should largely be governed by a desire to achieve the best possible data to address the aims and objectives of the research.

## Multi-strategy research

Combining methods, or *employing triangulation*, in a single research project is a strategy that is not without its problems. However, it is increasingly advocated on the grounds that it helps to facilitate a more valid and holistic picture of society than that which could be acquired by remaining true to only one set of methods (Definition 1.4).

### Definition 1.4 Multi-strategy research

Many social researchers use 'multiple strategies of field research in order to overcome the problems that stem from studies relying upon a single theory, single method, single set of data and single investigator' (Burgess 1984, p.144). This approach is frequently referred to as triangulation. It suggests that research conclusions that are derived from converging evidence – using a variety of different research methods – are likely to be more credible than research findings which are based on only one source of evidence. As Denzin and Lincoln (1998b, p.4) claim: 'The combination of multiple methods, empirical materials, perspectives and observers in a single study is best understood, then, as a strategy that adds rigor, breadth, and depth to any investigation.'

Classifying an approach as quantitative or qualitative does not mean that once an approach has been selected, the researcher may not move from the methods normally associated with that style. Each approach has its strengths and weaknesses and each is particularly suitable for a particular context. The approach adopted and the methods of data collection selected will depend on the nature of the inquiry and type of information required.

All the time, however, we have at the forefront of our minds that for some topics, our methods are context-specific. That is, that some methods really will not work by themselves in some situations. For instance, using a questionnaire survey to investigate why some young people feel alienated from the political system may not work all that effectively by itself – questionnaires may tell you the numbers of young people who are disengaged, but not necessarily why they *feel* this way. Alternatively, unstructured interviews are unlikely to give you precise measurements of the relationship between educational attainment and political alienation, neither will they necessarily be generalisable, or reliable, and they may even be accused of producing subjective (or anecdotal) accounts.

## Why combine methods?

One obvious advantage of employing a combined methods or multi-strategy approach in your research is that it helps to compensate for the fact that there is no consensus in research. According to Denzin (2009, p.298):

> Each research method implies a different line of action toward reality – and hence each will reveal different aspects of it, as much as a kaleidoscope, depending on the angle at which it is held, will reveal different colors and configurations of objects to the viewer. Methods are like the kaleidoscope: depending on how they are approached, held, and acted toward, different observations will be revealed.

As Brewer and Hunter (1989, p.17) note, mixing methods is all about trying to attain validity in research:

> Triangulated measurement tries to pinpoint the values of a phenomenon more accurately by sighting in on it from different methodological viewpoints ... when two reliable instruments yield conflicting results, then the validity of each is cast into doubt. When the findings of different methods agree, we are more confident.

The logic of multi-strategy research is to try to overcome any deficiencies that may derive from a dependence upon any one particular (single) method, 'to attack a research problem with an arsenal of methods that have non-overlapping weaknesses in addition to their complementary strengths' (Brewer and Hunter 1989, p.17). Methods are combined not only to gain their individual strengths, but also to compensate for the particular faults and limitations of any single method.

Another reason for combining approaches using triangulation is to overcome bias in research. A key point to note about the limitations of being locked into only one research perspective and strategy is that all researchers bring to the study their own interpretations of how the research should be structured and interpreted, and to an extent, these interpretations are unique. This unique perspective is likely to influence the people observed, the questions asked, and ultimately the results themselves:

> Triangulation, or the use of multiple methods, is a plan of action that will raise sociologists above the personal biases that stem from single methodologies. (Denzin 2009, p.300)

The third key advantage for adopting a multi-strategy approach in your research is that it is likely to assist us in gaining a complete overview of the matter under investigation. According to Burgess (1982, p.163), triangulation, like the kaleidoscope, can help to provide a holistic view of the area under study: 'Different methods can be used, and different data collected, in order to address a variety of theoretical and substantive problems.'

In a study by Henn et al. (1997) on the reaction of grassroots members of the British Labour Party to organisational and policy changes initiated by the party leadership, the researchers combined quantitative questionnaire data with qualitative focus group data. From the questionnaire results, the researchers found that party members seemed to give overwhelming support to the party leader, Tony Blair. Over three-quarters (78%) stated that he had had a positive impact on the party's fortunes, a further 88% claimed that he was a potential 'election winner', and 76% referred to him as a 'strong leader'. However, the data from the focus groups helped to clarify and contextualise the responses of the party members to Tony Blair's 'New Labour' project by confirming their overall suspicion of the modernisation process initiated by the party leadership. A typical reaction expressed by one party activist that met with support among most others participating in the various focus groups was that: 'I don't necessarily agree with everything Tony Blair says or does, but if it means defeating the Tories then I'm all for it' (Henn et al. 1997, p.506).

The multi-strategy research approach therefore enables (and encourages) the researcher to investigate a particular research area from a variety of different angles and perspectives, focusing on different questions and issues, collecting different types of data, analysing these data using different techniques, and interpreting the results from a variety of different positions. In this way, it is argued, no stone will be left unturned – all possible dimensions of the research field will be examined, and all possible meaning extracted from the data. As a consequence, by the end of the project, a thorough and comprehensive research study will have been completed.

So, should alternative research perspectives be seen as inherently dichotomous? Laurie and Sullivan (1990) examine some of the questions raised by the debate on using different methods in the same study. They conclude that: 'the tendency to see qualitative and quantitative methodologies as mutually exclusive and antagonistic paradigms is a misleading representation of the reality of social research practice' (Laurie and Sullivan 1990, p.113).

## Reflection

Think about what would be involved in adopting a triangulated or multi-strategy research approach in a research project on a topic that is of interest to you, and as you do so, ask yourself:

- What is the underlying logic and rationale for combining methods in such a research project?
- What is entailed in adopting such a strategy?
- What are the epistemological questions that arise?
- What are the methodological questions that arise?

How do advocates of triangulated research strategies support their claims that such an approach tends to:

- increase the validity of a research study?
- overcome problems of bias in a research study?
- improve the 'wholeness' of a research study?

What are the arguments against using a multi-strategy research approach in your intended project?

## Summary

This chapter has introduced you to what social research is, how it compares with research that is carried out in the natural sciences, and to the different styles of research that are available to the researcher. We have seen that there are, broadly speaking, two dominant and apparently irreconcilable approaches to what counts as knowledge within the social sciences, and how best to acquire it. These are positivist and interpretive epistemologies.

Different epistemological positions have in the past tended to steer the types of method and technique employed in research, and created a dichotomy between quantitative and qualitative research approaches in the social sciences. Thus, positivism is usually associated with techniques such as experiments and surveys, which emphasise controlled conditions in which the research programme is standardised and heavily structured, and where there is respondent/subject detachment. These are usually called quantitative methods. The interpretive approach tends to emphasise naturally occurring phenomena, and adopts unstructured research approaches in which there is an interaction between the respondent and the researcher so that meaning can be fully explored and articulated. These qualitative methods and approaches include (among many others) participant observation, in-depth interviewing, focus-group interviewing, projective interviewing and personal documentary analysis.

*(Continued)*

*(Continued)*

At an epistemological level, the quantitative–qualitative methods divide appears insurmountable, given that the approaches are based on contrasting ideas about what society is, how knowledge about it is to be properly gained, and on the aims of research (whether one is predicting, explaining or understanding). However, at a technical level, the debate is more concerned with which research tools are best suited to the discovery of particular aspects of society. That is, which research approach and research methods will most usefully enable the researcher(s) to address their research question? Here, then, some social researchers note the possibilities of combining quantitative and qualitative methods in a single research study.

In the next chapter we shall consider in more detail the critical social research position reviewed earlier. However, we shall also return to the positivist and interpretivist perspectives throughout the different chapters of this book, particularly (but not only) in Chapters 6 and 7.

## Chapter research task

Carry out a critical review of an empirically-based research study of your choice. A journal article should suffice for this task, providing it has a section on the methodology and methods employed. This could be something which is already familiar to you, which you wish to revisit, or something entirely new. A critical review involves integrating the approach, findings and conclusions of a study. Ask some or all of the following questions in order to structure your review:

1. What are the aims and objectives of the research? (Are there any hypotheses? How well are these set out? Are they grounded in theory? Do the results have practical implications? Was the research worth doing and well conceived?) You are likely to find these most easily by scanning the article's introduction and conclusion.
2. Is the study located within a particular theoretical context? (Hint: it probably is!) Is the study informed by particular assumptions about the world? If so, this may impact upon the focus of the research, the data gathered and the structuring of the conclusions that are drawn.
3. Provide a detailed critique of the methodology employed. As well as commenting upon the general research strategy, this may include an examination of the epistemological framework the author(s) is/are using.
4. Are there any ethical issues that you would like to comment upon?
5. How about the findings of the study. Are the data accurately reported? How are the data presented? (Accurately? Lucidly? Is it too technical?)
6. Conclusions. What claims does the author make? Do the analyses bear out these claims? Are competing hypotheses addressed and satisfactorily eliminated? Have

other plausible hypotheses been ignored? If so, does (and how) this invalidate the conclusions?

7. Is it possible to draw conclusions which the author missed or overlooked? Is what has been said probably true/false/undecidable?

As you can see, a critical review is not a descriptive summary of the text, but a detailed analytical examination.

## Recommended Reading

Brewer, J. and Hunter, A. 1989. *Multimethod Research: A Synthesis of Styles.* Newbury Park, CA: Sage.

Bryman, A. 1988. *Quantity and Quality in Social Research*. London: Unwin Hyman. pp.11–44.

Burgess, R.G. 1982. *Field Research: A Sourcebook and Field Manual.* London: Allen and Unwin. pp.163–7.

Denzin, N. 2009. The Research Act: A Theoretical Introduction to Sociological Methods. New Brunswick, NJ: Transaction.

Hammersley, M. 1992. *What's Wrong with Ethnography?* London: Routledge. pp.1–22.

Kolakowski, L. 1993. An Overall View of Positivism. In: M. Hammersley (ed.), *Social Research: Philosophy, Politics and Practice*. London: Sage. pp.1–8.

Laurie, H. and Sullivan, O. 1990. Combining Qualitative and Quantitative Data in the Longitudinal Study of Household Allocations, *Sociological Review*, 39, 113–30.

von Wright, G.H. 1993. Two Traditions. In: M. Hammersley (ed.), *Social Research: Philosophy, Politics and Practice*. London: Sage. pp.9–13.

# TWO

# Critical Social Research

- To introduce readers to emancipatory approaches to social research
- To consider the implications that critical theory might have for the goals of social research
- To investigate the rationale for, and characteristics of, feminist approaches to social research
- To introduce readers to the main features of qualitative and quantitative approaches to research
- To consider the characteristics of emancipatory disability research and the implications that these have for the conduct of research
- To encourage readers to reflect on relationships of power within the research process
- To emphasise the role of politics and values within the research process



## Introduction

In Chapter 1 we addressed the two central questions of 'What is social research?' and 'Why do we carry out social research?' In looking at these questions, we discussed the ideas associated with the two major social research perspectives – *positivism* and *interpretivism*. The views of these two approaches are summarised in Review boxes 2.1 and 2.2.

### Review Box 2.1 Positivism

The positivist approach is based on an application of the scientific method used in the natural sciences (physics, chemistry, and so on). As such, social scientists carry out their research with a firm commitment to objectivity, concerning themselves only with those phenomena that are tangible/measurable. Positivism is associated with predominately quantitative approaches (surveys, experiments, and so on) that stress reliability and generalisability. The purpose of social research is to establish the scientific laws of society (i.e. causal relationships) which are arrived at by testing research hypotheses.

### Review Box 2.2 Interpretivism

Interpretivism holds that to explain human behaviour, social researchers need to understand the meanings and interpretations that people attach to phenomena in the social world. Thus social research cannot proceed by simply applying the methods that are used in the natural sciences. Rather, research is designed to explore the motivations, perceptions and experiences of social actors. Interpretivism is associated with predominately qualitative methods (in-depth interviews, observation studies, and so on) that place a high emphasis on validity. The purpose of social research is to build an understanding of the motives and intentions that underpin social behaviour.

It was also noted in Chapter 1 that there is another approach to social research – that which can broadly be classified as *critical social research*. Those researchers who identify with a critical approach reject both the positivist and interpretivist approaches to social research, arguing that the aim of social research should be to change society for the better. Drawing their inspiration from ideas of critical theory, as developed by the Frankfurt School of Social Research, critical social researchers contend that social research should serve a particular purpose in emancipating oppressed groups within society.

In this chapter we are going to look at the characteristics of a critical approach to social research by focusing on two significant contributions: those that come under the banners of feminist methodology and emancipatory disability research. In examining the development of these critical approaches to social research, we shall examine their distinctive features, while addressing some of the debates that have taken place as a consequence. We shall also address some of the criticisms that have been levelled at emancipatory and critical social researchers and consider the general methodological implications that can be drawn from this debate.

## The Frankfurt School and critical social research

The theoretical framework for critical social research lies within the critical theory of society that was developed by scholars such as Jürgen Habermas, Max Horkheimer, Theodor Adorno and Eric Fromm, who were associated with the Institute of Social Research at the University of Frankfurt (Crotty 1998). In offering a Marxist critique of the changing nature of capitalism in the post-war period, the Frankfurt School attacked what they perceived to be the inherent class bias of orthodox social inquiry which, they argued, benefited the ruling capitalist class.

Kincheloe and McLaren (1998, p.263) offer a summary of the central propositions of critical theory:

- All thought is mediated by power relations that are socially and historically constructed;
- Facts cannot be isolated from the domain of values;
- Language is central to the formation of subjectivity;
- Certain groups in society are privileged;
- The oppression that characterises contemporary society is most forcibly reproduced when subordinates accept their social status as natural, i.e., oppressed groups labour under a false consciousness;
- Oppression is multi-dimensional;
- Mainstream research practice is unwittingly implicated in the reproduction of systems of oppression.

The Frankfurt School, therefore, raised universal questions of importance and relevance for all researchers: why is research conducted? What constitutes valid knowledge? And what are the consequences of research? In challenging the dominant ideas that were associated with positivism, the Frankfurt School attacked prevailing notions of value neutrality and argued that it is the responsibility of social researchers to generate knowledge that aims to reveal the underlying mechanisms and structures that perpetuate the subordination of oppressed groups.

Critical social researchers, therefore, are committed to raising emancipatory consciousness, to the empowerment of individuals and the confronting of injustice in society. While traditional researchers 'cling to the guardrail of neutrality, critical researchers frequently announce their partisanship in the struggle for a better world' (Kincheloe and McLaren 1998, p.264). Hence, Neuman (2006, p.95) defines critical social science as:

> A critical process of inquiry that goes beyond surface illusions to uncover the real structures in the material world in order to help people change conditions and build a better world for themselves.

From this perspective, traditional positivist and interpretivist approaches to research are seen as essentially passive activities that leave power relations undisturbed. For critical social researchers, the researcher's skills in the field of knowledge creation should be used to advance emancipatory goals. This view is typified by Humphries (1997, 2.6), who says that the point of social research is 'to understand the world in order to change it'. Social research can and should become a powerful vehicle for challenging the existence of racial prejudice, campaigning for the removal of gender inequalities, for the emancipation of people with disabilities, and to generally give voice to oppressed groups in society (Schostak and Schostak 2008).

## The origins of feminist methodology

With the rise of the women's movement in the 1970s, many feminist scholars argued that traditional social science reflected a deep-rooted male bias that defined society and science in terms of male values, knowledge and experience (Stanley and Wise 1983). Universities were criticised as largely male domains that colluded in the systematic privileging of male interests and the exclusion and marginalisation of women.

In critiquing the hitherto conventional practice of social inquiry, feminist researchers advanced a number of arguments (Harding and Norberg 2005):

- Traditional social scientific inquiry had focused predominately on visible and public phenomena as identified by men. Thus, issues in the supposedly 'private' domain that were important to feminists, such as the sexual division of labour within the household, sexual harassment and domestic violence, were largely invisible in the research community.
- While certain aspects of women's experience had been omitted from social inquiry altogether, women had generally been assigned largely passive and subsidiary roles as wives, daughters and mothers. Consequently, women's contribution to economic, political, social and cultural life had been downplayed and marginalised.
- Male social science had underplayed gender as a fundamental social division and had overlooked it as a key explanatory variable in comparison, for example, to social class.
- In using overwhelmingly male points of research, the traditional model of social research had over-generalised from mens' experience of the family, employment, and society in general, to the experience of all people, thus creating incomplete knowledge.
- A scientific approach based on traditional notions of rationality had resulted in a dismissal of the emotional dimensions of experience that were particularly important in women's lives.
- A commitment to conventional ideas of objectivity had resulted in the separation of researchers and research participants in such a manner that hierarchical and exploitative relationships were typical in the conduct of research.
- By failing to challenge exploitative gender roles, traditional social scientific inquiry had been guilty of perpetuating unequal gender relations in all spheres of women's lives.

In summary, the feminist movement of the late twentieth century argued that social science had been complicit in the control of women, and that feminist researchers were effectively steered towards a different way of conducting research by the realities of the social science that preceded feminism.

## How should feminists conduct their research?

Feminist researchers of the 1970s and 1980s focused their research on issues that had previously been neglected by the male-dominated research establishment. Kitzinger (2007), for example, discusses the way in which early research on sexual harassment allowed feminist researchers to take something that had previously been seen as restricted to the private domain of women's lives, name it and transform it into an issue of social concern for feminists and social science generally. As well as debating the issues that emergent feminist research should concentrate on, a great deal of thought and reflection was given to the methods that feminists should use in conducting their research.

### Feminist critiques of quantitative research

There has been a strong tradition among feminist researchers to critique quantitative approaches to research as ones that are unsuitable when seeking to understand the nature of women's lives. Quantification and positivist techniques of measurement, in the form of surveys and experiments, have been associated with a detached approach to research, in which 'research subjects' are treated as information-bearing units that need to be controlled within a standardised and highly structured research process (Jayaratne and Stewart 1991). Feminist researchers argue that women are not simply disembodied sources of data, but rather that their humanity should be emphasised in the process of carrying out research. They question the value and relevance of pre-coded questionnaire-based research which assumes that researchers already know the full range of responses that they are likely to receive and simply need to apply their skill in the coding and analysis of data. Such approaches to research are seen to discount the exploration that is necessary in understanding the fragmented and complex nature of women's lives. Many feminists have, therefore, argued against the use of quantitative research methods which they see as misrepresenting women's experience and as being fundamentally inconsistent with the goals of the feminist movement (Jayaratne and Stewart 1991).

### The association of feminism with qualitative methods

Given that many feminists have argued that the ideal of disengagement – the separation of reason and emotion as embodied in the process of quantitative research – is rooted in masculinist assumptions concerning the conduct of research, feminist researchers have traditionally tended to favour those methods of research that have been associated with the generation of qualitative data. While Oakley (2000) offers a comprehensive and critical review of the general attraction that feminist researchers have towards qualitative methods, Rabinowitz and Martin (2001) advocate qualitative interviewing as a method that validates women's experiences, Reinharz (1992) and Wilkinson (1999) both argue that the focus group is a method that is particularly sympathetic to the nature of feminist research, and Kitzinger (2007) contends that conversation analysis allows feminist researchers to access the interactional context of women's lives.

In summary, qualitative methods are seen as inherently more suited to the goals of feminist research for a number of reasons:

- Qualitative research allows for an exploration and understanding of women's lives as they are really lived and provide for access to experience from the actor's perspective rather than an externally imposed 'truth':

  > Qualitative studies maximise understandings of women's activities and beliefs and the process through which these are structured. Such research tends to be oriented towards the interior of women's lives, focusing on 'the meanings and interpretations of those being researched' (Maynard 1998, p.128).

- In qualitative research, there is a closer degree of involvement with those who participate in the research, and consequently a greater sensitivity to the rights of participants as people, rather than as objects of research. The bottom-up and more accountable nature of qualitative research enables more democratic ways of knowing to be opened up.
- Women are seen to be more sensitised to many of the features of a qualitative style of research – an understanding of interaction, context, experience, and so on. Douglas (1976, p.214) says that this is the case because women are 'sociability specialists', who possess an intuitive ability to relate to people through the traditional tools of qualitative research. Smart (1984, p.155) concurs with this view, suggesting that the job of qualitative interviewing is 'intrinsically feminine', with women being natural facilitators of conversation.

## Revisiting the legitimacy of quantitative methods

However, while the view that feminists should use qualitative rather than quantitative methods prevails in much of the literature on feminist methodology, this is not universally the case. Indeed, Oakley has voiced her concern for the way in which a caricatured, pure positivist position is often conflated with quantitative research to the extent that the use of quantitative methods by feminist researchers is deemed to be virtually unacceptable:

> Anyone who believes that hypotheses need to be warranted, anyone who uses numerical data or statistics, anyone who is concerned about representativeness or generalisability or the credibility of research findings is liable to be deemed a 'positivist'. (2000, p.156)

While embracing the ability of qualitative research to enable the diversity of women's voices and experiences to be heard, Oakley (2000, p.161) poses the question of whether the 'hegemony of qualitative methods as the dominant epistemological assumption' in contemporary feminist research is entirely healthy. Similarly, Ramazanoglu (2002) challenges the conventional norms of feminist inquiry, whereby feminists automatically adopt qualitative techniques as the default position. While qualitative methods may remain predominant among feminist researchers – due in large part to the realisation that many of the emotional and complex subjects that feminists typically choose to address lend themselves to qualitative inquiry – a growing body of opinion raises the value of quantitative research as a vehicle for influencing public policy.

Such views, voiced historically by Jayaratne (1993), have more recently been addressed by Fonow and Cook (2005), who contend that governments and policy-makers remain far less attentive to the concerns of individuals as reflected in qualitative work, repeatedly demonstrating their preference for the generalised statistical analysis that is delivered through large-scale survey research. Furthermore, they argue positively for the power of quantitative research to address matters of particular concern to feminists, such as the prevalence of domestic violence, the sharing of household responsibilities, occupation segmentation and wage differentials in the labour market, and so on. In questioning the suitability of qualitative research in all instances, Oakley (2000) suggests that a well-crafted quantitative research project is far more likely to contribute towards feminist outcomes than a poorly crafted and inappropriate qualitative project which is unlikely to achieve funding or influence policy-makers.

Furthermore, it has consistently been argued (Finch 1993; Collins 1998) that while qualitative methods such as in-depth interviews may be attractive given their *potentially* less exploitative relationships in the conduct of fieldwork, this does not necessarily mean that this will always be the case:

> Seemingly abstract, impersonal questions could lead interviewees to reveal deeply personal, emotionally charged information as if to a friend. … The more successful I was at forming close relationships with interviewees, the more likely they were to reveal personal thoughts or feelings … intimate details about their lives that they may later regret having shared. (Kirsch 2005, pp.2164–5)

In revisiting the debate over the appropriateness of methods, Oakley (2000) and Kesby (2005) have argued that the principled issue is not the choice between quantitative or qualitative techniques, but issues of democracy, involvement and participation in the research process. Thus Letherby contends that rather than an adherence to particular qualitative methods, the key question remains:

> ...the relationship between the process and the product, i.e. how what we do affects what we get (in both qualitative and quantitative work), is the central concern of feminist researchers. Thus, the key issue here is the relationship between doing and knowing: how the way that we undertake research (the process) relates to the knowledge we present at the end (the product). (2004, p.176)

One particular aspect of the research process that has attracted much debate concerns the nature of relationships that feminist researchers form when conducting their fieldwork.

## The nature of research relationships

The 'it's not what you do but the way that you do it' mentality referred to by Letherby (2004, pp.178–9) brings feminist research back to one of the central concerns of feminism: the hierarchical and unhealthy power relationships that are held to characterise the typical research process. For Maynard (1998, p.130), an approach to research which exhibits these characteristics is incompatible with the political goals of feminism:

> A central issue has been the structural relationship between researcher and researched and the extent to which these might be minimised. It is argued that it is hypocritical, and undermining of the knowledge produced, for feminists to replicate, during their research, the kind of power relations of which they are critical elsewhere.

Feminist researchers seek, therefore, to break down the traditional patterns that structure research relationships, to humanise the research process, and to work towards the establishment of more reciprocal and non-hierarchical research relationships such as those that are 'derived from authentic relations' (Reinharz 1983, p.186). Gelsthorpe (1992, p.192) calls this an 'interactive methodology', and Romm (1997, 6.4) talks of the development of a 'more collaborative knowledge-construction process'.

For example, Oakley (1981) discusses how she shared with her interviewees her own experiences of childbirth, and the effect that this had on her research. She argues that by exploring her own experiences, and incorporating these into her research, the relationships she established with her research participants were transformed, and thus led to better research. Oakley argues that the social rapport that was established between herself and her research participants, and the manner in which they opened up to her in their interviews, was a direct consequence of her decision to reveal such personal details about her own life.

In a seminal contribution to the debate, Harding (1987, p.8), suggests that feminist research demands that researchers place themselves 'in the same critical plane as the overt subject matter' and in doing so recognise their own personal, cultural, political and social biography, and the role that this has played in shaping their research. In bringing their own lives into the research process in this manner, it is argued that feminist researchers will be better able to comprehend the experiences of their research participants, while sharing their own feelings and experiences. Moreover, such an approach is held to facilitate new 'ways of knowing which avoid subordination' (Ramazanoglu 1992, p.210).

There are some feminists, however, who, while being sympathetic to the development of less hierarchical research relationships, suggest that professional researchers will continue to occupy a privileged position given their possession of specialised research skills and knowledge. For example, Kelly et al. argue that the highly developed knowledge and skills learnt within the academic community mean that while researchers may not consciously seek superiority over their research participants, they will always be seen as different: 'It is an illusion to think that ... participants can have anything approaching "equal" knowledge to the researcher' (1994, p.37).

Others, while identifying with a feminist position, maintain, a defence of what they see as their hard-won theoretical knowledge and research expertise (Millen 1997), and raise questions about the advisability of disowning theoretical and methodological privilege when studying powerful elites (Smart 1984). Furthermore, Cotterill (1992) also suggests that while it may be possible to negotiate power relationships within the research encounter, once the researcher walks away with the data they then re-assume control.

While feminists continue to grapple with these issues, Martyn Hammersley, a leading critic of the case for a distinctly feminist methodology, argues that for feminist researchers to suggest that they are no better or different from their research participants demonstrates an immaturity and lack of realism by those who refute their own intellectual authority. Rather, Hammersley (1992a, pp.200–1) asserts that it is in *everyone's* best interests that some people (researchers) have expertise in knowledge production as 'successful action depends on accurate information'; good knowledge is reliably produced by people who really know what they are doing, and good knowledge is better than bad knowledge.

For Hammersley, the way in which researchers go about their research, the relationships they form in the field, and their attention to ethically sound principles are most definitely to be scrutinised. But that does not mean that it is unreasonable for the researcher to define the research question, select the method of data collection, carry out the analysis, and write up the research report *without* consultation with the research participants. While Hammersley has a degree of sympathy for a more personal approach to research, he states that: 'The proper relationship between researcher and researched is not something that can be legislated by methodology, feminist or otherwise, but will be determined by the specifics of each particular case' (1992a, p.199).

## Objectivity, subjectivity and emancipatory research goals

Harding's (1987) contention that feminists should place themselves on the same critical plane as those they are researching marks a clear break with conventional approaches to research that emphasise detachment and objectivity in the research process. Furthermore, in explicitly rejecting what is held to be an 'objectivist' stance and embracing the role of subjective experience, feminist researchers raise fundamental challenges concerning the purpose of social research. Whereas a traditional model of research endeavour upholds impartiality and objectivity in the pursuit of knowledge as one of the guiding principles of science, feminists commit themselves to taking sides in challenging unequal and exploitative gender relations and consciously facilitating social change through the adoption of emancipatory goals. Such an approach rejects the contention that 'truth is the only value that constitutes the goal of research' (Hammersley and Gomm 1997, 4.12).

In arguing that research should be designed *for* women, the goals of feminist research are bound up with the self-empowerment of women as individuals while seeking emancipation at the societal level (Harding 1987; Fonow and Cook 1991; Olesen 1998). The goal of feminist research cannot therefore be the production of knowledge *per se*, but 'useful knowledge' (Kelly et al. 1994, p.25) which can 'serve the interests of dominated, exploited and oppressed groups, particularly women' (Mies 1993, pp.68–9). Feminist social research is therefore seen as a vehicle that can be used to reveal the inequalities inherent in gender relations, to critique the implications that these inequalities have in relation to power differentials in society, and to seek a transformation of women's position: to 'win, defeat or neutralise those forces that are arrayed against its [women's] emancipation, growth or development' (Harding 1987, p.8).

Such ideas explicitly challenge conventional notions of objectivity, which contend that scientists can control the research process so as to produce neutral knowledge of social reality. However, it is important to note that feminist researchers do not see the conscious adoption of emancipatory goals for their own research as marking them out as being 'political' researchers in contrast to 'neutral' and 'scientific' researchers who allegedly avoid a cultural and political location. Rather, they contend that they are simply acknowledging the socially constructed and intrinsically subjective character of all knowledge creation. Thus, the traditional or 'objectivist' approach is critiqued for the notion that 'scientific' researchers approach their research with an 'empty head' which allows them to conduct uncontaminated research (Stanley and Wise 1983, p.22). Haraway (1991) likens this view of science to a 'God-trick' because it proposes to see everything from nowhere, as value-free and omnipresent.

In contrast, the feminist way of knowing is akin to vision; it always looks from somewhere. For feminist researchers, as with all critical social researchers, research is a political activity that requires all researchers to align to particular value positions whether these be consciously expressed or not. Given that value-freedom is a myth, feminist researchers lay claim to the moral high ground in declaring the explicitly emancipatory goals of their research. Reinharz, for example, declares her support for such an approach that enables feminists to conduct 'honest' research:

> I for one, feel most satisfied by a stance that acknowledges the researcher's position right up front, and that does not think of objectivity and subjectivity as warring with each other. I have feminist distrust for research reports that include no statement about the researcher's experience. Reading such reports, I feel that the researcher is hiding from me or does not know how important personal experience is. Such reports seem woefully incomplete and even dishonest. (1992, p.263)

In contrast to Reinharz's view, however, Hammersley and Gomm argue that by bringing political objectives to the fore and adopting emancipatory goals, feminist researchers have abrogated the scientific pursuit of the truth as the only valid goal of research, and are guilty of introducing motivated bias into the research process. They define motivated bias as systematic error:

> deriving from a conscious or unconscious tendency on the part of the researcher to produce data, and/or interpret and present them, in a way as to favour false results that are in line with their pre-judgements and political or practical commitments. This may consist of a positive tendency towards a particular, but false, conclusion. Equally, it may involve the exclusion from consideration of some set of possible conclusions that happen to include the truth. (Hammersley and Gomm 1997, 1.7)

The feminist response to Hammersley and Gomm's charge of motivated bias has been to re-emphasise the way in which feminists see *all* research as incorporating 'subjectivity', partiality, bias and political commitment (Ramazanoglu 2002, p.49). Indeed, in characterising Hammersley and Gomm's position as remaining embedded in a 'masculinist' conception of science, feminist researchers deny that objectivity and the control of bias can remain as a reasonable and achievable goal for the social research community (see Harding 2003). While feminists may pursue a version of the truth which they may hold to be a 'better story', Ramazanoglu (2002) refutes the idea that feminists, or anyone else, can claim to be objective.

## Feminist standpoint epistemology

Central to the argument for a distinctive feminist methodology is the placing of women's experiences at the heart of their research. In that feminist research generates problematics from the perspectives of women's experiences, it uses these experiences as a significant indicator of the 'reality' against which knowledge is assessed. Thus, there is a shift from the 'context of justification' (the importance that traditional social research places on validity and reliability in the research process) to the 'context of discovery' that enables feminist researchers to address women's lives and experiences in their own terms. In this respect, feminist researchers say that they adopt a feminist standpoint from which they see the world and assess the value of research.

### How does one determine whether an explanation is true or false?

In rejecting the traditional scientific model of research, feminists are confronted with the challenge of justifying what counts as reliable knowledge – that which can be replicated by others – and what is held to be valid knowledge – that which can be judged to represent reality. In the absence of an externally verifiable reality, feminist standpoint theory holds that knowledge is constructed out of, is grounded in, and must be tested against women's experience of gendered power relations (Harding 1997). Standpoint theory therefore explores relations between knowledge and power in contrast to the scientific method, which seeks direct verification of knowledge against a known and universal reality. Feminist researchers acknowledge that their knowledge derives from a 'specific and partial social location, and so is socially constituted as a "knowing self"' (Ramazanoglu 2002, p.65) rather than claiming that their knowledge can be validated against generally accepted scientific criteria.

### Feminist standpoint debates concerning knowledge claims

Harding (1987, 2003) has consistently argued that the adoption of a feminist standpoint provides for access to 'socially situated knowledge' in which the experiences of women's lives provide an epistemologically advantaged starting point in the knowledge creation process. Thus, she contends that feminist knowledge is not just different from non-feminist knowledge, but that the truth obtained via feminist endeavour is 'less partial and distorted' than existing (male-centred) knowledge. Furthermore, she suggests that the more oppressed a group is, the more objective will be their knowledge. She terms this 'strong objectivity'.

Not surprisingly, there has been much debate within the feminist research community as to whether some knowledge claims are better founded than others. Harding's view that there is a hierarchy of access to the truth, with some knowledge claims being 'less false' than others, is supported, among others, by Mies (1993), Haraway (1991), Gillespie (1994) and Millen (1997, 7.2), who claims that the more holistic, integrative and connected knowledge that is created by feminists forms the basis for a 'successor science'. This is not a view that is shared by all feminist researchers, however. Gelsthorpe (1992), for example, while fully supportive of the case for a distinctly feminist methodology, does not consider the knowledge that is generated from a feminist standpoint to result in a knowledge that is better than that created by men. In a wide-ranging discussion, Ramazanoglu (2002) questions whether feminists can authoritatively claim privileged ways of accessing reality in the absence of justifying the specific criteria against which their truth can be tested.

Furthermore, the primacy of feminist standpoint knowledge has been challenged by postmodernism, which argues that it is not possible to adjudicate between different versions of 'truth', but that all that exists are a multiplicity of unstable, diverse and locally negotiated versions of the truth (Hekman 1997). In arguing that no methodology is able to produce a universal knowledge that adequately describes the fractured and deconstructed nature of social reality, postmodernism has 'made it particularly difficult for feminists to claim that any one story is better than another' (Ramazanoglu 2002, p.166).

### Can men conduct feminist research?

Of course, standpoint feminism raises the obvious question of whether men are able to carry out feminist research. Is this, as Stanley and Wise (1983) have suggested, an activity that can only be carried out by women? Ramazanoglu (2002) questions the relatively unsophisticated way in which some feminists remain wedded to two mutually exclusive gender categories of 'women' and 'men' that deny the socially constructed nature of gender. She argues that once this is recognised, and once feminists accept that feminist consciousness is not derived solely from a female body, it no longer remains the case that only women can conduct feminist research. This is a view that is shared by Smart (1984), who cautions against rigidity among feminists that would lead to the dismissal of feminist-sympathetic research carried out by men. Similarly, Henwood and Pidgeon (1993) contend that feminist-conscious men can adopt a perspective that is sympathetic to the feminist standpoint, and Cain (1990) argues that men can participate in feminist research, providing they remain 'gendered' throughout the research process.

### The privileging of gender?

Debates have also addressed the manner in which the dominant Anglo-American academic community have taken a relatively undifferentiated category of 'women' and assumed that all women experience male power the same way. Consequently, there is now much more of an appreciation of the differences that exist between women and that gendered power relations are only one aspect of women's lives. When one accepts that women are distinguished (and possibly separated) by social class, disability, race, ethnicity, sexual orientation and nationality, then it becomes clear that there can be no such thing as a single feminist standpoint (see Collins 1991; Harding 2003).

In a thoughtful contribution to this debate, Warren (1981) discusses the way in which the complexity of gender roles impact differentially on the conduct of research. She gives an extensive review of the differential impact of gender in a variety of cultural locations, questioning many *western* feminist conceptions of sex and gender. She provides a number of illuminating examples where, for example:

- it was vital for the researcher to be seen as part of a family with children (Sudan);
- race was an issue, but gender was not (Nigeria);
- a researcher had initially found it very difficult to gain access to a research site, but had achieved this on returning at a later date when pregnant (Kenya).

As part of his general critique of feminist methodology, Hammersley (1992a, p.192) takes the debates on such issues to argue against the notion that any individual factor or variable such as gender can be given 'pre-established priority over other variables' in the research process. In considering the complex relationships of gender, class, ethnicity, and other such characteristics, Hammersley poses the question of how one untangles the complexities of *real* relationships to construct a hierarchy of oppression: 'Given this, we find that many people will be classed as both oppressors and oppressed from different points of view' (1992a, p.203).

However, an acknowledgement of the intersecting relationships that exist between gender, disability, race, social class, and so on has not weakened the resolve of feminist scholars towards feminist methodology. Rather, we have seen an invigorating debate concerning the complex matrix of social 'variables' with which gender intersects in the research process (Humphries 1998; Ramazanoglu 2002; Harding 2003).

> Although feminism has a lot to contribute to our understanding of how we should know the social world, feminist thinking in this regard is not some kind of uniform and linear affair. There are healthy and vibrant disputes between feminists about these matters, just as there are between other philosophers, social theorists, methodologists and empirical researchers. (Maynard 1998, p.120)

## Emancipatory disability research

Where the debates of the embryonic women's movement of the late 1960s and early 1970s fed directly into a debate on feminist methodology, it was not until the 1980s and further into the 1990s that the modern disability rights movement resulted in a group of researchers coming together under a banner of emancipatory disability research. Oliver (2002a) argues that prior to this happening research in the area of disability had failed to:

- accurately capture and reflect the experience of disability from the perspective of disabled people themselves;
- make a meaningful contribution to the policy-making process and therefore the material conditions of disabled people;
- acknowledge the struggles of disabled people, thus opting for an apolitical approach to disability.

In common with feminist researchers, those working within the field of emancipatory disability research contested that the research agenda for disability research needed to be wrested free from academics who remained wedded to traditional methodologies and the distorted knowledge that these generated.

Let us look, therefore, at how emancipatory disability research has been characterised before going on to consider some of the central debates within this area.

## What is emancipatory disability research?

In a much-quoted passage, Stone and Priestly (1996, p.706) characterise emancipatory disability research as research which accepts the following:

- The adoption of the social model of disablement as the epistemological basis for research production.
- The surrender of claims to objectivity through overt political commitment to the struggles of disabled people and/or the removal of disabling barriers.
- The willingness only to undertake research where it will be of practical benefit to the self-empowerment of disabled people and/or the removal of disabling barriers.
- The evolution of control over research production to ensure full accountability to disabled people and their organisations.
- The giving of voice to the personal as political while endeavouring to collectivise the political commonality of individual experiences.
- The willingness to adopt a plurality of methods for data collection and analysis in response to the changing needs of disabled people.

As might be expected, many of the debates within the field of emancipatory disability research share a great deal in common with those that have taken place between feminist researchers. For example, discussions around objectivity and subjectivity in the research process that have adopted similar frames of reference to those used by feminists. In a typical contribution, Barnes poses the fundamental incompatibility of conducting anti-oppressive research while seeking to uphold notions of researcher independence:

> Researchers should be espousing commitment not value freedom, engagement not objectivity, and solidarity not independence. There is no independent haven or middle ground when researching oppression: academics and researchers can only be with the oppressors or with the oppressed. (1996, p.110)

Given that critical social researchers working from within the feminist and disability rights movements do indeed share many overlapping concerns about the design and conduct of research practice, it is not necessary to revisit some of the debates that have already been discussed in this chapter. Rather than do this, it will be more valuable to consider some distinctive areas where emancipatory disability researchers have addressed issues that have greater salience in relation to their particular issue agenda. Specifically, these concern the vibrant debate that has taken place concerning the difference between emancipatory disability research and alternative participatory action research approaches, and associated issues over control within the research process.

First, however, it is necessary to summarise what is generally referred to as the social model of disability, upon which much emancipatory disability research is based.

## The social model of disability

The social model of disability was developed as a challenge to the prevailing medical model of disability, which framed the 'problem' of disability as an individual impairment and an inevitable consequence of either medical illness or personal injury. Acceptance of this medical model had, allegedly, led to solutions that focused on the mediation of the specific disabling effects of individual impairment: disabled people could, therefore, be fixed, cured or rehabilitated at the individual level (Barnes and Mercer 1997).

The social model of disability, however, reverses this causal chain to explore how socially constructed barriers have had the effect of disabling people with a perceived impairment. Rather than the individual being inevitably 'disabled' by their impairment, disability is seen as a social construction. Adherence to the social model of disability forces researchers to reassess social, political and cultural arrangements that have hitherto been taken for granted, and expose the nature of disabling structures throughout society (Oliver 2002a). In accepting a false medical model of disability, it was argued that conventional research methodology had effectively perpetuated an individualistic operationalisation of the disabled 'problem' and accepted subordinate and exploitative relationships in the research process (Swain et al. 2004). Meaningful disability research, therefore, must become inherently political and be guided by a commitment to end the in-built marginalisation of disabled people: it must become emancipatory (Barnes 1996).

In common with feminist methodology, emancipatory disability research has generally been seen to favour the use of qualitative methods as those that are more likely to be capable of capturing the complexity of disabled people's lives. However, while there may, historically, have been a preference for the use of narrative methods and life histories (Engel and Munger 2003), adherents of the social model have tended to distance themselves from such methods in recent years. In doing so, they have argued that such research reinforces popular conceptions of disability as tragic and unbearable, and those who strive to overcome their disability as inspirational and heroic (Finkelstein 1996; Barnes and Mercer 1997). Rather than using such individualised and potentially sentimental methods, it has been argued that emancipatory disability research should remain focused on the structures of disablement through methods that capture collective experience wherever possible.

Before going on to explore the nature of emancipatory disability research *vis-à-vis* more conventional models of participatory action research, it is important to note that the relative supremacy of the social model in contemporary disability research has not gone unchallenged. For example, Danieli and Woodhams (2005) have questioned whether the domination of the social model within disability research has resulted in the silencing of dissenting voices who do not subscribe to an emancipatory paradigm. Furthermore, they question whether emancipatory researchers may only produce research which supports the social model of disability and ignore those voices who, for example, may not see themselves in need of emancipation.

### Delivering empowerment and emancipation

Emancipatory disability researchers contend that research strategies need to be both empowering (seeking positive individual change through participation) and emancipatory (seeking positive societal change) (Barnes 2003). Such research, therefore, must contribute towards the tangible transformation of the lives of disabled people rather than simply giving voice to marginalised groups and hoping that positive outcomes will result.

For disability research to be seen as emancipatory, and therefore worthwhile, Oliver (1996) argues that the researchers involved in the proposed research need to demonstrate the way in which the research outcomes will improve the material circumstances of disabled people and the conditions of their experience. Kitchen emphasises the contrast between consciously pursuing meaningful outcomes and relying purely on hopeful intentions: '…for academia and research to become truly emancipatory and empowering it has to actively seek change rather than hoping that the "right people" read the work and act on it' (2000, p.44).

### Emancipatory research: moving beyond participation to cede control

In a typical participatory model of research, where the researchers aim to advance positive images of disability and meaningful change on behalf of disabled people, professional academic researchers work in such a way to involve disabled people in the research process. Thus, disabled people may be invited to comment on the research questions being posed, to provide feedback during the fieldwork phase of the research, and to act in a general consultative role in preparing the report of research findings. Beresford (2002) casts this as a managerialist and instrumental practice, which avoids the explicit framing of disability research as a political act. Emancipatory research, in contrast, moves beyond this partnership mentality and fully integrates disabled people into the research process in such a way that the research process becomes 'collectivised' (Priestly 1997, p.89).

While sympathy towards a participatory outlook may therefore be a necessary prerequisite for emancipatory research, it is not sufficient to deliver the goal of change. To this end, Zarb (2002, p.128) argues that the well-meaning involvement of disabled people in the research process is unlikely to lead to emancipatory outcomes unless disabled people themselves are 'controlling the research and deciding who should be involved and how'. He suggests that emancipatory and participatory research can be distinguished by asking four questions:

1. Who controls what the research is about and how it will be carried out?
2. To what extent are disabled people involved in the research process?
3. What opportunities exist for disabled people to shape the research outputs and influence future research?
4. What happens to the research outputs?

At the heart of the matter, therefore, lies the thorny issue of control of the research process. Beresford (2002) suggests that the domain of genuinely user-controlled research runs throughout the whole research process, from the origination and initiation of research through to the subsequent evaluation once the research has been concluded. This includes:

- the generation of research questions;
- the planning, design and execution of fieldwork;
- data collection and analysis; and
- the writing and dissemination of the research findings.

In addition, Oliver (2002a) argues that disabled people and their organisations should have control of the funding of disability research. Kitchen (2000) characterises this transfer of control through true involvement as a democratisation of the research process. Furthermore, through his own research with disabled advocates and activists, he claims strong support from disabled people for this important component of the emancipatory paradigm.

## A transformed role for research expertise

Within this model of the research process, the role of the academic is transformed from the expert and professional methodologist who designs and runs the research in their own terms, to a skilled enabler of research. Those who subscribe to an emancipatory outlook are urged to place their expertise at the disposal of disabled people in a recasting of the active/passive relationship. Along with complex methodological skills, the academic may also, for example, possess the communication skills and personal contacts with policy-makers that may be necessary to translate the research outputs into meaningful outcomes.

Oliver criticises those researchers who may be broadly sympathetic to the aims of emancipatory disability research, but who are unwilling to place their methodological expertise at the disposal of disabled people: '...failing to give disabled people through their own representative organisations complete control over the research resources and agendas inevitably positions disabled people as inferior to those who are in control' (2002a, p.5). It has been suggested that such reticence on the part of professional academic researchers to cede their control of the research process may be explained by a number of factors:

- While voicing support for emancipatory goals, some supposedly sympathetic researchers see the primary function of their research as the promotion of their individual research career (Oliver 2002b).
- As a consequence of pressure from within the higher education sector for research outputs to serve institutional ends such as the Research Assessment Exercise that governs research funding in British universities (Goodley and Moore 2000).
- Because giving up control of research questions throws doubt on the wisdom of people who see themselves as experts and specialists (Priestly 1997).

In addition, Oliver (2002a) argues that disabled people and their organisations should have control of the funding of disability research. Kitchen (2000) characterises this transfer of control through true involvement as a democratisation of the research process. Furthermore, through his own research with disabled advocates and activists, he claims strong support from disabled people for this important component of the emancipatory paradigm. Such a comprehensive redistribution of power and control in the research process has led Oliver (2002a) to claim the transformation of the material and social relations of research production as a legitimate goal of emancipatory disability research.

Clearly, there are significant obstacles to the realisation of such an emancipatory model of research practice, outside the institutional pressures that confront many academic researchers. Some of these are about changes in academic behaviour. Rodgers (1999), for example, discusses the way in which the typically complex and specialist language that is used in the academic community can be modified and simplified to ensure that issues of ownership and accessibility can be adequately addressed. Other issues are somewhat more challenging. Thus, while entirely committed to the emancipatory model, Walmsley and Johnson (2003) pose some very real questions concerning the extent to which people with learning disabilities are precluded from direct engagement in terms of planning, implementation and dissemination due to the nature of their disability.

Within the field of emancipatory disability research, a healthy and vibrant debate continues over matters such as these. While there may be many differing views as to how to realise a truly emancipatory model of research, there is broad agreement that it is no longer acceptable to consciously rest power in the hands of methodologically skilled but experientially ignorant non-disabled researchers, and that to do so runs the risk of replicating the traditional and uncritical model of the research process which has historically perpetuated the disempowerment and disenfranchisement of disabled people.

## Summary

Over the past 30 years, traditional models of the research process have been challenged by critical social researchers for studying the social world from the perspective of a white male, able-bodied and middle-class universe. They have argued that this has had a profound influence on what has been regarded as significant for study, how it has been structured and ordered, and the outcomes and consequences of research. Fundamentally, critical social research has challenged the theoretical contention that it is possible to produce scientific knowledge of social life that can claim to be politically neutral. Many would argue, therefore, that the challenges that critical social researchers have presented to the 'research establishment' have proved to be the start of a necessary corrective.

This chapter has reviewed some of the debates that have taken place among and between feminist and disability scholars concerning:

- the role afforded to gender and disability *vis-à-vis* other such 'variables' of analysis, such as social class, race, age, and so on;
- the nature of knowledge construction and conventional notions of testing knowledge against reality;
- the role of research in promoting social change through the adoption of emancipatory goals;
- the methods that are most appropriate for critical social researchers to use;
- the nature of the relationships that researchers tend to form with their research participants.

Within this chapter we have reviewed the key features of feminist methodology and emancipatory disability research, indicating where key points of contention exist and considering some of the criticisms that have been made of these approaches. Of central importance is the claim that in adopting explicitly political goals, critical social researchers discard accepted notions of objectivity as a central concern of social research inquiry.

While the debate over emancipatory disability research and, more extensively, feminist methodology has been a lively and at times a somewhat potentially divisive one, it is surely a positive sign that as we reach the end of the first decade of the new millennium, discussion of critical and participatory approaches to research are increasingly being addressed in mainstream undergraduate research methods textbooks (see, for example, Sarantakos 2005; Silver 2008). Whichever 'side' one may be tempted to take in relation to these issues, we would argue that the inclusion of such debates within more mainstream texts should be seen as a positive development that will strengthen research methodology.

## Chapter research task

(The following scenario is based on an article by Hamner and Hearn (1993), entitled 'Gendered Research and Researching Gender: Women, Men and Violence'.)

Imagine you are to carry out a research project which looks at the area of violence against women by men who are known to them.

The aim of the project is to gain an understanding of the experiences of violence from the perspectives of both men and women, and to try to identify what 'violence' means to both groups. In addition to this, the project seeks to understand the relationship various agencies have with the victims and perpetrators of violence, and the social role they play. As such, it is hoped that the project will provide rich data upon which social policy can be reviewed and perhaps updated.

Women are to be accessed through a women's refuge which offers support to women who have been victims of violence. Men are to be accessed through a variety of different agencies, including the police, probation services, prison services, social services, counselling groups. (You may want to consult the section in Chapter 4 which discusses vulnerable groups and external agencies.)

In thinking about how you would carry out this project, consider the theoretical, methodological, practical and ethical issues for feminists in the area of violence against women.

You may want to reflect on some of the following questions:

- What should be the purpose of conducting research of this nature?
- Should social science research such as this be used to empower people?
- What would it mean to carry out 'objective' research in such a setting?
- Given the particular circumstances posed by this scenario, do you think that it is possible for male researchers to have access to 'the truth'?
- Is it possible for sympathetic men to do 'feminist research' or for able-bodied researchers to do emancipatory disability research?
- What is the character of knowledge that is generated by what would commonly be regarded as non-oppressed groups, i.e. white, male and able-bodied researchers? Is it of a different or a lesser quality?
- Are there methods and techniques of research that are inherently gendered or unsuitable for research with disabled people?
- Is the experience that the research is grounded more important than the methodological validity/reliability of the research methods that are used?
- How much of yourself should you reveal to your research participants?
- Should you adopt a different style for researching different people/groups?

## Recommended Reading

Barnes, C. 1996. Disability and the Myth of the Independent Researcher, *Disability and Society*, 11, 107–10.

French, S. and Swain, J. 1997. Changing Disabled Research: Participatory and Emancipatory Research with Disabled People, *Physiotherapy*, 83 (1), 26–32.

Hammersley, M. 1992. On Feminist Methodology, *Sociology*, 26 (2), 187–206.
Harding, S. (ed.) 2003. *The Feminist Standpoint Theory Reader: Intellectual and Political Controversies*. London: Routledge.
Kitzinger, C. 2007. Feminist Approaches. In: C. Seale, G. Gobo, J. Gubrium and D. Silverman (eds), *Qualitative Research Practice*. London: Sage. pp.113–28.
Maynard, M. 1998. Feminists' Knowledge and Knowledge of Feminisms: Epistemology, Theory, Methodology and Method. In: T. May and M. Williams (eds), *Knowing the Social World*. Buckingham: Open University Press. pp.120–37.
Mies, M. 1993. Towards a Methodology for Feminist Research. In: M. Hammersley (ed.), *Social Research: Philosophy, Politics and Practice*. London: Sage. pp.64–82.
Oakley, A. 2000. *Experiments in Knowing: Gender and Methods in the Social Sciences*. Cambridge: Polity Press.
Oliver, M. 1996. *Understanding Disability: From Theory to Practice*. Basingstoke: Macmillan.
Oliver, M. 2002. Changing the Social Relations of Research Production, *Disability, Handicap and Society*, 7 (2), 101–15.
Ramazanoglu, C. 2002. *Feminist Methodology: Challenges and Choices*. London: Sage.

# THREE

# Getting Started in Research: The Research Process

- To provide an overview of the research process
- To provide an appraisal of the relationship between theory and research practice
- To enable readers to be able to formulate their ideas as research problems and hypotheses
- To introduce readers to different research design models
- To provide an overview of different approaches to the selection of participants for involvement in the research process

- **Introduction**
- **Research design**
- **Getting started in research: the research problem**
- **Hypotheses, concepts, indicators and measurement**
- **Research designs**
- **Case selection**
- **Constraints on achieving credible conclusions: power, politics and values**
- **Summary**
- **Chapter research task**
- **Recommended reading**

## Introduction

This chapter will focus upon what is often considered to be a relatively practical aspect in research, that is research design. Typically, this is associated with the notion that there are various stages that research goes through, from taking a theory, focusing upon different aspects of it, designing appropriate research tools for collecting the data, and then, having analysed the findings, drawing conclusions which are written up in a research report or academic paper.

Of course, all of these elements are important in research, but research design itself is much more than this. This chapter will consider the idea that research is not a linear process, but rather it is cyclical and ongoing, or iterative. Furthermore, in designing our research, we should consider the various constraints that may impinge upon social science investigations, and the role of values, politics and power in research.

This chapter is concerned with the general approaches involved in research design, moving from clear initial questions via appropriate evidence to credible conclusions. This is dependent on:

- clearly formulated and expressed research problems;
- the research design chosen;
- the way in which cases are selected for investigation;
- the research argument.

In later chapters, we shall look carefully at various data collection techniques to complete the research argument that: 'This problem, investigated in this way using these cases, leads inescapably to these conclusions' (Sapsford 1993, p.11).

## Research design

Research design essentially refers to the plan or strategy of shaping the research, or as Hakim puts it:

> Design deals primarily with aim, purposes, intentions and plans within the practical constraints of location, time, money and availability of staff. (1987, p.1)

Just as there is a wide variety of views as to what research consists of (compare the positivist and interpretive positions assessed in Chapter 1), and great differences in actual practices as to what people research and how they do this, so there are alternative perspectives of what the process of undertaking research should actually look like.

### The research process

Perhaps the first key point to note is that all research projects embody an argument. For some (such as those using a broadly quantitative approach) the argument will be structured in the initial stages of the research. This general approach may be referred to as a *theory-then-research* method of constructing arguments (this approach is outlined in more detail later in this chapter).

For research that utilises a more qualitative approach, the argument proceeds incrementally, and is constructed in the course of the research itself – the

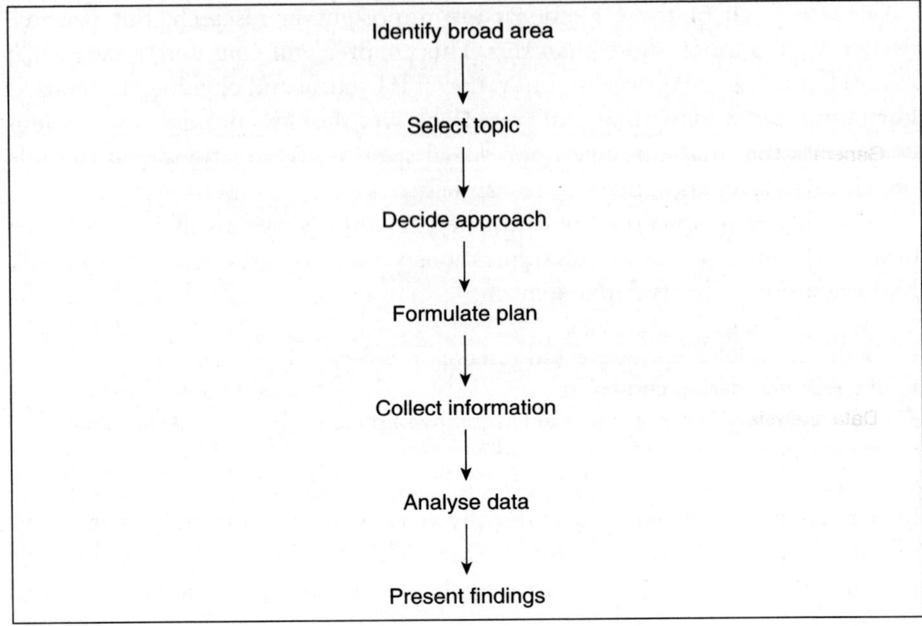


Figure 3.1 The sequential model of research (Gill and Johnson, 1997, p.3)

*research-then-theory* approach (see later in this chapter). In such emergent research strategies, many of the questions, aims and formulations of problems in the research will be developed in the data collection phase, interacting with the researchers' initial ideas or hunches. Thus the final design *emerges* through the course of the research. As Hakim states: 'The builder, and the materials he has available, takes a stronger role in the design than in the usual architect-designed study' (1987, pp.37–8). Related to this idea is the notion that there are different models of the research process. In the following pages, we shall look at two commonly used models.

## Sequential model

This model suggests that research passes through specific stages in pursuit of (at least tentative) answers to stated research questions. In this model, the research process is considered to take a relatively fixed, linear path, with a clear start and end. Gill and Johnson (1997) provide an example of this sequential model (shown in Figure 3.1).

## Cyclical model

Another common representation portrays the research process as cyclical. Here, many of the same aspects of the research process are included, and in

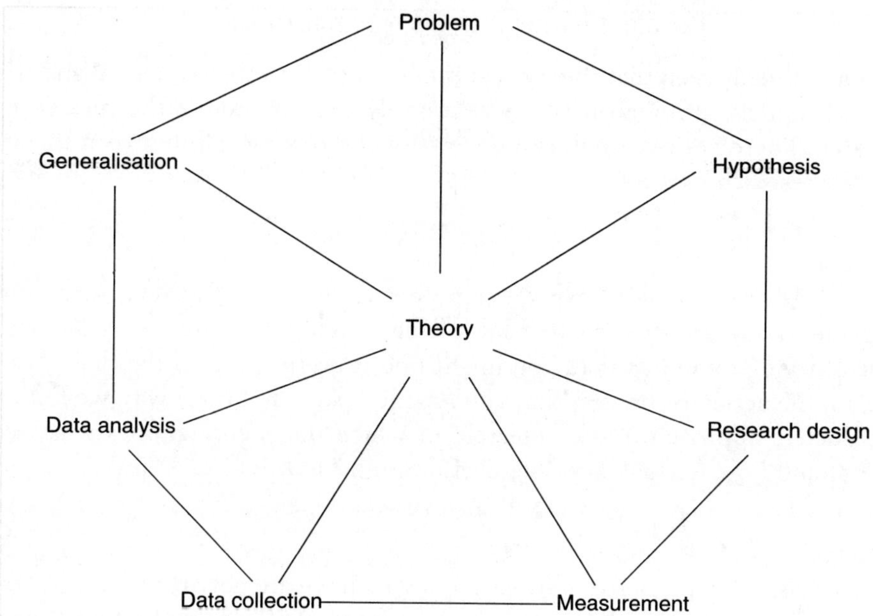


Figure 3.2 The cyclical model of the research process (Frankfort-Nachmias and Nachmias, 1996, p.20)

much the same order. Usually the cycle begins with a problem and finishes in a tentative generalisation. This marks the end of one cycle and forms the start of another.

This process may continue indefinitely, reflecting the progress of scientific knowledge. In this respect, the process is said to be *iterative*. There is an implication, however, that the process might be entered at a number of points, and that the experience of later stages might lead to a reinterpretation or revisiting of earlier stages. There is therefore no determinable chronological sequence to the process of research, and often there is an overlap between the different aspects of the research cycle.

As we shall see in Chapter 7, this is particularly the case for qualitative research, where data collection, analysis and problem formulation are closely bound up with each other. For instance, analysis of early interview data may lead the researcher into revising her or his line of questioning in later interviews. Thus, in the course of the research process, questions may be reconsidered, revised or even discarded as a result of earlier research. Figure 3.2 provides an illustration of the cyclical model.

So, the pursuit of knowledge is not necessarily as straightforward as the sequential model would imply. The reality for the practising researcher is that research will not always follow a clear and logical path, and at times it may even appear somewhat chaotic.

## The place of theory in the research process

We have already seen that theory is at the heart of both the sequential and the cyclical models, although it is not necessarily the initiator of the process of research. There are two contrasting views of the relationship between theory and the research process.

### *Deduction*

Usually we are seeking to explain some particular type of action or process, and often there are theories that have been developed already with the purpose of trying to do just that. You might find it useful to see if the theory can explain the action or process that you are interested in. In this way, we follow a deductive approach to our research, in which the theory defines what we look at and how we look at it (see Definition 3.1).

### *Induction*

Sometimes, we come across a situation in which we are not attempting to test how useful a particular theory is, but instead are seeking to understand a particular phenomenon, and through this, trying to build up an explanation of it. In this process – often rather loosely termed induction – we begin with a rather general research problem and, in the course of collecting and analysing data, we look for common themes or patterns in the data. Ultimately, we aim to draw some conclusions about the issue we are investigating, and perhaps to develop a tentative theory of our own (see Definition 3.1).

### Definition 3.1 Deduction and induction

**Deduction**: If you begin with theory, and use it to explain particular observation(s), this is known as deduction. Theory is applied in order to deduce explanations for the data. Basically, deduction begins with the construction of a theory or model, research is designed around the model, and data collected explains or refutes the model. This approach is often referred to as using the *hypothetico-deductive method*, associated with the *theory-then-research* strategy, in which:

- theory is consulted, and then guides the formulation of specific research questions;
- research questions are constructed as propositions, or hypotheses, which are then tested with empirical data.

If the data that has been collected demonstrates that the theory is lacking in some way, we may conclude that it has been falsified in its present form and needs to be revised. This process of falsification forces us to look at data in other ways to improve theories.

**Induction**: Contrary to deduction, induction moves from a set of observations to a theory, and is at the core of social scientific theory development. Induction allows a theory to be constructed from emerging patterns in the research data. It is associated with an *analytic-inductive method*, which is part of the *research-then-theory* strategy:

> The person doing such research assumes that he does not know enough before beginning his study to identify relevant problems and hypotheses in the organisation chosen for study, or to recognise valid indicators of the theoretical variables in which he is interested. He believes that a major part of his research must consist of finding out what problems he can best study in this organisation, what hypotheses will be fruitful and worth pursuing, what observations will best serve him as an indicator of the presence of such phenomena as, for example, cohesiveness or deviance. (Becker and Geer, cited in Burgess 1982, p.239)

## Getting started in research: the research problem

### The research problem

A research project usually begins with a broad idea that you want to explore – an idea about which you may have some initial thoughts. You start with a research problem. In this respect, Frankfort-Nachmias and Nachmias define the research problem as 'an intellectual stimulus calling for a response in the form of scientific inquiry' (1996, p.52).

Examples of research problems might include:

- Does educational attainment influence lifestyle preferences?
- What causes aggressive behaviour?
- Why do organisations relocate?
- What measures should government take to break the cycle of continuing political apathy among young people?

These are all problems that are amenable to some sort of research investigation in that the researcher may collect information in order to try to construct a plausible and credible answer to the question.

However, in addition to being empirically grounded, research problems have to be clearly specified. For example, the research problem 'What measures should government take to most effectively break the cycle of continuing political apathy among young people?' is rather too vague to research effectively. As a research question, its weakness is manifest in that:

- it is too ambiguous a statement to direct a research project;
- it is open to interpretation because of the lack of clarity in the meanings embedded within the research problem;
- it does not define who these young people actually are, in terms of age, gender, residence, social class, ethnic group, education, and so on;
- it does not indicate what is meant by 'political', or 'apathy', let alone what is meant by 'political apathy'– the latter could refer to all sorts of things, including (among many others), non-voting at elections, non-attendance at meetings of political parties, non-participation in demonstrations and protest rallies;
- it is unclear about the types of measure that may be considered. Assuming that political apathy refers to non-voting, measures might be cajoling or coercive in nature:
  - from making voting easier for young people (by changing the election rules to allow voting via the Internet);
  - through to more draconian and punitive approaches, such as imposing fines for those who do not cast a vote.

Deciding what you want to know through your research efforts, and then focusing this into a manageable and coherent research problem, is arguably the most difficult aspect of any research project.

### Focus your problem

Once you have chosen a topic, the next step in any research study is to set out clearly your research problem, which should:

- be specific;
- have a narrow focus;
- define all terms carefully.

An example of a well-designed research problem is provided by Kane (1990, p.19):

> *Changes (1950/1990) in Selected Characteristics of Convicted Juvenile Delinquents aged 13–18 years in St Michael's Correctional Institution.*

The research problem is clear about all aspects of the intended study and of its parameters, in terms of:

- the timeframe;
- the category of juvenile delinquent examined;
- the age of those to be researched;
- that only certain selected characteristics of the target group will be investigated;
- the particular site chosen as the setting for the research.

Kane (1990, p.20) suggests some useful steps for developing a clearly specified research problem:

i. Choose your topic and decide what aspect of it you wish to study. Ask: Who? What? Where? When? Why? How?
ii. State what you want to study in one sentence.
iii. Look at every word, and define each that you feel necessary.
iv. Rewrite your sentence, taking into account all the decisions you made in step (iii).

This involves a focusing process of moving from the general to the specific. Focusing is not an instantaneous process, but takes place over time. It will occur through consulting existing theories, debates and general issues emanating from the academic and/or professional literature. This will enable the researcher to generate issues for investigation, gain a sense of how to delimit the area into one that is specific and manageable, and develop an awareness of how others have sought to explain the issue(s). Furthermore, it may well take place in the course of actually collecting and analysing your data (perhaps as a result of carrying out and analysing your interviews and observations), especially where the research design is an emergent–qualitative one.

### Activity 3.1 The research problem

Think of an issue that you might be interested in examining through research — this may be something of general academic interest to you, or an issue related to your work, or a local issue. Define your research problem in no more than two sentences. Ask: Who? What? Where? When? Why? How? Then revise your research problem so that it can be summarised in a single sentence.

## Hypotheses, concepts, indicators and measurement

### Research hypotheses

You may find it helpful to set out a series of hypotheses to structure your research study, or these may emerge later during the course of a qualitative-based research project:

> A hypothesis is a tentative answer to a research problem, expressed in the form of a clearly stated relation between the independent and the dependent variables. Hypotheses are tentative answers because they can be verified only after they have been tested empirically. (Frankfort-Nachmias and Nachmias 1996, p.62)

As was noted above, research problems are usually too general by themselves to enable us to carry out meaningful analysis; they need to be specified in a more focused way. Hypotheses are specific statements that relate to the problem, the answers to which are likely to be yes or no, depending upon what is uncovered from the research. Examples of hypotheses might be:

- Suicide is related to the general level of religiosity/secularisation of society.
- Alienation and political participation are negatively related.

Such statements specify links between different phenomena, in order to explain different patterns of behaviour that appear to occur. However, such patterns of association do not necessarily demonstrate that a causal relationship exists. We cannot, for instance, say, 'socio-economic deprivation causes suicide'. If that was the case, then all those in Britain defined by various yardsticks as living in a state of relative poverty would inevitably commit suicide. This is, of course, highly unlikely to happen in the present climate!

## Concepts and measurement

In these hypotheses, there are a number of terms that are being used which are rather imprecise. They are commonly used, and there is a common understanding of what they mean. Nonetheless, they are rather abstract, and need to be clarified. We call these shorthand terms 'concepts'.

A concept is an abstract summary of a particular phenomenon that is of interest to a researcher – a representation of an object or one of its properties. Researchers have an idea of what they mean, and they are a useful way of describing and understanding different types of action, behaviour, characteristic, attitude, or other phenomenon that we come across.

Each scientific discipline develops its own concepts which constitute an accepted language. For example, 'inequality', 'racism', 'citizenship', 'power', and 'ideology' are concepts that are often explored in social and political science. Concepts such as 'aggression' and 'happiness' are common to psychologists. In business studies, researchers might encounter such abstract ideas as 'efficiency', workplace 'morale', and 're-skilling'. Hypotheses contain concepts that are the product of our reflections on the world.

Concepts are extremely useful in helping us to communicate succinctly. We can talk about the importance of social class in influencing our children's life-chances, for example, in terms of:

- the sorts of schools to which we are able to send our children;
- the types of qualification they might achieve;
- their chances of finding work;
- the type of employment they enter;
- the types of social circles we mix in;
- the goods and services we consume;
- and so on.

Of course, we will all have slightly different ways in which we understand social class, but using this concept enables researchers to communicate with each other, particularly with colleagues in the same profession.

But concepts need clarification if they are to be used effectively in research. They must be defined in terms of how they relate to a particular study. The general process for doing this is as follows.

## Conceptual definitions

The first step is to define what we mean by any particular concept. Once that has been done, it will then be possible to develop indicators for that concept as it has been defined.

A useful starting point is to look at the range of definitions of the concept that other researchers have used to tackle the problem. De Vaus (1996, p.50) discusses religiousness, and notes that some conceptualisations may regard it as about *belief*, and others about *behaviour*. Any set of beliefs that provides people with meaning in life may be defined as religious. What about those people who do not attend any religious services but who have a deep personal spiritual belief? Does belief have to include some notion of a supernatural being? At some point you have actually to decide on a single conceptual definition that encompasses the nature of your research.

## Delineate the dimensions of the concept

For many concepts, there will be different dimensions that it may be useful to distinguish in your research. Poverty, for instance, may be conceptualised in economic terms, perhaps using income (or rather the lack of it!) to assess its existence or not. But it may also be thought of as having a social dimension (such as living in a high-crime area), or an environmental dimension (perhaps the levels of noise or traffic pollution in an area). Determining these different dimensions, distinguishing between them, and then devising relevant questions to ask about them are likely to assist you greatly in conducting your research project:

> Distinguishing between dimensions can lead to more sophisticated theorising and more useful analysis. (De Vaus 1996, p.50)

## Defining concepts in practice

Seeman (1972, cited in Frankfort-Nachmias and Nachmias 1996, p.32) developed a conceptualisation of alienation that delineated five different dimensions:

1. *Powerlessness* – the expectation of individuals that their behaviour cannot bring about or influence the outcomes they desire.
2. *Meaningless* – the perception by individuals that they do not understand decisions made by others or events taking place around them.

3. *Normlessness* – the expectation that socially unacceptable behaviour (cheating) is now required to achieve certain goals.
4. *Isolation* – the feeling of separateness that comes from rejecting socially approved values and goals.
5. *Self-estrangement* – the denial of the image of the 'self' as defined by the immediate group or the society at large.

### From conceptual definition to operational definition

Once you have been able to specify the different dimensions of your concepts, you will be at the point where you can move from the abstract to the concrete. The operationalisation of concepts refers to the process through which indicators are developed to measure your concepts, – i.e. to transform them into observable phenomena.

From each of his five dimensions of alienation, Seeman developed a set of questions that were used to operationalise each one. For example, the following were used to operationalise 'powerlessness':

- 'Suppose your town was considering a regulation that you believed to be very unjust or harmful. What do you think you could do?' [People who responded that they could do nothing were categorised as powerless.]
- 'If you made an effort to change this regulation how likely do you think you would succeed?'
- 'If such a case arose how likely is it that you would actually do something about it?'
- 'Would you ever try to influence a local decision?'

Although alienation can never be empirically *observed*, the questionnaire items serve as indicators through which it can be inferred.

De Vaus (1996, pp.47–8) provides a useful overview of what the process entails. He asks, 'if we are interested in testing the hypothesis that religiousness is a response to deprivation, where might we begin?' The proposed relationship is a positive one, where an increase in deprivation (the independent variable) *causes* people to be more religious (dependent variable). To test the research hypothesis we must work out who is religious and who is not, and classify people according to whether or not they are 'deprived'. Income might be used to determine who is deprived and who is not: those earning less than £6,000 a year could be classified as deprived and those earning £6,000 and more could be classified as non-deprived. Church attendance might be used to denote religiousness, with monthly or more frequent attendees being identified as religious and all others as non-religious.

### How many indicators to use?

Typically, concepts are complex and are best measured with a number of indicators to encompass their full scope. There is often a need to establish multiple indicators to infer the existence or not of a particular concept.

For instance, religiousness cannot be measured simply by asking how often people attend religious services. This is just one way in which a person's commitment to their religion could be expressed. The single indicator of church attendance does not address the many other aspects of 'religiousness', for example:

- observance of religious festivals;
- having a good knowledge about one's faith;
- how often a person prays;
- whether someone believes in life after death;
- whether one adheres to the central tenets of the faith.

If we only ask one question, then we run the risk of only discovering one facet of the phenomenon under investigation. There may be many highly religious people who for a variety of reasons do not attend religious services.

### Activity 3.2 Operationalisation of concepts

Take the research problem that you defined in Activity 3.1. Provide two examples of conceptual definitions that such a research area would lead you to examine, and for *each*, provide two operational definitions:

**Concept 1:**
Operational definition 1
Operational definition 2

**Concept 2:**
Operational definition 1
Operational definition 2

## Research designs

Having discussed the process through which we transform a research idea into a manageable research question, the next step in any project is to decide upon the framework that is to be followed in conducting the research – or the *research design*:

> Research design situates the researcher in the empirical world, and connects the research questions to data. ... [It] is the basic plan for a piece of research, and includes four main ideas. The first is the strategy. The second is the conceptual framework. The third is the question of whom or what will be studied. The fourth concerns the tools and procedures to be used for collecting and analysing empirical materials. Research design thus deals with four main questions, corresponding to these ideas: the data will be collected (and analysed) following what strategy? Within what framework? From whom? How? (M. Punch 1998, p.66).

As we can see from this definition, there is an important distinction to be made here, between what we have defined as research design and what we define as research methods. The latter is merely an aspect of research design, including techniques for drawing samples as well as methods for collecting and analysing data.

There are numerous research designs open to the researcher. The main research designs are:

- comparative design;
- experimental research design;
- cross-sectional design;
- longitudinal design;
- case study design;
- action research design;
- evaluation research design.

## Comparative design

Comparison lies at the heart of all social research activity. In order to make inferences about social life, we need to make comparisons between cases that we are studying (whether they be individuals, groups, organisations or even nations), and often over time. Thus, Émile Durkheim was interested in examining the drivers and patterns of suicide. Writing in 1897, he compared suicide rates in different European countries over time, and within those countries he examined differences according to people's contexts – their family groupings, whether they lived in towns or in the countryside, whether or not they lived in Catholic or Protestant communities, the degree to which they were socially integrated within their community, the extent of social support available to them, and many other variables.

Durkheim used national government statistics (including death certificates) in his examination of suicide rates, but comparative designs might use all manner of different methods and sources of data – and they might not necessarily be cross-national in nature. As May (2001, p.206) indicates:

> At an analytic level, we make comparisons between the influences of variables from questionnaire results, or accounts in interview transcripts, or documentary sources and field notes on observational settings. On a more general level, we compare within societies (*intra-societal* comparison) and between societies (*inter-societal* comparison). [original emphasis]

There are some important issues to consider when conducting comparative research studies. These include:

- There is a need to be sensitive to the diversity and specificities of individual cases selected for study, particularly in cross-national studies. For instance, consider a pan-European study of poverty rates that are based on indicators developed by the statistical agencies of different national governments. In such a project, researchers would need to be aware that key indicators, such as unemployment figures, might be measured differently in the various countries examined. The absence of universal criteria against which to measure phenomena undermines both direct comparative analysis and validity.

- Related to this point is the issue that generalisation from cross-national studies to other cases is not always possible because of the array of political, social, economic and cultural forms apparent in different countries. Thus, a study which examines the historical relationship between social class and political power in Western Europe may have only limited application to a nation outside that region, where the historical-cultural determinants of political power may, for instance, have their roots in ethnicity.
- Comparative research does not always need to be cross-*national* in nature. For example, a study of the location and social mobility decisions of dual career households might compare data from different regions of a country, or it might compare the sectors within which participants work, such as education, industrial manufacturing, the banking service sector and the blue-chip, hi-tech sector.
- The comparative design is often thought of as quantitative in nature, involving large-scale analysis of multiple observations from within two or more cases. For instance, a comparison of the impact of labour market reform legislation initiated by the European Commission in different member states might involve comparable large-scale samples of car assembly workers in six different countries. Such a study might use a cross-sectional research design format (see below for a discussion of cross-sectional research designs). However, a comparative study might equally take a qualitative form, involving a multi-case study design. For instance, researchers might examine the impact of the EU labour market reforms in different UK workplaces, with detailed investigation in three large, three medium and three small industrial enterprises (see below for an overview of case study designs).

## Experimental research design

This particular research design is the benchmark against which all others are assessed, and it is dealt with at length in Chapter 6. Considered to be the archetypal scientific method, it is at its simplest a design that has as its purpose to make sense of the social world by identifying underlying patterns of behaviour, and establishing causal relationships between phenomena, to determine what are the factors that govern human behaviour and shape beliefs and attitudes.

As an example, an experimental research design might be used by researchers to make inferences about the predictive effect of exposure to television news messages (independent variables) on people's attitudes regarding migrant workers in the UK (the dependent variable), and from there to assert the more or less general applicability of the findings to the public at large. In the experiment, a small number of participants would be carefully and systematically selected. The sample might also take account of variables such as gender, age and ethnicity, if these were considered to be relevant.

Participants would then complete a *pre-test* – an opinion questionnaire that was designed to measure their views about the issue. Once this data was established, they would then be exposed to an intervention in the form of televised news broadcasts about East European migrant workers. These interventions would be broadcast within a controlled environment, whereby the participants had no access to other sources of information about the matter. Finally, an identical opinion questionnaire would be reissued to participants as a *post-test*. Any differences in responses recorded in the *pre-* and *post-tests* would then be interpreted by the researcher as evidence of a causal impact of the television news broadcasts on the participants' views about East European migrant workers settling in the UK.

Note that because of the way the experimental research design has been organised, it will be possible to factor in an analysis of the potential impact of additional independent variables on the relationship between exposure to news messages and the formation of attitudes. Does the *strength* of impact vary according to participants' ethnicity or whether they are male or female?

It was mentioned in the example that the experiment would be conducted within a *controlled environment*. For researchers working within this tradition, the emphasis on control is a very important feature of the research process. Such control is important for the reliability of the study, as it enables the manipulation of study conditions to minimise the impact of extraneous variables on the study, and uphold the integrity of the data. It is important, therefore, to disentangle the experiment from its context so that only the key variables of interest in the study are subject to investigation. With this in mind, the research team would aim to ensure that any change in responses recorded in the post-test were actually a direct function of the result of exposure to the intervention. What this means is that participants would not have any opportunity to look at other sources of political information (such as newspapers or television news items) that might otherwise influence their views on East European migrant workers as measured in the post-test questionnaire.

## Cross-sectional design

The purpose of a cross-sectional research design is to examine variation across cases (whether they be people, households or organisations), usually in terms of a range of variables of interest to the researcher. Often considered to be synonymous with survey research, the cross-sectional design will aim to take quantitative measures on the topic of interest from a relatively large number of cases and at a single point in time.

An opinion poll provides a useful illustration. Here, the pollster (the researcher) will aim to gather data relating to people's (cases) political views (variables) in order to examine how these views vary across different subgroups of people. Such polls will often take soundings from several hundred members of the electorate. For instance, political parties might commission a polling agency to survey the political party preferences of first-time voters and older groups during an election campaign period. Potential voters will be carefully selected according to key criteria to ensure that, taken together, they represent a broad cross-section of the voting public, and that the findings from the study approximate the political party preferences of voters across the country. The record of the pollsters is very good when it comes to forecasting the voting intentions of citizens in European and US elections (see Henn 1998).[1] Indeed, in the final week of the 2008 USA presidential election, the average of 15 national polls published gave the eventual victor, Democrat Barrack Obama, a 7.6% lead over Republican John McCain, within 1% of the final 6.7% margin of victory. With over 127 million people voting, estimating the election outcome to such a close point using polls with an average sample size of only 1,400 is testament to the reliability of well-prepared cross-sectional research designs.

A key feature of cross-sectional research designs is that data should be collected at the same point in time. This is to mitigate against the possibility that external time-related events and variables impact on the data. Take as an example a situation whereby mid-way during the data collection process of an opinion poll that is spread over an extended period of time, a national party leader makes a radical and controversial policy announcement with the conscious intention to shift people's voting allegiances. Those people interviewed by the pollsters prior to the policy announcement may well have expressed different views if they had had a chance to hear the policy announcement. In such a scenario, the final opinion poll would include views that were out of date – the poll would not accurately represent the views of these voters.

## Longitudinal design

In contrast to the cross-sectional research design, longitudinal designs are deployed to measure *change* in attitudes or behaviour by comparing data from studies conducted at two (or more) points in time. A key feature of longitudinal designs, therefore, is that they enable examination of social processes and change, and, as such, allow the researcher to gain insight as to the relationships between variables and, in some cases, even to infer causality.

For instance, Henn et al. (2002) conducted a two-wave panel survey of young people to assess, among other things, the impact of elections on their political views and orientations. A probability random sampling method was

[1] However, notable exceptions include the UK general elections of 1951, 1970 and particularly 1992, where the 50 pre-election polls provided a relatively stable forecast of a narrow Labour win prior to the eventual landslide victory of John Major's Conservative party (see Chapter 6).

used to select 1,597 young people aged 18 from a regional electoral register, and a detailed self-completion questionnaire was sent to them one year prior to the 1999 European Assembly elections – the first such contest for which they were old enough to vote. A further questionnaire was posted to the same individuals one year later and shortly after the election, with 425 of the original respondents taking part in this second-wave. The findings revealed a broad pattern in the data which, although not statistically significant, indicated an increasing dislocation from mainstream and electoral politics, with young people critical of the way that political parties and professional politicians conducted themselves.[2]

This example is useful in that it raises several noteworthy points of methodological interest concerning longitudinal designs:

- There are different types of longitudinal design. The most commonly used are *panel designs* (outlined in the example above), which involve collecting data on different occasions from the exact same individuals. *Cohort designs* investigate people because they share particular characteristics or life experiences; they can be distinguished from panel designs because each wave comprises entirely new people. In Britain, the Youth Cohort Survey samples a different group of 16 year olds annually to investigate (changing) patterns of activity among those who are at a stage in life when they can make decisions about further education, work or training.
- Longitudinal designs are typically (but not exclusively) based on highly structured quantitative research approaches (often with a large sample, or 'large *N*'). Thus, the research design will often draw on an examination of a carefully selected sample, in which views and behaviours are quantified in order to precisely monitor patterns of change over time.
- There are two potential problems associated with panel designs – those of panel attrition and panel conditioning:

    1. *Panel attrition*: As panel designs aim to study the same individuals on different occasions, there is always the danger that people exit from the study (perhaps through changes in circumstance, boredom or even death). Where this is the case, subsequent panel waves become increasingly unrepresentative of the initial wave. Although it will remain appropriate to examine changes in individual-level data, making survey-wide comparisons becomes potentially less reliable, particularly if those who leave the study are different in important ways from those who remain. If the decision is taken to analyse data only from those who remain in the final round of data collection, it is important to recognise that this sample may no longer be representative of the original population from which they were drawn.
    2. *Panel conditioning*: This represents a further threat to validity in that the more that individuals take part in successive waves of a panel survey, the greater the

[2] This was also reflected in follow-up focus group work conducted as part of the project, with young people claiming that the election had left them feeling even more marginalised from the political process.

risk that they become sensitised to the issues that they are questioned about. If this happens, the sample group may become increasingly atypical of the population that they were originally chosen to represent. For instance, where an individual is repeatedly questioned about their political views in a pre-election panel survey, the more likely they are to then seek out information about politics and the election. If this happens, they will become better informed than the broader electorate about such matters, and consequently may respond differently to questions as a result of participating in the survey.

## Case study design

While the previous research designs are often associated with more structured approaches and with the use of quantitative methods, the case study design is commonly characterised as having a more *qualitative* orientation – although as we shall see, it may often deploy quantitative methods and use relatively structured data.

Unlike cross-sectional and longitudinal designs, the case study will involve intensive, detailed and in-depth research among a small sample of carefully selected cases (what is often referred to as 'small *N*'), or even of a single case. The cases themselves may include a variety of different types of setting, situation or group (or even individual), such as:

- a single organisation – a hospice, in which the purpose of the study is to investigate the ways in which volunteers are provided with structured emotional support mechanisms;
- a particular community – perhaps a rural village which has been the setting for a prolonged dispute between land developers and a direct action environmental protection group;
- a particular group – a case study design might consider the psychological impact on protagonists of their involvement in a long-term industrial strike;
- an individual – for example, an in-depth examination designed to understand the motivations and offending dynamics of a career criminal;
- a decision – such as a local authority's decision to merge two schools (why was the decision taken, how was it implemented and what was the outcome);
- an event – for instance, a fiercely fought national election campaign.

The purpose for using a case study design will be to examine the intricacies and complexities of the situation (or setting or group) selected for study in order to reveal its most important features. Unlike the experimental research design, the case study design will consider contextual conditions in order to discover whether or not they are relevant to and impact upon the topic of investigation. The research will be systematic and extremely detailed, and researchers will tend to draw upon a wide variety of data, not hesitating to deploy more than one research method if doing so enables the development of a complete account of the social process(es) under investigation. For example, Corrigan (1979) used both qualitative and quantitative methods for capturing the life and school experiences of his 'Smash Street kids' in Sunderland during the 1970s. His period of fieldwork was prolonged, and his experience was common for researchers working within this tradition, whose studies tend to be conducted over an extended period of time in order to probe and dissect the area of investigation.

Inevitably, there will be a trade-off for researchers using a case study design; the benefits of richness and insight that derive from investigating a situation in such fine detail will come with the cost that such projects will tend to lack breadth of coverage. Thus the case study design is typically small *N*, implying that the findings that emerge will likely be particularistic and even unique – often with comparatively little scope for application to other situations, settings or groups, or what we often refer to as *external validity* or *generalisability* (see Chapters 6 and 7). This issue of the extent to which inferences may be drawn from such research is a contentious and defining one for researchers using case study designs. Indeed, many researchers would argue that a shortfall in any capacity for identifying general laws of human behaviour is but a small price to pay for the richness and depth of theoretical insight that follows from a well-designed and well-executed case study.

## Action research design

Action research has as its primary objective to identify a specific practice-based problem, and then to undertake research in order to identify the means (or *action*) through which to resolve it. Thus, it has an action-orientation that emphasises change rather than a descriptive-orientation. The research is based in practice and is commonly used in organisational, educational, and also increasingly in health and social care settings. However, it is also used by those working within a critical social research tradition for emancipatory ends, usually to initiate change (see Chapter 2). Reinharz (1992), for instance, argues that feminist research is linked to action, with a politicising purpose to enlighten participants and help them to change their situations. However, while action research can be emancipatory, many studies using this approach are quite practical, with the intention to improve efficiency and processes within an organisation.

Winter and Munn-Giddings characterise action research as a process that 'alternates continuously between inquiry and action, practice and innovative thinking – a developmental spiral of practical decision making and evaluative reflection' (2001, p.5). Kurt Lewin is credited with first developing the term 'action research' (1946). He conceptualised it as a spiral of cycles of planning, acting, observing and reflecting on the project outcomes. The approach is considered to be cyclical in that reflection is likely to lead to a revised plan, which requires further acting, observing and reflecting. Implicit in this definition is the notion of improvement. For Carr and Kemmis, this involves 'firstly, the improvement of a *practice* of some kind; secondly, the improvement of the *understanding* of the practice by its practitioners; and thirdly, the improvement of the *situation* in which the practice takes place' (1986, p.165).

A key feature of the action research design is that it has a democratic and user orientation. It is collaborative and participative, and emphasises the involvement of both the researcher and the research participant(s) in the research process. This aspect of the action research design runs counter to the strict separation of roles that is advocated by many researchers working within the scientific tradition as outlined in Chapter 1. Instead, the research aims, design and strategy in action research are jointly negotiated at the outset and throughout the duration of the study. It is this participative and democratic approach that makes the action research design so attractive to critical social researchers, as it implies a radical redefinition of research roles and a research design that is non-hierarchical.

### Example 3.1 The Management of Workplace Stress

An action research project might focus on developing an initiative within a particular hospital that has a high incidence of stress-related staff absenteeism. In such a research scenario, the researcher would collaborate with various key stakeholders in the design and implementation of the project. These would include the hospital's senior management team, the branch committees of the various recognised trades unions and a patient support group. The brief of the action research partnership would be to identify the key stress drivers and to formulate interventions aimed at reducing the impact of these. The research strategy would involve collection and analysis of numerous types of data, using observations, an online quantitative questionnaire survey and focus groups.

In many respects, the action research design is similar to the case study design in that it takes a particular situation and examines it in fine detail. Furthermore, while it will adopt a systematic research approach, the actual choice of methods deployed will be a flexible and pragmatic one. Thus, the research inquiry may involve either quantitative or qualitative data methods and designs, or it may use a combination of both in a triangulated research study (see Chapter 1).

## Evaluation research design

Evaluation studies are an increasingly prominent feature of the contemporary public service landscape across the USA, Europe and Australasia. They are commonly used by government departments and by public service agencies for the purposes of examining the effectiveness of policies, initiatives, services and social programmes, and for determining whether or not these are achieving their stated aims. Evaluation projects are also commissioned with the intention of attaining transparency in the conduct, efficiency and performance of programme activities. The findings of such studies are often published to enable external scrutiny and public accountability of an agency's activities.

Evaluation studies can be distinguished from action research studies on two key fronts. First, while action research projects are designed to identify and resolve practice-based problems, the purpose of an evaluation study is to measure the impact of an intervention that has previously been initiated. Thus, researchers will be commissioned to undertake an assessment of a policy or programme such as the impact of CCTV on crime rates, by measuring the programme's performance against certain carefully defined criteria.

Secondly, evaluation researchers are not involved in the type of *collaborative* relationships that are so typical in action research. Instead, evaluation researchers will normally adopt an autonomous and professional role that is distanced from the strategic interests and, indeed, the politics of the commissioning agency and those that observe it. This is important if the outcomes from the research are to be adjudged as objective and free from external influence and bias. However, where a project brief is specified in advance by the agency, it will likely reflect the agency's assumptions concerning what it considers to be worthy of investigation, its ideas about how performance should be measured and who should be consulted and questioned as part of the measurement process, and how the agency regards success or failure. Furthermore, if the outcomes of the research contradict the interests of the commissioning agency, there is every possibility that the research is kept out of the public domain to avoid external criticism.

Where the commissioning agency takes such a guiding and interventionist role, there is always a risk to the researcher that the integrity of the evaluation outcomes will be called into question. This will be particularly so in a charged political climate where the motivation behind the social programme is subject to controversy. It is therefore an obligation of the evaluation researcher to take a proactive role in the management of expectations of all parties involved in the research, and to establish from the outset transparency in terms of the aims of the research, how the study is to be designed and conducted, copyright matters, and how the data are to be published. An evaluation commission should therefore only be accepted by a researcher if the proposed project outline can be demonstrated to be professional, fair and ethically sound.

Much evaluation research has traditionally been experimental in nature, using random control trials in which the findings from two groups – one that has experience of the social programme and one that has not – are compared to assess the impact or effectiveness of the programme. However, the value of an exclusively experimental approach in evaluation research has been questioned in some quarters. For instance, Pawson and Tilley conclude from their examination of numerous experimental evaluation studies, including Martinson's review of offender rehabilitation schemes that, '[f]or us, the experimental paradigm constitutes a heroic failure, promising so much and yet ending up in ironic anti-climax' (1997, p.8). They claim that evidence indicates an inconsistency in outcomes across experimental evaluations of similar programmes. They interpret this as a consequence of the method's failure to account for context, and specifically to ask, '"why" or "how" the measure has its effect' (1997, p.11). Perhaps not surprisingly, the approaches used in evaluation studies are now increasingly likely to be diverse, and often researchers will deploy a range of both quantitative and qualitative approaches and methods in a single evaluation project.

### Example 3.2 Martinson's 'What works? Questions and answers about prison reform' (1974)

In 1974, Robert Martinson published a review of 231 experimental-based evaluations of prison rehabilitation schemes that had been conducted between 1945 and 1967. The conclusion from this meta-analysis was that these reform measures were broadly unsuccessful: '...with few and isolated exceptions, the rehabilitative efforts that have been reported so far have had no appreciable effect on recidivism' (1974, p.25).

The political fallout from Martinson's report was intense, and it received significant publicity and generated much controversy. The findings were used vigorously by the anti-rehabilitation lobby in an attempt to evidence support for their position that the prison system was too lenient, and to try to influence policy-making. Indeed, in 1989, the US Supreme Court upheld federal sentencing guidelines which removed rehabilitation from serious consideration when sentencing offenders.

Pawson and Tilley contend that due to Martinson's subscription to an 'impossibly stringent' research design that excluded all non-experimental studies and included only those programmes which 'provide[d] positive changes in favour of the experimental group in all trials in all contexts' (1997, p.9), it was perhaps not surprising that Martinson's review concluded that such prison rehabilitation schemes were likely to fail.

## Case selection

The initial question posed at the beginning of this chapter concerned the extent to which it was possible to obtain credible conclusions from research.

We have considered two of the core elements of this: the research problem and how this can be transformed into a manageable and measurable area for inquiry; and the research design, the general approach through which data should be collected and analysed. The third major element to be addressed is how do we select cases for study so that we can have confidence in any conclusions that we draw from the findings? That is, who should be our target group, and how should we select members from that group to include in our research project?

## Representative cases

When focusing on one single case in a research project – for instance, how decisions are made in a local group campaigning against the closure of a school – then the way in which that case has been selected is largely unproblematic.

However, when you are selecting a subset of cases with the intention of making claims about – or of generalising to – a larger group or population, then the way in which you choose these cases is fraught with potential problems. These might possibly undermine any conclusion(s) that you draw from subsequent research. For instance, if you are conducting a city-wide study on the extent to which people have been victims of crime, you are likely to find it prohibitively expensive to conduct a census – a study of the entire population of the city that you are examining. An alternative approach might be to carry out a sample survey – a subset of the target group that you are investigating. Yet this can only be a description of the city's population in so far as it is representative of it.

We need to be assured that the sample is made up of the same kinds of people, in the same proportions, as the population.

Consequently, the credibility of a project's findings and conclusions will rest largely on the cases selected for investigation (Definition 3.2). Such an evaluation will be based upon an assessment of whether or not the study is externally valid:

> External validity ... [is] the extent to which the conclusions of the study generalise beyond the immediate subjects and circumstances of the investigation. (Sapsford 1993, p.19)

### Definition 3.2 Cases

Cases are the units of investigation. They are often people who may be studied at different levels – as individuals, within communities and within groups (such as trade unionists or owners of small firms). But cases may also refer to other units of analysis, including organisations (schools, businesses, political parties), localities, regions, countries. They may also include 'incidences' – political scientists, for example, might focus upon political riots, sociologists might compare different instances of suicide or police drugs raids, while business studies students might focus on company mergers or company closures.

**Aside**: There is considerable debate on ethical grounds as to how 'people as cases' should be conceptualised in research, as respondents, subjects, citizens, participants, or in some other way (see Finch 1993, pp.174–9).

There are various sampling procedures which have been developed in an attempt to achieve representative samples and external validity, and these include both probability and non-probability sampling methods. See Chapter 6 for a discussion of different sampling methods.

## Typical cases

In circumstances in which only a small number of cases are investigated (such as environmental policies within three selected countries), or even a single case (a particular factory or hospital), there is often an implicit assumption held by the researcher that the findings can, to a certain extent, be generalised to other situations. It is not possible to guarantee that these cases will be representative, but the researcher should make an attempt to establish that the case or cases are at least typical – that other cases are likely to resemble it sufficiently for general conclusions to be drawn.

## Theoretical sampling

A final kind of sampling which does not need to demonstrate either typicality or representativeness is theoretical sampling. Here, cases are selected specifically because the analysis is intended to shed light on some aspect of theory that you are interested in. Such cases are often referred to as *critical cases*. Qualitative researchers, whose studies are likely to be small-scale and intensive, commonly use this method of selecting cases.

For example, Henn (1998) wanted to show that the processes of social and political restructuring in contemporary societies were such that electorates were becoming progressively volatile and unpredictable. Consequently, opinion polls would find it increasingly difficult to measure voting behaviour.

Henn took as his starting point an analysis of electoral developments in Britain, which was chosen theoretically and strategically as a critical case. He made the claim that Britain served as a useful analytical benchmark in which the processes of what he referred to as 'Complex Politics' were historically least pronounced; if the processes of complexity were causing concern for pollsters here, it would be likely that the scenario for pollsters in other late-capitalist countries would be more marked.

For comparative purposes, he then conducted research in cases where the processes of political complexity were most advanced as far as opinion polling was concerned – the European post-communist societies. He stopped sampling cases when it was clear that no new theoretical insight could be gained, i.e. when theoretical saturation had been reached. Extract 3.1 (taken from Henn 1998, pp.6–7) outlines the method of theoretical sampling used in this example.

## Extract 3.1 Theoretical sampling for the comparison of opinion polling contexts in late-capitalist and post-communist societies (Henn 1998)

**Countries chosen for analysis**

The analyses of the role, status and functions of political opinion polling in this book are confined primarily to capitalist and post-communist contexts, and are based largely upon case studies. To represent post-communist political systems which have developed from their communist roots, there will be a focus on the former Soviet Union, Bulgaria, Romania, Poland, Hungary and the former Czechoslovakia. As an example of a capitalist political system, there will be a focus on Britain, although polling developments elsewhere in Europe, the USA, and Australasia will be referred to. The inference here is that where political landscapes are complex, such as in late-capitalist and post-communist political systems, then pollsters will confront a number of problematic factors which will combine to make their tasks increasingly arduous. At the same time, where political landscapes are less complex, then the problems for opinion pollsters will be less defined. Britain is regarded as a critical methodological case here to test the shift toward Complex Politics in late-capitalist societies. According to Almond and Verba, it came closest to their conception of the ideal 'civic culture' in the 1950s and 1960s. They suggested that there was a high degree of political consensus relating to the post-war British state and its system of government, a strong sense of deference to political authority, and significant trust and confidence in Britain's political institutions and political arrangements (Almond and Verba 1963, pp.197–198). Furthermore, it can be argued that traditionally Britain has had a comparatively stable, majoritarian system, with a limited number of well-established parties competing for governmental office and forming traditional alliances with blocs of voters. Indeed, Britain possessed, certainly up until the early 1970s, one of the most stable and enduring political systems within the advanced capitalist world (Crewe 1977). At the heart of this stability, was the largely homogeneous nature of society, with cleavages which were based predominantly on social class lines underpinning party-voter alliances. Finally, Britain has always been more tolerant of polls than many of its capitalist counterparts, such as Spain, Portugal, Italy, Belgium, France, Switzerland, Germany and others, where polling is either banned at particular times within the electoral cycle or else subject to external regulation.

Consequently, if Britain's political landscape begins to display features similar to those found in the post-communist societies, then it can be assumed that those other European capitalist political systems whose political landscapes are more complex historically than Britain's, are likely to undergo such changes more rapidly. The implications are that, if the developing processes of political complexity serve to undermine the ability of pollsters to effectively carry out their tasks in Britain in ways which reflect the situation in the post-communist political systems, then the situation will be more critical for Britain's more complex late-capitalist neighbours in Western Europe. Such developments may precipitate the need to reappraise methodological techniques, and develop new styles of measuring public opinion so as to prepare for these shifts toward more complex political landscapes throughout Europe. The analysis of polling in post-Second World War capitalist and post-communist societies which follows will give an indication of these developments and the likely scenarios for political opinion polling in the future in a variety of European contexts.

## Activity 3.3 Selecting cases

Take the research problem that you defined and operationalised in Activities 3.1 and 3.2, and *briefly*:

1. Outline and justify the method or combination of methods that you would use to investigate your research problem(s).
2. Define and justify which cases you would select for study.
3. Describe the process that you would take in order to include your chosen cases.
4. How would you classify your method for the selection of your cases — representative sampling, typicality sampling, or theoretical sampling? Why have you chosen this approach?
5. To what extent do you consider that the findings which would be generated by this method are generalisable?

## Constraints on achieving credible conclusions: power, politics and values

In any research, there will be certain decisions made about, and influences imposed upon, the research design which need to be addressed and laid bare if the conclusions which the study generates are to be considered as credible. For instance, the early choices which underlie research design and the way the design is manifested in the research process are not merely technical questions. They relate intimately to the underlying values and assumptions of the researcher, and of other more structural factors such as the priorities and agendas of the sponsors of the research.

For instance, Bilton et al. (1987, pp.505–6) recount how the Social Science Research Council (the main source of funding for academics in higher education since 1966) was reorganised in 1983, and renamed as the Economic and Social Research Council. Bilton et al. imply that deletion of the label 'science' from the ESRC's name and the substantial reduction in the level of financial support to the agency were largely due to concerns among leading members of the government with the direction that much academic research was seen to be taking. First, there appeared to be a marked shift within these research fields to a more 'qualitative' and, it was perceived, 'unscientific' style of research. Secondly, the Secretary of State for Education, acting on behalf of the government, was concerned with the radical nature of much of the research that was conducted.

Gatekeepers may also wield extensive power over your research – they do, after all, have the ability to deny you access to the target group or research site that you are interested in studying. You may need to negotiate certain aspects of your proposed research design and, in so doing, compromise your research plans to some degree. This was the experience of a team of researchers when conducting a collaborative project exploring the perceptions of rank-and-file members to the leadership of one of the two main British political parties (Henn et al. 1997). Negotiations were held with the local, regional and national party offices. Intended research questions were carefully scrutinised and the merits of many were debated. Access to the membership database – crucial for the research – was eventually granted, subject to compromises made in terms of the method and timing of publication.

What we can derive from this discussion is that data is *not* 'asocial', waiting to be gathered in by some mechanical and neutral process. There is a process involved in deciding what to research and how to research it, which is affected by the interests and values of the researcher and of the funders of the research.

Furthermore, the power of certain people and groups to resist a researcher's investigations is also likely to affect the outcome of any research study. For example, Stavenhagen (1993, p.59) claims that much social science research tends to focus upon relatively powerless, marginalised and vulnerable groups precisely because they do not have the resources at their disposal to deflect the attentions of inquisitive researchers. This is in stark contrast with elites, who are able to wield considerable power to avoid coming under scrutiny by researchers:

> How many studies do we have of political elites and their decision-making processes; of the functioning of bureaucracies; of entrepreneurs (not only as innovators or modernizers but as political and economic groups); of foreign business communities in underdeveloped countries; of corruption among labor leaders; of advertising and the manipulation of ideologies, opinions, attitudes, tastes and the innermost emotions ... of the role of the mass media; of oppressive educational systems; or simply of the varied and multiple aspects of repression (physical, cultural, psychological, economic) that dominant groups use to maintain the *status quo*? ... Admittedly, these are difficult areas for the fieldworker to get involved in. And by tradition we have chosen the path of least resistance. It is easier to walk into a peasant hut than into an executive office; besides, the peasant is not likely to ever read our field report. (Stavenhagen 1993, p.59)

And many would argue that there is much about the social world that is left masked by mainstream social science research. As we have seen in Chapter 2, many researchers call for positive steps to address this:

> Many feminists have argued for a specifically feminist methodology: one which emphasises the omni-relevance of gender, a respect for personal experience as against scientific method, a rejection of 'hierarchical' forms of research, and the emancipation of women as the goal of research. (Hammersley 1995, p.x)

## Summary

The research design of your project should take into account all the issues that have been addressed in this chapter. In particular, for research conclusions to be plausible and credible they need to be based upon carefully formulated and expressed research problems. Without such clarity and precision about the focus of your study it is very difficult to develop a manageable research project. It is all too easy to find oneself embroiled in an overly ambitious, confusing and potentially messy process.

Theory plays a particularly important role in research; it may shape and itself be shaped by the research process. Deduction involves a theory-then-research approach in which the researcher consults current thinking about a particular issue and uses this as a starting point for the development of specific research questions (and often hypotheses) that are to be examined with empirical data. Thus, existing theory is deployed to help define the parameters of a research investigation – what is to be studied and how.

Induction is an approach that may be used by the researcher when there is less known about the phenomenon that is to be studied, the purpose being to collect data in order to develop theoretical insights. Using a research-then-theory approach, this exploratory process is at the heart of social scientific theory-building, and involves the researcher searching for meaning and emerging concepts from data in order to contribute to theoretical knowledge about a topic that has previously been under-researched. Often researchers will make use of both inductive and deductive approaches, either in the same study or in further research – a theory developed about a particular case inductively may be tested on other cases deductively. This leads to an interdependency between both approaches and between researchers.

In all research studies, there is always a danger that the outcome will be influenced by the values of the researcher or some other external force, whether that be the agency that has commissioned the research, or an organisation or individual that has the power to grant or not our access to the research site and the potential sample group. Values and preferences may impact upon the choices made in terms of the topic to be investigated, the approach and methods deployed, the interpretation given to the data, and the manner in which the results are written-up and disseminated. The researcher who aims to convince others that they should have confidence in his or her work should be aware of the potential impact of these pressures, and should reflect upon their research thinking and practice in order to conduct fair and balanced inquiry. This is necessary to minimise the potential of personal or political values affecting what is discovered and reported.

## Chapter research task

Using Activities 3.1–3.3 as a starting point, design the outline of a research project. To do this, you should think carefully about the following issues and write out your proposed project plans (use no more than 2–3 sides of paper in order to maintain focus):

- your title;
- the objectives of the proposed study;
- the research questions you would like to explore;
- your chosen research design (which should be justified);
- who you will include in your study (and why);
- how you will select these people for inclusion;
- what your methods are (which should be justified), and how you are actually to carry out your research;
- any problems or constraints you anticipate in conducting the research;
- any ethical issues that you think are likely to need to be addressed through your research.

## Recommended Reading

Bryman, A. 2004. *Social Research Methods*, 2nd edn. Oxford: Oxford University Press.

Frankfort-Nachmias, C. and Nachmias, D. 1996. *Research Methods in the Social Sciences*, 5th edn. New York: St Martin's Press.

Hakim, C. 1987. *Research Design: Strategies and Choices in the Design of Social Research*. London: Routledge.

Kane, E. 1990. *Doing Your Own Research: Basic Descriptive Research in the Social Sciences and Humanities*. London: Boyars.

Sapsford, R. 1993. Problems, Cases and the Logic of Research Studies. In: M. Hammersley (ed.), *Principles of Social and Educational Research*. Milton Keynes: Open University Press.

Stavenhagen, R. 1993. Decolonializing Applied Social Sciences. In: M. Hammersley (ed.), *Social Research: Philosophy, Politics and Practice*. London: Sage. pp.52–63.

Ward Schofield, J. 1993. Increasing the Generalisability of Qualitative Research. In: M. Hammersley (ed.), *Social Research: Philosophy, Politics and Practice*. London: Sage. pp.200–25.

# FOUR

# Ethics in Social Research

- To sensitise readers to key ethical issues which may arise during the research process
- To highlight the two extremes of the ethical debate, and the emphasis upon the pursuit of knowledge within this debate
- To provide a historical overview of the development of ethical codes of practice
- To make readers aware of power relationships, both evident and hidden, which may exist within the research process
- To make readers aware of the responsibilities they have to themselves, their participants and other parties involved in the research process



## Introduction

Science is neither neutral nor always beneficial.

> Controlling science ... raises resilient practical, ethical and legal issues that are a matter of constant debate. The questions involved confront us with fundamental dilemmas,

> such as the protection of the subjects versus the freedoms to conduct research and publish research findings. (M. Punch 1998, p.167)

Barnes (1979) contends that the concern about ethics in social research has only come about in the latter part of the twentieth century because of a historic shift in the balance of power *from* the research establishment *towards* ordinary citizens. He argues that the broad civil rights gained by British citizens from the 1950s onwards led them to question the activities that were carried out in the name of science. Previous to this, Barnes argues that citizens had virtually no part to play in what should be investigated, by whom, and how. He cites Mayhew's research as an example of this 'old-style' research: 'I made up my mind to deal with human nature as a natural philosopher or a chemist deals with any material object' (Henry Mayhew, in *London Labour and the London Poor*, 1861–2, cited in Barnes 1979, p.31).

In the past decade, methods of data collection and analysis have become far more sophisticated, owing largely to the advanced utilisation of computer technology. Social research has widened its scope and now has the potential to be far more intrusive and penetrating. Such capabilities have given rise to a greater concern in some quarters about the potential that those in positions of power now possess.

In addition, M. Punch (1998) identifies three developments that he says have led to a much greater awareness of the ethical dimension of social research:

1. The influence of critical social researchers from the feminist and disability rights movements who have encouraged a scholarship that is based on trust, openness and non-exploitative relationships (see Chapter 2).
2. Interventionist or 'action' research has promoted those who were previously regarded as the 'subjects' of research to be seen as equal partners – 'participants' and 'respondents'.
3. The financing of research by public bodies is commonly dependent on researchers signing an agreement on ethical standards.

## Defining ethical considerations

Barnes (1979, p.16) defines ethical factors as those which:

> arise when we try to decide between one course of action and another not in terms of expediency or efficiency but by reference to standards of what is morally right or wrong.

This definition makes an important distinction between matters of *principle* and matters of *expediency* – what is right or just in the interests of those who are the focus of research. Ethical considerations place the research participants, rather than the researcher, at the centre of the research design when deciding what is appropriate and acceptable conduct.

However, if we say that decisions need to be made and research planned on the basis of what is right or wrong, then we shall obviously encounter problems with the meanings of such words. Knowledge is not simply a neutral product – the values of individual researchers will have a significant impact on the decisions that they take in all aspects of their research.

All research raises ethical issues. When we talk about 'ethics' in social research we are addressing those issues that concern the behaviour of social researchers and the consequences that their research brings to the people they study. As such, ethical issues have the potential to impact at *every* stage of the research process and within any research project. Therefore, all social researchers need to have a clear understanding of the ways in which ethical dilemmas can arise when carrying out their research.

Frankfort-Nachmias and Nachmias (1996, p.77) draw attention to the way in which ethical issues can arise during the course of the research process. They suggest that ethical issues may arise from:

- the research problem itself – determinants of intelligence, alcoholism or child sexual abuse;
- the setting in which the research takes place – hospitals, prisons or schools;
- the procedures required by the research design – an experiment that may, for example, have negative effects on the research participants;
- the method of data collection – covert observation methods;
- the kinds of people serving as research participants – homeless people, mental health patients and children who may be vulnerable and relatively powerless to resist being studied;
- the type of data collected – sensitive, personal or financial information;
- the communication of results – are the sponsors of research likely to attempt to withhold certain results that do not accord with their organisational or commercial objectives?
- the pressures that external agencies (such as governments, employers or service provides) may place upon research participants to become involved in research;
- the (mis)representation of others' experiences by the researcher – application of cultural norms during the interpretation of data.

Typically, we tend to be more conscious of these issues when conducting qualitative research, which is assumed to be more intrusive given the face-to-face contact that the researcher and research participants experience (Punch 2005), but it would be false to restrict our concerns to such cases. In this chapter we shall consider the ways in which major ethical issues impinge upon research using quantitative methods, such as survey and experimental research, as well as observation, ethnography and documentary research.

Many of the issues that will be discussed in this chapter arise out of debate between researchers over a number of notorious and often controversial research projects. These debates have served to put the spotlight on certain key dilemmas that face the social researcher. Burgess (1984, p.185) summarises these key ethical questions as follows:

- How can research take place without the influence of the state, which may aim to produce certain findings to suit its political needs?
- What are the risks and benefits for those individuals who take part in research?
- What should people be told about the conduct of social research?
- Is secret research justifiable?
- What limits, if any, ought to be placed on what data is collected?
- How should data be disseminated?
- What protection can research participants expect from social researchers?

To a large extent discussions about ethics in social research tend to focus on issues of consent, privacy, consequentiality, harm, and confidentiality and anonymity.

It is intended that this chapter will:

- encourage you to think about some of the problems that are inherent in studying human behaviour;
- enable you to assess critically the ways in which other researchers have carried out their research;
- prepare you for any possible criticism of your own research in the future;
- encourage you to think about the relationship between you and your participants, and how this may impact upon your research.

We shall identify the principles that help to differentiate ethical research from unethical research, and consider some of the important debates that have taken place in recent years, such as that between the supporters and opponents of 'covert' research. We shall also seek to address the key question that is posed when carrying out social research – do the ends (research findings) always justify the means?

## The two extremes of the ethical argument

### The responsibility of science

Some commentators contend that strict rules of conduct must be adhered to at all times and that no information is so valuable that it should be obtained at the expense of eroding an individual's personal liberty. From this perspective, deception of any kind is a violation of the personal rights of citizens and debases professional research inquiry:

> Social research involving deception and manipulation ultimately helps to produce a society of cynics, liars and manipulators, and undermines the trust which is essential to a just social order. (Warwick 1983, p.58)

Similarly, Bulmer (1982, p.217) argues that through a process of patient negotiation a sympathetic and resourceful researcher will eventually gain the necessary agreement of all those involved in order to be able to carry out her or his research. The use of covert research is therefore 'neither ethically justified, nor practically necessary, nor in the best interests of sociology as an academic pursuit'. From this perspective, the rights of the individual *always* override the rights of science.

### The rights of the researcher

For other researchers, however, the view that research should always be based unambiguously on truth, openness and trust ignores the reality of the real world where conflict and inequalities in power condition all relationships. As such, Douglas (1976) argues that social research needs to come to terms with the world as it exists and 'get its hands dirty' in a world of deception and mistrust. Given that the researcher engages in a social world in which people employ lies, fraud and a variety of deceptive techniques, Douglas (1976, p.55) suggests that the social scientist is justified in using the same methods in the pursuit of scientific truth:

> Profound conflicts of interest, values, feelings and activities pervade social life. Instead of trusting people and expecting trust in return, one suspects them and expects others to suspect us. Conflict is the reality of life; suspicion is the guiding principle.

Furthermore, Fielding (1981, p.94) argues that the deception involved in assuming a participant observer role in ethnography is 'mild compared to that practised daily by official and business organisations'.

This, then, is the researcher's fundamental dilemma: how to weigh one's ethical obligations towards those who participate in research against the quest for scientific knowledge. In an attempt to resolve these conflicts and to provide researchers with clear guidance on the ethical conduct of research, a series of professional codes of ethical practice have been developed since the 1980s.

## Ethical codes of practice

### The historical context supporting codes of practice

Ethical codes of practice for researchers can be traced back to one of the Nuremberg Trials, known as 'The Doctor's Trial'. This trial considered the actions of Karl Brandt, Adolf Hitler's personal physician, as well as a number of others involved in human experimentation for the Nazis throughout the Second World War. The extent of the experimentation was boundless, and often resulted in physical and psychological harm to the participants, or even death. The trial resulted in a 10-point code, the Nuremberg Code, being drawn up in order to protect participants in medical research. The core components of this code still underlie many ethical codes of practice today, and included:

- informed voluntary consent of the participant;
- the results should be 'for the good of society, not random and unnecessary';
- research should be 'conducted as to avoid all unnecessary physical and mental suffering and injury';
- participants should be allowed to terminate their involvement at any time;
- researchers should terminate research if any ethical concerns arise.

Despite the development of the Nuremberg Code, unethical research on humans continued, and the 1960s saw a number of now infamous examples of unethical studies which resulted in public outcry. Between 1963 and 1966, children at Willowbrook School in New York were deliberately infected with hepatitis as part of a medical research programme. Parents who wished for their children to be admitted to the school, a specialist school offering support for mentally ill children, had to provide consent for them to take part in the study. In some cases parents were told that it was a vaccination programme and were unaware of the true nature of the research.

In an equally disturbing study, carried out in 1963, patients at the Jewish Chronic Disease Hospital in New York were injected with live human cancer cells in an experiment to study the rejection of human transplants (Katz 1972). Patients were not informed of what was going on at the time, but the study contributed to growing concerns among elements of the medical profession regarding research and its effects on patients.

In 1964 the World Medical Association responded to these concerns by adopting the Declaration of Helsinki. The ethical principles outlined by the declaration expanded upon those first proposed by the Nuremberg Code, but emphasised the importance of prioritising the research participants' interests above those of wider society. The Declaration of Helsinki continues to be revised and updated, and, along with the founding principles of the Nuremberg Code, it has led to the development of a number of ethical guidelines which span disciplines to also cover non-medical research (see Example 4.1 for a guide to the major codes relevant to research in Britain).

### Example 4.1 Ethical codes of practice

The following ethical codes can be found at these Internet locations:

Market Research Society – www.marketresearch.org.uk/standards/codeconduct.htm

Social Research Association – www.the-sra.org.uk/documents/pdfs/ethics03.pdf

British Psychological Society – www.bps.org.uk/thesociety/code-of-conduct/code-of-conduct_home.cfm

British Sociological Association – www.britsoc.co.uk/equality/Statement+Ethical+Practice.htm

For example, the British Sociological Association (BSA) first adopted a Statement of Ethical Principles in 1973. The BSA has since revised its guidance on a number of occasions, seeing it as organic rather than a set of fixed rules.

The issues that are dealt with by the BSA's *Statement of Ethical Principles* can be summarised around three general themes:

- The maintenance of professional integrity – researchers are encouraged to explain their work as fully as possible to all sponsors, facilitators and research participants in ways that are likely to be meaningful to them.
- Protecting the interests of research participants – these are taken to include individuals and groups of all kinds. This is commonly manifested in a call for researchers to adhere to the doctrine of informed consent.
- Relations with sponsoring bodies, colleagues, employers, employees and members of other professions – researchers are urged to reflect on the implications of their research given the organisation for which they may be working and the nature of the research itself. The intention here is to ensure that research remains independent when commissioned by an external body.

Typically, ethical codes of practice attempt to lay down certain fundamental principles governing the conduct of research within a particular professional setting.

The Social Research Association (SRA), whose statement of *Ethical Guidelines* seeks to inform the work of all social science researchers, says that its intention is to:

> enable the social researcher's individual ethical judgements and decisions to be informed by shared values and experience, rather than to be imposed by the profession. ... They offer a framework within which the conscientious social researcher should, for the most part, be able to work comfortably. Where departures from the framework of principles are contemplated, they should be the result of deliberation rather than of ignorance. (SRA 2003, p.10)

The SRA states clearly that it has no intention of establishing a set of 'authoritarian or rigidly prescriptive' regulations (SRA 2003, p.11). Rather, it sees it as its responsibility to assist those researchers who are struggling to come to grips with a series of difficult decisions, and who are searching for reassurance in relation to certain key issues.

In recent years a number of other important bodies in the UK have also published ethical codes and guidelines that govern the conduct of research in particular domains. Anyone who wishes to conduct research in the National Health Service (NHS) needs to work to the Ethics and Research Guidance of the Medial Research Council and also needs to gain approval from a local ethics committee under the terms laid down by the Research Governance Framework for Health and Social Care (Gomm 2008). Similarly, researchers who accept research grant funding from the Economic and Social Research Council (ESRC) do so under the condition that they will abide by the ESRC's *Research Ethics Framework* (ESRC 2005). Indeed, the ESRC framework requires that any individual seeking to carry out empirical social research within the UK university sector needs to submit their detailed research plans for scrutiny by a formally constituted ethics committee. Only once this has been done and the researcher – whether an undergraduate student embarking on her or his dissertation, a doctoral student seeking to undertake her or his fieldwork, or an academic member of staff working with a local agency – has satisfied the university ethics committee of their ethical competence and sensitivity will the researcher be given approval to proceed with their research.

## Arguments against the use of ethical codes

Many researchers now accept the regulation of research conduct by ethics committees, even though they may do so somewhat reluctantly: 'Counting all the committee memberships in the UK at any one time, there are now probably more people involved in the ethical supervision of research than actively involved in doing research' (Gomm 2008, p.366). However, a number of arguments are raised against the presence of ethical codes of practice. Douglas (1976) asserts that ethical codes are objectionable in principle in that they are used wrongly to protect the powerful in society against the weak. Douglas maintains that a code of ethics assumes that there is an open society, when the reality is quite different in that powerful groups and organisations, such as governments and corporations, operate against the greater good under a shroud of secrecy. In these cases, Douglas argues that it is the job of researchers to expose corruption and dishonesty. Rather, the existence of such codes encourages researchers to give their fullest attention to reaching an ethical research design, while restricting themselves to innocuous topics that leave unequal power relations undisturbed. This is a view that may be shared by many of those who approach research from a critical perspective (see Chapter 2).

Allied to this is the criticism that ethical codes of practice stifle researchers' creativity and their 'freedom of truth-seeking' (Douglas 1976, p.31). For those who share Douglas's commitment that social research should be a creative and cultured process, ethical codes of practice are viewed with the suspicion that they are an attempt at a blueprint or a 'recipe book' for 'good' research.

Some researchers also criticise codes of practice for being too general to be able to provide for practical application. For example, M. Punch (1998, p.168) argues that the generality of codes:

> often does not help us to make the fine distinctions that arise at the *interactional* level in participant observation studies, where the reality of the field setting may feel far removed from the refinements of scholarly debate and ethical niceties. [original emphasis]

Thus, for Punch, codes of practice are effectively unworkable in certain situations. He quotes the situation that was faced by Powdermaker in the American Deep South (Powdermaker 1966). In an entirely unanticipated event, Powdermaker suddenly came face to face with a lynch mob. What, Punch asks, was she supposed to do in this situation? Should she:

- flash her identity card at the crowd and coolly outline her presence and then continue to observe events?
- walk away from the situation?
- seek out the victim and aid his escape?
- try to talk the crowd out of their intentions?
- inform the police in the hope that they would intervene?

Powdermaker agonised over the situation, having a sleepless night worrying about what to do. In the end, she did nothing and was very relieved when the man (who turned out to be entirely innocent) escaped from the clutches of the gang the following day. In such situations, making the 'right' decision is obviously very difficult – a decision that many researchers would be glad not to have to face.

While ethical codes of practice *can* be useful as guides, once engaged in the process of research, the onus is placed on the individual researcher – it is the researcher's duty to take responsibility for her or his own actions: 'Ethics begins with you, the researcher. A researcher's personal moral code is the strongest defence against unethical behaviour' (Neuman 2006, p.130).

## The doctrine of informed consent and the use of deception in research

Central to the case for ethically sound research is the principle that research participants are able to consent positively to their involvement in research, free from coercion and based on full and accurate information about the research to be undertaken (Bulmer 2008). In order to do this, people who are the focus of research must be informed of certain key points in a manner that is intelligible to them. This is referred to as the doctrine of informed consent. Essentially, this means that people should not be under the impression that they are required to participate in a research project and that they should not be deceived into doing so. Such an approach is held to show respect for the dignity and autonomy of human beings in the research process (Bulmer 1982).

The SRA (2003, pp.27–30) suggests that the following points are those that ought to be communicated to potential research participants to gain their consent:

- The purpose of the study, its policy implications, and so on.
- The identity of the funder(s).
- The anticipated use of the data and the form of publication that may result.
- The identity of the interviewer/experimenter and their organisational base.
- How the individual was chosen, e.g. the sampling method used.
- What the individual's role in the study will be.
- Any possible harm or discomfort that may result from the research;
- The degree of anonymity and confidentiality assured.
- The proposed data storage arrangements, the degree of security, and so on.
- The procedures of the study, e.g. the time involved, the setting, and so on.
- Whether their participation is voluntary or compulsory:
  - if participation is compulsory, the potential consequences of non-compliance;
  - if participation is voluntary, their entitlement to withdraw consent.

It is important to note that while people may agree to take part in a research project by, for example, being interviewed as part of a survey, this does not mean that they have then to answer *all* of the questions that may be put to them. Rather, research participants should be informed of their right to decline to answer any questions that they wish to do so, and that they are able to withdraw from the research at any point up to the publication of the research findings. Consent is not a 'once and for all' obligation, and individuals should be aware of their entitlement to refuse their consent at any stage of the research. Similarly, it would be unethical to tell a potential survey respondent that an interview will take five minutes when the researcher is aware that it is likely to take 15 minutes instead. While it may be tempting to improve response rates by misleading potential research participants in this way, it should be resisted.

## Issues and problems in gaining consent

However, there are instances where the gaining of informed consent may be problematic for a variety of reasons. For example, there may be some situations in which it may not be possible for those who are being researched to give their consent due to a lack of capacity. By informed consent, we understand the right of individuals to choose whether to participate in research free from any element of duress, coercion, fraud or deceit. However, in the case of minors (children under the age of 11), those people suffering from mental health illnesses, or otherwise in some form of institutional care, whose exercise of choice is legally governed, consent will need to be obtained from the person or agency legally authorised to represent the best interests of the individual.

Where consent is gained via a proxy, it could still be argued that those granting consent (such as a parent or legal guardian) might not always be able to represent the best interests of their child. For example, Denscombe and Aubrook (1992) report that even though the children in their study had been told about the research by their teachers, and had been given the choice as to whether or not to participate, it was unclear whether the children had felt constrained to do so given that they were in a classroom situation.

Allied to this situation is the issue of subtle coercion. It may be that as a researcher you are in a more powerful situation than those people that you intend to research. Where this is the case, and you are 'studying down' among relatively powerless and vulnerable groups, such as children or homeless people, it would be easy for a professional researcher to use powers of persuasion to coax people to take part in research; for some people it may be very hard for them to refuse. Under these conditions, even though they have consented, this may be far from freely, and may be the result of some duress, which may cause anxiety in the future. As the SRA (2003, p.29) says, 'the boundary between tactical persuasion and duress is sometimes very fine and is probably easier to recognise than to stipulate'.

Some researchers contend that where research is being conducted with the aim of exposing a powerful group in society (often known as 'studying up'), it can be argued that the ends justify the means in using deception. M. Punch (1998, p.173), for example, rhetorically poses the question of whether '...certain institutions get what they deserve?' In this view, different standards of conduct ought to apply when the focus of research is upon organisations such as governments and multinational corporations which allegedly engage in deceitful and questionable activities as a matter of course. Researchers of such a disposition are likely to lend a sympathetic interpretation of Reiss's (1971) research on the British police force. Reiss led the police to believe that his ethnographic study concerned the public's perception of the police force, when in reality the research was really focusing on how the police treat citizens. In the process of the research, Reiss observed the police carrying out substantial mistreatment and brutality against members of the public. The police officers were unaware that they were the object of the study, and were shocked when Reiss published his findings.

There also tends to be a far less critical reaction to covert research when the researcher's focus is trained on those targets that are commonly regarded as undesirable. For example, Fielding's (1981) research on the British fascist political party, the National Front, saw him adopting the role of a party enthusiast to allow him to observe the inner workings of the organisation over a period of time. He argued that his research enabled people to understand the appeal of violent far-right organisations such as the National Front and thus persuade those vulnerable to their propaganda to resist their overtures.

There may also be a variety of practical and logistical issues that may impinge on the ability of the researcher to gain prior consent. Thus, Hammersley and Atkinson (1995) discuss the problems in seeking to obtain the free consent of all of one's research participants at all times, pointing out how complicated and potentially disruptive this can be. Indeed, with some types of research, particularly ethnography and observation studies, explaining your presence to everyone, the purpose of your research, and so on may be physically impossible. This is a point that is reinforced by Punch (1986, p.36):

> In a large organisation engaged in constant interaction with a considerable number of clients it is physically impossible to seek consent from everyone and seeking it will kill many a research project stone dead.

In such circumstances, where the research participants' consent has not been obtained prior to the research taking place, it is usually suggested that the researcher should ensure that consent is gained as soon as possible after the research has finished. This commonly means that the research participant is made aware of the research, what has taken place, and the uses to which the researcher wants to put the data. Ryen (2007, p.219) refers to this as 'an honest description of the study once it is over'. While the research participants cannot wind back time to erase their involuntary participation in the research, they do at this point have the ability to regain ownership of 'their' data and deny its use for the purposes of analysis and publication.

As the SRA (2003, pp.34–5) maintains:

> Once the methodological advantage of covert observation, of deception, or of withholding information has been achieved, it is rarely defensible to allow the omission to stand.

The SRA's firm and consistent guidance on covert research and deception, which is shared by all other professional associations, arose out of significant debates on research ethics in the late 1960s and early 1970s following a number of high-profile research projects where it was widely believed that researchers had unethically manipulated people who had volunteered to participate in their research.

### Informed consent and experimental research: the Milgram experiments

It may be the case that gaining informed consent in some situations, such as when using experimental research, is detrimental to the research design to such an extent that the research would become pointless.

Experiments are especially problematic because their effectiveness often depends on those taking part not being aware of all of the details of the research. Experimental research is based on the researcher manipulating certain controlled conditions to be able to identify the relationship between certain variables that it is hoped will explain 'cause and effect' relationships. The classic experiment involves placing research participants in an artificial setting and attempting to manipulate their behaviour in a manner that will shed light on certain phenomena. Thus, it is argued that a certain level of deception is necessary to prevent research participants from learning the true hypothesis of the research and thus adjusting their behaviour.

One of the most well-known cases concerns the research of Milgram (1963). Milgram wanted to discover how the horrors of the Holocaust in Nazi Germany occurred, and so set out to examine the strength of social pressure to obey authority. To do this he conducted a series of experiments in which volunteers were recruited and falsely led to believe that they were involved in research on the effects of punishment on learning. The recruits were assigned the role of 'teacher' to test an individual's memory of words and lists, and to administer electric shocks (up to a near fatal 450 volts) to 'pupils' when they made mistakes. The 'teachers' could not actually see the 'pupils' while the experiment was taking place, but they could hear the outcome of the electric shocks that they thought they were administering. At specified points, the 'pupils' were prompted to feign noises of great pain. Where the 'teachers' showed signs of unease, the researcher made reassuring comments such as 'you must go on'.

The true aim of the study was to observe the limits to which the 'teachers' were willing to obey the authority of the researcher – the authority figure. The study demonstrated a surprisingly high level of willingness among people to administer supposed electric shocks at very dangerous levels. Milgram's 'teachers' were fully debriefed after the event, and were offered to have their data withheld from the final report of the research.

Milgram's research has been heavily criticised over the years for its use of deception and for generating feelings of guilt and substantial levels of stress among its research participants. It has also been suggested that such research may have affected the research participants' ability to trust authority figures in the future. Even though Milgram claimed that 80% of his participants retrospectively said that they were glad to have taken part in the research (Gomm 2008, p.381), it is highly unlikely that such research would be given clearance by a university or other research ethics committee today.

### Informed consent and ethnographic research: Humphreys, *Tea room* Trade

In the field of ethnography, the research of Humphreys (1970) is equally notorious for the way in which the researcher used deception in pursuit of his goals. Humphreys used deceptive means to observe male sexual encounters in public toilets. Attending a number of gatherings in this manner, Humphreys adopted the role of 'watchqueen' (a third man who serves as a lookout for those engaged in homosexual sex and who obtains voyeuristic pleasure from his observations). He then followed the men he had observed back to their cars to obtain their car registration numbers. Following this, he used police contacts to trace the names and home addresses of 134 men, deceiving the police by saying that his work was 'market research'. Having obtained their personal details, Humphreys then visited the men whom he had observed at their homes a year later having changed his physical appearance. In doing so he posed as a researcher who was carrying out a project into social health.

Not only did Humphreys employ deception, misrepresentation and manipulation in his research, but also he has been criticised for taking advantage of a relatively powerless group (Babbie 2004). In his defence, he argued that the men's names had been kept in a locked safe, completely anonymised, and that these records were destroyed very soon after the data was aggregated. Furthermore, he defended his research saying that it had brought into the public domain an activity that was hitherto shrouded in negative stereotypical images, and that he had helped further understanding of an issue that had previously been repressed.

While Milgram and Humphreys may have sought to defend their ethical approach, arguing that their research findings justified their unconventional means, the consensus within the social science research community is that such tactics are generally not defensible and ought to be avoided wherever possible (Ali and Kelly 2004). Of course, these two examples are rather extreme cases and the great majority of research is far less controversial in nature. Given that this is the case, the SRA maintains a strong position against the use of covert methods wherever possible:

> It remains the duty of social researchers and their collaborators ... not to pursue methods of inquiry that are likely to infringe human values and sensibilities. To do so, whatever the methodological advantages, would be to endanger the reputation of social research and the mutual trust between social researchers and society which is a prerequisite for much research. ... Social inquiries involving deliberate deception of subjects (by omission or commission) are rare and extremely difficult to defend. (SRA 2003, pp.34–5)

However, this stops short of saying that covert research and deception should *never* be employed, leaving it open to some researchers to maintain a degree of pragmatism and flexibility in weighing up such decisions:

> Perhaps some measure of deception is acceptable in some areas where the benefits of the knowledge outweigh the harms that have been minimised by following convention on confidentiality and identity. ... One need not always be brutally honest, direct and explicit about one's research purpose, but one should not normally engage in disguise. One should not steal documents. One should not directly lie to people. And, although one may disguise identity to a certain extent, one should not break promises made to people. Academics, in weighing up the balancing edge between overt–covert, and between openness–less than open, should take into account the consequences for the subjects, the profession, and, not least, for themselves. (M. Punch 1998, p.172)

### Activity 4.1 The use of deception in research

You are carrying out a study of court procedures to see whether the courts discriminate against people from black, minority and ethnic groups. To do this you decide to sit in a court's public gallery and observe events over a period of time. Do you tell the magistrates what you are doing, knowing that this is likely to affect the way that they act, or do you decide not to tell them on the grounds that the potential uncovering of institutional racism is for the greater public good? Make some notes outlining the advantages and disadvantages of this particular research strategy. (Adapted from Crow 2000, p.69)

## Harm

Another central area of concern in the design of ethical research is the recognition that social research can harm an individual in many different ways – physically, psychologically, legally and professionally. The SRA's *Ethical Guidelines* (SRA 2003, p.17) maintain that:

> No generic formula or guidelines exist for assessing the likely benefit or risk of various types of social inquiry. Nonetheless, the social researcher has to be sensitive to the possible consequences of his or her work and should, as far as possible, guard against predictably harmful effects.

Furthermore, it is recognised that gaining the free consent of research participants does not absolve the researcher from an obligation to protect those participants against any potentially harmful effects of participating. In this respect, the researcher has a duty to inform individuals of the potential consequences of participating in their research.

### Physical harm

Physical harm that may arise through the process of actually doing the research is the most readily identifiable type of harm for a researcher to perceive and therefore ought to be the easiest to protect against. In terms of physical harm, a researcher should make every effort to identify the basic safety risks associated with her or his research.

Researchers most definitely ought to refrain from any research where physical harm is central to the project. While this might seem an unnecessarily obvious statement to make, the history of social research contains some startling examples where this has been done. For example, as mentioned earlier, several patients who were already ill were injected with live cancer cells in research into resistance to the illness (Katz 1972). Furthermore, the American military was responsible for giving the hallucinogenic drug LSD to unsuspecting individuals and then recording the results using hidden cameras (Sieber 1992). Several of these people subsequently became mentally ill from the experience and one person committed suicide.

## Psychological harm

Even though they rarely set out to deliberately do so, it is clearly the case that in many instances researchers may unwittingly place people in stressful, embarrassing and anxiety-producing situations (Neuman 2006). Placing research participants in such stressful situations may be considered harmful in some eyes, and so it is generally accepted that researchers should seek, wherever possible, to apprise their research participants if they feel that there is a potential of this likelihood occurring. For example, Hammersley and Atkinson (1995) raise the prospect of research on terminal illness and the impact that this may have on those who are dying as well as their friends and relatives. Simply asking someone to take part in a questionnaire-based study by approaching them in the street may create anxiety or put pressure on highly sensitive people. The actual questions asked may also cause distress and offence.

Zimbardo's (1973) research provides a classic case of a project that placed its research participants in a highly stressful situation. This was an experiment that took place in a simulated prison environment. Volunteers signed up for two weeks, during which they were told that they would be under surveillance and would have some of their civil rights suspended, but that no physical harm would come to them. The participants were divided into two groups – 'guards' and 'prisoners'. The 'prisoners' were dressed in standard uniforms and referred to only by their prison number, and the 'guards' were given militarised uniforms, truncheons and reflective sunglasses. The two groups were then asked to act out their respective roles. However, the experiment had to be abandoned after six days when both the 'guards' and 'prisoners' significantly over-identified with their roles. The 'prisoners' became passive and disorganised and the 'guards' became aggressive and threatening.

## Harm through publication

The SRA's statement of *Ethical Guidelines* (SRA 2003, p.17) recognises that 'all information ... is subject to misuse and no information is devoid of possible harm to one interest or another'. For example, a particular district may be negatively stereotyped by an inquiry that finds that it contains a very high incidence of crime. Similarly, publication of research findings may affect both the public reputation of individuals and their material circumstances.

At stake here is not whether the information published is true but what implications the publication carries. Of course, it should be recognised that who the publication of research findings harms is a highly contentious issue. Critical social researchers may well argue that causing harm to powerful interests in capitalist societies is a valid goal of social research (see Chapter 2).

### Harm to the researcher

While researchers need to pay due attention to protecting their research participants from harm, it is important to remember that over the course of the research process, researchers can inadvertently place themselves in harmful situations. Thompson (1967) got beaten up by the Hell's Angels he was studying because he refused to pay them any money for the privilege of observing their violent activities; Yablonsky (1968) was threatened with violence in a commune; and Schwartz (1964) was attacked verbally and physically during his study in a mental hospital when seen as a 'spy' by both patients and staff.

### Harm to the research profession

Another aspect of harm that needs to be considered is the harmful implications that the conduct of research may have on one's own profession itself. All researchers ought to be aware of the obligations that they have to their fellow researchers. If the process of the research is found to be objectionable or the publication of research is held to be damaging, then future research is likely to be denied. Such sentiments are prominent in the SRA's *Ethical Guidelines* under the heading 'Obligations to Colleagues'. Hammersley and Atkinson (1995, p.275) remind researchers that they have an ethical obligation not to 'spoil the field' in this way. The research of Reiss (1971) (reviewed earlier in this chapter) has been criticised for jeopardising the future of further research studies with the police owing to the distrust that has been generated.

Associated with the question of causing harm to the research profession itself is the controversial issue of the individual researcher's obligation to obey the law. The reputation of social research is brought into question where a researcher breaks the law in the course of her or his research. Once again, the various codes of ethical research practice are quite clear on this point, maintaining that social research does not stand above the law. However, some researchers argue that once engaged in research the issue is far from clear. Douglas (1976) rhetorically asks:

- To what extent does a researcher's inaction condone illegal activities?
- If a citizen can assist the police, do they have a moral obligation to do so?

Similarly, Adler (1985) talks explicitly about gaining 'guilty knowledge' in the process of her research into drug dealing communities on the West Coast of America. This includes:

> Information about crimes that are committed ... guilty observations, by being present at the scene of a crime and witnessing its occurrence ... guilty actions, by taking part in illegal behaviour ourselves. (Adler 1985, p.27)

This is, indeed, a very important area for consideration, particularly where action research is being pursued.

For example, the situation might arise where a social worker is interviewing adult clients and during the course of an interview it becomes apparent that one of the research participants is involved in some sort of criminal activity. In such a situation the researcher will need to make a judgement that will be informed by:

- the relevant ethical code of conduct;
- the researcher's commitment to the confidentiality of the research participant;
- the demands of the organisation for whom the researcher is working;
- their legal obligation to inform the police of specific illegal activities;
- the researcher's own personal sense of what is 'right' and what is 'wrong'.

Such a decision would be an extremely difficult one to take.

### Activity 4.2 Protecting research participants from harm

You want to study why it is that some children are frightened of the dark and others are not. In order to do this, you decide to carry out a controlled experiment exposing children to such situations. Make some notes on what you consider the main ethical issues to be. For example, to what extent are the children being placed in harm? Are the children able to understand all of the implications of the procedure? Are they able to give their informed consent to the research? Is there any coercion involved in the experiment? How might you deal with any anxiety that may result? (Adapted from Graziano and Raulin 1997, p.287)

## Confidentiality and anonymity

These two terms are often used interchangeably, but they do have quite distinct meanings. Confidentiality is an active attempt to remove from the research records any identifying features of the research participants and anonymity means that those who participate in the research remain nameless. Both of these terms are connected with separating an individual's identity from her or his responses. Anonymity ensures that a person remains nameless and unidentifiable. Confidentiality means that the researcher holds the data in confidence and keeps it from public consumption. A researcher may provide one without the other, but they usually go together.

## Anonymity

It is important to take any precautions that are necessary to protect the identity of the people who take part in your research, even though it can be the case that some research participants *do* want to be identified in research publications (Neuman 2006). Thus researchers commonly use pseudonyms to prevent research participants from being individually identifiable.

However, researchers need to be more conscientious than simply changing people's or organisation's names. The inclusion of geographic locations, workplaces and other characteristics can often be used to identify people. For example, although Holdaway (1982) used pseudonyms for the police stations in which his research took place, he left many other details unchanged. As a result, it was easy to identify his research as being conducted with the Metropolitan Police. Evidently, researchers should not give assurances that cannot be fulfilled.

Cavendish (1982), on the other hand, provides a model example where a researcher has taken every precaution to ensure that the research participants would not be identified on publication of the research. In her study of working women in a factory, she changed all the names of the individuals involved, used a pseudonym to ensure that the company was not identifiable, invented a name for the workers' trade union, changed the location of the factory, and made up a product that was different from the one that the company actually made.

Of course, the smaller and more specialised the group, community or organisation under investigation, the more difficult it becomes to keep the identity of participants protected (Ryen 2007). Indeed, with some types of qualitative research it is almost impossible to assure a potential research participant of absolute anonymity. In these instances it will be necessary to assure people a high degree of confidentiality.

## Confidentiality

Having granted anonymity to the research participants, the researcher must be prepared to protect their identity and any information that arises from their participation in the research. This is what we mean when we assure people of confidentiality. Guba and Lincoln (1989, p.236) argue that people have a right to control the information relating to them and that researchers ought to recognise this:

> When participants do not 'own' the data they have furnished about themselves, they have been robbed of some essential element of dignity, in addition to having been abandoned in harm's way.

In the majority of cases, maintaining confidentiality is relatively uncontentious. However, this may not always be the case. For example, what happens when, in the course of the research, a research participant informs you of something that implicates that participant or another person in illegal activities? If you become aware of a crime that is about to take place, are you bound by your pledge of confidentiality to the research participant or your law-abiding duty as a citizen to inform the police?

It is quite common for researchers to assure their research participants that anything discussed between them 'will be treated with the strictest confidence' without reflecting on the full implications of this statement. For example, while carrying out research on police reporting methods, Van Maanen (1979) witnessed a variety of illegal procedures, among them seeing police officers beat people. Even though he had given an assurance of confidentiality, Van Maanen decided to publicise his findings (in the name of wider justice) rather than maintain the confidence of the police.

A contrasting case is reported by Neuman (2006, p.140) of a sociology doctoral student who was jailed for 16 weeks after he refused to testify on the illegal activities of a radical animal rights organisation with whom he was conducting research. The judges refused to acknowledge his plea that he was bound by his assurance of confidentiality.

Another aspect of confidentiality that needs to be considered is that which relates to records that exist prior to embarking on one's own research. This is obviously an issue that arises when carrying out research based on documentary data. Researchers may well wish to gain access to confidential records held on patients in hospitals, children in schools, or clients of a social services department to aid them in their research. However, while the institution itself may grant access to such files, it would be unethical for a researcher to use these documents without the consent of the individuals involved.

The assurance of anonymity and confidentiality is something that researchers should seek to maintain throughout the entire research process. The time at which this assurance is at its most vulnerable to being compromised occurs when it comes to placing research in the public domain. This issue is dealt with in Chapter 9.

## Privacy

It is important to remember that social researchers do not have a special right to study people. In everyday life we draw distinctions between public places, such as parks, libraries and the high street, and private places, such as people's houses. In the scope of social research, what is public and what is private is rarely so clear-cut. Indeed, many highly experienced researchers find themselves unable to establish hard-and-fast rules. Hammersley and Atkinson (1995, p.267), for example, pose the question 'is talk in a bar public or private?' while freely admitting that the answer to such a question is far from easy and 'depends on one's point of view'. According to Ruebhausen and Brim (1966, p.432), the right to privacy involves:

> The freedom of the individual to pick and choose for themselves the time and circumstances under which, and the extent to which, their attitudes, beliefs, behaviours and opinions are to be shared with, or withheld from others.

Do individuals have an absolute right to privacy or is this overridden by the search for knowledge? Of course, this is the central question that lies at the heart of the controversy over research ethics – the debate between those researchers who contest the respective rights of the individual when counterpoised against the prerogative of science.

Marsh (1982) suggests that privacy is the major ethical issue to be confronted in survey research. While it is relatively easy to identify those questions that are liable to be seen as an invasion of most people's privacy – things such as sexual behaviour or personal relationships – many less contentious questions may also be seen in an unfavourable light by some people. For example, survey questions concerning standard socio-demographic variables such as age, income and marital status may be regarded as an invasion of privacy by some (Bulmer 2008). Indeed, Ali and Kelly (2004) suggest that the act of simply being stopped in the street and asked to participate in a survey could be seen as an invasion of privacy by some people.

Issues surrounding privacy are very complex and involve many subtleties, including the manner in which research is carried out and the relations that are established between the researcher and the research participants. As Cassell (1982) points out, people can feel *wronged* without being *harmed* by research. This may happen if they feel that they have been treated as objects of measurement without respect for their individual values and sense of privacy. (For a detailed overview of the impact of the Data Protection Act 1998 and rights to privacy, see Townend 2000, pp.113–21.)

## Power relations between researcher and researched

The various issues that have been reviewed in this chapter so far have raised a number of highly contentious questions concerning power and politics in society and the way in which this impacts on the course of research. Indeed, many of the issues that are the focus of consideration can, and are, seen in a different light depending on the contrasting views with regard to the kind of society in which we live. Against those who advocate a clearly defined ethical path of research (Bulmer 1982) are ranged other researchers who suggest that such unequivocal statements are not possible given the deficiencies that are evident in Western democracies (Douglas 1976).

However, while the greater focus has been on the way in which politics and power intervene in the research process at the societal level, it is also the case that they impact at the individual level. This is manifested in the choice of research participants and the unequal relations that exist 'in the field'.

### The focus of research

It is often the case that research shines the spotlight on relatively powerless groups or individuals in society. The focus of much social research, therefore, has been on those people who are seen to be marginalised and disadvantaged in society, such as 'deviant' youth, people who are unemployed, the homeless, those in poverty, or those suffering drug or alcohol abuse (Kelman 1972). This is often justified in terms of the benefits that accrue from the research, in 'helping' people with identified social problems.

However, it is argued (Berg 2001) that the lack of political, social and financial power experienced by those such as homeless people means that they have far lesser means by which to protect themselves from the investigations of researchers than do powerful elites in government, business or the military. See, for example, the case made by Stavenhagen (1993) in Chapter 3, where a comparison is made between the power of different groups to resist being the focus of research.

### Exploitative potential

Researchers also need to consider the ethical implications of power, authority and influence within the research process in the relationships that are formed during research. Although equal relations may be intended – especially in qualitative research (Oakley 2000) – it is hard to escape from the subtle persuasive influences that permeate the research process, making the reality of research relationships far less equal than might be intentioned (Mason 2002).

The potential for such inequalities to arise is far more likely in those situations where researchers are 'studying down', i.e. carrying out research on those who are in some way less experienced, more vulnerable or open to exploitation. This may be the case when carrying out research with, for example, people with mental health problems, children/young people, the victims of physical/sexual abuse, homeless people, and so on.

## Relations with the sponsors of research

There are many potential sponsors of research with an even wider diversity of interests. Those who sponsor research often do so because they are seeking some form of 'evidence' with which to pursue their particular interests. It is also quite common for such sponsors to enter into negotiations with researchers from a position of strength (Neuman 2006). Thus, a motoring organisation may sponsor a study with the intention of defending the use of the private motor car. At the same time an environmental organisation may sponsor a study that, it hopes, will demonstrate the harm that cars bring to society. Although this is a hypothetical example, there are plenty of instances where such clashes do occur, with the contestants calling upon scientific research to illustrate and confirm their particular interests and campaigns.

What, if any, constraints ought to be placed on research by a sponsor who provides the financial and material resources to enable the research to take place? The SRA specifically warns social researchers against accepting 'contractual conditions that are contingent upon a particular outcome from a proposed inquiry' (SRA 2003, p.19). In this respect, it is important to agree the details of publication and dissemination at the outset of a research project. This may prove to be of great value if your findings are in any way contrary to the interests of the sponsor, with the sponsor then deciding that it does not want to release the results.

Wherever possible, researchers ought not to accept research from a sponsor who has requested that their findings will need to be vetted prior to publication. Indeed, it may be advisable to ensure that the contract for the research is written in such a way as to preclude such a censoring role for the sponsor. Other questions that will need to be considered when entering a contract for research are:

- What if the sponsor insists on a method of data collection that the researcher considers inappropriate or invalid?
- What if the sponsor insists on asking certain questions in a study or asking them in particular ways that the researcher considers will lead to biased results?
- What if the sponsor wants to hide its support for the study, thus denying potential research participants full information on which to decide whether or not to participate in the research?

### Activity 4.3 Relations with the sponsors of research

You have been awarded £50,000 by a large sponsor of social research to conduct research into the characteristics of young people who commit crime. You are told that the results of your research will be used by the police and social and probation services in 'tackling' offending. Make some notes outlining the ethical dilemmas that you would be likely to face in conducting this research. (Adapted from May 2001, p.68)

## Power relationships with external agencies and vulnerable groups

As social researchers, our concerns are with the things that make up the social world: the people and organisations that form society, and the structures within which these operate. With this in mind, it is important to recognise the place that politics and values have for both the participants of our research and the agencies with which these people are connected. When considering research participants, we must recognise that:

> People who are the objects of research interest – by funders, policy makers and researchers – are predominantly members of socially disadvantaged groups. Advantaged groups, by their nature, are not commonly available for critical scrutiny; they are protected from research by powerful majority interests. But other groups of people come into designation as problems, as threats to the social order, so warranting intervention to restore harmony; or they are variously identified as socially, economically or politically disadvantaged and in need of help or redress. (Hood et al. 1999, p.1)

In these 'problem' or 'disadvantaged' groups, we might place such people as offenders, the unemployed, teenage mothers, children, ethnic minority groups, the disabled, and so forth. Such generalisation about these groups being either problematic or disadvantaged may seem somewhat crude, until we consider the agencies that exist to work with these groups. The probation service exists to 'deal' with offenders by assisting their transition back into society. Teenage mothers receive extra advice and guidance from social services based on the particular circumstances of being a young mother, not usually afforded to older women. Schools are a dominant force in the lives of children, and the Immigration and Nationality Directorate oversees issues which concern those seeking British citizenship.

There is an assumption underpinning these agencies' existence that the people that use their services are in need of some form of assistance. The position these agencies hold, as providers of support and guidance, regardless of how well intentioned they may be, is one of power. There is a reliance upon these agencies by the vulnerable people they are set up to help, and this is a particular kind of relationship which we must be aware of when carrying out research with such groups.

When researching vulnerable people, it is often such agencies that we call upon in order to access our research participants. In doing so, we are making use of a gatekeeper, upon whom our participants depend. If we were to carry out research on homeless people, we may wish to access our participants through a housing association which provides beds in hostels, food and support to help people to find homes. This is a useful way of gaining access to an otherwise hidden group of people, and the opportunities that it may open up through snowball sampling are good reasons to use this pathway. However, when an agency such as this is acting as an intermediary between the researcher and the participant, certain effects can occur as a result of the dependency the participant has on the agency.

First, participants may feel an obligation to take part in the research. If approached to take part via the agency which offers them support, they may find it difficult to resist, whatever reservations they may have. This can be particularly problematic if incentives are offered, such as giving vouchers to homeless people in return for their participation. This is, of course, true of any incentives, regardless of the involvement of an external agency. There may be instances when such incentives are not so visible, however. If research was being carried out involving unemployed people, taking part in a series of interviews might be considered as demonstrating a willingness to embark on voluntary projects in order to gain experience. The individual may then be looked upon more favourably as taking a proactive approach to finding work, which in turn might result in more lenient treatment by agencies such as the employment services. This indirect type of reward for participating in research is embedded in the nature of the relationship of dependency vulnerable people can have on external agencies.

Having accessed our participants through an agency, we must ask ourselves how the participants were chosen. One of the consequences of using gatekeepers to gain access to research participants is the possibility of losing control over the sampling strategy. Participants may be chosen because they are known to view the agency in a positive light, and so it is anticipated that this will be reflected in the research. Even if this is not the case, participants may feel inclined to give a positive account of the services of the agency. One way around this is simply not to include anything in our research objectives which directly deals with the services of the agency. In practice, however, this is difficult to achieve, since the agency will play such a central role in the lives of our participants. It is difficult to conceive of a research project involving children that did not tackle the issue of school at some point in one form or another, or research with offenders that did not deal with the probation service in some way.

There may be situations where access to participants via an agency is closely monitored beyond the sampling stage. Imagine that we wanted to carry out a series of interviews with patients in a psychiatric hospital. We may be allowed access to such individuals on the condition that a nurse is present during the interviews. This has perfectly good reasoning behind it, in that should the participant become upset or uncomfortable during the interview, the nurse, being a professional and having built up a level of trust with the patients, would be in the best position to reassure the participant. The very presence of agency figures in the interview situation will, however, have an effect on the dynamics of the interview, and adds another element which needs to be taken into consideration when interpreting the data. The interviewee may feel unable to divulge certain feelings or views in such a situation. Ironically, the presence of agency representatives during data collection is usually in response to ethical concerns about harm to participants or researcher. However, this very presence can introduce power relations between participant and agency which may influence participants in unseen ways.

If such power relations are unseen, and manifest themselves in a dependency of participant on agency, how can we as researchers account for them? Careful consideration of the way power is exerted over vulnerable individuals by agencies is required if we are to understand fully the dynamics of such relations. May suggests that:

> The definition that there exists a problem will often depend on the relative power that the people who define the social problem have over those who are defined. ... Given these factors, rather than simply accepting given definitions, it is equally valid to examine the process through which a phenomenon became defined as a problem in terms of the power of social groups. (2001, p.52)

When carrying out research with vulnerable individuals, it is necessary to be aware that what they tell us may be affected by social norms which have been established by agencies in positions of power. Given that this may be the case, it is important, as May suggests, to examine how phenomena become labelled as problems. In a school where much emphasis is placed on academic achievement in such subjects as maths and science, a child who excels in creative arts, but lacks an interest in the sciences, could be labelled as a failure. The child, being powerless against the school as an agency, is not in a position to argue for the various merits of the arts, but perhaps shows frustration and disaffection in a tendency for truancy from maths and science classes.

It is easy to see how this chain of circumstances quickly takes on the definition of a 'problem'. If we are to understand the ways in which such problems are defined, we need to scrutinise the relationship between individuals and agencies. This is a form of reflexivity (see Chapter 7 for a further exploration of this term). Rather than reflecting on one's own role as researcher and our own relationship with research participants, we need to reflect on the presence of other external factors which may introduce imbalances of power into the research scenario.

Reflexivity is a key analytical tool for understanding how different power relations exist, so that our interpretations of data can take these into account. Failure to reflect on differences between the cultural norms of researcher and participant can lead to misrepresentation. This was particularly evident in the work of Hans Eysenck's studies of intelligence (1971). The quantitative study made use of intelligence quotient (IQ) measures in order to test a hypothesis that intelligence was linked to race. The conclusions, which have since come up against much criticism, suggested that intelligence was linked to race, with white individuals demonstrating higher IQ levels than black and Hispanic people. Many of the measures used for the IQ tests made references to ideas which were firmly situated within white, Western cultural norms, thereby discriminating against the participants from other cultures.

Quantitative approaches are often defended for being value-free and objective, although in the case of Eysenck's study, this was clearly not the case. With qualitative research approaches, which tend to be far more value-laden, it is even more important that we reflect on our own cultural norms and our relative power in relation to our participants. In doing so, it is hoped that we might minimise the problems brought about by power imbalance and misrepresentation.

## Ethical issues in online research

Concerns over data confidentiality have risen with the increase in electronic storage and transferral of data. Identity fraud and a number of well-publicised incidents of misplaced databases containing personal details have heightened public awareness of the potential for electronic data to go missing or be intercepted. This in itself may lead to reservations on the part of participants in disclosing information if it is to be stored electronically. While some of these reservations are undoubtedly fuelled by media sensationalism, they do emphasise the need for researchers to be aware of data confidentiality issues which are particularly pertinent to electronic storage. Mann and Stewart (2000, p.43) alert us to the fact that 'although researchers can promise confidentiality in the way they use the data, they cannot promise that electronic communication will not be accessed and used by others'.

Increasingly, companies are monitoring employees' emails and website viewing habits, even when logged in to the company network from home. Such activity is often justified on disciplinary grounds analogous to a site manager touring the factory floor to oversee productivity (Chadwick 2006). In many private companies, and increasingly in the public sector, web monitoring software which blocks sites containing certain content is now commonplace. In the academic community, researchers will often wish to investigate sensitive topics, and may need to access websites relating to, for example, racial violence or sexual assault. Such sites are likely to be flagged by blocking software, and the researcher required to submit a special request to gain access, citing the legitimate reasons for doing so. Despite opposition calling such surveillance a personal intrusion, the argument for continued monitoring remains a forceful one, and the disciplinary/security versus civil liberties debate will doubtless rage on for many years to come. The implication for researchers is that online communication that might appear to be private cannot always be *guaranteed* as such.

Early in 2009, the social networking site, *Facebook*, introduced a change to its terms and conditions relating to the storage of user-created content. The new terms stated that the site could keep copies of messages, photos and other content that users had posted *after* the user had deactivated their account. The change provoked a strong reaction from users, who formed online protest groups claiming that it was a breach of privacy. Very shortly after this event, *Facebook* retracted the policy and reverted to its previous terms and conditions, which stated that such content *would* be deleted upon the deactivation of an account. This incident highlighted the problem of information ownership online. The users claimed that any content posted on the site was owned by them, but in a public blog post, *Facebook* CEO Mark Zuckerberg responded by saying:

> When a person shares something like a message with a friend, two copies of that information are created – one in the person's sent messages box and the other in their friend's inbox. Even if the person deactivates their account, their friend still has a copy of that message. (Zuckerberg 2009)

The central issue appears to be the sharing of information. Although *Facebook* users can choose to share information only with specified users – their 'friends' – Zuckerberg is suggesting that once shared, the content is then effectively also 'owned' by whomever it has been shared with. *Facebook* is presented as a platform which enables that sharing, and so for it to continue working effectively, some level of individual ownership must be surrendered. There are parallels with offline information ownership here. If we join a club and share stories with people we meet through the club, when we leave would we expect that information to be taken back from those with whom we have shared it, effectively erasing any memory of that information? Of course, this would be impossible, but if we had contributed to a group discussion to which minutes were recorded, then left the group, would we be within our rights to request that our name and contribution were struck from the minutes?

Questions of information ownership rights inevitably inform questions of information access rights, which, for a researcher, is a key ethical question. If someone posts information on a publicly accessible area of the Internet, and a researcher is able to access it, is there any reason why that information should not be used for research purposes? Mann and Stewart (2000) point out that, due to the textual and visual nature of a lot of online secondary data, many of the ethical questions around ownership or use of information are interwoven with copyright guidelines, but this remains problematic because of the uncertain status of much of the information we might be dealing with. Should a post on a discussion board be treated in the same way as a published book, for example, or as a conversation held in a public place? The distinction is one which is not always clear.

The Association of Internet Researchers (AOIR: www.aoir.org) have produced ethical guidelines for Internet researchers, although they are keen to reinforce the point that they are not legislative, just as with most ethical guidelines, but should be taken as guiding principles which the researcher needs to interpret within the context of the specific research project in question. Tackling the issue of whether information posted on the Internet should be perceived as private or public, the ethical guidelines state that 'the greater the acknowledged publicity of the venue, the less obligation there may be to protect individual privacy, confidentiality, right to informed consent, etc.' (Ess et al. 2002, p.5). An example of a very public 'venue' might be a newspaper site on which readers' comments in response to articles are posted, whereas a private venue might be a chat room, entry to which is by invitation only from select users. The AOIR recommends close inspection of a site's copyright and usage terms since these will provide some of the basis for site users' expectations of the extent to which their contributions should be considered public. Once again, drawing parallels with the offline world, if someone were appearing in the audience of a televised public debate, it would be reasonable to expect that anything said could be recorded and repeated outside that debate by anyone watching. Contrast this situation with a conversation that took place within a meeting of a local support group and a clearer distinction begins to become apparent.

The topic of the online communication is also important, as is consideration of the vulnerability of the users. Young children, for example, may disclose more private information in public online spaces because of a naïve lack of understanding of the online space. Fortunately, it would seem that site owners and users are becoming more aware of how freely accessible the information they post on Internet sites is. Many online support groups, which are set up with an express purpose of helping the vulnerable, put in measures to protect their users. Some require participants to take part in a telephone interview as part of the registration process, for example, while others will prevent 'lurking' in chat rooms (the practice of reading what others are saying without contributing).

The message to researchers considering using content that has been posted online is to look very closely at the copyright terms on the site in question and read the guidelines for use. Also consider all of the ethical issues covered elsewhere in this chapter, as these are just as relevant to online research. Discussion forums posts and blogs are somewhat different from offline archival sources because the authors will often return to the site at which the data are found, possibly with a view to adding to it. It is, therefore, perhaps easier to gain consent by expressly asking for it, and if there is any doubt as to whether the information we wish to use should be considered as private or public, gaining consent for its use may offer a useful solution.

Gaining consent for the collection of primary data is equally important in online research, but there can be difficulties that are particularly associated with an online environment. Hewson et al. (2003) note how online mediated communication can hide the true identity of participants. This, they say, has the potential for the recruitment of underage participants without the researchers' knowledge. Of course, this could be true of other forms of research, but the problem is perhaps exaggerated by the apparent frequency with which people do adopt alternative identities when online. (See Chapter 7 for a further discussion of the problems associated with anonymity and identity in online qualitative research.)

The freedom with which people can publish their thoughts and intentions in blogs or in discussion forums also leads to the possibility of encountering information on the Internet during the course of research which may call into question ethical responsibilities. Stern (2003) provides a hypothetical example in which a researcher, watching the news, realises that a high-school massacre was carried out by the authors of a web page that the researcher had visited while searching for secondary data. On the web page, the authors had outlined their intentions to kill, and so the researchers were privy to information in advance of the event. The obvious question that is raised by such an example is what are the legal and ethical responsibilities of a researcher in such a situation? Although an extreme example, it does help to highlight the degree to which information relating to private thoughts and behaviour is more openly available online. There are no guidelines as to what we should do if faced with such situations. Should we even be especially concerned? After all, the same dilemma would apply to *anyone* who reads distressing information online, not just researchers. However, as researchers actively seeking out secondary data, we are possibly more likely to be confronted with information that may challenge our own sense of ethical responsibility, and we do therefore have the responsibility of at least having a raised awareness.

All of the ethical issues which apply to any research do so equally online, but the uncertainty over the public/private categorisation of online information remains a topic of specific debate. The appeal of online research – easy access to large quantities of data, global coverage, relatively low administrative costs – should not overshadow the need to be particularly conscientious with regards to the ethical dimensions of the Internet.

## Summary

As we have seen in this chapter, ethical problems can relate to both the subject matter and the conduct of the research – *what* is researched and *how* it is done. There are many issues that need to be addressed if we are to ensure that we produce an ethically sound research design as well as one that is intellectually coherent and compelling.

While it is very difficult to anticipate *all* that may happen during the execution of a research project, the sensitive and intelligent researcher is charged with thinking through all of the possible areas in which ethics *may* impinge on the research. This is something that should be done during the initial planning stages when the research project is first articulated and considered in detail.

Where possible, ethical issues should be identified and worked through, weighing the costs and benefits of particular courses of action. In this respect, Denzin (2009) emphasises that ethical considerations ought to be interwoven through every step of the methodology and should not be pigeon-holed, i.e. confined to a particular section of the research strategy or considered as an afterthought. However, it is evidently the case that, if done conscientiously, 'ethical research takes longer to complete, costs more money, is more complicated, and is more likely to be terminated before completion' (Neuman 2006, p.130).

We have also seen that there is a heated debate concerning ethical issues in research, one that is inextricably linked with the question of power and politics in the research process. The ethical implications of some of the celebrated cases that we have reviewed in this chapter, such as Humphreys (1970) and Reiss (1971), tend to be viewed differently depending on the contrasting levels of power that reside in those who have been deceived. It is also the case that the political values of individual researchers are likely to impact upon the judgement that is made concerning what is acceptable behaviour when dealing with such groups or organisations: 'The specific circumstances of a research project and the moral and political values of the researcher will inevitably have a powerful effect on the ethical stance that is taken'. (O'Connell Davidson and Layder 1994, p.58). As such, some researchers have argued that it is not possible to define a set of universally acceptable ethical principles that can guide all those who engage in research, motivated by disparate interests and viewing the social world from many different perspectives.

Many of the ethical issues that we have reviewed raise extremely complex questions that demand careful consideration of both context and principle. In reality, the literature concerning research ethics does not provide clear-cut answers to many of the ethical dilemmas that researchers will confront in the course of their research.

This is the case, for example, when the researcher is confronted with making the 'right' choice between the confidentiality assured to the participants and issues of legality. Such dilemmas that face researchers in the field will ultimately need to be resolved in the process of carrying out research, balancing the search for knowledge against a commitment to ethical research.

When embarking upon research it is important to recognise other agencies that are at work and that may affect participants. While an ethical code of practice provides good guidelines for how researchers can protect themselves and their participants, there will always be other factors outside the control of the researcher which need to be considered. Pressures upon participants to take part in research can lead to invalidating the research findings, as can a feeling of insubordination during the research process. Careful choice of methods which involve participants more directly in the research process can help to overcome this problem, at least in part.

When interpreting data, it is important to be aware of cultural norms which may affect how people's experiences are presented. This is particularly problematic when the researcher is dealing with unfamiliar cultures or organisations. In order to ensure validity in the research, great care must be taken in presenting a true and accurate reading of the data, in order to avoid misrepresentation.

While the literature on ethics may fall short on ready-made answers, it does act as a guide, steering a path through the complex problems and issues that arise in the process of doing research. In this respect, researchers are advised of certain fundamental safeguards against the practice of unethical research:

- that the bounds of the research are negotiated with their research participants;
- that they safeguard the privacy and identity of their research participants and settings;
- that they ensure that their research participants do not suffer harm or embarrassment from the research;
- that they carry out their research in a manner that will not preclude further/future academic research.

## Chapter research task

Take the code of ethics for the professional association that is most appropriate for your research. If in any doubt, use the *Ethical Guidelines* of the SRA. Try to think of research examples where deception might be justified or warranted in gaining data. Are there areas where some measure of deception is justified in gaining data? Are there institutions that deserve what they get, i.e. where devious means are legitimate in exposing 'bad' practices? Are codes of practice too limiting? If so, how might they be modified? Are there any issues/organisations/cultures that you would never research on ethical grounds because to do so would make you feel that you were giving them some sort of credence?

## Recommended Reading

Barnes, J. 1979. *Who Should Know What? Social Science, Privacy and Ethics*. Harmondsworth: Penguin.

Bulmer, M. (ed.) 1982. *Social Research Ethics*. London: Macmillan.

Diener, E. and Crandall, R. 1978. *Ethics in Social and Behavioural Research*. Chicago: Chicago University Press.

Finch, J. 1993. 'It's Great To Have Someone To Talk To': Ethics and Politics of Interviewing Women. In: M. Hammersley (ed.), *Social Research: Philosophy, Politics and Practice*. London: Sage. pp.166–80.

Gomm, R. 2008. *Social Research Methods: A Critical Introduction*, 2nd edn. Basingstoke: Palgrave Macmillan. pp.365–90.

Homan, R. 1991. *The Ethics of Social Research*. London: Longman.

May, T. 2001. *Social Research: Issues, Methods and Process*, 3rd edn. Buckingham: Open University Press. pp.46–68.

Punch, M. 1998. Politics and Ethics in Qualitative Research. In: N. Denzin and Y. Lincoln (eds), *The Landscape of Qualitative Research: Theories and Issues*. Thousand Oaks, CA: Sage. pp.156–84.

SRA (Social Research Association) 2003. *Ethical Guidelines* [online]. Available at: www.the-sra.org.uk/documents/pdfs/ethics03.pdf (Accessed 7 April 2009).

# FIVE

# Documentary Sources, Official Statistics and Secondary Data

- To introduce readers to the variety of documents available to researchers as primary and secondary data
- To identify the ways in which positivist, interpretivist and critical approaches inform the use of documentary sources in research
- To alert readers to potential limitations of the use of documents in research and to highlight the advantages of their use
- To make readers aware of how, and for what purposes, official statistics are produced
- To encourage readers to approach official statistics critically



## Introduction

The idea of documentary research conjures up an old-fashioned image of a researcher digging away in a dusty archive, wading through piles of paper. Nowadays we tend to think of surveys and field research, in the form of interviews and observation studies, as the key methods of inquiry for social science researchers. However, documentary research in its various forms has a longer history than either of these approaches – public records from ancient civilisations record some of the oldest writings in existence. Such documents describe places and social relationships at a previous time when we could not have conducted our research, or in environments to which we had no meaningful access.

Even now the existence of such documents and the place of documentary research is no less important, providing us with direct accounts of people involved in their social situations. With such research there is no intermediary to influence this account, to report it, or change it. Rather, such documents provide a first-hand account from the 'inside'.

As Webb et al. (1984) inform us, documentary research remains a valuable research tool in its own right, and has only been eclipsed by survey research and field research because of recent changes in technology. Such changes now allow for the collection, handling and analysis of large sets of data, and the recording of speech and interaction using audio- and video-recording devices. However, these very same technological developments in electronic data storage and retrieval have seen something of a resurgence in the use of documentary data, by making use of the considerable number of online documents now available, whether they simply be electronic versions of traditional records or new media such as blogs and personal video.

In this chapter, we shall examine what constitutes a document and how social researchers classify the different types of document that are used in the research process. We shall also look at the way in which different epistemologies impact on the use to which documents are put in the research process. This will be followed by a discussion of the general merits of documentary research before taking a more detailed look at the main documentary sources that are used. Attention will be brought to some general problems that arise when conducting documentary research.

Within this chapter, official statistics are given special attention because of their wide but often controversial usage within the social sciences. The very substantial benefits of official statistics are discussed as well as their weaknesses. Most importantly, we shall examine the claim that official statistics often employ unexamined assumptions about social life which social science researchers may inherit and reproduce in their studies if they do not guard against them. Indeed, some critics of official statistics maintain that they are not simply social 'facts', but also social and political constructions, which may be based upon the interests of those who commissioned the research in the first place in order to reinforce and promote a particular ideological agenda.

This chapter will examine some of these issues and hopefully provide you with an understanding of the need to interrogate rigorously the rich seam of data which, potentially, documentary sources (and in particular official statistics) can provide.

## Doing documentary research

At the very outset of your research you will need to ask yourself what you really want to know as well as what the documents that you will obtain might be able to tell you about the phenomena in which you are interested. Do you expect them to tell you in a very literal sense about the phenomena under investigation (e.g. in the way you might use *Hansard* to inform you of the number of speakers in a parliamentary debate), or are you intending to 'read' them for some other purpose? You may see them as representations of something else – as the textual manifestations of cultural discourses (e.g. in examining the advertising campaigns of car manufacturers), or you might expect to be able to detect something about the underlying norms or rules of society (e.g. by examining the manifestos of political parties at election time).

Conducting secondary research has a long tradition within the social sciences and there are a number of different approaches that reflect the different epistemological positions discussed in Chapter 1. Jupp and Norris (1993) usefully contrast three such approaches as, first, content analysis, secondly, an interpretivist approach, and thirdly, a critical tradition including reflexive critical analysis and discourse analysis.

### Positivism: content analysis

The positivist paradigm dominated documentary analysis up until the 1960s. This approach views documents as objective indicators of phenomena to which they refer, and is therefore concerned with analysing the content of a document. Such content analysis also, to a certain extent, seeks to uncover the attitudes and values of the author and the effects of the communication on the intended recipient. In a nutshell, it is concerned with 'who says what to whom and with what effect' (Lasswell 1942, p.12).

The key characteristics of content analysis are:

- A concern with what can be seen on the page of a document or in a communication – the manifest content. It is not concerned with the meanings or intentions of the message. An example of this type of documentary research is the work of Platt and Kreitman (1985, cited in Hakim 1993, p.138), who used health service records to study patterns of attempted suicide.
- Quantitative counting. The literal meaning is measured by counting certain predetermined things within a document, such as the number of readers' letters that are published on a particular issue in a newspaper or the column inches devoted to a certain topic.
- The document itself is seen as a research resource.

### The interpretivist tradition

This approach also focuses on the document, the sender and the recipient, but with a different theoretical emphasis. The document is viewed not as a neutral resource, but as a social construction that represents the way some people (the people who produced the document) see the world. In this sense, documents are not objective sources of information. Rather, they will need to be read and interpreted to bring out the evidence that is within them.

Instead of confining themselves to an examination of the literal meaning of a document, interpretivist researchers seek to understand the nature of the document itself. In this respect, the emphasis is on understanding the deeper latent meaning that must be arrived at by an interpretivist analysis.

A good example of the interpretivist approach is the work of McRobbie (1991), who studied the teenage girls' magazine *Jackie* as a key part of her analysis of adolescent femininity. For McRobbie, the importance of the magazine is not in its surface meaning, but lies in the authors' meaning and intentions. The key to understanding the true meaning of the document is to uncover the latent messages that are hidden in the text. She found, for instance, that the magazine nourished a romantic outlook among its readership, and encouraged young girls into accepting traditional gender roles within the family.

## The critical tradition

Like the interpretivist tradition, critical social researchers see documents and text not simply as a resource to help explain the world, but as objects of research in their own right. However, critical social researchers criticise both positivists and intrepretivists for playing down the place of social structure in the generation of documents, text and discourse. In particular, they point to the key structural influence of social class relationships in capitalist society, and hold that positivist and interpretivist approaches ignore the key issues of power and ideology. (These issues have already been examined in more detail in Chapter 3.)

For example, reflexive critical researchers contend that the state's crime control apparatus plays a central role in maintaining the existing social order by focusing on and emphasising working-class crime: the crime statistics that are produced and used by the police and courts in capitalist societies reveal the assumptions of the criminal justice system. For example, in 1995 the Metropolitan Police Commissioner, Sir Paul Condon, was criticised for suggesting that police statistics provided evidence that black people were responsible for a disproportionate share of street crime in London. Academic social researchers disputed this conclusion, claiming that Sir Paul Condon's assertions were based upon subjective and limited definitions of street crime, and ignored economic and social deprivation variables which were more strongly associated with these crimes than was race (Campbell 1995).

Critical social researchers seek to emphasise the relationship between the document itself and the society in which it was produced. By undertaking a critical analysis of the process by which such documents are constructed, critical social researchers seek to lay bare the role that documents play in maintaining and promoting unequal social relationships. In this way, critical social researchers use documentary analysis as part of their overall critique of capitalist social relations, and this analysis thus becomes a vehicle for changing social relationships.

This critical paradigm, which focuses primarily on the relationship between documents and social structure, class relations, ideology and power, has evolved into an area of discourse analysis. Leading this movement, the French social theorist Michel Foucault (1980) treats text as a discourse that reveals the mechanisms by which power is exercised in capitalist societies. (For a more detailed discussion of discourse analysis, see Chapter 8.)

## Forms of documentary data

There are many forms of text-based and non-textual documents that are available to the social science researcher. Macdonald and Tipton (1993, p.188) define documents as 'things that we can read and which relate to some aspect of the social world'.

Such documents may include minutes of meetings, law reports, transcripts of parliamentary debates, diaries, autobiographies, newspapers, photographs, websites, songs, posters, wills, bills, maps, films, official records and logs of decisions. Indeed, this is just a very brief list of some of the documents that have been used by researchers in the past.

### Classifying documents

Documents can be classified according to a variety of criteria. The most common characterisations are between public and private documents, primary and secondary documents, and solicited and unsolicited documents.

#### Public/private documents

Public documents are mostly produced by governments and their agencies, and are intended for public consumption. These include such things as court and police records and newspaper reports. Webb et al. (1984) identify four types of public document:

a. Actuarial records on the public, e.g., certificates of births, deaths and marriages.
b. Political and judicial records, e.g., decisions of courts, and by government.
c. Other government records, e.g., records on the weather, hospital records.
d. Mass media, e.g., news content, editorial columns and advertising.

Private documents are those that were not originally meant for public scrutiny. These include such things as letters, diaries, photographs, and so on. Of course, it is quite common for documents that were originally of a private nature to find their way into the public domain.

The Internet has led to a blurring of the public/private divide, with many people publishing apparently private documents in the very public domain of the Internet. Media-sharing sites, such as YouTube (video) and Flickr (photo and video), contain millions of insights into people's private lives, posted for anyone to see. Personal *blogs* (web-logs) are often built around a personal diary format, regularly updated and shared with millions of people. This cross-over of the private into the public has implications for how the researcher approaches the documents, as we shall see later in this chapter.

## Primary/secondary documents

Primary materials are those that are written or collected by those who actually witnessed the events which they describe. They are gathered first-hand and have a direct relationship with the people, situations or events that are studied. For example, court records, minutes, contracts, letters, memoranda, notes, memoirs, diaries, autobiographies, and other reports all provide a first-hand account of a situation.

Secondary documents are those that are produced *after* the event which the author had not personally witnessed, and as such they provide a summary of primary source materials. Therefore, secondary documents may include materials such as newspaper articles that *report* the correspondence between two people, or a television programme that is based on the memoirs of a leading politician. Secondary quantitative data are produced as an outcome of either data-gathering processes which are part of the machinery of the state, or from prior research. Such data might include official statistics in their aggregated or raw forms, or survey data collected as part of a research project conducted by another researcher.

Hakim (1982, p.1) defines secondary research as:

> Any further analysis of an existing data set which presents interpretations of, conclusions of knowledge additional to, or different from, those presented in the first report on the inquiry as a whole and its main results.

## Solicited/unsolicited documents

Solicited documents are those that are produced for the purpose of research, and at the request of the researcher, for example diaries. These can be generated by you, the researcher, or by those whom you have asked to generate them for you (see Example 5.1).

Unsolicited documents are those that have been produced for a purpose other than research. For example, while an advertisement is designed to encourage sales of a particular product, it may subsequently become the subject of research itself.

All of these documents tell us something about the society, culture or organisation in which they were produced as well as the values, interests and purposes of those who commissioned or produced them. For instance, Durand's (1960) study of mortality estimates from Roman tombstone inscriptions indicated more than just the life expectancy of Romans: it also revealed important insights as to the position of females in society: 'Possibly a wife was more likely to get an inscribed tablet if she died before her husband than if she outlived him' (Durand 1960, cited in Webb et al. 1984, p.113). Of itself, much documentary data may appear sterile, but as Webb et al. explain, it can be transformed into powerful forms of research data, provided the researcher asks insightful questions:

> There is little explicit in patient records, city-water archives, parking meter collection records, or children's readers to suggest their research utility. It required imagination to perceive the application and a willingness to follow an unconventional line of data collection. (Webb et al. 1984, p.129)

## Diaries

Diaries offer a reliable alternative to interviews for 'retrospective data' in that they provide a direct account of events rather than one that relies on the fallibility of human memory. They can also be preferable to interviews for collecting sensitive data, where people may feel uncomfortable about talking to a researcher. Diaries are used to collect very detailed information about behaviour, events and other aspects of people's daily lives. They offer a view or a picture of reality from an individual actor's perspective and may tell us several things about the way people spend their time.

There are three types of diary used for research:

1. The intimate *journal* is regarded as a valuable document providing an insight into thoughts, events and feelings that are considered important to an individual. Such diaries can provide rare insights into the thoughts and feelings of a variety of people, and can prove highly valuable for collecting sensitive data on a whole range of personal and social issues, such as health, happiness, social networks, crime, and alcohol and drug consumption. See, for example, the research of Coxon (1988), who used personal diaries to study the changing lifestyle patterns of people who were diagnosed as suffering from AIDS. A personal diary is a thing that is usually produced spontaneously and in private, and is not therefore usually intended for publication at the time of its writing.
2. The *memoir* is most commonly associated with the accounts of political decision-making recounted by senior politicians. While these may be similar to personal diaries, they are often written with publication in mind. For example, Richard Crossman's (1975) *The Diaries of a Cabinet Minister (1964–66)* and Tony Benn's (1988) *Out of the Wilderness: Diaries 1963–67*.
3. A *log* is a record of events, meetings, visits, and so on. It is quite common for a researcher to persuade the research participants to keep such documents. For

example, Burgess (1984, p.130) asked schoolteachers to keep diaries to obtain an account of what happened in their classes. In doing so he gained access to events that were previously denied to him (see Example 5.1).

### Example 5.1 A solicited diary (Burgess 1984, p.130)

I am interested in what actually happens in the course of your classes with members of the 5th Year Newsom group. I would therefore appreciate it if you would keep this diary over the next four weeks. It would be interesting to know what the lesson is about, what members of the group say and do (or do not do). Finally, it might be useful to write up what one or two pupils (selected at random) do in the course of your lesson. If you would like to chat to me about the notes you keep I shall be interested to hear from you.

Many thanks,
Bob Burgess

## Blogs

The Internet has gradually evolved, to the extent that it is now generally agreed that we have reached a second generation, known as 'Web 2.0'. This new generation has brought with it a wealth of 'online services that, among other things, integrate writer and reader, producer and consumer and blur the boundary between both' (Ó Dochartaigh 2007, p.99). Authorship of online content is now available to anyone with access to the Internet, without the need to know anything about the language of website programming, html. Perhaps the most successful example of this is the online, publicly authored encyclopaedia, *Wikipedia*. As with all 'wikis', contributors can update and alter the site at will, a feature which must be borne in mind by anyone considering using it. As a source of reliable information about a subject, wikis may not be particularly helpful, but they can perhaps tell us something about the way the Internet is fulfilling its early promise of democratising knowledge, by enabling anyone to contribute to knowledge formation and transfer.

For a documentary researcher, a more interesting aspect of Web 2.0 which has proliferated in recent years is the web-log, commonly referred to as a *blog*. Blogs enable users to post messages on a website, to which site visitors can respond. They tend to centre around current events, sometimes personal – they have been described as 'little more than an online diary that you can create or access via the web' (Dolowitz et al. 2008, p.101) – but often political. As a means of public address, blogs offer any individual with access to relatively rudimentary technology the opportunity to post their thoughts to a potential audience of millions. Many journalists now make use of blogs to offer comment on news stories, which can then be debated by readers posting comments.

Similarly, politicians are increasingly using blogs as a means of campaigning, a trend which really took off with the 2004 US Presidential elections. It is, though, the opportunity for the layperson to instigate and contribute to public debate that leads Chadwick (2006, p.316) to conclude that:

> It is highly unlikely that most Internet users will give up visiting CNN.com (for example) in favour of a diet of blogs, but at the margins, do-it-yourself journalism seems likely to continue to play a role, even if this is often indirect, as mainstream journalists increasingly pick up stories from the blogosphere. In this sense, the Internet does appear to be contributing to a more pluralistic public sphere of communication – one less constrained by commercial values.

For researchers interested in understanding how this new form of democratic public debate contributes to new discourses, blogs can provide an extremely useful resource.

## Letters

Letters are indicative of different types of social relationship – they can be ceremonial, personal, literary, business-related, or provide information, and so on.

The classic case of documentary research that is based primarily on letters is that of Thomas and Znaniecki (1918–20), who examined Polish immigration into the USA at the turn of the twentieth century. They used letters and other documents that *émigrés* sent back home (including agency documents, newspaper articles, records and reports from public agencies) to show how traditional family solidarity was maintained or altered as family members moved to the USA.

While groundbreaking, their research has been criticised in terms of the representativeness of their material. How did they get hold of it? They advertised and paid for letters from individuals obtained newspapers when they could from isolated individuals and visited official agencies. This raises some doubts about the reliability and validity of their data.

## Emails

Emails, like letters, come in many forms and styles, from the informal correspondence between friends to the message announcing departmental restructuring sent out to staff by managers. Despite being described as 'letter-like documents' (Mann and Stewart 2000, p.9), there are important differences. First, emails can, and often are, sent to multiple recipients, and in this sense bear a closer resemblance to memoranda traditionally distributed within organisations. Email distribution can therefore provide valuable data about organisational structure and authorial intent: if a message is sent to a restricted group of recipients, what might this tell us about the intended outcomes of the communication?

The convenience with which emails can be sent, and the rapid send/reply nature of a lot of email communication has also drawn comparisons with conversational exchanges. In a study of forwarded emails, Kibby (2005, p.771) noted that 'senders exhibit reduced constraints about the type of messages sent electronically and are inclined to post more frequently, to more people and on a wider variety of topics via email than via print or phone'.

Kibby also notes how the forwarding of email messages is often done without any modification to the message by the person doing the forwarding. This is in contrast to spoken segments of information, which are rarely repeated faithfully, word-for-word, but are modified by each person who passes on the information. Whereas spoken messages may be accidentally modified as they are passed on, when emails are modified it is often with a specific intention, as Ó Dochartaigh (2007, p.152) warns us:

> People often forward by email news stories or other items they've gleamed from the web. In some cases people edit or alter the stories, for legitimate reasons, highlighting the section they want to bring to your attention. In many cases, though, people edit to make news reports appear more favourable to their argument or political position.

The forwarding of emails presents interesting questions over authorship and intent, and suggests that we need to locate the origin of emails as well as any modifications to the messages that have been made during transit from one person to another.

A particular difficulty in using emails as sources of documentary data is that they are not always archived. The disposable nature of emails, combined with a need to keep email inboxes from becoming full up will often lead to the deletion of emails which are less formal. Lengthier emails, containing detailed communications or information are, however, more likely to be retained and can provide valuable information.

## Autobiographies

An autobiography allows an individual to give an account of her or his own life and the events she or he experiences. As such, autobiographies can be from people who want to 'put the record straight' and should be viewed with some caution. Allport (1942) distinguishes three types of autobiography:

1. *Comprehensive autobiographies* cover the main trends in an individual's life, from earliest recall to the time of writing. These include descriptions of life experiences, personal insights and anecdotal reminiscences, such as that provided by one of the leaders of the 1917 Russian Revolution, Leon Trotsky (1975), in his autobiography entitled *My Life*.
2. *Topical autobiographies* select a particular theme around which an individual constructs a story. These will offer a partial picture of an individual's life. An example of this is provided by the research of Burgess (1984, pp.127–8) who asked some of his research participants in the Newsom School to keep 'a brief autobiography on two sides of A4 paper' for a short period of time (see Example 5.2). The autobiographies

that Burgess generated allowed for comparisons to be made between the teachers' social and educational backgrounds, their experiences and their approach to teaching.
3. *Edited autobiographies* highlight certain areas while deleting other less relevant segments. An example of this type of autobiography is provided by Bogdan (1974, cited in Burgess 1984, p.127), who carried out one of the first studies of transsexuality.

The subject matter of autobiographies can, similarly, be divided into three main groups:

1. The reflections of the powerful, such as politicians. These may give you insight into how decisions are taken, such as former British Prime Minister Mrs Thatcher's (1993) *The Downing Street Years*.
2. The lives of rich and famous celebrities.
3. The life experiences of ordinary people. For example, Ellen Kuzwayo's (1985) *Call Me Woman* provides an account of a black woman in apartheid South Africa. Such autobiographies are less common owing to a lack of interest by publishers.

### Example 5.2 Solicited autobiographies (Burgess 1984, pp.127–8)

As part of my research I am interested in the kind of things you have done before coming into teaching, your teaching experience and the work that you do now. I am also interested in your contact with the 5th Year Newsom pupils. In writing about these things on the attached sheet, the following suggestions might help: The people in your family – the work they did, the area they lived in, their religion. The schools you went to and what you did at school. The college or university you went to and what you did. Anything you have done other than teaching. The places you have taught. Your work in McGregor and your contact with the 5th Year Newsom pupils. I hope this will help – if you would like to chat about this I shall be interested to hear from you.

Many thanks,
Bob Burgess

## Visual documents

These can include a very wide variety of materials such as photographs, advertisements, posters, films, architecture, and so on. For example, there is a very rich photographic archive of the twentieth century that charts the many and various wars, revolutionary struggles, discoveries, cultural highpoints, and unforeseeable events that have taken place over the past 100 years (Bernard 1999). More recently, with the vast increase in storage capacities of

Internet servers, we have seen the development of online photo archives. The photo storage and sharing site, Flickr, has entered into a collaborative project with The Library of Congress called *The Commons* (www.flickr.com/commons). This online repository contains photographs from the archives of a large number of museums and cultural heritage organisations, and is fully searchable.

Online video storage has also become popular, and as well as enabling individuals to upload personal videos, organisations such as broadcasters and newspapers are increasingly placing archival video footage online. The Internet Archive (www.archive.org) is a project which seeks to provide digitally archived visual (and audio/textual) documentary sources for use by researchers, including news and documentary footage.

However, when using visual documents, we should always be aware that the old adage that 'the camera never lies' is somewhat out of date (Becker 1974). For example, Stalin famously airbrushed Trotsky out of pictures of the Russian Revolution (Macdonald and Tipton 1993, p.193). We should also be aware that in contemporary times, computer-generated and modified images make it difficult to know what is actually 'real'. When using video footage, the manner in which it is edited may actually tell us something about the authorial intent of the document. Are certain scenes cut shorter than others? Are particular angles chosen from which to shoot in order to emphasise a certain aspect of the scene? As with all documents, when analysing the visual, we must ask questions about *how* the documents were produced and for what purpose, not just about what is contained within them.

### Activity 5.1

Thinking about all the documents you have read about so far, list five different documentary sources that you could use specifically for researching the issue of employee absenteeism.

## Problems and issues in using documents

It is important to be aware of a range of potential problems involved in using documentary data in research. These include what are termed selective deposit and selective survival, both of which are concerned with 'missing' data that can invalidate findings if the researcher is not sensitive to both their extent and to their implications (Webb et al. 1984).

Selective deposit occurs where only an unrepresentative selection of documentary data is stored. For example, this often happens in relation to official statistics:

1. Crime statistics – the official measurement of domestic violence and many sexual offences underestimate the actual rate of such crimes as many cases are not reported to the police and therefore are not included in published statistics.
2. Census data, such as the effect that was produced at the introduction of the 'poll tax' in Britain in the 1990s. When this happened many people in lower income groups decided not to register in the 1991 Census for fear that they would be traced and prosecuted for non-payment of their 'poll tax'.
3. Suicide statistics – only a quarter of suicides actually leave a suicide note, so it is not possible to gain a definite account of why the suicide took place.

Selective survival involves an editing process, which more often than not is governed by the values, perspectives and assumptions of those who are in a position to decide what should and should not be made available to researchers. These processes are social in character, and involve decisions being made which may have detrimental consequences for the research if the researcher is unable to identify and acknowledge the bias that may be associated with the data. In such circumstances, the ability to estimate from the data may be limited by such problems.

When conducting documentary research, it is important to ask yourself whether the document is the real thing or whether it may have been innocently, carelessly or deliberately changed or falsified by someone in the process of its production or reproduction. Platt (1981) suggests that you ask a series of questions to determine whether the material that you are using is trustworthy and representative or whether it is atypical or has been significantly edited or refined:

- Does the document make sense or does it contain any glaring errors?
- Are there differing versions of the document available?
- Is there a consistency of literary style, handwriting or typeface?
- Have many copyists transcribed the document?
- Has the author engaged in any distortion or deception to achieve her or his own ends?
- Has the document been through several hands after leaving the author?
- Has someone who has a material interest in passing it off as the real thing circulated the document?
- Has a long time occurred between the event and the account of it?
- What do you know about the representativeness of the materials that are available for use, and what do you know about those that are not available? Is there any significance to be attached to the presence or absence of materials?

## Official statistics

The most obvious source of documentary data for research purposes is in the form of government-produced official statistics, such as the national Census, as well as various reports detailing demographic, social, economic, business and political trends. Thus, the Census, the General Household Survey, the Family Expenditure Survey, Regional Trends, and the many other government statistics are major sources of data on crime, employment and unemployment, housing, health and illness, and birth and death rates, to name just a few areas.

These figures are collected and produced by official agencies, chiefly agencies of the state, such as the various departments and ministries of central governments, as well as their central statistical offices, for example the British government's own National Statistics organisation. However, such data are also collected by other official organizations, including local authorities regional health authorities and local education authorities.

## Activity 5.2 The range of official statistics

Take a brief look at the National Statistics website at www.statistics.gov.uk/. Within the site you can access resources and statistical data under a number of different categories. At the time of writing, these are:

- Agriculture and Environment
- Business and Energy
- Children, Education and Skills
- Crime and Justice
- Economy
- Government
- Health and Social Care
- Labour Market
- People and Places
- Population
- Travel and Transport
- Equality and Diversity

Take a look at some of the resources that are available under these headings to get an idea of the enormous amount of information that is generated by central government, the range of fields that is covered, and the possibilities for researchers.

### The British Census

Undoubtedly, the largest statistical operation conducted within Britain (and probably the most frequently used source of official statistics by the British social science community) is the decennial Census of population, carried out by National Statistics. The Census has been conducted every 10 years since 1801 – the last in 2001. It is a vast undertaking, covering 20 million households in the country, at a cost of £140 million in 1991, and £259 million in 2001.

It is a population count of the entire number of people in each area of the country (census districts), the number of men and women (together with their marital status and ethnicity), of particular groups such as children, teenagers, retired people, and so on. It also includes specific population characteristics, such as people's occupations, qualifications, housing tenure, car ownership, and many other variables.

As the Census is legally compulsory to complete, it is therefore seen as an authoritative source of data for planning purposes. It is used in the fields of housing, health and other local services, the planning of future spending, welfare provision and pensions, and by the British academic community.

However, the Census is not without its problems. As such a large-scale operation, it is subject to certain inaccuracies and data errors:

- The information it contains covers a 10-year period, yet becomes out of date comparatively quickly as people move homes, change jobs and make other life changes on a regular basis.
- Some people are inevitably double-counted (the 1991 Census states that 'People staying temporarily with the household are included', and these temporary persons may earlier or later be counted at their permanent residence) while some others may be missed entirely.
- Very importantly in the field of policy, its deficiencies mean that it is often difficult for policy-makers to forecast accurately the resource needs of communities and regions.

'Unofficial' sources of statistics are far more wide ranging than official statistics. They include regular studies, such as media viewing figures, and one-off studies designed for a specific purpose. These are likely to appear within the publications and reports of various bodies such as the Low Pay Unit, trade unions, charities, and so on. Increasingly, they are available through the various higher education funding councils, such as the Economic and Social Research Council's data archive at Essex University (www.data-archive.ac.uk/).

### Activity 5.3 Unofficial statistics

List three different types of unofficial statistic. Write brief notes on: (a) why you think they are produced; and (b) what you think they are used for. When you have done this, look back at Activity 5.2 and note any differences that are apparent between these 'official' and 'unofficial' sources.

## Advantages and disadvantages of official statistics as a research source

### Advantages of official statistics as a research source

There are several major benefits that official statistics hold for social researchers:

- There is a great wealth of information available on a wide range of social, political and economic issues.
- Much of the information that a researcher might want is readily available.
- Many of the government's official statistics are available to the researcher without cost through university or public libraries, or on the Internet.
- The government's official statistics are collected by technical 'experts' at the Office for National Statistics (ONS) (and elsewhere) who are highly skilled in their jobs, thus suggesting a high degree of proficiency.
- Official statistics data sets are often very large, enabling detailed analysis of sample subsets. Hence it is possible to get representative samples of numerically small populations when in normal circumstances you may have difficulty in obtaining a

sampling frame. Such groups may, for instance, include cohabitees, one-parent families, the elderly disabled, and so on.

- Sometimes official statistics may be the only source of information that is available for particular topics. This would be the case, for example, with the retail price index.
- Because official statistics are collected systematically over time, and usually across the whole country, they permit comparative analysis in terms of:
    - time – enabling the measurement of change, such as fluctuations in crime levels or changing patterns of share ownership;
    - 'before and after' studies that monitor the impact of particular policy changes, such as the introduction of CCTV in specified areas, or curfews for young people;
    - different socio-demographic groupings based on gender, age, occupation, and so on, such as hours of training at work or variations in levels of pay;
    - geographic areas, for example by examining the allocation of the National Lottery's Board grants to different regions of Britain.

## Disadvantages of official statistics as a research source

However, while official statistics provide the social science researcher with a wealth of readily available data, caution needs to be exercised in relation to a number of points:

1. Official statistics are collected for administrative purposes to suit the needs of politicians and bureaucrats, not for social researchers. They may therefore be limited or shaped in particular ways that are not always suitable for particular research studies to be undertaken by social scientists.
2. Official definitions are often non-sociological. Thus crime figures are based on reported cases of law-breaking whereas social scientists might be interested in broader definitions, including crimes not always reported to the police, such as racial abuse or domestic violence.
3. Official statistics often do not cover areas of interest to social science researchers, or are presented in ways that are unsuitable for research purposes. For example, official statistics on health and illness may be available on a regional basis only. They may not, therefore, be appropriate for social researchers who are interested in making comparisons between different socio-economic groups.
4. Comparison across different official statistics sources is often difficult because they are often collected on a different methodological basis. Therefore, where, for example, different sampling methods have been used, comparison between these samples would not be methodologically sound. It is also not uncommon to find key analytical concepts measured in different ways across studies. Thus social class may be defined using the Registrar General's social class schema in a study of crime, but by socio-economic group in research on housing issues, resulting in incompatible data sets.
5. In practice, official statistics rarely provide complete coverage of the population, and under-enumeration occurs. Though this may be small in terms of percentages, the effect can be a significant one and can have adverse consequences for the use of the data (e.g. in the allocation of public monies to localities).
6. There is a tendency for official statistics to become outdated quickly, given the extent of the usual time-lag between collection and publication of results.

7. A substantial amount of official data is quantitative, with virtually no figures on public opinion or attitudes. Instead, statistics are usually of a 'factual' nature. This is not necessarily a problem, but it may be an issue for the researcher.
8. There is a strong reliance on the survey method, which entails difficulties in terms of sampling error, the limitations of structured questionnaire formats and standardised pre-coded questions, and possible interviewer bias. (These, and other issues connected to survey research, are explored in detail in Chapter 6.)

### Theoretical criticisms of official statistics as a research source

There are then a number of practical problems involved with employing official statistics in research, but there are also a number of more general theoretical problems associated with them that have been highlighted by critics.

According to critics, much of the problem with official statistics arises precisely because they are official. This reflects the fact that only the state has the capacity (the economic resources and political authority) to collect large quantities of information on a national scale. Because official statistics are generated by the state, it is relatively easy to slip into the view that they are somehow an authoritative and neutral source of information, a view summed up in the phrase 'stats are facts' – that they are a clear representation of the external social world. Hence, if one wishes to know the British 'crime rate', then official crime statistics will reveal the full extent of this.

This view is fairly widespread within the social science community, but is one that some critics see as highly problematic. Irvine et al. (1979), in their collection of articles *Demystifying Social Statistics,* have presented a critical analysis of the collection and construction of official statistics from a radical perspective. They claim that official statistics are not just neutrally gathered, authoritative summaries of the social, economic and political world. Rather, official statistics are socially constructed in various ways, and reflect the assumptions and interests of particular dominant groups in ways that combine to reinforce the *status quo* within society. They describe official statistics as 'social products', which perform an ideological role within society:

> Statistics do not, in some mysterious way, emanate directly from the social conditions they appear to describe, but that between the two lie the assumptions, conceptions and priorities of the state and the social order. (Government Statisticians' Collective 1993, p.163)

Two major criticisms have been levelled at central government-generated official statistics. These are, first, that '[t]he nature of the modern capitalist state and the significance of official data for its operation determine the range, volume and orientation of the official data produced' (Irvine et al. 1979, p.6). Thus, for instance, the British government changed the definition of unemployment on over 30 occasions between 1979 and 1991, and its critics argued that this was done in order to create the impression of falling unemployment.

It did this by excluding from the statistics married women, school-leavers, part-time workers, and so on. The result of these changes was to reduce the actual level of reported unemployment for Britain in all but one case (Macdonald and Tipton 1993, p.189). Irvine et al. are, however, at pains to point out that deliberate *political* falsification is rare. More common is non-publication, delay of publication, misleading commentaries on figures, and so on. They claim, for example, that only the most presentable figures will be highlighted.

At a second level, critics claim that the statistics that are published often have certain assumptions built into them that reflect the views and interests of dominant groups within society – a powerful elite that is usually white, male and middle-class. Thus Oakley and Oakley (1979, p.173) maintain that '[s]exism may enter into the production of official statistics at [various] level[s]', including the topics chosen for analysis, the concepts used to present the statistics, the data collection process, the processing and analysis of figures, the presentation of figures, and the classification of women's social class.

## Is it possible to use official statistics in social research?

While many critics have drawn attention to important problems and issues that need to be addressed when using official statistics (and other documents) in research, few would argue that they should be rejected wholesale. Bulmer (1984), for instance, claims that while there may be flaws in the way in which unemployment figures are collected and disseminated, they still have meaning, and important uses can be made of them despite their deficiencies and limitations. Many social science researchers conclude that, for research purposes, published statistics can and should be used in a critical and informed way.

There are, however, a number of important questions that might be asked of official statistics when used in research, although it may not always be possible to answer all of them! These include:

1. What is the source of the data? Is it a reputable and authoritative source? Are the figures and conclusions likely to be reliable and trustworthy?
2. Who commissioned or sponsored the statistics? What purpose lay behind the collection of the data? Is there any likelihood that the figures have been manipulated or distorted in some way, or have they been collected to support a particular case or argument?
3. What has influenced the selection of the areas chosen for investigation?
4. Are the figures accurate? As far as you are able, you should check them for any possible errors, omissions or distortions. Are particular findings being exaggerated to emphasise a particular interpretation? Have charts or graphs been distorted to make findings appear more impressive than they really are?
5. Are the figures valid? This is perhaps the most important question. How are the concepts defined? Do they really represent what they are purporting to measure? For example,

is the social class of women measured by reference to their own circumstances or that of a male spouse? How adequate are the definitions used in the research (say, of social class)? Are there implicit assumptions built into such data?

6. How were the data collected? What method was used, and what problems were encountered? (Were the data collected via a sample survey or a record-keeping form or a census?) What can you find out about the appropriateness of the sampling strategy that was employed?
7. Are the interpretations and conclusions that may accompany the data supported by the actual statistics? Check that any such argument makes sense and is properly based on the findings, rather than mere opinion or conjecture.
8. How are the figures presented and analysed? Are they in the most appropriate form for research purposes? For example, are graphs employed when full tables of the data are needed?
9. Is there any significant omission of data? Check why any information may have been missed out. Would inclusion of such data have altered the final picture?

## Other forms of secondary quantitative data

Official statistics provide one source of quantitative data, and these, as we have seen, have their strengths as well as their weaknesses. One particular characteristic of a lot of official statistics is that they are often presented, and only available to the researcher, as aggregated statistical tables. For example, population totals for different geographical areas may be listed, possibly broken down by socio-demographic variables, but data for individual cases will not be available. This might be because of data protection, or possibly because of the data collection methods (central government departments might require that local and regional bodies submit aggregated figures to them, which are then published collectively, for example). Since much statistical analysis requires that data are available at the case level, rather than aggregated, researchers can find that they are limited as to what they can achieve with aggregated statistics. An alternative is to make use of the increasingly diverse number of quantitative data sets which are made available online for the purpose of secondary analysis in academic research. Often these data sets will be based on large, national or even international surveys: the British Election Surveys, General Household Survey, European Social Survey, for example. In the UK, many of these are available at the UK Data Archive (www.data-archive.ac.uk).

The raw data themselves, alongside extensive documentation, are usually available. In order to download data, it is necessary to register a particular project for which the data are to be used. The Data Archive does allow browsing without signing in, however, and this alone can provide a valuable insight into the nature of the data sets available. In addition to the data, each set is accompanied by documentation about the methods employed to generate the data, the sample and the objectives of the original research. This is particularly useful for evaluating the quality of the data, as we shall see later.

The Data Archive, while expansive in its collection of data sets, does not offer everything a researcher will want. Some data sets will have to be obtained directly from the organisation responsible for the original study. Usually, this can be achieved by writing to them and requesting the data. Other data sets are available for download from different websites, following payment or disclosure of details of the project for which you wish to use the data. Use of data stored at the Data Archive is also dependent upon acknowledgement of the source of the data, and notification of any publications which result.

## Secondary data quality

When we generate our own data we are a lot closer to the methods employed – the sampling strategies, the operationalisation of variables, the interviewing process, and so forth – than when relying on data produced by someone else. This closeness enables us to offer an evaluation based upon a thorough understanding of the research design. When these parts of the process are in the hands of others, however, extra care must be taken to ensure we fully evaluate the quality of the data. Arber (2001, pp.279–80) suggests that:

> When considering a potential survey for secondary analysis it is necessary to subject its methodology to critical scrutiny, including the developmental and pilot work, interviewer training and fieldwork control, the method of sample selection, the nature of the sampling frame and the response rate. The secondary analyst needs to obtain as much documentation as possible about the collection of the survey data and be aware of any potential data limitations.

With this in mind, it is important that we are able to access as much background information as possible. Fortunately, the way in which much secondary data are archived involves extensive documentation about the research design, including more specific details of data collection and how the sample was selected, as well as any weighting that was necessary or booster samples which have been used.

Weighting is an extremely important consideration since it is used to counteract the problems encountered when respondents in a random sample do not have an equal chance of being selected, or if a sample is found to be underrepresentative of a particular subgroup. In these cases, certain individuals are weighted to effectively count as a fraction more or less than one case, and hence their characteristics, attitudes and behaviours are given more or less weight in the final analysis to ensure that they are properly represented.

In addition to weighting and sampling, details about non-response, sampling error and piloting of measures should be included. In evaluating these points we can begin to assess the validity and reliability of the data. Validity in secondary analysis has a lot to do with whether our research objectives, variables of interest and indicators match those used in the original research. Let us assume we were interested in finding out how popular a rise in income tax was. We may find a data set which includes a measure based upon a question which asks 'Is the government right to introduce the proposed rise in income tax?'. This might tell us that on the whole, people feel that the government is right to introduce the tax, but this does not necessarily mean it is popular – it may just be felt to be necessary in order to avoid charges for certain health services or decreases in the funding available for education, for instance. So here we have an example where the operationalisation and measurement of the concept may have been suited to its original purpose, but not for ours. When evaluating the suitability of data, this is something that must be taken into consideration.

As with the analysis of official statistics, one of the advantages to using secondary data is the access it provides us to data derived from large cross-sections of the population. More often than not, secondary data from government and other surveys will consist of large samples. However, care must be taken to ensure that the sample is large enough, and that if we are intending to look at subgroups, they do actually consist of enough cases to make analysis worthwhile.

Arber (2001) mentions three more concerns when evaluating the quality of data: timeliness, size and complexity. Secondary data, by its nature, will not be made available until some time after the primary research for which it is being used has been completed. This means that if our research is heavily reliant upon up-to-the-minute data, then secondary analysis will not be appropriate. However, it may also be that we wish to study a phenomenon from a particular time (or different times in the case of longitudinal studies), in which case such matters become less important. It is also often the case that using data which are a year old will not affect the research outcomes dramatically. However, in looking at annual surveys such as the British Social Attitudes survey, it is worth noting that those studies which took place at certain times – in election years, for example – may well be influenced by key events, such as party political activity. Attitudes may change in response to events such as election campaigning, and so it is worth considering the social climate in which the data were collected if using data that are some years old; it is easy to forget when key historical and social events took place and for oversights to occur.

The number of variables in a data set, combined with the complexity of the way in which the data are arranged can be confusing to someone who was not involved in the design of the original data collection and recording strategy. It is a good idea to read the documentation first, and try to locate a copy of the original research instrument, if there is one. Having a questionnaire by your side will help to make sense of the data.

As discussed in relation to official statistics, data are the outcome of a process, and that process will have been instigated for a particular purpose. The same applies when analysing raw secondary data; it is just as important to consider whether any variables have been excluded as it is to scrutinise those which are included. If, for example, a study were carried out which was intended to identify failing schools, it may well be that the data would not include any measures of strengths within such schools. It is important to recognise that data sets are the results of decisions based upon social constructs. A failing school, for instance, is one which is defined by a lack of *academic* success; success in other areas may well be overlooked.

The problem with social constructions is that they are based upon established assumptions that have become normalised. Thomas (1996) points to many problems associated with the construction of data sets, and illustrates these with a number of examples. One such example involves the National Food Survey, which began in 1940 in response to concerns over nutrition as a result of rationing. Thomas points out that initially, as a survey of household food consumption, it would have provided a fairly good indicator of individual food consumption because of the way in which households were organised. Extended families lived together and ate together, resulting in an individual diet which resembled that of the household. However, 30 years later it became apparent that the makeup of households had changed. Assumptions about the way in which households operated had become outdated, and so the social construct of the household was no longer relevant, although it continued to shape the way in which the National Food Survey was carried out. This has since changed, but it highlights the way in which social constructs help to shape the way data sets are produced. Close examination of our own operational definitions in relation to those used to produce the data we are employing, and broader social discourses, is vital if we are to ensure that the data we are analysing provides a valid measure of the variables of interest to our own research.

To fully understand the political discourse that surrounds the creation of data, we must first identify the agencies responsible for the production of the data set, and any sponsors. We also must be aware of the political climate at the time the data were generated (particularly if we are making use of data from some years ago). Having considered these factors, it is important to be critical of the operational definitions used to create the measures, and to be aware of our own understanding of the topics we are investigating. In short, although secondary data provide a valuable resource to researchers, we must always remember that they came into existence primarily to tackle a different problem from that which we wish to investigate, and on different terms from our own.

## Summary

This chapter has reviewed the wealth of documentary material that is available to social researchers. Indeed, many of the documents that we have discussed are resources that we might not previously have considered to be likely sources of research data. The wide range of documents that exist in society provide a rich seam of data that can be used in the process of research.

We have also seen how the documents that have been reviewed in this chapter may be approached and used in very different ways by researchers who come from a variety of different research traditions. Such backgrounds may influence researchers to 'read' the document in a literal, interpretive or critical manner.

In assessing the role that documents can play in the research process, we have looked at the strengths and weakness of different types of document. While some of these are specific to the type of document, there is a general set of issues that need to be addressed when carrying out documentary research.

In each case, where a document is used for the purpose of research, it has been noted that care needs to be taken to think about the possible limitations of those particular documents. While documents may provide the researcher with a valuable source of data that might not be otherwise obtainable through qualitative means (such as in-depth interviews and observation studies) or quantitative methods (such as surveys and experiments), a great deal of care and attention needs to be taken when employing them for research purposes. In all instances, it has been seen how important it is to ask some very important questions of the documents that you want to use.

However, while it is the case that you will want to interrogate the documentary data to establish their trustworthiness and representativeness, this in no way suggests that documents cannot be put to very good use by the reflexive researcher.

## Chapter research task

For this task you are required to use documentary sources to ascertain how much 'poverty' there was in Britain in 1981. Furthermore, you should go on to compare your findings for 1981 with the situation in 2001.

To answer the above questions you will need to search those official statistics that are available in libraries and on the Internet. The aim is to provide a *general figure* for overall poverty. A good starting point would be to begin by consulting the general literature to get an idea of the different ways in which 'poverty' can be understood before you attempt to measure it. Once you have done this you may want to use the following points as a guide:

1. How is the concept (in this case, 'poverty') defined (or, technically speaking, 'operationalised')?
   (a) Were there different 'levels' of the concept? (For example, if you used *Unemployment* as a proxy variable, did you need to define it at all? Who is 'officially' included in this category and, perhaps just as importantly, who is not?)
   (b) Were there different 'dimensions' of poverty? (For example, is poverty just about how much *money* people have? Or is it about other issues, such as *homelessness*? Or is it about issues to do with *relative poverty*?)
2. Were there any 'holes' or omissions in the data?
3. Is it possible to achieve different *quantities* of poverty from different statistical sources? (For instance, are the Census figures and those reported in *Social Trends*

the same? If not, why do you think that might be the case? Might it be because different methods are used?)

4. How are the *indicators* of poverty actually developed?
5. What difference does it make to the *quantity* of poverty you derive if you measure either absolute poverty (say, those on supplementary benefit) or relative poverty (say, numbers of people living on less than half median male earnings)? Do you have a preference, and if so why?
6. What are the general issues (and problems) raised by using your chosen sources of documentary data for measuring poverty?
7. How have the data been collected (by survey, or by some type of census)? What do you consider to be the strengths and weaknesses of the method(s) chosen?
8. Are the data (a) reliable, and (b) valid?
9. How *complete* are the findings on, say, unemployment and homelessness (or whatever dimensions of poverty you chose)?
10. What general impressions do you have of your data?

## Recommended Reading

Arber, A. 2001. Secondary Analysis of Survey Data. In: N. Gilbert (ed.), *Researching Social Life*, 2nd edn. London: Sage. pp.269–86.

Bulmer, M. 1984. Why Don't Sociologists Make More Use of Official Statistics? In: M. Bulmer (ed.), *Sociological Research Methods*. London: Macmillan. pp.131–52.

Government Statisticians' Collective 1993. How Official Statistics Are Produced: Views from the Inside. In: M. Hammersley (ed.), *Social Research: Philosophy, Politics and Practice*. London: Sage. pp.146–65.

Hakim, C. 1993. Research Analysis of Administrative Records. In: M. Hammersley (ed.), *Social Research: Philosophy, Politics and Practice*. London: Sage. pp.131–45.

Jupp, V. and Norris, C. 1993. Traditions in Documentary Analysis. In: M. Hammersley (ed.), *Social Research: Philosophy, Politics and Practice*. London: Sage. pp.37–51.

Levitas, R. and Guy, W. 1996. *Interpreting Official Statistics*. London: Routledge.

Macdonald, K. and Tipton, C. 2001. Using Documents. In: N. Gilbert (ed.), *Researching Social Life*, 2nd edn. London: Sage. pp.194–210.

May, T. 2001. *Social Research: Issues, Methods and Process*, 3rd edn. Maidenhead: Open University Press. pp.71–87.

# SIX

# Quantitative Approaches in Social Science Research

- To review the positivist tradition and its influence over quantitative approaches to research
- To provide an overview of the characteristics of quantitative approaches
- To investigate the different stages of the research process in experimental and sample survey methods
- To examine the process for drawing an accurate and representative sample of the population
- To provide an appraisal of the different question types, measures and indicators which are used in the design of questionnaires
- To highlight the main issues confronting social researchers when using quantitative approaches and methods in research projects



## Introduction

Quantitative approaches are typically associated with positivist perspectives in social research. Hammersley (1993a, p.39) provides a useful definition of this approach:

The term 'quantitative method' refers in large part to the adoption of the natural science experiment as the model for scientific research, its key features being quantitative measurement of the phenomena studied and systematic control of the theoretical variables influencing those phenomena.

Thus, the logic of such research is to:

- collect data using standardised approaches on a range of variables;
- search for patterns of causal relationships between these variables; and
- test given theory by confirming or denying precise hypotheses.

The methods employed in this type of quantitative social research are most typically the sample survey and the experiment, a method that is particularly popular in psychological research.

The sample survey is *the* most commonly used technique for gathering information, whether by quantitative or qualitative means. Surveys are based on using statistical sampling methods. By taking a representative sample from a given population and applying a standardised research instrument in the form of a structured questionnaire, surveys enable descriptive and explanatory generalisations to be made about the population in question.

Quantitative approaches differ from qualitative approaches in a number of important respects, and these are discussed in detail in Chapter 1. Importantly, there is a relatively high degree of preconceptualisation associated with quantitative-based studies. Adopting the theory-then-research approach (as reviewed in Chapter 3), researchers working within this tradition will have certain *a priori* assumptions about:

- exactly what research questions to address and how these should be formulated;
- how the study should be designed (including which research tools to use, how data collection is to be organised and the intended methods of analysis);
- the range of likely findings to be expected.

This approach contrasts sharply with qualitative approaches which, as we have seen, are typically involved in exploratory research, in which the objective is to open up a research question. Here, the research strategy is guided by the reality of conducting a research project. Decisions about how a qualitative-based research study is to progress often take place *during* the course of the research itself, rather than before it has begun.

In this chapter, we shall begin by considering a series of landmark studies and projects that have been developed using predominantly quantitative approaches and methods. The purpose for doing so will be not only to illustrate the potential value of quantitative approaches in social research, but also to examine the methods in action – their strengths and limits, and how the broader academic and practitioner communities have responded to these.

We will then look at the use of both experiments and sample surveys, some of their advantages and disadvantages, and the issues that arise by their use. Design issues and techniques in experiments and sample surveys will be reviewed (types of method used, differing sampling strategies, and so on), together with an overview of the debate concerning the legitimacy of these quantitative methods within the social sciences.

We shall also take a look at the opinion poll as an example of an application of the general sample survey method designed for uncovering peoples' political values and orientations. In particular, we shall consider the role and effectiveness of political opinion polls at recent British electoral contests in order to develop insights into the value of the sample survey method for researchers.

## Quantitative research exemplars

The quantitative style has a long tradition in the social sciences, and has been deployed in a number of classic research studies and projects. In the following section, we review Durkheim's nineteenth-century investigation, *Suicide*, which used official government statistics from across a number of different European countries. We then consider a more contemporary and questionnaire-based quantitative study – Parry, Moyser and Day's renowned *Political Participation and Democracy in Britain*. Finally, we look at a major UK government-funded study, *The British Crime Survey*. First conducted in 1982, this ongoing national survey is an important source of information about levels of crime and public attitudes to crime, and is hugely influential within both academic and practitioner circles alike.

### Émile Durkheim, Suicide

One of the pre-eminent studies published within the social sciences is Émile Durkheim's classic investigation of the antecedents of suicide. Conducted at the end of the nineteenth century, his aims were to examine patterns in suicide rates and to identify whether or not there was evidence to suggest that victims' backgrounds and circumstances impacted on their actions. His analyses of religious affiliation, of marriage and the family, and of political and national communities, led him to develop three broad categories of suicide:

- egoistic suicide – the degree to which individuals are integrated or not within socially-supportive networks, communities and societies in general;
- altruistic suicide – the sense of sacrifice that one has for a higher purpose;
- anomic suicide – in which individuals find themselves disconnected from their normal life routine and from the broader society because of a dramatic change in circumstance (such as divorce).

The study is arguably better known for the methodological approach that Durkheim deployed than it is for the nature of its subject matter. In the preface to the 1952 edition of *Suicide*, Simpson refers to Durkheim's study as the 'prototype of systematic, rigorous and unrelenting attack on the subject of the data, techniques, and accumulated knowledge available at any given period... [his approach was] among the very first modern examples of consistent and organised use of statistical method in social investigation' (1952, p.9). *Suicide* has often been characterised as a manual for positivist methodology, seeking to uncover causal relationships between social phenomena in order to determine underlying laws of social behaviour, and privileging observable social facts over other less tangible data. As Durkheim described his approach: 'Sociological method as we practise it rests wholly on the basic principle that social facts must be studied as things, that is, as realities external to the individual' (1952, pp.37–8). He rejected methodological individualism which placed individuals and consciousness at the centre of social analysis:

> Of course, it may occasionally be interesting to see how these eternal sentiments of humanity have been outwardly manifested at different times in history; but as all such manifestations are imperfect, not much importance may be attached to them. (1952, p.38)

Instead, Durkheim prioritised external social forces as structuring private attitudes and behaviours. Using official government statistics from across Europe as objective indicators of the suicide counts in those countries, he contended that only social facts that were themselves directly observable and measurable – such as a person's marital status, or their religious affiliation, or their suicidal demise – should be treated as data in research studies. According to Durkheim, the integrity and reliability of other data, such as individual motivations and subjective predispositions, were at best questionable, and such data should be avoided in sociological studies.

The research approach at the heart of *Suicide* has, over time, generated some of the fiercest methodological debates within the social science community. One of the most cogent critiques of Durkheim's approach has been articulated by Douglas (1967). His major concern was that Durkheim appeared to have used the official statistics on suicide rates in an uncritical way without due regard to either their validity or their reliability. In essence, the position of Douglas and other critics is that official statistics are not simply objective, reliable measures of suicide counts. Instead, they are constructs, having been socially produced by coroners, police officers and other such official agents, by doctors, and by relatives and acquaintances of the victims. It was these observers rather than the victims themselves who had determined that the cause of death had been by suicide, rather than by homicide or by accident. Douglas summarises his primary concern in using official statistics in this way:

> The difficulty, however, is that one is still relying upon human judgement for the data, not simply upon sensory experience, which one also used to observe the mercury expansion and contraction against a calibrated scale, but actually upon the complex faculties of human judgements in interaction with each other. (1967, p.170)

According to interpretivist critics of Durkheim's use of official statistics and of the causal explanatory approach he deployed in *Suicide*, the fundamental question to ask of data relating to suicide counts is not what causes suicide, but how (and indeed why) have decisions been made to categorise observed deaths as such (Atkinson 1978)? The logical extension of this question requires the inquisitive researcher to investigate and interrogate a world in which subjective verdicts are alleged to have been manufactured on the basis of subjective interpretations of available evidence concerning subjectively derived definitions of the phenomena in question—in Durkheim's case, of suicide.

Despite these criticisms, *Suicide* remains one of the foremost sociological and methodological works, and continues to form part of the bedrock of study and research training for successive generations of social scientists.

## Geraint Parry, George Moyser and Neil Day, Political Participation and Democracy in Britain

Gerraint Parry, George Moyser and Neil Day carried out the fieldwork for the British Political Participation Study between October 1984 and January 1985, and subsequently published their full findings in *Political Participation and Democracy in Britain* in 1992 (Parry et al. 1992). This study, which was funded by the Economic and Social Research Council, was the first systematic national study of political participation in Britain. It addressed a number of areas, including:

- Who is most likely to participate in conventional electoral politics?
- Who is most likely to participate in unconventional protest/direct action politics?
- What, if anything, is the relation between these two different types of political activity?
- What is the importance of individual resources, such as personal wealth or education, in promoting participation in different types of political activity?
- What is the importance of group resources, such as membership of voluntary groups or trade unions, in promoting participation in different types of political activity?
- Do individual or group resources have a greater impact on participation rates?
- What issues are of greatest importance to citizens?
- What roles do citizens see themselves playing in a modern democracy?
- Which citizens are most likely to have a high degree of political efficacy, i.e. they have a greater sense that their own actions can have an impact on the political process?
- Which types of people can be classified as political cynics, i.e. those who are distrustful of political parties, career politicians and the government?

As well as examining these issues, the study also looked at the interrelations between these factors and sought to address a number of research questions. For example, they examined the extent to which differing combinations of political efficacy and political cynicism combined to influence people's participation in different types of politics. In another area, they used their data to interrogate variations in age-related participation in electoral and protest-style politics and determine whether these were a consequence of either life-cycle factors (as suggested, among others, by Verba and Nie (1972)) or generational factors (as suggested by Inglehart (1977), among others).

To generate the data to answer these questions the research team carried out:

- a sample survey of 1,578 people aged 18 and over, selected using a random sampling strategy, from 120 polling districts across England, Scotland and Wales;
- a further sample survey of 1,641 adults in six local communities, selected for their typicality using cluster analysis of 36 variables from the 1981 Census data;
- 300 structured interviews with community leaders in the same six locations.

Both sample surveys were conducted face to face using a pre-piloted questionnaire of mixed open and closed questions that took approximately an hour to complete. While there was some variation of questions due to the nature of the local surveys, the two surveys were closely coordinated to ensure a high degree of comparability between the findings. While somewhat more open than the sample surveys, the local elite interviews were structured in such a way that they generated 'standardised and comparable information' (Parry et al. 1992, p.53).

In offering a critical assessment of their own research approach, Parry et al. (1992) make some complimentary statements about the value of qualitative methods to uncover richer, more varied and complex contextual data than that which is available through surveys, but do so while defending the ability of the sample survey to make generalisable claims to the (then) adult population of approximately 43 million people. While claiming 'relative precision' for their survey and commenting that 'quantification has its limitations and even distortions', Parry et al. (1992, p.32) caution against the abandonment of survey techniques, favouring the 'more careful' use of statistical techniques as a remedy for these potential deficiencies.

Since the publication of this landmark study, a variety of criticisms have been levelled at Parry et al.'s research. Many of these revolve around issues of validity and whether the specific questions that have been used in their questionnaire adequately measure the things that they seek to measure. Similarly, Parry et al. have been critiqued for their definition of what constitutes 'politics', which they define as 'action taken by citizens which is aimed at influencing decisions which are, in most cases, ultimately taken by public representatives and officials' (1992, p.16).

Some have censured such a definition for what they suggest is an essentially top-down notion of politics as mediated by formal political institutions (Henn et al. 2002; White et al. 2000; O'Toole et al. 2003). Others, on the other hand, have suggested that such a definition effectively discounts a variety of actions, such as volunteering, and other such social actions that, while 'political' in the wider sense of the concept, have invariably been overlooked in official definitions of politics (Bhavnani 1994; Roker and Eden 2002). Furthermore, Parry et al.'s exclusion from 'politics' of those actions that are 'not aimed at influencing public representatives' would apparently discount the actions of the anti-globalisation and anti-capitalist movement, whose primary target has been transnational corporations, such as Microsoft and Nike, and supranational bodies, such as the International Monetary Fund and the World Bank (Todd and Taylor 2003).

Parry et al. (1992) have also been criticised for a lack of appreciation of social movement and direct action participation. While their operationalisation of direct action includes activities such as attending protest meetings and participating in protest marches that many in the direct action community would classify as relatively conventional and non-radical interest group activity (McKay 1998), they also tend to suggest, inaccurately, that all social movements are organisations that can be joined (Wall 1999).

While their study has been reproached on these counts, the great majority of those in the academic political science community place great historical store in the value of their work. As they had intended, their study did indeed provide benchmark data against which most types of political action and participatory trends could be compared in the future. While providing a comprehensive picture of political participation in Britain – where none had existed previously – Parry et al. were also able to provide strong conclusions about the nature of political participation in Britain at the time of their study:

> The general conclusion is, therefore, that high levels of overall participation, which substantially means taking part in collective action, contacting and party campaigning, are associated with well developed links to formal networks, strong party commitments, feeling politically efficacious, espousing a consistent array of political values (especially of the left variety) and, not least, being well educated. (1992, p.226)

Furthermore, they asked some extremely important questions concerning the nature of representative democracy in Britain. For example, they raised the question of the health of British democracy in the face of relatively low levels of participation among the electorate. Considering that only just over one in four Britons were found to 'actively sustain the citizenry's role in political life' (Parry et al. 1992, p.228) by participating in some form of political activity outside voting in elections, they asked whether the quality of British democracy was adversely affected when so few participated and when those who did were highly unrepresentative of the population as a whole.

Similarly, they posed a series of questions that did indeed exercise both the academic community in the years to come as well as government and its agencies:

- What will be the shape of political participation in the future *vis-à-vis* the balance between conventional and unconventional political participation?
- How will citizens of the future interact with government and other official agencies?
- How can political parties encourage greater turnout in elections?

*Political Participation and Democracy in Britain* is, therefore, regarded as a landmark contribution to the political science discipline in Britain and internationally.

### The UK Government Home Office, The British Crime Survey

*The British Crime Survey* (BCS) is one of a number of large-scale quantitative studies conducted by the British government on a regular basis. Its purpose is to measure perceptions and experiences of crime within the general population of England and Wales. The information is used, alongside official statistics produced by the police and other institutions within the criminal justice system, to inform social policy. In this respect, the BCS is very much a 'working' survey, the findings of which are used to directly inform government action as well as contributing to the development of criminological theory.

One of the primary reasons for the initial development of the BCS was as a response to claims that official statistics produced by the police were unreliable. The accuracy of police crime reporting can be affected by a variety of factors: an unwillingness on the part of a victim to report the crime – which might be due to fear of recriminations, lack of faith in the criminal justice system or the sensitive nature of the crime – or incorrect classification of crimes by the police themselves (Wolhuter et al. 2008). Since 1982, when the first BCS was carried out, it

> has provided a very valuable database for both estimating the 'dark' figure of crime and informing the policy-making process. Its questions, particularly in relation to the patterning of criminal victimization [have made it] possible to construct images of who is more likely to be criminally victimized and which challenge conventional media images: the young male who uses public transport and goes out drinking two or three times a week as opposed to the elderly female, for example. (Walklate 2007, p.46)

The dark figure of unreported crimes becomes startlingly apparent when we consider that 'overall less than half of BCS crime is reported to the police' (Kershaw et al. 2008, p.4). Given the concerns over the reliability of official crime statistics, the BCS must be seen to provide a reliable alternative, and this is achieved through a research design that is almost certainly beyond the resource capabilities of most surveys.

The sheer size and scale of the BCS are perhaps the foremost characteristics that differentiate it from most other surveys; the 2007/08 survey obtained interviews with a total of 46,773 individuals (Bolling et al. 2008), at a cost of £4.6 million (HC Deb 2008). Based on a random probability sample, stratified by police force area and other variables, the survey achieves a lower sampling error than many national surveys. A useful implication of such a large overall sample is that it enables analysis of single geographical areas, or of minority groups, while still including a large enough number of cases to make statistical analysis meaningful. Since the BCS informs policies that are very much in the public consciousness (such as the allocation of policing resources), it is also important that such policies are seen to be based upon scientific studies. A national survey of nearly 47,000 is likely to be perceived by the layperson as supplying credible evidence upon which to base decisions.

The resources to carry out a survey giving this coverage are usually only available to governments, but one of the notable outcomes of the BCS is the sharing of data with the academic community. Data are made available by the Economic and Social Data Service (ESDS) soon after the initial primary analysis and reporting are complete. Researchers wishing to conduct secondary analysis are free to do so, on the basis of due credit being given to the original source. The availability of such a rich quantity of data is both democratic and transparent. It is, of course, in the interest of any government to demonstrate that its decisions are based on data that are accurate and reliable, and it could be argued that open access to the data merely serves the purpose of instilling trust in the government's decision-making process. But there can be no denying the contribution to criminological theory that data from the BCS has had. Users of the data are required to notify the ESDS of any publications that cite the BCS (a search of the ESDS website conducted on 27 March 2009 revealed 102 publications citing the survey). These publications are drawn from a range of disciplines, including, most obviously, criminology, but also psychology, sociology, politics, economics and the broader sphere of social policy.

Some of the issues covered in the BCS are sensitive, and while the rest of the survey is administered by an interviewer, questions relating to illicit drug use, drinking behaviour, sexual assault, domestic violence and stolen goods can all be answered by the respondent entering their answers directly into a laptop themselves. This enables a more accurate collection of data, which are likely to reveal a picture which more closely matches that of the hidden figures, but there are still problems which are inherent with investigating some sensitive topics.

Myhill and Allen (2002, p.2) identify a number of limitations to the reliability of BCS data relating to sexual assault on women, for example. Particularly 'high-risk' women, such as 'the homeless or women under the age of 16' are not covered by the survey. Women are also unlikely to report incidents if they were perpetrated by a partner who is present during data collection. Finally, there is the question of whether the respondents understand their experiences in the context of that of the survey. Do they consider the incident as a criminal activity, or do they fully understand sexual assault in the same terms in which it is framed in the survey questions, for example? The same can be said of the other self-completion modules. Asking a respondent to remember how often in the past month they have felt very drunk is unlikely to lead to a reliable measure, particularly if the respondent has been routinely drunk.

Perhaps the largest criticism of the BCS is its reliance upon the self-reporting of incidents. One of the tests of reliability of any survey is that the questions lack ambiguity, yet what one respondent considers to be a criminal activity may be perceived differently by another. However, the BCS was never intended to be used as a replacement for official crime statistics, but to complement them. Despite some potential flaws relating to the interpretation of criminal activity, the BCS does offer a valuable insight into the true scale of criminal activity in Britain. As an example of how to design a survey on a truly grand scale, it faces little competition, and its application to both applied policy and theory through secondary analysis must make it one of the most widely scrutinised survey data sets available.

The BCS is just one example of a number of large-scale quantitative studies conducted by government and other organisations. What these studies offer to the researcher working with tightly constrained resources is the possibility of secondary analysis, a research technique well worth considering in the absence of primary data.

## Experimental research

Experiments are most commonly used in psychological research and in the broad field of business studies (particularly in organisational research). Experimental research is based on the researcher manipulating certain controlled conditions in order to identify the relationship between particular variables that it is hoped will explain cause-and-effect relationships. In seeking to measure the impact that one factor has on another by controlling all other factors that might have an effect, experimental research builds on the principles of a positivist approach to science more than any other research technique.

Experiments can be carried out in either a laboratory or a field setting. Laboratory experimentation is the most closely regulated method of experiment, involving the introduction of certain conditions into a controlled environment that simulates key characteristics of a natural environment. An example might be examining the extent to which the responses of a group of voters to questions about political attitudes *after* exposure to a series of party election broadcasts might be different from another (yet identical) group's responses when it has *not* been confronted with such images. Such experiments allow for very considerable control on behalf of the researcher, who is able to effect change and observe the research participants' subsequent behaviour.

A classic example of such a laboratory experiment is Asch's (1965) study of interpersonal influence. Here, the experiment was designed to create conditions of intense disagreement within a group, and measure the effect of this on an individual's behaviour. Eight participants were asked to match the length of a given line with three unequal lines. However, unbeknown to one of the members, Asch had instructed the other seven participants to contradict this individual. The objective was to measure the extent to which this unwitting *critical subject* would modify her or his response when confronted by this group pressure and move towards the majority opinion, even when it appeared obvious to the individual that the group was in fact wrong in its matching line assessments.

In this laboratory experiment, Asch was able to maintain tight control over the research environment to test the effect of interpersonal influence. Asch was able to manipulate the experimental conditions so that variables which might otherwise have influenced the critical subject's behaviour were removed from the experiment – any change in behaviour could therefore be unambiguously assumed to be the result of the interpersonal influence.

Experiments conducted outside the laboratory take place in a natural environment under as carefully controlled conditions as possible. An example might be a situation in which researchers 'stage' a physical attack in a public place to examine people's responses to the 'incident', as an investigation of bystander apathy.

Harari's staged attempted rape was an experiment conducted at an isolated university campus. It was designed to measure the actions of passers-by who witnessed the act (Harari et al. 1985). Unlike Asch's laboratory experiment, the group of researchers had little control over the situation – they were unable to dictate who the passers-by were, or exactly what these witnesses heard or saw. It therefore had low internal validity. However, as the experiment was carried out in a 'real-life' – or naturalistic – setting, the findings were more generalisable, and the study had high external validity. The reactions of passers-by were considered to be good predictors of the type of behaviour that members of the public would follow if they were to witness a similar rape attempt. These concepts of internal and external validity are discussed in the next section. These types of naturalistic experiment are rare these days because of the ethics of deception and lack of informed consent (see Chapter 4).

Field experiments are somewhat different. Here, experimental principles are applied to 'live' social events and therefore permit the study of phenomena which ethical or practical considerations would normally rule out. Essentially, the researcher measures the effect of an intervention which is occurring naturally. Such projects, which measure variables without actually manipulating them, are often called quasi-experiments or non-experimental designs. An example might be a comparison of voter turnout for local elections in two different areas, one where a new initiative has been introduced by a local authority (voting by telephone) and one where it has not. The role of the researcher will be to measure any change in the voting levels that follow from the initiative, to examine whether there is a cause-and-effect relationship between the two variables (which, in this case, are voting method and voter turnout rate).

## Establishing causality

Experimental research is based on testing a hypothesis stating a relationship between a dependent variable (the variable that the researcher wishes to explain) and an independent variable (the variable that the researcher expects to explain the change in the dependent variable). If we can determine that the two variables or phenomena vary, then we can say that we have established covariation. For example, we may be able to establish covariation between personal income and political conservatism.

However, simply being able to say that a change in the level of income is associated with a change in conservatism is rather limited in terms of scientific explanation. In the majority of cases researchers will want to go beyond covariation to demonstrate causality – that a change in the independent variable *causes* a change in the dependent variable. To be able to establish causality it must be possible to establish the time order of events – that the effect follows the cause.

In the natural sciences, where experiments are carried out under highly controlled conditions, the verification of causality is not particularly problematic. For example, it is relatively straightforward to determine that the application of heat to water causes it to boil. However, in the social world we are often faced with covarying relationships where causality is far from clear-cut. To return to our example of income and political conservatism, it is possible to argue that either of the variables may cause the other:

- As a person's income increases, they become more conservative in both outlook and behaviour.
- If a person adopts conservative values and lifestyle, they are likely to see an increase in their income.

The chain of causality in this example is difficult to establish, even though covariation is relatively easy to identify. Even where we can demonstrate a clear covariation between two variables *and* we are capable of asserting that one predates the other, we do not necessarily have sufficient conditions in which to infer causality. Other variables must first be ruled out for this to be the case. For example, it would be a weak explanation of the relationship between these two phenomena that did not take into account age. It may be that a person's age is a major determinant factor in relation both to people's political views and the level of personal income that they are able to earn. Where a causal relation between two variables could possibly be explained by a third variable, we say that the relationship is a *spurious* one. Thus researchers seek to establish non-spuriousness – that causality is not violated by the existence of another variable.

| Pre-test | Stimulus | Post-test |
|---|---|---|
| $O_1 \rightarrow$ | $\rightarrow X$ | $\rightarrow O_2$ |

Figure 6.1 Pre-test–post-test single-group experiment

## Experimental and control groups

In conducting an experiment we use an experimental group and a control group to test our research hypothesis. It may be, for example, that we want to determine the effect of a new management initiative in a particular company. We may want to see whether such an initiative leads to an increase in morale and productivity.

To be able to measure the impact of this change, it will be necessary to conduct a pre-test and a post-test. Figure 6.1 illustrates this method diagrammatically. Here, a measure ($O_1$) is taken of the dependent variable as a pre-test. A stimulus is then applied (the independent variable, X), and then a further measure (the post-test, $O_2$) of the dependent variable is taken to determine the extent to which it has been affected by the intervention.

Take as an example a project involving measuring morale and productivity both before (the pre-test) and after (the post-test) the management initiative. In order to conclude that the practice has had a causal effect on employee morale and productivity, it will be necessary to note any differences between measurements. But this will not tell us *why* a change has occurred, only that it has. It may be very difficult to conclude definitively that the change we have observed was as a result of the treatment, i.e. that the change in workplace practices has been initiated. It may be possible that the observed change may have occurred as a result of any number of other factors that may have happened at the same time – such as a pay rise or a change in national employment law that confers new rights on employees.

In order to account for such a situation, it will be necessary to establish a control group, which should be as similar to the experimental group as possible in all its characteristics. Perhaps the experimental and control groups could be made up of different workplaces of the same company? Problems will occur if the two groups have not been selected carefully. Any change in subsequent morale and productivity levels may be the result perhaps of the experimental group being predominately women, say, who might perhaps be more receptive than men to the new management initiative.

In allocating membership of both experimental and control groups, the researcher is able to choose between a strictly randomised method and the decision to match the two groups as closely as possible. If the two groups are to be assigned by matching, then the variables that will need to be taken into consideration will vary from study to study to take account of particular contextual factors. In our example, it would be necessary to consider factors such as work role,

| Group | Pre-test | Stimulus | Post-test |
|---|---|---|---|
| Experimental | $O_1 \rightarrow$ | x | $\rightarrow O_2$ |
| Control | $O_3 \rightarrow$ | $\rightarrow$ | $\rightarrow O_4$ |

Figure 6.2 Pre-test–post-test two-group experiment

level or grade of employee and length of service as well as the most important socio-demographic variables, such as gender, age and ethnicity.

The control group should be subject to exactly the same experiences as the experimental group, with the crucial exception of the treatment (management initiative) that the experimental group is exposed to. If the two groups are assigned with enough care and attention to ensure their comparability, then any difference in morale and productivity levels after the retest can be held to be a result of the management initiative. This approach is illustrated in Figure 6.2, which diagrammatically represents the classic pre-test, post-test, two-group experiment.

Here, measures are taken of morale and productivity for the experimental group ($O_1$) and the control group ($O_3$). If the groups have been carefully selected to ensure that they match each other, the likelihood is that the morale and productivity levels as measured in $O_1$ and $O_3$ will be more or less the same. The new initiative (X) is applied for the experimental group only. After a period designated by the research team, new measures of morale and productivity are taken for both the experimental group ($O_2$) and the control group ($O_4$). Observations $O_2$ and $O_4$ are then compared in order to assess the impact of the management initiative.

Guaranteeing such similarity between the two groups is far from straightforward given the difficulty that social researchers have with manipulating and controlling an individual's circumstances. It should be borne in mind that the laboratory conditions that are available to those working in the natural sciences can often be difficult to replicate when studying phenomena in the social world.

The steps to be taken when conducting an experiment are set out in Figure 6.3.

1. Determine the dependent variable and independent variable in your study.
2. Choose the level of treatment to be applied (i.e. what test to use and how often to conduct it).
3. Draw a representative sample from your target population.
4. Impose as many controls as are possible on other parameters that could affect the conditions of the experiment.
5. Divide the research participants into an experimental group and a control group.
6. Pre-test both the experimental group and the control group using an appropriate instrument.
7. Expose the experimental group to the treatment.
8. Measure both the experimental and control group again using the same instrument.
9. Collect data from both the pre-testing and post-testing of both groups.
10. Analyse data to determine the effect of the treatment on the experimental group.

Figure 6.3 The 10 steps in an experiment

## Issues in conducting experimental research

All experiments are subject to threats to their validity in ways that may severely detract from their findings. These are expressed in terms of threats to an experiment's internal validity (those things that may affect whether a true measurement has been obtained using the measuring instrument) and threats to external validity (concerning the generalisability of the findings to the intended population).

### Internal validity

There are a number of events and occurrences that could affect the integrity of the experiment. All of these can be limited to a certain extent by ensuring that the experimental and control groups are as identical as possible in every respect, with the obvious exception of the exposure of the experimental group to the treatment. However, many events may be outside the control of even the most careful and resourceful experimenter:

1. History – events that may occur in society between the first and second measurements which could explain the change in the dependent variable. For example, in carrying out an experiment on workplace morale something may happen in the experimental group's workplace and not in the control group's workplace. Even outside influences such as particularly good or bad weather (most definitely outside the control of the experimenter) may impact on the experiment.
2. Maturation – other processes that may be influenced by the passage of time between the two tests. This obviously depends on the time that elapses between the pre-test and the post-test. Where the gap is a considerable one, a variety of factors, including personal life events, may need to be taken into account.
3. Mortality – this happens when some of the experimental or control group leave the experiment, thus affecting the two groups' comparability. Again, this will be a function of the length of the experiment, and will be more of an issue where the experiment takes place over a longer period.
4. Instrumentation – any variation in the test whether between the two groups or over the two tests. It will be very important to ensure that the same instrument is used for both the pre-test and the post-test. If this is not the case, then the observed difference could be the result of a variation in the measurement process.
5. Testing – the possibility that the test itself may explain the change in the dependent variable. For example, in the course of carrying out an experiment on the extent to which exposure to party election broadcasts might affect the level of people's political knowledge, the very act of actually taking part in the experiment itself might affect people's test score. It might get them into the 'mode' of being tested – perhaps by relieving any pre-test nerves and increasing their general pre-test level of confidence. If this is the case, it is possible that any change you record may actually be the result of your conducting the research, not of showing them the party election broadcasts.

### External validity

The main threat to external validity is that the knowledge that people are participating in a study is likely to impact on the behaviour of the research participants. If, for example, the people in the study know that you are observing them to see whether their morale has improved after the introduction of a new management initiative, they may deliberately act in a particular way. This is known as the problem of reactivity. They may display markedly positive or negative reactions, depending on their disposition towards their employer. This phenomenon has become known as the 'Hawthorn Effect' after a research project that was carried out at the Hawthorne Works in Chicago in the 1920s, where the workers in question 'acted up' for the benefit of the researchers. Reactivity is used as a methodological justification for using a level of deception in experimental research. As we shall see in Chapter 7, it is an issue that confronts the researcher intent on using a qualitative participant observation approach – whether to do so overtly or covertly.

### Ethical issues in experimental research

Experimental research raises a number of ethical dilemmas concerning the manner in which researchers treat people. For example, some researchers may consider it inappropriate to 'manipulate' human beings in the same way as laboratory animals such as mice and guinea pigs are treated. An extensive discussion of the ethical implications of experimental research can be found in Chapter 4.

An additional ethical consideration in relation to experimental research is the question of including or excluding people from a study in which some may benefit. For example, an experiment may be designed to measure the effect that the introduction of CCTV has in reducing crime in certain residential neighbourhoods. In this instance, it may be argued that researchers occupy a too powerful position in being able to decide which area (and therefore which residents) will benefit from the experiment and which will not benefit. One way around such a charge of unethical abuse of power by the researcher is to take a change that is occurring anyway, and collect or obtain statistics from before the change, during it and after it. This is known as a quasi-experiment.

### Defining change accurately

Another problem that confronts social scientists in using experiments is being able to accurately establish exactly what it is that they will be looking for as an outcome in their research. Experimentation in the natural sciences is not usually faced with such a problem. For example, a chemist may want to know whether heating a particular object causes its temperature to rise above a definite point. In this case, the experimenter will know exactly what she or he is seeking to measure – a precise temperature at a predetermined time. After this temperature has been taken, the experimenter will be able to state clearly the outcome of the experiment.

However, in the great majority of cases the social world does not offer such clear-cut situations. What if our social experiment wants to measure the effect of changing practices in the workplace? In implementing some new practice at work, perhaps to enhance morale, the experimenter will need to define what will count as an improvement before starting to make any measure. This must be done in advance of the experiment. Otherwise, defining what counts as success *after* you have carried out the experiment, i.e. initiated the programme of workplace changes, is likely to be influenced by what you see happening in the early stages of the new initiatives.

One obvious way of determining measurement outcomes is to consult the literature in the chosen field of research to see what the expert or professional convention regards as acceptable. You may, for instance, want to establish what counts as 'improved morale at work'. Before you initiate your experiment you will need to think very carefully about the outcome measures that you will use to identify changes in employee morale.

### Activity 6.1 Experimental research design

Design an experiment to investigate the hypothesis that attending staff development seminars on equal opportunities issues will affect a person's attitudes towards racism. As you do so, follow the steps and consider the issues set out in Figure 6.3, earlier. What ethical issues, if any, do you think that you will need to consider in this experiment?

## Sample surveys

### The origins of social surveys in Britain

Social surveys can be traced back to the production of the Domesday Book, and were used widely by the Romans. In more recent times, the development of social surveys in Britain can be seen at the turn of the twentieth century through the work of a number of social anthropologists, led by Charles Booth and Joseph Rowntree (Tonkiss 1998). These early social researchers quantified the income, hours and conditions of work, housing, standards of living, size of family and dwelling, frequency of sickness, leisure activities, and club and union membership of Britain's poor.

An important development in the evolution of the sample survey method was the introduction of public opinion polls. The Gallup Organisation introduced public opinion polling into Britain in 1937, and 1946 saw the formation of the Market Research Society in Britain. The impetus for social-survey-style research after the Second World War was maintained by an increased role for government with the advent of the welfare state, and by the expansion of the social sciences in further and higher education (Tonkiss 1998). Sample surveys played an important role in academic circles by providing social science researchers with the means for collecting large-scale data about different aspects of social life.

## Purposes and characteristics of the sample survey

Sample surveys are conducted in order to provide the researcher (or the sponsor of the research) with statistical information, either on a particular issue or problem that needs resolving, or to test the robustness (or not) of an existing theory. This involves measuring various phenomena and drawing conclusions about any relationship(s) between them to establish patterns of cause and effect. For instance, in a study of industrial relations, we might compare different workplaces in terms of a number of variables that we hypothesise are likely to be associated with industrial dissent. These might be:

- the size of the firm or organisation;
- the type of industry;
- the 'inclusiveness' of the decision-making process;
- whether the organisation is unionised or not;
- the skill level of the employees;
- the gender mix within the organisation;
- the balance between part-time and full-time employees;
- the unemployment rate in the local area;
- and so on.

To analyse such relationships and draw widespread conclusions requires the researcher to generate large amounts of data, so that conclusions can be generalised from the sample survey to the wider population from which the survey respondents were drawn. In order to have confidence in the results generated from a sample survey, and to eliminate (or minimise) bias, the researcher should aim to maximise the response rate and, in so doing, ensure that the study is representative of the population group.

Sample surveys are a method of gathering information by means of personal interviews or questionnaires. They are sometimes referred to as 'mass interviews' because they are a way of collecting similar information from a large number of people at the same time. Sample surveys are based on standardised approaches, using standardised instruments, such as questionnaires. These research instruments employ fixed question-and-answer formats so that there is a consistency of data collection approach, regardless of who is actually asking the questions.

The sample survey is therefore akin to a structured dialogue between (usually two) people, in which the researcher asks a series of pre-planned (standardised) questions and the respondent's answers are recorded precisely on a form, and (ultimately) turned into numbers for statistical analysis. In this way, the studies are said to be quantitative.

## The users of survey research

Academic researchers conduct surveys to test out various research hypotheses. For example, they may want to explore the relationship between age and political conservatism, or why it is that some children play truant from schools, or under what circumstances people become addicted to gambling. By gathering statistical evidence, survey research may help to support a particular theory by shedding light on the connections and associations that exist between such variables. In this way, researchers look for patterns that may explain social phenomena.

Academics are not the only ones who use survey research. Other users of surveys can be broadly categorised as follows:

- Government and its agencies, voluntary sector organisations and campaigning groups use survey research to inform and influence the political, economic and social policy-making process.
- Businesses of all sizes carry out surveys in their quest for gaining a lead in the market for their product by differentiating their product against those of their competitors.
- The media and political parties carry out public opinion polls on voting intentions, party political leaders and their policies.

## Types of data gathered in a survey

Survey research can be used to obtain multifaceted data from an individual:

- Behaviour – straightforward questions on what the respondent has done, is doing and may do in the future. For example, it is possible to ask people if they use public transport for certain journeys, or if they are vegetarian.
- Beliefs – what people think will happen. What do they believe is true or false? Do people believe that the National Health Service is safer in the hands of the current government than it was under the previous administration?
- Attitudes – how people think and feel about certain things. For example, whether people consider that women with pre-school children should participate in the workforce.
- Attributes – these are the personal questions that concern the characteristics of the respondent, such as her or his age, sex, ethnicity, religion and employment status. As such, these questions have the potential to be viewed as sensitive questions. They are often referred to as *classification* questions.

By employing a combination of such questions in a survey, the skilful researcher opens up the possibility of describing and explaining complex social phenomena.

### Different methods of data collection in survey research

There are four main types of data collection methods for a social survey:

1. The face-to-face interview, where the respondent is questioned in person by an interviewer. The main advantage of this method is that it usually results in a relatively high response rate. However, such interviewing commonly incurs high costs due to the number of interviewers that need to be employed, and it is also argued that personal interaction between the interviewer and the respondent can lead to biased responses. In a study that considers questions of child discipline and punishment, it may be that respondents will offer the 'socially acceptable' response – the answer that they believe the interviewer wants to hear.
2. Postal questionnaires are widely used because they are relatively cheap to administer and they enable coverage of a wide geographic area. Also, given that they avoid direct personal contact, they have the advantage of ensuring a degree of privacy for the respondent. The main disadvantage associated with postal questionnaires is that they perform poorly in relation to response rate.
3. Telephone interviews have become more common in the past decade, as technological advances have allowed researchers to draw samples with greater accuracy. They are also very quick to administer. However, they are limited to researchers who have access to the relevant technology (such as random digit dialling technology) to carry them out.
4. Online surveys, which are delivered by email or make use of a web-based form in place of a questionnaire are now widely used. They share some of the characteristics of postal surveys in that they are inexpensive to administer, but may have lower response rates than interviewer-administered surveys. Access to data the instant a response is sent and being able to draw samples on a global scale are also attractive benefits, but the differences between characteristics of Internet users and non-users can result in Internet-based samples which are not representative of the general population.

Each of these methods of data collection has its own strengths and weaknesses in relation to design, cost, and so on, and in crude terms one's weaknesses are often the other's strengths. The method that is selected will depend on the type of population you aim to research, the nature of the research question and the resources at your disposal.

## The process of survey research 1 – sampling for survey research

Surveys are often referred to as sample surveys because the information that the researcher wishes to gather is usually collected from a selected group of people – a sample. It is very unusual for researchers to question all of the people that they wish to study owing to both time and cost considerations. For example, it would be extremely expensive and would take a very long time to ask all adults in Britain how they intend to vote in the next general election. Rather, a survey researcher will select a sample in such a way so as to achieve closeness of fit between the sample and the population (Definition 6.1). If this can be realised, then the findings that are based upon the sample group can be generalised for the population from which the sample comes. That is to say, the researchers can be relatively confident that their findings will broadly reflect the findings they would have obtained if they had collected information from the entire group they were studying.

To take an often used analogy, one does not need to eat an entire fruit cake to gain an idea of its taste – a single slice will do, although the larger the slice, the better! The same is the case with sampling. The researcher will *not* need to include all members of the targeted group in her or his study. A subset will do, providing it has been selected carefully. However, the usual rule is that the larger the subset selected, the higher the level of accuracy to be expected in the findings from the sample survey. Thus, in survey sampling, the margin of difference between the results from the sample and the population values – referred to as *sampling error* – is attributable primarily to:

- the method of sample selection; and
- the size of the sample.

### Definition 6.1 Population and sample

**Population** – the entire group that you want to study.
**Sample** – a subsection of the population, chosen in such a way that their characteristics reflect those of the group from which they are chosen.

## Methods of sample selection

Traditional sampling for survey research is based on the mathematical theory of probability in that it employs methods of random selection. Such sampling is usually referred to as probability sampling. Where probability sampling is used, researchers tend to employ the devices of stratifying and clustering their sample in order to increase their accuracy and cut down on the cost of the survey. The main alternative to probability sampling is the use of non-probability sampling, including especially quota sampling. This is where the researcher sets quotas for the sample based on the known characteristics of the population (such as age, sex and occupation) to ensure that the correct number of certain types of person is included in the sample. However, where these characteristics are not known, then quota sampling is not possible.

Probability sampling methods have considerable advantages over non-probability sampling methods like quota samples, not least of which is that 'there is plenty of empirical evidence to show that when selections are made by non-probability methods results are liable to distortions that may be serious' (Hoinville and Jowell 1978, p.57). For instance, with such approaches individual respondents are selected not by random, but according to the discretion of the interviewer. As a consequence, there is considerable scope for interviewers to select only those people who look 'agreeable'. In a study of youth, this might include only students in a relatively 'safe' environment, such as a university building, rather than young people from areas which may have high incidences of youth crime. The implication is that the voices of young people living in such areas may not be heard in the study.

In addition, probability sampling methods enable researchers to make reliable estimates of sampling error involving the statistical process, the randomisation of error variation. It is for this reason that attention is now given to probability sampling methods (although non-probability sampling methods will be described in more detail in due course).

## Probability sampling methods

Probability sampling methods involve randomised selection, in which all members of your population, or target group, have an equal chance of being selected for inclusion in your research study.

### *Simple random sampling*

Simple random sampling involves a process in which all members of the population are assigned a number, and then random numbers are chosen (and people selected) until you have created your sample list. The numbers chosen may be determined by a table of random numbers or randomly generated using a computer.

### *Systematic sampling*

An alternative to this approach is systematic sampling, which is generally considered to be a simpler and more cost-efficient system. Again, all members of the population are numbered, but here the *method* of selecting respondents from the numbered list differs. With systematic sampling, the population is divided by the required sample size – perhaps 200 employees from a company list of 1,000, or one-fifth as a proportion. This creates the sampling interval, in this case of five. Consequently, every fifth employee is selected from the list, the first one randomly from the first five employees listed, and the subsequent sample members are chosen by counting every fifth person from that point onwards. Thus, if the first member chosen (from the first sampling interval, i.e. those assigned a number between 1 and 5) was 3, then those selected for inclusion within the study would be those numbered 3, 8, 13, 18, ... until the person numbered 498. This method would provide you with the required sample size of 200 employees, in which all members of the workforce had been given an equal opportunity of selection.

### *Stratified random sampling*

To ensure that key groups within the population are adequately represented in the sample, proportionate stratified random sampling may be used. Perhaps you want to ensure that the final sample reflects the make-up of the company workforce in terms of the proportions of manual workers and non-manual workers. Here, the initial list of potential sample members is divided into these two groups (or strata), and then systematic sampling is used to select members from each group. Using the example above, if manual workers comprise 750 members of the workforce, and non-manual workers 250, then 150 employees will be chosen from the former, and 50 from the latter (using the sampling interval of five to ensure the sample size of 200 from the 1,000 employees).

Disproportionate stratified random sampling may be used in circumstances where the size of a particular key stratum may be too small for meaningful statistical analysis, if its size within the sample is directly proportional to its size within the population. For instance, if 50 of the 750 manual workers were temporary staff, using a sampling interval of five would result in only 10 being selected for investigation. It is generally accepted that 50 is the minimum size necessary if a particular subgroup is to be subjected to detailed analysis (Hoinville and Jowell 1978, p.61). (Notice here how a *second* level of stratification has been administered to separate temporary employees from permanent employees when creating the sample. It is not uncommon to stratify by several key variables when using probability sampling methods.)

In such circumstances, the actual size of the stratum in question is *boosted* so that its presence within the sample is disproportionate to its presence within the population. Here you may decide to include *all* 50 temporary manual staff in your sample, rather than only the 10 that you would have done had you wanted the size of this subgroup to be directly proportionate to its size within the population. You might decide to select members of all other strata so that they are proportionate to their size within the population. Table 6.1 illustrates the implications of using proportionate stratified random sampling and disproportionate stratified random sampling for this example. Notice how the sample size and the sampling fraction for the two groups other than the temporary manual workers remain constant – only the latter group has been boosted in size, leading to an increase in the overall sample size than would have been achieved had the different strata been selected proportionately.

It is important to ensure that whenever disproportionate stratified random sampling is used adjustments are made *before* the different strata are analysed together. If you have adopted this disproportionate approach, your overall

Table 6.1 Proportionate and disproportionate stratified random sampling

| Work status | | Population size | Percentage total in each stratum | Proportionate | | Disproportionate | |
|---|---|---|---|---|---|---|---|
| | | | | Sample size | Sampling fraction | Sample size | Sampling fraction |
| Manual | Permanent | 700 | 70 | 140 | 1/5 | 140 | 1/5 |
| | Temporary | 50 | 5 | 10 | 1/5 | 50 | 1/1 |
| Non-manual* | Permanent | 250 | 25 | 50 | 1/5 | 50 | 1/5 |
| Total | | 1,000 | 100 | 200 | | 240 | |

* There are no temporary non-manual staff employed at the company.

sample will be distorted. In this example, as you have increased the size of the temporary manual staff by a factor of 10, you will need to restore the balance by weighting, so that each individual member of this particular stratum is treated so that her or his views are worth only one-tenth of the views of a colleague from one of the other strata. Unless you are planning to use weighting to restore the balance, you are advised against boosting your sample in this way because your sample will become unrepresentative of the population.

A commonly used approach, especially where a large geographic area is to be sampled, is multi-stage cluster sampling. Here, the first stage involves dividing the area for study into primary sampling units or 'clusters'. For instance, in a national study of 1,500 people, the first stage of the research may involve the researcher in dividing the country into parliamentary constituencies and then randomly selecting a sample of these areas using the systematic sampling method – perhaps 50 of the 651 constituencies in Britain. The next stage of the sampling method could involve dividing each constituency into smaller geographic areas (perhaps wards, or even smaller areas such as polling districts) and using systematic sampling to select one such area to represent the entire constituency. The 1,500 people to be surveyed would be equally divided into these 50 areas so that 30 interviews are to take place in each, with usually one interviewer per area. Finally, the interviewer could then select the 30 people for this area from an appropriate list of residents – perhaps an electoral register. Again, the systematic sampling method could be used for this purpose. Thus, the multi-stage cluster sampling method could be said to be random, with interviews taking place in geographic clusters. This reduces the cost, time and effort involved in a national sample where the 1,500 people to be interviewed are dispersed across the country.

## Non-probability sampling methods

So far, we have seen that the essential logic of the probability sampling method is to provide each member of the chosen population group with an equal opportunity of being selected. In this way, it is possible to specify the probability

Table 6.2 Interviewer quotas

| | Age | | |
|---|---|---|---|
| | *18–34* | *35–49* | *50+* |
| **Male** | Below degree 3 | Below degree 4 | Below degree 3 |
| | Degree 2 | Degree 2 | Degree 1 |
| **Female** | Below degree 3 | Below degree 4 | Below degree 3 |
| | Degree 3 | Degree 2 | Degree 0 |

that any person will be included in the survey, and an estimate of the extent of sampling error. Small-scale surveys often use non-probability sampling methods, in which it is not possible to do this. There are a variety of such methods.

### *Quota sampling*

Like probability sampling methods, the quota sampling method aims to achieve statistically representative samples, but where there is no list of potential respondents (or sampling frame) or where resources do not permit the use of a random probability method. Quota sampling is the most commonly used non-probability method. The task of the researcher is to ensure that key features of the population are proportionately reflected in the sample, as is the approach with stratified sampling. Certain key variables of relevance to the topic of investigation are specified. In a study of voting behaviour, these might be 'educational qualifications', 'gender' and 'age', all of which, theories suggest, are claimed to be closely related to a person's party preference. The interviewer will be given a quota of interviews that she or he should achieve for each category of each variable (male and female for 'gender').

An example of an interviewer's 'quotas' is given in Table 6.2. The interviewer is instructed to approach and interview 30 people who match these characteristics until the quota is filled, and is usually given much latitude in how she or he does this. On completing the fieldwork, the sample will be broadly representative of the population in terms of the proportions of people interviewed for each of the key quota variables selected.

### *Convenience sampling*

There are other methods of non-probability sampling available to the researcher, but none of these are able to achieve samples which might even loosely be characterised as 'representative' of the population. Convenience sampling involves the researcher selecting whichever cases are conveniently available. In a study of workplace morale, these might be work colleagues, for instance. As a method, this is useful when piloting a study – perhaps to build up a picture of which questions might be included in a questionnaire, or to test out the questions in terms of their clarity or meaning. However, the method is not an especially robust one, and the researcher has no way of estimating either the sample's level of representativeness or the population's values.

### *Snowball sampling*

With snowball sampling, the researcher will typically build up a network of respondents through an initial group of informants, who introduce the researcher to other members of the same population. These then serve as additional informants who may introduce the researcher to other potential respondents. This approach is often used to develop samples from groups which are difficult to contact (disabled people, political activists, members of business elites, and so on). Snowball sampling is a form of purposive (or judgement) sampling, where the intention is to obtain a pool of respondents that is appropriate for the study, and which is largely determined by the judgement of the researcher.

## Sample size

Prior to this discussion of different sampling methods, it was mentioned that sampling error is largely attributable to two key features of survey research design: methods of sample selection (which we have now discussed) and the size of the sample.

Providing the sample is chosen carefully, the general rule is that the accuracy of a sample estimate will be increased with an increase in sample size. However, it would be wrong to assume that increases in accuracy will follow proportionately with increases in sample size, or that the sample size should be in proportion to the size of the population. Similarly, there is no optimum sample size – often it will be driven as much as by the level of research resources available to the researcher as it is by the level of precision required in the results. Nonetheless, it is possible to give an indication of the link between sample size and sampling error. Table 6.3 is taken from Hoinville and Jowell (1978, p.69), and enables the researcher to estimate the degree of accuracy – or range of error – in the results from a sample survey study. For instance, in a study of 200 employees selected from within an organisation using a simple random sampling method, where 60% report having attended three hourly meetings or more within the last week, the finding will be subject to a margin of sampling error of 7.1%. This means that the actual figure that will have attended this number of meetings within the organisation over the period will be between 52.9% and 67.1%. Interpreting this table will become easier once you have read the next section, but suffice it to say, the higher the sampling error recorded, the lower the level of accuracy in the study.

## Estimating values and sampling error

Notice that the level of sampling error for any given sample size is greater for multi-stage sample designs than it is for simple random sampling. This is largely

Table 6.3 Range of error (±) for 95% confidence level

| | | *Percentage found by survey* | | | | |
|---|---|---|---|---|---|---|
| | *Sample size* | *5% or 95%* | *10% or 90%* | *20% or 80%* | *30% or 70%* | *40% or 60%* |
| **Simple random sample** | 100 | 4.4 | 6.0 | 8.0 | 9.2 | 10.0 |
| | 200 | 3.1 | 4.2 | 5.7 | 6.5 | 7.1 |
| | 500 | 1.9 | 2.7 | 3.6 | 4.1 | 4.5 |
| | 1,000 | 1.4 | 1.9 | 2.5 | 2.9 | 3.2 |
| | 2,000 | 1.0 | 1.3 | 1.8 | 2.0 | 2.2 |
| | 5,000 | 0.6 | 0.8 | 1.1 | 1.3 | 1.4 |
| | 10,000 | 0.4 | 0.6 | 0.8 | 0.9 | 1.0 |
| **Stratified multi-stage sample** | 100 | 6.5 | 9.0 | 12.0 | 13.7 | 15.0 |
| | 200 | 4.6 | 6.4 | 8.5 | 9.7 | 10.6 |
| | 500 | 2.9 | 4.0 | 5.4 | 6.2 | 6.7 |
| | 1,000 | 2.1 | 2.9 | 3.8 | 4.4 | 4.7 |
| | 2,000 | 1.5 | 2.0 | 2.9 | 3.1 | 3.4 |
| | 5,000 | 0.9 | 1.3 | 1.7 | 2.0 | 2.1 |
| | 10,000 | 0.7 | 0.9 | 1.2 | 1.4 | 1.5 |

because clustering carries with it the possibility that selected areas will contain people of a particular type rather than a group which is broadly representative of the wider population. For instance, in a study of political attitudes across a city, clustering in two or three small areas might result in a situation in which one of these has a class bias – perhaps the area is unusually affluent compared to the rest of the city, containing a disproportionately high number of Conservative-supporting, upper-middle-class people when the majority of the city's population is typically lower-middle-class and tends towards the Labour Party. This is an example of sampling error for which multi-stage sample designs are more prone than the simple random sampling method.

As we have noted earlier, certain methods of survey sampling which are based upon the principle of random probability enable researchers to make an estimate of the accuracy of their findings, or, put another way, to assess the degree of sampling error in their study. For instance, in a survey, we might ask a number of questions designed to work out an average score for people's knowledge of political affairs. It is possible, when using a random probability sampling method, to estimate the degree of error on the political knowledge score recorded in our sample.

We might take a sample of 100 adults in Britain, note the average political knowledge score, and use this as an *estimate* of the average score across the entire adult population in the country. If we were to repeat the exercise, albeit with a new sample of 100 adults, we might find that the political knowledge score within the sample is somewhat different from that achieved in the first study. However, if we were to continue drawing fresh samples and measuring the political knowledge score in each, we would ultimately begin to see a pattern emerging. Most likely, there would be a small number of sample surveys recording unusually high, and a similar small number recording unusually low, scores. Most sample studies, however, would likely be very similar in terms of the political knowledge scores they generate – the amount of actual variation in the sample surveys would be relatively small.

Providing we have used a random probability sampling method, if we were to take the average score from these numerous samples (or what is termed the mean distribution of the samples), it would very closely approximate the *actual* political knowledge score across the country. In technical terms, the mean distribution of our sample scores would provide an accurate estimation of the population parameter (i.e. of political knowledge).

The extent of variation in our sample means is referred to as the *standard error.* To put this simply, the higher the variation in scores across the different samples, the lower the level of confidence we can have in actually predicting from our sample studies how much knowledge of political affairs people in our country actually have, and the more therefore will be the *error* in our sample predictions.

Typically, however, we would take only *one* sample to estimate the population value (the public's knowledge of political matters). This means that in reality, we cannot calculate the standard error because this depends on our having taken more than one sample (remember – it is the *average* variation in *average* political knowledge scores recorded in different samples). This might create a problem because sampling theory tells us that without the standard error, we cannot estimate the population parameter. That is, we cannot estimate the accuracy of our sample findings. Fortunately, convention allows us to approximate the standard error by using the *standard deviation* (the amount of, or average, variation) in political knowledge scores from a single sample. Computer programs can very easily calculate this measure of variation, from which we can estimate the standard error (SE) using the formula:

$$SE = s/\sqrt{n}$$

If the average (mean) political knowledge score from a sample of 100 British adults was 4.2 (out of 10), but with some variation in the range of scores recorded (with a standard deviation of 1.3), then it follows that the standard error (SE) would be the standard deviation (*s*) of our sample score, divided by the square root of the sample size:

$$\begin{aligned} SE &= 1.3/\sqrt{100} \\ &= 1.3/10 \\ &= 0.13 \end{aligned}$$

From this standard error (of 0.13), we are able to provide an approximation of the *actual* political knowledge score across the country, by establishing the confidence interval. The confidence interval is a margin of sampling accuracy (or a margin of sampling error, depending on how pessimistic you are!). While researchers can never be entirely sure of the reliability of their sample findings, they can have a high degree of confidence in them. Typically, researchers tend to work within 95% confidence limits or, to put it another way, to assert that they are 95% sure that a finding from their sample survey is within *x*% (±) of the actual figure for the population. Establishing this confidence interval is a straightforward process once the standard error has been calculated – it is the range of political knowledge scores between 1.96 standard errors higher or lower than the sample score (in our example, the average political knowledge score is 4.2). The formula is:

$$\pm 1.96 \times 0.13 = 0.25$$

How does this translate for our political knowledge score example? As above, the researcher has derived a political knowledge score of 4.2 (out of 10) for the sample of 100 British adults, with a standard deviation of 1.3. Using the formula to calculate the confidence interval, the researcher can establish with a high degree of confidence (i.e. the researcher can be 95% sure) that the actual political knowledge score across the country would be within the range 3.95 to 4.45 (i.e. 4.2 ± 0.25).

To summarise this discussion, then, we can say that, providing a sample has been randomly drawn using a probability sampling method, it is possible to estimate the accuracy of a survey's findings, or the margin of sampling error. Computers can quickly calculate standard errors and confidence levels, although without understanding how such figures have been derived or their meaning, it would be hard to adjudge the validity of sample survey results.

## Non-response

Throughout this section, it has been noted on a number of occasions that the ability to generalise from a sample to the population from which it is drawn is based on the extent to which that sample is representative. However, when using random sampling techniques the problem of selective non-response is a threat to the representativeness of the sample. This problem can arise from people's refusal to participate or an inability to contact those people who have been randomly selected to take part.

Social researchers may do their utmost to persuade people to participate in their studies, but people may decline for a variety of reasons. Chief among these is the importance of the issue under investigation to the individual who has been approached – the higher the salience of the topic, the more likely it is that an individual will take part in the research. Other factors that will influence the decision of whether or not to participate in the research include, for example, the skill of the interviewer in persuading people to take part, the appearance of the questionnaire that is used, and the time commitment that is necessary to complete the questionnaire.

As well as those who decide not to participate in a survey, the researcher is faced with the problem of not being able to contact a certain number of people who will form part of their sample. The people who are less likely to be contacted in a survey include those who are in some way socially excluded or marginalised from mainstream society. Such people may include those who are homeless, those who are highly geographically mobile, the elderly, poorer people, or those people for whom English is not their first language. This would not be a problem for survey researchers if people from such groups were evenly distributed across the population. However, in reality there is a likelihood that their particular life experiences will have a significant influence on their behaviour and attitudes (Sapsford 1999).

## The process of survey research 2 – the design of questionnaires

For every conceivable question there are several possible and theoretically acceptable forms it can take. Questions can be asked in either a closed or open format, and may employ the use of attitude scales.

Closed questions are those in which the respondents are simply asked to choose a reply from a number of predetermined options. These can be as simple as 'Yes/No' questions, or can be more lengthy and complex, such as the standard classification of ethnicity which allows for eighteen different responses. Closed questions are:

- easily asked;
- easily understood;
- quick to answer;
- quick to code for the purposes of analysis.

Some examples of closed questions are:

HOW MUCH INTEREST DO YOU NORMALLY HAVE IN *LOCAL* POLITICAL ISSUES?

A great deal [ ] 1
Quite a lot [ ] 2
Some [ ] 3
Not very much [ ] 4
None at all [ ] 5

DID YOU VOTE IN THE LOCAL ELECTION THAT WAS HELD EARLIER THIS YEAR?

Yes [ ] 1
No [ ] 2

However, closed questions are criticised for forcing respondents into a predetermined response rather than letting them answer in their own words. If closed questions are used, then it is important to ensure that the choices offered respondents are:

- Mutually exclusive – it must not be possible for an answer to fall into two categories. For instance, in a closed question which asked a respondent their age, the following must be avoided, in which a 35 year-old has the opportunity to assign herself to both category 3 *and* category 4:

  WHAT IS YOUR AGE?

  | | |
  |---|---|
  | Under 18 | [] 1 |
  | 18–24 | [] 2 |
  | 25–35 | [] 3 |
  | 35–44 | [] 4 |
  | 45–54 | [] 5 |
  | 55–64 | [] 6 |
  | 65 and over | [] 7 |

- Exhaustive – you must ensure that *all* of the possible answers are catered for in the response options, and that you have not left something important out. For example, in a question asking people what issue would most influence their vote in a forthcoming election, the researcher needs to ensure that the list of options is not so short that it does not include the full range of issues likely to be important to respondents. Piloting the question before the full survey is conducted will provide the researcher with a clear idea of the range of answers likely to be given to the question, and which should therefore be included in the list of issues. At the very least, there must be an 'Other' option available to any respondents for whom the list of options does not include the issue of most importance to them.

An open question is one where the researcher asks the question and leaves a blank space for the respondents to record their response. In this sense, the questions are good because they do not force the respondent into a predetermined category that can obscure nuances. They also allow the respondent greater freedom of expression, and open up the possibility for more qualitative-style data to be generated. An example of an open question used in a questionnaire is:

WHICH COMMUNITY, NATIONAL, OR INTERNATIONAL ISSUE ARE YOU *MOST* CONCERNED ABOUT?
*(PLEASE WRITE IN FULLY USING THE SPACE PROVIDED)*

________________________________________

________________________________________

________________________________________

However, responses to open questions may be long and complex, and where written in by the respondent they may be hard to read. For these reasons, open questions may be difficult to code and analyse. Open questions are used less often than closed questions because of their time-consuming (and therefore *costly*) nature.

Attitude scales consist of a number of statements that the respondent is asked to agree or disagree with, to differing degrees. An example is given below:

HOW MUCH DO YOU AGREE OR DISAGREE WITH THE FOLLOWING STATEMENT?
*I THINK THAT IT'S IMPORTANT TO VOTE IN LOCAL ELECTIONS:*

| | |
|---|---|
| Strongly agree | [ ] 1 |
| Agree | [ ] 2 |
| Neither agree nor disagree | [ ] 3 |
| Disagree | [ ] 4 |
| Strongly disagree | [ ] 5 |

The use of scales is a way of measuring an individual's position on an attitude continuum and thus generates more quasi-qualitative data. The most commonly used scale is the Likert scale. When used, a scaled question must be balanced, ensuring that the responses should range from positive through neutral to negative in a unidimensional manner. When respondents are offered a scale that is skewed in some way, this is likely to induce a biased response.

A good questionnaire should include a mix of closed, open and scaled questions. Furthermore, it will take into account the type of data to be collected and the resources (time and money) that are available for the study. A good questionnaire is also one in which the questions that have been asked are well crafted and are the product of careful consideration. In designing questionnaires, researchers should do their utmost to avoid the many pitfalls that present themselves, including the use of:

- ambiguous language;
- language that is not appropriate for the targeted audience;
- prejudicial language;
- questions which lead respondents to answer in ways that could result in biased data.

Of equal importance is the need to structure the questionnaire so that it aids the progression of the interview. Asking the questions in a relatively logical order enables a sensible flow to develop. It should also be borne in mind that overly lengthy questionnaires are likely to put many people off from participating in a study. It is important, therefore, to be concise and economic with the subject areas in a survey as well as the language used in the actual questions.

The postal questionnaire used for the Youth and Politics project is given as an example in Extract 6.1. Notice the instructions given for respondents on how to complete the questionnaire, the general layout, the mix of question type, and the use of both open and closed questions.

## Extract 6.1 Questionnaire from the Youth and Politics project (Henn et al. 2002)

Please answer as many of the following questions as you are able. For all questions (except where asked otherwise), please indicate your answer by ticking the relevant box. So, if you voted in the recent European parliamentary election, you would tick the response box number one, as in the example here …

**7. Did you vote in the recent European parliamentary election on June 10th 1999? Yes ☑1 No ☐2**

1. Are you (please tick all that come close to describing your situation):

| | | | |
|---|---|---|---|
| In education (full-time) | ☐1 | In education (part-time) | ☐2 |
| In paid work (full-time) | ☐3 | In paid work (part-time) | ☐4 |
| On an apprenticeship | ☐5 | On a government training scheme/New Deal | ☐6 |
| Unemployed | ☐7 | Self employed | ☐8 |
| Other (please write in) | ☐9 | | |

2. How much interest do you normally have in local political issues?

| A great deal ☐1 | Quite a lot ☐2 | Some ☐3 | Not very much ☐4 | None at all ☐5 |
|---|---|---|---|---|

3. How much interest do you normally have in national political issues?

| A great deal ☐1 | Quite a lot ☐2 | Some ☐3 | Not very much ☐4 | None at all ☐5 |
|---|---|---|---|---|

4. Generally speaking, how often would you say you talk about political issues with your friends or family?

| A great deal ☐1 | Quite a lot ☐2 | Some ☐3 | Not very much ☐4 | None at all ☐5 |
|---|---|---|---|---|

5. How much do you agree or disagree with the following statements?

a) I think that it's important to vote in local elections:

| Strongly agree ☐1 | Agree ☐2 | Neither agree nor disagree ☐3 | Disagree ☐4 | Strongly disagree ☐5 |
|---|---|---|---|---|

b) I think that it's important to vote in national elections:

| Strongly agree ☐1 | Agree ☐2 | Neither agree nor disagree ☐3 | Disagree ☐4 | Strongly disagree ☐5 |
|---|---|---|---|---|

c) I think that voting is a waste of time:

| Strongly agree ☐1 | Agree ☐2 | Neither agree nor disagree ☐3 | Disagree ☐4 | Strongly disagree ☐5 |
|---|---|---|---|---|

6. Did you vote in the recent local election on May 6th 1999?

Yes ☐1 No ☐2

*(Continued)*

*(Continued)*

7. Did you vote in the recent European parliamentary election on June 10th 1999? Yes ☐1 No ☐2
8a. Do you intend to vote in the next parliamentary general election (for a Member of Parliament)? Yes ☐1 No ☐2
8b. If you do intend to vote in the next parliamentary general election, do you know which party you will vote for? Yes ☐1 No ☐2
9. Which community, national or international issue are you most concerned about? (please write in fully using the space provided)

________________________________________________

________________________________________________

## Issues in conducting sample surveys

While the sample survey is the most commonly used research method within the social sciences, it has been criticised on a number of levels.

### The logic of sample surveys

Critics argue that the logic of sample surveys in attempting to isolate causal connections between different variables is in itself deficient. Given the complexity of human consciousness and behaviour, critics hold that survey researchers will not be able to gain access to the process through which people adopt particular views, or act in particular ways, by simply posing a series of highly structured questions.

Thus, collecting numerous items of information about the world of, for example, industrial relations, and subjecting these to various statistical tests in order to identify which variables appear to have the highest degree of association with the key variable 'industrial dissent', fails to uncover:

- the history of industrial relations in a particular organisation;
- what the working conditions are like for employees; and
- how these experiences may have shaped the outlook and attitudes of employees to new work practices that are being introduced by the management of the organisation.

It may, of course, be that it is these very processes that have had the most significant effect on industrial relations within an organisation, but they may not be revealed in a questionnaire survey that actively avoids two-way dialogue.

### The value content of surveys

Another major criticism levelled at survey research is that, far from being an objective method for dispassionately collecting 'social facts', it employs techniques which both reflect and reproduce assumptions that the researcher holds about the social world, and in particular the phenomenon under investigation. Thus, the structured format of the questionnaire-based study suggests that the researcher has made certain choices about the overall research design, the issues which should (and by implication should not) be raised, and the format of their mode of delivery (self-completion forms or interviews).

In this way, critics of the sample survey claim that the study (and its conclusions) is largely a function of the values and presuppositions of the researcher. Those who criticise surveys from this perspective may advocate the use of qualitative research as an alternative in that such methods are more likely to let the respondents speak for themselves.

### Lack of depth or context

Furthermore, because the question-and-answer systems employed are highly structured, respondents are denied the opportunity to elaborate on issues – especially those of a complex nature – or to qualify any answers given. Thus, critics would claim that this failure to gain an holistic appreciation of a respondent's views concerning an issue or phenomenon inevitably results in only partial data, and fails to tap into the reality which exists within the inner consciousness of the respondent.

For example, this may happen when a respondent is forced to reply literally to the question:

DO YOU AGREE OR DISAGREE THAT THE UK GOVERNMENT WAS RIGHT TO SIGN UP TO THE SOCIAL CHAPTER OF THE MAASTRICHT TREATY?

Agree [ ] 1
Disagree [ ] 2
Don't know [ ] 3

Individuals may answer that they 'agree', when in reality they only mean that they supported the government's actions *under certain circumstances*. For instance, the respondent might be concerned that any such action was tantamount to ceding further sovereign powers to the European Union, but at the same time be actually in favour of certain principles and policies enshrined within the Social Chapter, such as ceilings on hours worked per week or the guarantee within law of employment rights for disabled people.

### The understanding and interpretation of questions

At an epistemological level, the highly structured approach employed in questionnaire-based studies undermines a researcher's ability to ensure that the respondent's understanding and interpretation of the questions is as intended by the researcher. Obviously, if there is no correspondence between the researcher and the respondent in terms of the meaning given to the questions posed, the research will be invalidated.

Thus, take a seemingly simple question such as *'What is your income?'* A respondent, denied the opportunity to elaborate or clarify the meaning that he or she holds of the question, and to ensure that it is the meaning expected by the researcher, might be unsure if the question refers to gross or net income, weekly or monthly income, income solely from earnings or from earnings and share dividends (or rent received on a second house), and so on. The rules of standardised interviewing do not necessarily correspond to the nature of everyday conversation, raising the question of *validity* – whether the question really does measure that which it purports to measure.

For Marsh, it is important to distinguish between two levels of criticism aimed at the sample survey: she considers that if the problems associated with survey-based research are intrinsically philosophical, this will therefore 'place absolute constraints on the method' (1979, p.294). Here, however, she claims that the fundamental problem is common for all social scientists. That is:

> The problem that the subject matter of our research is conscious, communicates in a language whose meaning is not capable of unique determination, and is capable of changing very rapidly. (Marsh 1979, p.294)

However, if the problems are essentially 'technical' in nature, this suggests that problems peculiar to this method can be overcome. Marsh's conclusion is that these problems are fundamentally of a practical technical character, and therefore capable of resolution through careful attention to design, measurement and pilot work. In this way, she states that surveys can provide the kind of evidence needed to test social science theories effectively, and make a valuable contribution to our knowledge of the social world.

## Conducting online surveys

Since postal surveys are so common in many areas of social research, there was a sense of inevitability that, with the advent of email, it was only a matter of time before email surveys also became popular. Instant responses are a notable advantage to a medium which delivers electronically, but the format in which emails are sent does present some problems. A postal survey arrives with the respondent in a fixed format, with boxes to be ticked, and spaces for responses clearly marked. When writing directly on a paper-based questionnaire the layout remains unaltered, but with an email, the insertion of textual responses is more problematic, since more often than not different respondents will have different ways of indicating their answers. For example, some may insert a tick symbol next to the relevant answer, others may underline the response they wish to choose and others might delete all of the unselected responses. This results in a lot of work for the researcher in deciphering the responses and can result in a drop in data quality. A preferable option is the questionnaire which appears on a web page. This can include options to be clicked as well as boxes into which text can be typed directly without altering the layout of the page.

Creating a web page is beyond the technical capabilities of most people, but there are a number of companies which offer survey creation services, many of which include a free basic service as well as more advanced subscription services. Two examples are Survey Monkey (www.surveymonkey.com) and Survey Gizmo (www.surveygizmo.com), and a Google search for 'online survey tools' will turn up a host of others. Surveys can generally be designed by selecting question types (multiple response, open-text questions, rating scales, etc.) and typing in wording for the questions and answer categories. A unique web address is then provided which can be emailed to the sample or included on a web page. Once respondents have provided their answers, they click a button to submit them, and the data are held on a server where they can be viewed using tables and charts, or downloaded to be opened up in packages such as Excel or SPSS for more sophisticated analysis.

There are a number of immediate advantages to adopting web-based surveys over postal surveys, perhaps the most obvious of which is the automation of data collection. As soon as respondents submit their answers, the data are ready to be analysed. This saves time and money, but also enables sample characteristics to be monitored as responses are received in real-time. Early speculative analysis may also be carried out.

Completing an online form does, however, require a certain amount of technical proficiency, which might impact upon a respondent's ability or willingness to participate. Hewson et al. (2003) highlight the lack of conclusive evidence in studies which have attempted to compare the response rates of online and traditional surveys, but Dolnicar et al. (2009) conclude that online surveys produce more complete data and fewer dropouts, and claim that this contradicts previous evidence to the contrary. Whether online surveys do indeed produce better response rates is difficult to gauge, but it would seem that all of the standard issues already addressed in relation to response rates, such as questionnaire design, salience of the topic, and sending of reminder letters, hold for online surveys as well.

In traditional surveys, one way of boosting responses is to begin with a much larger sample than is required, thus anticipating a certain level of refusal. This, of course, is resource-heavy in traditional survey research, but the ease with which Internet users can be contacted either via email or by posting a message on a message board or website means that over-sampling is a potentially quick and cost-effective way of boosting response rates. Over-sampling should always be adopted with caution, however, since it can result in an all-too-easy reliance upon the willingness of certain types of respondent to take part, and may in turn introduce sample bias.

Access to samples can present one of the main stumbling blocks for any researcher, and so the attraction of the Internet as a source of potential respondents is easy to understand. Internet use is becoming more widespread in the developed world, with 65% of UK households having access in 2008 and 71% of US households in 2007 (Office for National Statistics 2008; US Census Bureau 2007). Despite this, there remains a significant proportion of the population who are unconnected and these people tend to fall into certain demographics. Even in the UK, which has one of the highest proportions of Internet users of any country in the world, 93% of adults under the age of 70 holding degree-level or higher qualifications enjoy household Internet access compared to only 56% of those with no formal qualifications (Office of National Statistics 2008). This suggests that the Internet user population is markedly different from the general population, even in those countries with high levels of access. In other countries, where access remains a privilege of the few, these differences will only be compounded.

Weisberg, Krosnick and Bowen (1996, p.39) point out that:

> [S]trictly speaking, sampling can just generalize to the sampling frame from which the sample was drawn, rather than to the full population, so the researcher should try to use a sampling frame that corresponds as close as possible to the population.

This highlights two important issues. First, it is a reminder that in order to draw a random sample, we require a sampling frame. These are difficult to come by, if the sample we wish to achieve is one from the general population of Internet users. General population sampling frames used in traditional surveys tend to make use of household addresses rather than individual names. A sampling frame of Internet users would most likely require personal email addresses, which are not generally available. The second issue is that, regardless of the sampling strategy we adopt, it is questionable whether the Internet can provide a reliable and representative sample of the general population anyway.

Hewson et al. (2003) identify a number of studies in which both Internet and non-Internet samples were used, and which suggest the resulting demographic characteristics of both samples were comparable. They also point out, however, that in a number of these studies, the samples were self-selecting and from micro-populations with specialist interests in the research topic. In some instances, for example, offline participants were drawn from a Psychology student population and online participants from specialist-interest Psychology websites. Both groups demonstrate a common interest in Psychology, the subject of the research in question, and both share similar educational and other socio-demographic characteristics.

It may be, then, that the Internet provides a rich source of respondents if we are conducting research which requires specialist samples, or if we are able to negotiate access to organisations in which the population being researched are based. A survey of students at a particular university could make use of a sampling frame of all email addresses provided by the university registrar's office, for example, and a trade union could survey its members by selecting a sample of email addresses from its membership list. Beyond this, convenience samples are likely to be the only option for much online research, and all of the usual limitations on inference associated with traditional convenience samples must be considered if these are to be used in online surveys.

In summary, online surveys provide useful means of generating a large amount of data at relatively little cost, but special attention must be paid to the design of online forms and potential bias in samples. That said, online research does, through specialist discussion forums and social networking sites, open up opportunities to access global samples large enough for meaningful analysis, which might not otherwise be possible.

## Political opinion polls

In the light of these issues, and some of the problems levelled at survey research, to what extent is it possible to trust the findings of studies which are based upon this approach? Such studies can be (at least partially) replicated to test whether the results of a particular study are verified in another similar study. But does this necessarily mean that both studies accurately reflect the reality that both aim to measure? For instance, if both studies suggest that people would rather the government increase taxes to improve the education service than reduce income tax, how can we be sure that people really hold such selfless beliefs?

One way in which the results from survey-based research can be tested is to look at the record of opinion polls in forecasting election outcomes – do the results of opinion polls (which aim to measure *expected* political behaviour) correspond with the way people behave when they *actually* come to cast their votes in an election? As Nick Moon of NOP (National Opinion Polls) explains: 'General Election opinion polls represent one of the few occasions when sample surveys are tested against actual figures' (Moon 1997, p.5).

Opinion polls are a form of social survey – they differ only in terms of the subject area upon which they focus. While social surveys are concerned with issues which might broadly be defined as 'social', polls investigate people's political beliefs, attitudes, opinions and behaviour. In terms of the methods employed and the general approaches followed, opinion polls and social surveys are broadly identical.

Generally, the performance of opinion polls in forecasting the share of votes achieved by the different political parties in British general elections is considered to be good. As a consequence, opinion pollsters have, until recently, been reluctant to consider changing their methods and techniques (Henn 1998, pp.117–35).

In the immediate post-war period, the pollsters achieved a reputation for effectively and accurately estimating electoral outcomes. However, the final polls at the general elections of 1951 and 1970 failed to anticipate the outcome of the electoral contests. In 1951, the three final-day polls suggested a Conservative victory of between 2.5% and 7.1%, when in fact Labour secured a larger share of electoral support by a margin of 0.8%:

> Were it not for the fact that the Conservatives won 26 more seats than Labour, despite taking fewer votes, the polls' failure would have been regarded at the time more seriously than it was. (Crewe 1983, p.11)

In 1970, however, the error on the final pre-election polls was more marked. The electorate eventually voted the Conservatives into office with a lead of 2.4%. However, 19 of the 20 pre-election polls had put the Labour Party ahead, and four of the five final polls gave Labour a lead of between 2.0% and 8.7%. To a lesser extent, the performance of the pre-election polls at the two general elections in 1974 were also short of the mark. In February, the polls indicated a comfortable Conservative victory, when in fact a hung parliament was the outcome; at the October election, a Labour landslide was forecast, yet only a three-seat majority was won.

In 1992, the opinion polls were widely perceived to have failed in their attempts to forecast the British general election accurately. Throughout the 1992 campaign period, there were 50 national opinion polls conducted, which collectively provided a fairly constant pattern of party support and suggested an average Labour lead over the Conservatives of 1.85%. These findings were widely interpreted as indicating that Labour would be the largest party in a hung parliament.

The final pre-election polls themselves provided a similar summary, with Labour at 40% (± 2%), the Conservatives at 38% (± 1%), and the Liberal Democrats at 18% (± 2%). These results were largely reinforced by the exit polls, which, when adjusted, suggested between 298 and 305 seats for the Conservatives, and 294 and 307 seats for Labour.

However, in the event, the Conservatives won 42.8% of the vote – a 7.6% lead over their nearest rivals, the Labour Party – and were returned to government with 336 seats and an overall majority of 21. The net effect of these results implied the most serious failure on the part of the opinion pollsters in general elections since polling began in Britain (Butler 1994, p.vii). The mean error per party at 2.6% was higher than any recorded in the post-war period, and the mean error on the gap between the Conservatives and Labour at 8.5% was well beyond the threshold of 4.2% which could be explained by sampling error alone with an average sample size of 2,102.

As a consequence of the pollsters' apparent poor performance in terms of both the scale and the direction of the error in their final forecast polls, a series of inquiries were set up to try to identify the factors which could account for the discrepancies. Of particular significance were the 1992 and 1994 reports of the Market Research Society. The 1992 report suggested that there was 'a prima facie case to support the claim that opinion polls are generally likely to slightly over-estimate Labour support and under-estimate Conservative support' (1992, p.15), and had indeed been doing so not only throughout the 1992 campaign, but more seriously at most general elections since 1959.

The polls were again criticised at the European Assembly elections in 1994 and the 1997 general election for failing to forecast accurately the levels of support achieved by the main British political parties (O'Muircheartaigh 1997).

All of this is not to suggest that opinion polls – and, by implication, the sample survey method itself – cannot be trusted to measure social and political phenomena necessarily. Instead, that like all research methods, surveys and opinion polls should be used carefully, and the findings derived from them interpreted cautiously.

## Summary

This chapter has focused on the main quantitative methods that are used in research – sample surveys and experiments. In particular, we have considered the usefulness and application of sample surveys in research.

In examining these questions, there is an explicit connection with many of the issues that were raised in Chapter 1, where the quantitative–qualitative debate was first encountered. We have seen that the logic of quantitative research is to *explain* social phenomena – why people behave in the way they do, or hold certain views and values – by reference to underlying causes. This emphasis on the search for causal connections between different phenomena (or variables) tends to steer researchers working within this tradition towards favouring highly structured research approaches and techniques such as experiments and questionnaire-based sample surveys.

Quantitative approaches, while comparatively dominant within the social sciences, have attracted significant criticism at both epistemological and technical levels. Largely, this criticism is levelled at the very structured nature of such methods, which, it is claimed, prevent any opportunities for respondents to seek clarification over the meaning of questions that are asked, and in turn to communicate their responses fully and clearly. This is said to threaten seriously the validity of any such research project. Such critics would therefore dispute the extent to which survey research can provide an accurate assessment of people's views and behaviour.

## Chapter research task

Design a survey on a topic that you are wanting to investigate.

Produce a structured questionnaire of 10–15 (mostly 'closed') questions that would elicit consistent information for your chosen topic. This must be a questionnaire suitable for a face-to-face interview. You also need to take into consideration the things you have learnt from your previous reading, such as bias, objectivity and operationalisation of concepts. In addition you need to: (a) outline how you would identify the (target) population; (b) outline a sample population; and (c) outline how you would go about 'finding' members of this group.

The final questionnaire should be 'piloted' on one other person, and you should then hold a debriefing session where you should discuss the following:

1. Did you successfully develop a rapport?
2. Did you have a sense that the person 'told the truth'?
3. How did *you* feel?
4. Did the questionnaire interview procede professionally? Were you taken seriously?
5. Did you have a sense that there was a hierarchical/power relationship involved?
6. Were the questions (a) clear and (b) unambiguous?
7. Was the data useful? Or was it too limiting?

You may find it useful to remind yourself of the following stages in a survey as you approach this task:

1. Choose the topic to be studied.
2. Review the literature.
3. Form hunches and hypotheses.
4. Identify the population to be surveyed and choose a sample selection strategy.
5. Carry out preparatory investigations and interviews.
6. Develop a questionnaire.
7. Conduct a pilot survey.
8. Finalise the questionnaire.
9. Select a sample of the population.
10. Select and train interviewers (if necessary).
11. Collect the data.
12. Process the data and analyse the results.
13. Write the research report, perhaps in the form of a book.
14. Publish the report.

## Recommended Reading

Arber, S. 1993. Designing Samples. In: N. Gilbert (ed.), *Researching Social Life*. London: Sage.

De Vaus, D. 1996. *Surveys in Social Research*, 2nd edn. London: UCL Press.

Fowler, F. 2002. *Survey Research Method*, 3rd edn. London: Routledge.

Hoinville, G. and Jowell, R. 1978. *Survey Research Practice*. London: Heinemann.

Marsh, C. 1979. Problems with Surveys: Method or Epistemology?, *Sociology*, 13 (2), 293–305.

Moser, C. and Kalton, G. 1971. *Survey Methods in Social Investigation*. London: Heinemann.

Newell, R. 1993. Questionnaires. In: N. Gilbert (ed.), *Researching Social Life*. London: Sage.

Schofield, W. 1993. Sample Surveys. In: M. Hammersley (ed.), *Principles of Social and Educational Research: Block 2*. Milton Keynes: The Open University. pp.75–108.

Tonkiss, F. 2004. The History of the Social Survey. In: C. Seale (ed.), *Researching Society and Culture*. London: Sage. pp.85–97.

# SEVEN

# Qualitative Approaches in Social Research

- To introduce readers to possibilities for using qualitative approaches and methods in research projects
- To provide an overview of the logic of qualitative research, and its origins within an interpretivist tradition within the social sciences
- To define the 'qualitative' research approach and contrast this with the 'quantitative' research approach
- To review the main methods for conducting qualitative research projects – in-depth, one-to-one and focus group interviews, and participant observation
- To highlight the main issues confronting social researchers when using qualitative approaches and methods in research projects

- **Introduction**
- **Qualitative research exemplars**
- **Defining qualitative research**
- **How is qualitative research conducted?**
- **Conducting qualitative research online**
- **Issues in conducting qualitative research studies**
- **Summary**
- **Chapter research task**
- **Recommended reading**

## Introduction

The qualitative research style is more often than not associated with an interpretive perspective in social research, in which the logic of research is not so much to test out given theories about what guides human behaviour, but instead to develop an appreciation of the underlying motivations that people have for doing what they do. Underlying the qualitative research style, then, is the assumption that in order to understand human behaviour, a researcher must first understand the meanings that people have of the world around them because these meanings tend to govern their actions. The emphasis given by qualitative researchers to their studies therefore involves an examination of the perspectives of the people or groups that are of interest to them – their ideas, attitudes, motives and intentions.

In a classic qualitative study of the behaviour and experiences of a group of schoolboys, Paul Willis, in his book *Learning to Labour* (1977), asked the question of why working-class boys tended to enter working-class occupations on leaving school. Following an intensive and lengthy period of observation of the schooling process and of the boys' behaviour both inside and outside the classroom, as well as numerous – and often informal – interviews, Willis began to gain an empathetic understanding of the boys' shared experiences of schooling. He concluded that the educational paths followed by the boys were partly shaped by these shared experiences. His research findings revealed to him the existence of a counter-school culture in which the boys rejected schooling as a process. Their behaviour was thus structured by their shared interpretations of schooling and of their perceived place within their school.

Qualitative research methods such as in-depth interviews and participant observation share some of the following characteristics:

- Research is carried out in 'real-life' settings. In order to build up an understanding of how people experience the world around them, and to identify what informs their behaviour, the researcher attempts to study action and talk as it naturally occurs, with as little disruption to people's lives as possible. Quantitative methods, such as questionnaire surveys and experiments, are eschewed as leading to the creation of relatively artificial research situations, in which it is not possible to study 'real' views and 'real' behaviour.
- The objective is to take detailed descriptions of people's behaviour and thoughts to illuminate their social meanings. This implies adopting an insider perspective in research, in which there is likely to be a closeness between the researcher and the people studied, rather than an impersonal and distanced relationship. For instance, an organisation-based study of absenteeism may entail a researcher spending considerable time at the workplace, observing how work is organised, the relationships between actors, and developing a non-threatening presence. From this vantage point, the researcher will aim to develop a rapport with employees (to gain their trust and confidence) in order to encourage them to speak fully and frankly about issues that may be associated with absenteeism.
- The researcher is likely to adopt an approach in which there is no precise initial specification of research issues and concepts. The focus of the research may change during the course of collecting data, as ideas develop and particular issues become important.
- The qualitative approach involves theory construction rather than theory testing. Theoretical ideas develop from initial data collection and then go on to influence future data collection – there is a cumulative spiral of theory development and data collection.

In this chapter, we shall begin by reviewing three classic social science-based research studies that have used a qualitative research design, often incorporating several research methods and techniques with the same project. The purpose in doing so will be to demonstrate the often eclectic nature of qualitative research designs – and how different methods in combination may complement each other in helping the researcher to develop deep insights into the topic investigated. Furthermore, reviewing these research exemplars will also demonstrate the various methodological issues confronting the researcher when using a qualitative research design, as well as the range of issues that one ought to be aware of when conducting qualitative research projects.

We shall then consider what a qualitative research design looks like in practice, and how it differs from a broadly quantitative research design in terms of the logic and operationalisation of the project. When compared to quantitative-based studies, such research designs are often relatively small in scale, adopting somewhat loosely structured approaches designed to encourage research participants to talk in detail about the meanings that they have of the world and the extent to which these influence their behaviour. Several methods commonly used within qualitative research strategies will then be reviewed, together with a discussion of their strengths and limits. These will include one-to-one, in-depth interviews, focus groups and qualitative observation-based studies. Finally, some of the key methodological issues and concerns raised by research practitioners about the use of qualitative research designs will be addressed, including such questions as validity and reliability, objectivity and subjectivity, and ethical matters.

## Qualitative research exemplars

As examples of the qualitative style of research, and the issues that are raised, we shall look at a number of oft-cited studies. These studies have been based upon a variety of research methods and this is something that is typical for the qualitative approach within the social sciences. However, the key methods are participant observation and in-depth interviewing.

### Eileen Barker, The Making of a Moonie

This study had as its overarching aim to examine what, at the time, were generally held beliefs about the Unification Church – or as members were commonly referred to by the mass media, the 'Moonies'. Barker conducted a six-year programme of research, designed to:

- answer questions about Moonie beliefs; and
- test whether media claims condemning the movement as a 'brainwashing, bizarre sect' were really justified.

She set herself several questions:

> Why and in what sort of circumstances, will what kind of people become Moonies? Why, and in what sorts of circumstances, will what kind of people leave the movement? What is life like in the Unification Church? What kinds of communication system and power structure does the organisation have? To what extent, and why, does the movement vary according to time and place? What is the range of the relationships which the church and its members have with the rest of society? And in what kind of ways can we best understand and explain the phenomenon of the Unification Church and public reaction to it? (Barker 1984, p.16)

She used a variety of approaches and methods to address these initial research questions. These included:

- *In-depth interviews*: Thirty British members of the Unification Church were randomly selected for taped interviews in local church centres. Each interview lasted between 6 and 8 hours. As is typical for this style of interviewing, Barker developed a provisional outline topic guide, but was flexible in terms of the way she asked her questions and the order in which she asked them.
- *Participant observation*: In order to deepen her understanding of the church, how it was organised and who its members were, Barker actually spent six years residing in various centres in a number of different countries. During this period, she followed three phases of participant observation-based study: a 'passive' phase of watching and listening; an 'interactive' phase of engaging in conversation to learn the concepts and language of the church and its members; and an 'active' stage where, having learned the social language, she could challenge and debate to understand better the essence, life and organisation of the church.
- *Questionnaire survey*: In the course of developing an understanding of her initial research questions (through her interviews and participant observations), Barker became sufficiently confident in her studies to begin to devise more structured questions. She then designed a large questionnaire that was sent to all English-speaking members in Britain, and some in other countries.

One of the key issues for the social science researcher to learn from this study is that the qualitative research approach is a *style* of research; it may involve more than one particular research method or technique, and often the research follows an iterative process. Here, Barker uses a combination of methods to gain cumulative insights into the life of the Unification Church and its members. And the insights gained from one method in her study informed the development of other methods – in particular, the questionnaire survey was informed by the participant observation aspect of her project.

## Maurice Punch, Observation and the Police

In his study of the police in Amsterdam, Punch was interested in examining their 'social' role – in particular, how they interacted with the public and how individual police officers themselves defined their role. He claimed that as they are a particularly secretive and secluded part of the criminal justice system, participant observation would be the only method that would fully enable researchers to appreciate policing:

> The essence of uniformed police work is relatively solitary patrolling, free of direct supervision, with a high degree of discretion in face-to-face interaction with the public, and with decision-making behaviour that is frequently not reviewable. ... Only observation can tap into that initial encounter on the streets, or in a private dwelling, with all its implications for the individual citizen concerned and for his potential passage through the criminal justice system. (Punch 1993, p.184)

Furthermore, Punch provides a series of detailed examples as insights into the possibilities that participant observation has as a method for social researchers:

> I could follow radio messages, conversations between policemen, and verbal exchanges during incidents. Additionally I could read the extensive documentary material in the station – telegrams, the station diary, reports, charge sheets, 'wanted' notices, telex messages etc. (Punch 1993, p.187)

These examples also indicate what conducting participant observation studies actually entails. The approach involves more than just observing action and interaction; instead it is a flexible research approach that involves using a variety of different methods and sources of data in order to aid the construction of a picture of the world according to the group or organisation under investigation.

In the course of his research, Punch notes that it was necessary for him to become involved in a social relationship with the police officers he was observing – to establish a rapport with them. This was crucial for his study. Without such a relationship, he would be incapable of convincing the officers that they had nothing to fear from revealing their world to him, and the part they had to play in it. Perhaps not surprisingly, such an approach raises the possibility of what is known as 'going native' – of over-identification with, in this case, the police officer's role:

> I had a strong identification with the work of the patrolmen. I considered them my colleagues, felt a unity with the group, and was prepared to defend them in case of physical (or intellectual) attack. (Punch 1993, p.191)

Elsewhere, he again raises the issue, and in doing so reveals the implications that this issue has in terms of his ability to conduct his research in an objective and credible way:

> The more I was accepted the more they expected me to act as a colleague. In my willingness to be accepted by the policemen I over-identified perhaps too readily and this doubtless endangered my research role. For the patrol group is a cohesive social unit and the policeman's world is full of seductive interests so that it is all too easy to 'go native'. (Punch 1993, pp.195–6)

As Punch carried out his research, it became increasingly clear to him that the police officers that he was studying were modifying their behaviour somewhat in order to shield some aspects of their 'world' from him. Such behaviour represents a real threat to a research project, as it undermines the ability of a researcher to record accurately complete details of the field that she or he is studying. In formal research terms, this issue is referred to as reactivity. Punch observes that it was only as rapport and trust developed between himself and the police officers that he came to learn that his initial observations were based on only a 'partial picture' of the data:

> I went to Hans's flat for a celebration and several policemen began talking excitedly about corruption. I learnt a lot more in that evening, thanks to the liberating effects of alcohol, than in all my field-work ... a subterranean police culture which had largely escaped me suddenly emerged. ... Hans and Tom explained, 'How much do you think you found out when you were with us? You wrote somewhere that you thought we were open-hearted. Well, we only let you see what we wanted you to see. You only saw about fifty per cent. We showed you only half of the story'. (Punch 1993, pp.192–3)

A final issue illuminated by Punch's paper concerns the ethical aspects of his study. In one notable episode, for instance, he recounts how he was asked on at least one occasion to hold the gun of one of the police officers and restrain people suspected of having committed a crime. It became almost routine for him to perform policing duties without the authority actually to carry these out:

> More and more I became involved in a participant role. I chased people, searched people, searched cars, searched houses, held people, and even shouted at people who abused my 'colleagues'. (Punch 1993, p.191)

### John Goldthorpe et al., The Affluent Worker in the Class Structure

This was a study of a group of upper-working-class manual workers based at the Vauxhall Motors plant in Luton during the 1960s. It was conducted in the aftermath of the British Labour Party's third successive electoral defeat in 1959, which led many commentators to argue that a process of 'embourgeoisement' was taking place, largely as a result of the growth of an increasingly affluent working class, and its apparent adoption of middle-class values and lifestyles. However, Goldthorpe and his colleagues were among 'those who regarded the thesis of the worker turning middle class with some marked degree of scepticism, or who at any rate, could see a number of serious difficulties in the thesis as it was being presented' (1969, pp.23–4).

The authors opted for a qualitative research design – an intensive case-study approach using both qualitative and quantitative methods that they hoped would yield considerable detail about the social lives of working-class people in Britain:

> Our intention, then, was to bring together data which pertained both to attitudes and to social behaviour and relationships, and to cover work and non-work milieu alike; the ultimate aim being that of forming some idea of the total life-situations and life-styles of the individuals and groups we studied. (Goldthorpe et al. 1969, p.31)

The immediate dilemma facing the authors is one that confronts all researchers intent on using case studies in qualitative projects. And that is, how to select a case study that would enable Goldthorpe and his colleagues to make broad generalisations about the new 'affluent' working class? From their literature review, they set up certain criteria which they considered might serve as measurable indicators to test the embourgeoisement thesis empirically. These included (Goldthorpe et al. 1969, pp.32–3) that:

- the population of workers should be relatively affluent, economically secure, physically mobile, and consumption minded,
- they should work in an industrial setting with advanced technology, 'progressive' employment policies, and harmonious industrial relations,
- their community should be characterised by its relative newness, instability and 'openness', it should be socially heterogeneous, and economically expanding.

The authors opted to select an ideal case that would be as favourable as possible for the confirmation of the embourgeoisement thesis. Their rationale for this sampling method was that should the thesis be confirmed through their data, then they would have detailed material about workers undergoing a process of class transformation. By way of contrast, should the thesis not be confirmed by the reality of working-class life in this most affluent of contexts, it would serve to undermine the argument that embourgeoisement was occurring across British society as a whole. This is similar to a theoretical sampling method using the critical case approach, in which settings (or people) are chosen for investigation precisely because they offer the researcher the clearest insight into the topic being investigated; there is no attempt at *random* probability sampling here, but rather the *strategic* selection of cases. This theoretical sampling method is outlined in the next section of this chapter.

A further important issue that readers should consider when studying this book is the researchers' use of sampling methods. Their sample of workers was based entirely of men. Their study might therefore be criticised for contributing to the relative 'invisibility' of women in social science research, especially in relation to studies of social class. It might be argued that such an approach assumes that women have no class at all, and that their role is dependent on their male partners. The questioning strategy employed might also be criticised on the same grounds. For instance, 7.(a) (section 1) of the interview schedule asks, 'What sort of work does your father do or what was his last job, if he is no longer alive or retired?' Elsewhere in section 3, question 3 asks, 'How many of the men who work near to you would you call close friends?' In neither of these two questions (nor indeed elsewhere) is there any reference to women, perhaps presupposing that women were not in paid work – or perhaps reflecting the gender division of (paid) labour in British society at that time.

One issue that the authors do acknowledge is in relation to *representativeness*. Theirs was not a random probability sample of the population, but included (male) workers chosen from only the major departments in the workplaces. As a consequence, some of the assembly workers were under-sampled. However, readers were left with a reliance upon the assurances of the authors, who claimed that these workers did not differ in terms of their characteristics from workers in other departments.

## Defining qualitative research

There is some disagreement about how to define a qualitative style of research. Perhaps the easiest way is to begin with what researchers do, and how this distinguishes them from researchers using other approaches. From this point of view, qualitative research has several important features. It involves:

1. The study of one or a small number of cases, often over a lengthy period of time (certainly days, but as we have seen from Barker's study of the Unification Church above, perhaps even years!). In organisational research, for instance, studies frequently focus on a single agency, or a small number of departments, or employees within the agency. In educational research, the focus may be on a single school, or perhaps a number of classrooms, teachers and/or pupils within a particular school.

In this context, the data collection process is characterised as being intensive; very detailed study involves the collection of large quantities of data from a small number of informants and settings. Research sites and participants are typically selected using theoretical sampling or snowball sampling. With snowball sampling, researchers aim for typicality rather than generalisability through their sampling strategy. However, while the principles of representativeness and generalisability, which are generally applied in quantitative research, are not appropriate for qualitative research, theoretical sampling, in which research participants and research sites are selected based on their relevance to the theoretical focus of the research, does allow for a degree of generalisation (Definition 7.1). While the quantitative researcher's concern lies with obtaining a statistically representative sample, a qualitative researcher employing theoretical sampling is focused on the representativeness of concepts in the research, and of being able to access the social processes in which she or he is interested. In that theoretical sampling leads to the selection of respondents where the phenomena in which the researcher is interested are most likely to occur, generalisation also follows a theoretical logic – with 'the generalisability of case to the theoretical proposition rather than to populations or universes' (Bryman 1988, p.90). Indeed, as Mason (2002, p.8) has argued, good qualitative research always aims to achieve 'wider resonance' rather than be content with findings that are 'idiosyncratic or particular to the limited empirical parameters of the study'.

### Definition 7.1 Qualitative sampling

In qualitative research, 'the researchers' primary goal is an understanding of social processes rather than obtaining a representative sample' (Arber 1993, p.73). Settings and participants are selected using snowball sampling and theoretical sampling. Snowball sampling is used where there is no obvious list to refer to in order to generate a participant base for a study. It relies on the researcher obtaining a strategically important contact who can recommend other possible participants who might be approached to take part in the study. Theoretical sampling is:

> Entirely governed by the selection of those respondents who will maximise theoretical development. The sampling should aim to locate strategic data which may refute emerging hypotheses. Sampling stops when 'theoretical saturation' is reached, that is, when no new analytical insights are forthcoming from a given situation. (Arber 1993, p.74)

This approach is in stark contrast with quantitative research studies using questionnaires, for instance; these are designed to investigate much larger numbers of cases, but which collect data for much shorter periods of time on each case.

Hakim (1987, p.28) has provided an interesting way to distinguish these two approaches:

> If surveys offer the bird's eye view, qualitative research offers the worm's eye view.

### Review box 7.1 Qualitative sampling

Look again at the discussions concerning the selection of cases in both Chapter 3 and also the section on sampling for survey research from Chapter 6. As you do so, remind yourself of the different approaches to sampling that are available to the researcher.

2. The adoption of a wide initial focus at the outset, rather than the testing of narrowly defined hypotheses. Qualitative researchers tend to begin with no more than a rather general interest in some type of social phenomenon or issue. It is only during the course of data collection and analysis that researchers narrow down their research problem and begin to formulate and test hypotheses. Thinking back to the

discussion of Eileen Barker's study, reviewed earlier in this chapter, the transition to the 'active' stage of her research was only possible because of what she previously learned through her 'passive' stage.

A commonly used approach is the method of 'grounded theory' developed by Glaser and Strauss (1967). Essentially, the researcher begins with a general problem that she or he would like to explore, conducts the fieldwork, examines this by looking for relationships and patterns in the data, and then turns to theory to try to explain any patterns. In this way, theory emerges from the data. The general strategy might be defined as a research-then-theory strategy. It adopts an iterative process, in which analysis takes place while the data is being collected rather than after it has been gathered. The grounded theory approach is outlined in detail in Chapter 8.

3. A range of types of data is employed, not just one. Results from observations and/or unstructured interviews are usually the main sources of data, but use may be made of public and private documents and even of official statistics and questionnaire data. For instance, an investigation into declining employee morale at a particular workplace may involve the researcher conducting observations, in-depth interviews, questionnaires, analysing internal memoranda and examining minutes of meetings. The guiding principle here is that utilising such an apparently eclectic set of methods and data places the researcher in a relatively strong position to develop a holistic account of the issue. (You might want to remind yourself about what is involved in using a combined methods approach, by referring to Chapter 1.) In combination, these methods might enable the researcher to:

- monitor the extent of declining workplace morale;
- identify the range of possible situational and contextual factors that may play a part in the trend;
- observe the relationships that exist between employees;
- develop an understanding of how employees experience work;
- examine how the organisation has previously approached the issue, what steps it has taken in the past to resolve it, and the impact of these approaches.

Such a research strategy contrasts with quantitative research work, which tends to rely on only a single source of data.

4. Minimal pre-structuring of the data that is collected. It is for this reason that the observations and interviews used by qualitative researchers are often referred to as 'unstructured'. On the basis of their observations, qualitative researchers usually write field notes in which they try to describe what they have seen and heard in detail, rather than entering with a list of categories and ticking those off when they observe instances.

Similarly, the questions that researchers ask in interview will usually be open-ended. They will try to note down exactly what informants say, rather than interpreting the responses in terms of predefined answers. In addition, observations and interviews are often audio- or even video-recorded.

In summary, categories for structuring and analysing the data are developed in the course of data collection and analysis, rather than beforehand.

5. The reporting of qualitative research data generally in the form of verbal descriptions and explanations, with quantification and statistical analysis taking a subordinate role at most. See Example 7.1 for a description of the approach taken in integrating qualitative data in the analysis of research findings. As you read through this extract, taken from the authors' Youth and Politics project, note how direct quotation is used to illuminate issues dealt with in the commentary as well as the rather liberal use of such quotations that is made.

## Example 7.1 Reporting qualitative interview data (from Henn et al. 2002)

A consistent message expressed in all of the focus groups was that politics is not aimed *at* young people. This reflects the findings of much previous qualitative research (Bhavnani 1994; White et al. 2000) that suggests that if young people appear to exhibit a lack of engagement with politics, it is because they perceive the world of formal politics to be distant from their lives, and broadly irrelevant – that politics has little *meaning* for them. A common complaint was that '*there is no encouragement for us to take an interest*'. An overwhelming majority of the participants agreed that if politics were targeted more at young people, then they would take a more active interest:

- 'All politicians complain that they are not getting through to the younger generation, but they don't give the younger generation any real reason to be interested in politics'.
- 'Young people choose to exclude themselves because they find no connection with themselves [and politicians]'.

There was a general consensus that political parties were at least partially responsible for any youth apathy that might exist, because they persistently failed to actively encourage young people to take an interest in politics: '*They don't give us any incentives to want to know about it [politics]*'. As a consequence, the focus group participants were concerned that young people were generally '*encouraged to be passive*'. The point was frequently made that, instead of blaming young people for a lack of interest in politics, politicians and political parties should take the lead both in trying to connect with young people, and in finding ways to transform politics into a more engaging and meaningful process and activity. At present, however, they were criticised for both failing to target their

*(Continued)*

*(Continued)*

communication towards youth, and for consistently ignoring 'youth' issues. Ambivalence to 'formal' politics was therefore less an indication that young people were apathetic or naturally disinterested in politics, and more a product of their frustration that their views and desires would not be addressed by politicians and officials. Some adopted a fatalistic approach, symptomatic of a general mood of powerlessness:

- *'Why bother – we're never really going to change things'*
- *'I'm not going to change their mind'*
- *'We've got no interest because we don't think there's going to be any change. If we thought there was a chance to change [things] we'd probably be interested'.*

## How is qualitative research conducted?

Qualitative research as a style of inquiry uses a wide variety of methods of data collection. As we have seen, the two most commonly used qualitative methods in social research are in-depth interviews and participant observation.

### In-depth interviewing

There are essentially two types of qualitative in-depth interviews. The first approach involves one-to-one interviews in which individual respondents are questioned at length about a particular issue, experience or event. The second method uses group discussions (or focus groups), which are designed 'to allow you to see how people interact in discussing topics, and how they react to disagreement' (Fielding and Thomas 2008, p.251).

There are two broadly different approaches to the way in which data from qualitative interviews may be read. The first, which Silverman (2005, p.154) refers to as a 'realist' approach, treats 'respondents' answers as describing some external reality (e.g. facts, events) or internal experience (e.g. feelings, meanings), as if such data provides factual accounts of people's lives. An alternative 'narrative' approach 'treats interview data as accessing various stories or narratives through which people describe their world … [where] interviewers and interviewees, in concert, generate plausible accounts of the world' (Silverman 2005, p.154).

What is central to in-depth interviews, regardless of how the emerging data is perceived, is that they provide qualitative depth by allowing interviewees to talk about the subject in terms of their own frames of reference. In so doing, the method enables the interviewer to maximise her or his understanding of the respondent's point of view.

Critics of the qualitative approach would argue that the closeness between the interviewer and interviewee that occurs in such interviews implies that the method is inevitably a subjective one that lacks scientific rigour. The informal 'conversational' process, it is argued, provides too much scope for the interviewer to influence the interviewee's responses, in terms of:

- revealing their own views on the matter;
- the questioning style used;
- the body language displayed;
- the behaviour and conduct throughout the interview.

However, researchers conducting qualitative-based studies can make use of procedures to increase scientific rigour and systemise their general approach. Issues such as observing over multiple sites and the recording of interviews are addressed later in this chapter. There are equally well-established methods for rigorously analysing data that are considered in Chapter 8.

Many qualitative researchers would also counter the criticisms mentioned above by asserting that it is not possible to achieve absolute objectivity in research. To condemn qualitative in-depth interviews in this way is to ignore the reality that all research is subjective. Indeed, quantitative research designs are influenced by the values and assumptions of those who commission and conduct the research in terms of:

- the questions asked (and, by implication, those that are not);
- the target group(s) and setting(s) selected for study;
- the research methods used;
- the methods of analysis that are used;
- the emphasis that is given to certain aspects of the data in the analysis of findings (and, by implication, the downgrading of other data);
- the interpretation given to the data;
- the reporting of the research, in terms of focus, selection and weighting given to different elements of the findings.

## In-depth one-to-one interviewing

Unlike structured interviews, qualitative in-depth, one-to-one interviews are open-ended, using interview schedules or *aide-mémoires*, rather than carefully crafted pre-structured questionnaires. The intention is therefore to capture the point of view of the respondent rather than the concerns of the researcher.

Such in-depth, one-to-one interviews are designed to explore issues in detail with the interviewee, using probes, prompts and flexible questioning styles (both in terms of the ways in which questions are asked and the order in which they are delivered). In many respects, qualitative semi-structured or unstructured interviews are conducted in situations where the researcher's intention is to share control of the data-gathering exercise with the respondent, to allow the respondent to craft her or his own account of the matter in question, rather than to gather highly structured data which can be directly compared to the results from interviews held with others. The use of probes and prompts in qualitative interviews enables the researcher and the respondent to enter into a dialogue about the topic in question. This can be helpful in that the researcher and the respondent are given the opportunity to query questions and answers, and to verify that they have a shared understanding of meaning.

Significant latitude is given to the respondent in the shaping of the interview agenda, and she or he is provided with the opportunity to discuss the topic using the respondent's own frame of reference, own language and own concepts. This is important as one of the major concerns of researchers conducting exploratory research is to uncover issues and concerns that they themselves had perhaps not previously thought of, or had little knowledge of or understanding about. These interviews therefore allow respondents to lead the researcher into exploring relatively uncharted terrain. Using this method, respondents are also encouraged to provide examples in order to ground their narrative. For an example of the questioning strategy used in a qualitative in-depth interview, see Example 7.2.

## Example 7.2 An interview schedule for in-depth, one-to-one interviewing (Weinstein 2005)

As an example of the questioning strategy used in qualitative interviews, consider the interview schedule below. Notice how the questions are written out in full, but unlike structured questionnaires, there are no pre-arranged answers. Instead, prompts and probes are used to encourage the respondent to elaborate, qualify and expand upon their answers, and to provide examples as evidence.

After my own introduction ...

A broad and open invitation for the respondent to tell me a little about their social background and history.

How did you take on/arrive at an activist role in politics? How did you get to where you are now?

- Influence of family or other important individual(s)?
- Sparked by events?

On reflection, do you feel that your involvement in politics was a discrete choice, or was it the outcome of a less conscious set of events/processes?

What motivated you to get active in politics? (Why?)

What motivates you now?

What sort of things do you do now as an activist?

- Types of action/time commitment?
- Sparked by events?

What political goals do you have?

- Policy oriented/personal?
- What is the balance between these?

What has been your experience of being active?

- Good or bad, enjoyable or frustrating?

What makes you positive about what you do? Examples?

What, if anything, makes you feel negative about what you do? Examples?

[ ... Other questions continue]

A related feature of this approach is that interviewers will aim to develop some form of social rapport with respondents: 'In any project involving unstructured interviews, the relationship between the researcher and those who are researched is crucial' (Burgess 1984, p.107). This is considered an essential requirement for this method. First, without such a rapport, it is difficult to convince respondents to participate in the interview, and to talk fully and frankly about the issues addressed. Secondly, many researchers – and in particular feminist researchers – would argue that developing such a relationship, as part of a wider humanist interviewing approach, assists in reducing unequal power relations in the research. Mies (1993, p.68), for example, argues that 'the vertical relationship between researcher and "research objects", the *view from above*, must be replaced by the *view from below*' (original emphasis). Here, interviews are less formal and less structured, and invite the interviewee to take part in setting the agenda. There is also a shared exchange of information, rather than the one-way extraction of data implied (according to critics) by the highly structured (and hierarchical) survey-type quantitative interviewing method (Finch 1993, p.167). Please refer back to Chapter 2 for a fuller discussion of these issues.

Wherever possible, qualitative interviewers will tend to aim to reach agreement with respondents to record the exchange. This serves several purposes. It enables the researcher to capture a full transcript of the interview, which is considerably more difficult when reliant on note-taking. This also frees the researcher to reflect more carefully on the course of the interview – to think about the responses given and to plan the next line of questioning, and also to take reflective notes and comments about issues raised in the interview that might fruitfully be returned to at a later stage. Researchers should also take notes on any interesting non-verbal data, such as body language and any particular episodes or events that occur during the course of the interview that may have a bearing on how the data should be contextualised and understood. Data from tape-recordings can also be open to public inspection by others, providing opportunities for interested peers to scrutinise and either validate or challenge reported findings and interpretations. This will also significantly increase data reliability. Making recordings and full transcripts publicly available also enables others to check that interviews have been conducted in a professional manner, with data that faithfully represents the voices of respondents rather than reflecting the values and biases of a manipulative researcher.

### Activity 7.1 The interview schedule

Design a qualitative interview schedule (for a one-to-one interview) for a subject that is of interest to you in your research. This may be related either to your academic study or to an issue at work or in your community that you would like to address. Write out a clear introductory and explanatory statement that will serve the purpose of 'opening up' the interview. Next, design a series of open-ended questions to address the issue in some depth for a 5–10 minute unstructured interview.

## Focus groups

Qualitative interviews that are held with a group of participants (a focus group) are done so with a different purpose in mind from those held with just one respondent. The central purpose for both is to collect data that accurately reflects the thoughts, feelings and opinions of respondents. However, in focus groups the intention is to stimulate discussion among people and bring to the surface responses that otherwise might lay dormant. Such discussions may enable participants to clarify their views and opinion positions or, on the basis of engaging with others, to articulate more clearly than they otherwise might. The interactive dynamic is therefore considered to be a crucial element of the focus group approach. The interviewer (or moderator) will use a variety of techniques to encourage respondents to debate topics and issues, to challenge opinions expressed by others, to identify areas of consensus and disagreement, and to collect examples with which to illuminate concepts.

The membership of focus groups is usually determined by some shared attribute among participants. This might be an experience, a known opinion position, a socio-demographic characteristic, or some other variable. Thus, some form of theoretical sampling method is used in the selection of focus group membership so that a degree of homogeneity is evident. This is important. Too much difference and heterogeneity and the focus groups may become unwieldy and unmanageable. By contrast, where participants in a particular focus group share an important attribute, it is possible for the researcher to identify shared positions (and areas of disagreement or potential discrepancies) and contrast broad group opinions with those emerging from other focus groups whose membership is based upon an alternative attribute. See Example 7.3.

## Example 7.3 Focus group memberships (from Henn et al. 2002)

In this study of young people's political attitudes, respondents' levels of political engagement were identified through responses to questions asked in a questionnaire. The questionnaire results indicated that there appeared to be two groups holding very different opinions about the way politics operated in Britain – one group that we labelled 'political enthusiasts' and another that we called the 'political sceptics'. We decided to hold separate focus group discussions for each with a view to understanding why these young people held such different views. The questionnaire survey also indicated that views differed according to several other important factors too, and this informed our decisions to hold focus groups with young people who were still in full-time education, those in work, those who had expressed postmaterialist value-positions (such as concerns about the environment and animal rights, anti-militarist positions, and solidarity with people living in developing countries), and a control group comprising a general mix of young people.

In focus groups, the role of moderator is to encourage participants to discuss topics, to challenge opinions expressed by others and to identify shared positions. To stimulate discussion, a variety of data collection methods may be used. Moderators will aim to gauge reactions to specific questions asked from a general topic guide, but may also use sentence completion exercises and visual aids such as show cards, leaflets, newspaper clippings and videos. Example 7.4 gives an example of a focus group interview schedule used in a study investigating young people's views about voting, and makes use of several techniques for this purpose.

## Example 7.4 Extract from focus group schedule (from Henn et al. 2002)

**C. VOTING** **(20 minutes)**

There is growing concern about the decline in the numbers of young people voting.

**SHOW PRESS HEADLINES HERE**

i. Do you think it is important to vote? What makes you say that?

**SENTENCE COMPLETION**

A. Now that I have had an opportunity to vote, I feel …

*(Continued)*

*(Continued)*

**Ask participants to share what they have written, and to talk about it.**

ii. Do you always vote (*if not, why don't you?*)

**SENTENCE COMPLETION**

B. I would be more likely to vote in the future if ...

**Ask participants to share what they have written, and to talk about it.**

iii. Which of the following do you think would encourage you personally to vote?

iv. And which would encourage young people in general to vote?

**SHOW CARDS**

- Allowing voting in supermarkets
- Allowing voting by telephone
- Allowing voting through the Internet
- Campaigns to raise awareness (SHOW 'Stick it in the Box' and 'Rock The Vote' leaflets)
- Making voting compulsory
- Lowering the voting age from 18 to 16
- Forming youth/school councils, etc. (EXPLAIN)

As with one-to-one interviews, focus groups are usually recorded. Participants should not be asked for their consent to this at the meeting itself, in case there are objections which, if not handled carefully, might result in mass abstention by the attendees. Instead, agreement for the recording of the session should be made in advance of the meeting by informing participants about how the session will be conducted.

Where it is possible, an assistant moderator (AS) should be asked to help in the focus groups. The role of the AS is likely to be varied, but will include, for example, ensuring operation of the recording process. It is very easy for the moderator to become so immersed in the focus group discussion that she or he forgets to attend to the recording, and the AS has a crucial role in taking responsibility for such practical matters. If you are able to organise an AS to help in the focus group, you might ask the AS to complete a field note reporting form (see Example 7.5). Here, the AS produces a summary of the focus group discussion and group dynamics. This should include any notable quotes and any terms participants spontaneously use that might be new to the researchers. The AS should also make careful reference to any major events that occur during the course of the discussion, such as expressions of friendship and agreement, noting how participants respond to particular points of view that are expressed – including gestures, facial expressions, posture, and so on. The AS will also aim to make a note of which topics seem to generate particular controversy, or general confusion, or little response from participants. Finally, it is useful if the AS finishes each section of the discussion and the full focus group session itself by providing a summary. The field note reporting form may serve this purpose. By asking for participants' responses to this summary, researchers may verify for the purposes of ensuring data validity that they have captured the full meaning and essence of the discussion. Such summaries also enable the researchers to ask for any final further insights from respondents to clarify and expand upon the data.

## Example 7.5 Field note reporting form (from Henn et al. 2002)

A. MEDIA AND POLITICIANS' VIEWS OF YOUNG PEOPLE'S POLITICS (20 minutes)

| **Brief summary/Notable points** | **Notable quotes** |
|---|---|
| Not informed about politics. Politicians' lack of encouragement of young people. Politics is not accessible, and nor is it inspiring. The media use stereotypes, and some people then conform to this stereotype. This reinforces the media stereotypes. There is a snowballing process. Young people are ignored by politicians, who do not target their communications at youth ...... the language used by politicians is alienating. There is a layer of youth that is apathetic **(lack of agreement here.)** ...... partly this is because people are not sufficiently educated about such matters to understand politics and to then take part in it (i.e., through voting). There is no independent information on the parties – only info *from* the parties, and this is only communicated immediately prior to elections. But it is not only youth who take a battering by the media – people generally are accused of being apathetic politically. | If there is apathy, it's the politicians's (fault) for not telling us enough about politics. All politicians are the same, so does it matter if you don't vote? Politicians only pay an interest in young people when there is an election (there was much agreement here). |

**Comments/Observations**

Focus groups can be difficult to manage. There is always a danger that in seeking to maximise the involvement of all participants in the discussion, some will see this as a signal to exert themselves in an attempt to attain a position of relative dominance to the exclusion of others. The moderator therefore needs to anticipate how to manage such a situation, to skilfully close down dominant talkers and involve all members without offending. There are questioning techniques available for this purpose (see Example 7.6, for instance), but the key to managing the group dynamics of a focus group is to explain the ground rules for the session at the outset, before the discussion has taken place. Here the moderator can explain in advance why she or he may at times need to ask some participants to curtail their contribution to allow others to offer views and observations to maximise the range of views recorded. See Example 7.7 for a description of how to establish the ground rules at the beginning of a focus group session.

### Example 7.6 Some useful questions or phrases (adapted from Krueger 1994)

Keeping to the point:
'That's an interesting point – we'll perhaps talk about that later'

Dominant talkers:
'Thank you X. Are there others who wish to comment on the question?'
'Does anyone feel differently?'
'That's one point of view. Does anyone have another point of view?'

Rambling respondents:
Discontinue eye contact after 15–20 seconds (the Assistant Moderator should do likewise).

Views: intensity and dis/agreement:
'That's a very clear view, now does anyone else agree with that? Why? How strongly do you feel about this?'
'And does anyone disagree with that view? Why? How strongly do you feel about this?'
Or
'Does anyone see it differently? Or, are there any other points of view?'
Sometimes ask the questions in turn to participants

Ending questions:
'All things considered. Suppose you had one minute to say what you considered to be the most important issue facing young people today, and why. What would you say?'
Give periodic summaries (to include all views – including minority ones)

Silence:
Often the best question is no question! Simply waiting for a response allows those who need more time to formulate an answer, or those who are uncertain, to do so.

Probing and prompting:
Try 5-second pauses (coupled with eye contact) after questions – this gives the respondent the opportunity to elaborate or make additional points of view.

Probing:
'Would you explain further? Would you give me an example of what you mean? Would you say more? Is there anything else? Please describe what you mean? I don't understand.'

## Example 7.7 An example introduction to focus group session (from Henn et al. 2002)

1. Welcome. Introductions
2. The purpose for our research
3. You were selected because you have certain things in common (details about the organisation of the focus groups/analytic rationale – 6 groups, and composition of each)
4. Explanation of the recording procedure and what will happen to the recording (prevent need to take notes). **Be brief here and move quickly to...**
5. Statement about confidentiality – first-name basis, but when we write the report, no names will be attached to your comments. **Be brief here and move quickly to...**
6. Purpose of the two Assistant Moderators
7. Incentives paid at start of the session and travel expenses at end
8. No smoking
9. Turn off mobile phones
10. Finish time
11. Rules for participants
    - Make clear that this is a group discussion ...
    - Views of all participants need to be heard – we value (and would like to hear) all views, regardless of how obvious they may seem, or how unusual
    - There are no right or wrong answers, but rather differing points of view. We would like to hear all your views

*(Continued)*

*(Continued)*

- We recognise some will have less to say/be more reluctant to talk than others
- The session is not about argument, but uncovering views/stances and positions/perceptions
- Nevertheless, feel free to elaborate/give examples/contradict the thoughts and views of others

– So please speak up so that we can hear you clearly, and for the tape
– Please don't speak over each other, so let one person speak at a time
– I will play the referee and try to make sure that everyone gets a turn
– So, don't worry about what I think or what your neighbour thinks – we're here to exchange information and have fun while we do it!
– Why don't we begin by introducing ourselves. X, why don't you start, and we'll go around the table and give our names and a little about what we enjoy doing – perhaps a hobby or activity

- **Don't** ask participants if they have questions before we start – this is **very risky**

## Activity 7.2 The focus group schedule

Design a focus group schedule on the same subject that you selected for Activity 7.1. Think about your opening remarks and your 'ground-rule making' and write these out. Think also about how to design a questioning strategy that will engage your participants so that they feel stimulated to contribute fully to the focus group session – you may want to use a variety of questioning techniques and visual aids. Next, design a series of open-ended questions to address the issue in some depth for a 30-minute session.

## Ethnography and observations

Apart from in-depth interviewing and focus groups, the other major method that is used by qualitative researchers is ethnography – study through the observation of institutions, cultures and customs. The researcher will aim to investigate an institution, group or setting that is relatively under-researched and about which relatively little is known. The ethnographic approach is used for this purpose, to inquire systematically about the world people see and to develop theories about the social world. This is an important point to note.

Researchers undertake ethnographic studies to see the world in a new way from the point of view of the people under investigation, not just to confirm their preconceptions about a particular issue or group (or organisation) that they are studying. This involves looking hard at all aspects of what is going on, not picking out one or two events and using them to confirm taken-for-granted views about the nature of the social world. Thus, the ethnographer does not just observe and record the unusual or 'extreme' behaviour, but joins in the everyday activities and life of those who are being studied.

The researcher observes social interaction, and talks informally with group members, aiming to acquire cultural knowledge and identify and make sense of patterns of social interaction in people's natural environment. This style of research is often referred to as 'naturalistic' (Hammersley 1992b, pp.163–5), and assumes that the study of people's behaviour can only be conducted in situations where people do not feel under surveillance. The task of the researcher, therefore, is to observe people in a sensitive and unobtrusive fashion. Usually, this involves spending time in the field so that the researcher gains acceptance among the community that she or he is investigating. As Bernard puts it, 'Hanging out builds trust, and trust results in ordinary conversation and ordinary behaviour in your presence' (1994, p.152). This is important as it helps to create the conditions necessary for both the researcher and the researched to gain a natural closeness and mutual trust that is free of self-consciousness and the dangers of behavioural adaptation that may occur in situations where people feel 'examined' by others. This potential threat to validity – or reactivity – was described earlier in this chapter in the section that reviewed Punch's work with the police in Amsterdam, and is considered in more detail in the pages that follow. On the other hand, where a researcher is drawn too deeply into the group under observation, then validity is threatened by the researcher over-identifying with the group and 'going native'. In situations where this happens, the objectivity of the study may become compromised.

Acquiring acceptance within a community provides the researcher with the potential to become fully appraised of and conversant with the culture in question. It is only when the researcher achieves such a status that *Verstehen* – an empathetic understanding of the lived experiences of people in their natural settings – can be achieved. Thus the researcher, when elevated to insider status, can ask questions for the purposes of gaining understanding and clarification of observed behaviour without fear that people will consider the questions prying and obtrusive, answering in a guarded and suspicious manner. In sharing over time the work and associated experiences of the machine shop workers that he was investigating, Roy (1952) gained an understanding of the norms, codes and culture of the group, and of the subtleties in which these operated. Through such participant observation, he learned the meanings of behaviour and language that an outsider would find difficult to access. Thus, the phrase 'don't rupture yourself' was not issued as a concern that a colleague was in danger of doing himself a physical injury; rather it was a request to work to a pace that conformed to the working patterns of his 'colleagues'. Similarly, Corrigan's acceptance by the 'Smash Street kids' (1979) in his ethnographic study of their life and school experiences enabled him to gain a sensitivity to the field, and an appreciation of the children's codified language and concepts, and of their meaning. It is only through acquiring understanding of such language and concepts that researchers are able to engage in exchanges with group members that are natural and result in *Verstehen*; without such understanding, the researcher is likely to remain an outsider, unable to appreciate fully the subtleties of the language and behaviour of the people in question, and ultimately incapable of fully tracing the cultural practices and world of the people under investigation.

Ethnography refers to more than just the process of observing; it includes holding interviews (either informal 'chats' or in-depth interviews with individuals or in group situations) whenever and wherever appropriate, and may include, for instance, the analysis of documents (such as organisational memoranda or personal documents). The ethnographic approach may also involve the use of quantitative methods, such as questionnaires. For example, in Corrigan's (1979) study of school children, he employed a number of different research methods in unison, including relatively structured questionnaires, qualitative interviews, observations, getting to know the pupils, 'and just plain chatting' (1979, p.14). Thus, the ethnographic researcher is a fieldwork pragmatist, flexible and resourceful in her or his approach to the use of whichever methods and sources of data are at her or his disposal – qualitative or quantitative. The key is to ensure that the research approach is one that is appropriate for the research question and also maximises *Verstehen*.

The main research method associated with ethnography, however, is participant observation. As noted above, participant observation involves the researcher in becoming part of a group or situation that is being studied, although not necessarily as a member of that group. Earlier in this chapter, we saw how Barker (1984) spent a number of years 'living' with the Unification Church, while Punch (1993) participated closely in the day-to-day operations of the Amsterdam policing world. In both of these studies, the researchers adopted an overt approach in their research, in which individuals and relevant organisations were informed that they were being studied. In other studies, researchers may be less open about their role and their purpose in conducting the research, preferring instead to adopt a covert role. For example, Patrick (1973) essentially joined a Glasgow gang in order to build up an understanding of who the members were as well as their motivations for taking part in what was often illegal, and occasionally violent, behaviour. Humphreys (1970) employed a disguised fieldwork role in his study of homosexual liaisons in public conveniences. He used deception by adopting the role of 'watchqueen' lookout so that he could observe the activities of these men. It is important to be both aware of and sensitive to the ethical implications of such covert approaches. Covert participant observation threatens to break important and agreed ethical research conventions. Researchers should pay careful attention to the issues that are raised in Chapter 4, as well as the particular code of conduct governing ethical research practice for their academic discipline or research area.

### Activity 7.3 Ethics and participant observation studies

Look back to Chapter 4, and if necessary consult the ethical code of practice for your general field. Make a list of the ethical conventions that might be threatened by adopting a covert participant observation approach, and for each, explain briefly why you are drawing this conclusion. Are there any circumstances under which you think that adopting a covert approach might be justified? If so, think of some examples.

When conducting ethnographic studies using participant observation, the researcher is confronted by several practical questions. One of the most important decisions open to the researcher is selection of a site for study. Owing to time and resource constraints, observations are often limited to only one or a small number of research sites, and as such the researcher should consider taking steps to ensure that this/these are typical of the many such settings available for study. The researcher will often find several possibilities, and the decision should be driven largely by the anticipated richness of data that particular sites offer. Beyond this, as an ethnographer, you should choose a setting that is relatively easier than others to gain access to, although preferably one that is not familiar, where you have no particular knowledge or expertise and where you are most open to record the unexpected. As Neuman states, '[i]t is easier to see cultural events and social relationships in a new site' (2006, p.386).

Having selected a site for study, the researcher needs to gain physical and social access. Physical access refers to the process through which the researcher is able actually to enter the site. This may involve the participant observer seeking permission from a gatekeeper to enter a particular setting, such as a school or a hospital, and may require some negotiation. Inevitably, there are political consequences in any such negotiation, and the researcher may have to cede some power and control over the research process – and may be required to compromise some aspect of the proposed research strategy.

Social access requires the researcher to gain a vantage point through which she or he can view the world as it is seen from the perspective of the people being studied. Having physical access to a site is one thing, but if particular aspects of the life-world under investigation are kept secret from the researcher by a suspicious community, then the data acquired will at best represent only a partial account of the real world of the culture or organisation. It is imperative, for the sake of *Verstehen*, that the researcher gains acceptance within the community and the trust of its members. Securing the support of a gatekeeper may help in achieving social access – unless the gatekeeper is viewed with suspicion by the community.

Finally, there is the stage of recording the behaviour and events that form the basis of the research data. The ethnographer will aim to record data from her or his observations in the form of field notes. These will be descriptive accounts of what has been seen and heard, reflective analytic notes that focus on themes and patterns that emerge from the data, and also methodological observations such as ethical issues and field strategies. In general, researchers should aim to take full field notes immediately after an observation session has been completed. Such notes should include details about the settings (perhaps maps or diagrams of rooms where the action has been observed), events, people's behaviour and talk. Notes will usually be recorded chronologically with full details about the date and time of the observed actions. They may also include initial impressions and thoughts about the fieldwork session as well as interpretations and analytic observations. See Example 7.8 for a sample of full field notes taken from a study of change in a small family business by Fletcher (1997).

## Example 7.8 Full field notes

**Field/observation note from April 5th, 1995**

Darren [General Manager] and Rob [Workshop Manager] were pulled into Lenny's [Managing Director] office for a telling off about profits being down. It seems this month the business had a turnover of £170,000 but they made a loss of £2,000. Anyway, Darren took this on the chin because, according to Darren, Lenny 'throws these wobblies from time to time', but then he was hauled back in again after he had just been down to xx to get some new business. This time, Darren was so annoyed and we heard him shout, 'Have you finished?' and then he left the room and went straight home. The next day Darren told Lenny that 'he was well out of order' and Lenny apologised. Lenny also apologised to Rob but Rob said, 'Don't worry about me, it is Darren who is thinking of leaving'. And Lenny was shook up by this.

**Field/observation note from April 30th, 1995**

The girl from maternity leave (Anne) is back but this has caused some concern for Jane and Carole because they have been job sharing the receptionist role. Now Anne has come back (the girls were hoping she wouldn't), this means that Jane will have to go back to a clerical role and Carole is no longer needed. Apparently, Carole burst into tears this morning when she was told this. I was sitting in Darren's office when Carole came in and sat down. Darren explained to her that things would not last forever and that changes were afoot. What this means is that Steve is going upstairs (into accounts) and that Anne has been asked to take his job, which means Jane and Carole can both stay on reception. But Darren tells her not to say anything. Later I go into the reception and Jane tells me something is afoot upstairs because Anne has been called in to see the Financial Controller. She is dying to know what is going on and tries to quiz me to see if I know.

At times it might not be feasible to take full notes as the action takes place, particularly when to do so might draw attention to your role as a researcher and result in people adapting their behaviour if they feel self-conscious. Given that the purpose of such field observation studies is to record natural behaviour, such reactivity would undermine the whole process and contaminate the field data. In such circumstances, the researcher will need to devise strategies for taking jotted notes in more surreptitious ways, such as short trigger prompts and key terms that can be expanded upon at a more convenient time as soon as possible after the close of the fieldwork session. Lofland and Lofland refer to these as comprising 'little phrases, quotes, key words, and the like' (1995, p.90). The threat to validity that derives from this method of recording observations is that data may be lost in the process if the researcher is unable to recall important events and actions.

## Conducting qualitative research online

In the previous chapter we discussed the ways in which the Internet has opened up various possibilities for conducting online surveys. The long-standing association that computer technology has had with processing numerical information hints at why the uptake of online methods by survey researchers is unsurprising. The Internet also offers a rich visual and textual universe, however, and therefore provides an easily accessible source of qualitative data. It has also had a large impact on how we communicate and interact with one another, and so forms a topic of interest to social researchers in its own right. Before discussing some of the issues that are particularly relevant to online qualitative research, it is worthwhile revisiting the methods already discussed and to consider how they might be enacted online, beginning with interviews and focus groups.

There are a large variety of ways in which exchanges take place online, either on a one-to-one basis or in groups. People use the Internet to send messages to one another all the time, but also communicate in groups by posting on discussion boards or in chat rooms. Dolowitz et al. (2008) identify three broad categories of technology which can be utilised for research interviews: email, instant messaging or video-conferencing. Although the latter might require specific hardware (web-cams, microphones and speakers) and software, email and instant messaging are more freely available to researchers and participants. We would add to this list the use of discussion boards and specialist software for conducting online focus groups.

Which technology is adopted will depend partly on whether an interview or focus group is required, but also on considerations of immediacy. Online communication does not always take place in real-time. In fact, much of it takes place over protracted periods of time. Email, for example, requires that we compose a message, send it and await a response. Discussion boards often begin with a single message, with replies posted over a series of days, weeks or even months. Such communication is described as 'asynchronous', and is to be differentiated from 'synchronous' communication, such as that which happens in chat rooms and in some instant messaging systems. With these systems, text can be seen by other participants as it is being typed or as soon as the enter key is hit, and it requires that participants are online at the same time.

The implications for adopting a synchronous or asynchronous method can be far-reaching. On the one hand, synchronous exchanges can mirror more closely the natural flow of conversations that take place in traditional face-to-face exchanges. However, unless video-conferencing is used, the time taken to type messages means that even synchronous communication can never really happen in the same natural, flowing way of a spoken interchange, as Davis et al. (2004, p.947) discovered in their study of HIV sufferers, which utilised both synchronous online and offline interviewing techniques (FTF refers to 'face-to-face'):

> Online interviews in the synchronous mode are slow. In our study, they took about twice the length of FTF interviews and produced far fewer words. For example, a 120-minute online interview produced about seven pages of text. A 90-minute FTF interview produced 30 to 40 pages of text. The exchange of questions and responses was clearly influenced by the reading, reflection and typing skills of the respondents. In some exchanges, quite some time elapsed before a response appeared, sometimes as a result of computer crashes.

Synchronous communication is clearly difficult to effectively maintain, whereas when using asynchronous communication, participants do not have to remain logged on for continuous periods of time in which the interview must be achieved, and technical proficiency and typing skill are less of a problem. Asynchronous communication can also afford other benefits, as Seymour (2001, p.152) discovered when making use of a discussion board for her research with disabled participants:

> Although unable to conduct real-time interviews, it seemed that the advantages ... clearly outweighed the disadvantages. Participants could enter and re-enter the site as often as they wished, enabling them to extend on a particular topic, to delete or qualify a point, or to clarify their responses over time. The evolution and development of the communication could be traced by reading each message in a threaded discussion. In contrast to the single scheduled interview of much traditional qualitative research, it is clear that this facility offered participants a much more generous opportunity to express their views and to influence the research outcomes.

The way in which disabled people make use of information technology was actually the central topic of Seymour's research, and by conducting interviews which took place over several weeks, she was able to maximise the involvement of disabled people in the research. This is very much in accord with the emancipatory disability research discussed in Chapter 2, and also reflects how asynchronous online interviewing offers not just an alternative to the face-to-face interview, but an extension of it, allowing for lengthy consideration of responses and detailed probing.

One might question the lack of spontaneity in the responses given during asynchronous interviews, and it may well be that enabling participants several days to contemplate a response to a question results in very different, 'unnatural' data, but the practicalities of synchronous communication do present certain difficulties which are altogether compounded when conducting online focus groups.

Focus groups are usually conducted online either by posting a message on a discussion board, to which the group members have been given exclusive access, by group email or by specialist software. One potential disadvantage of using specialist software is that it may require each member to download it, although some systems make use of web-based interfaces, which can be accessed by visiting a particular web page and logging in. Focus group software tends to present a screen consisting of a number of windows. Individuals type their contributions in one window, while the text responses from the whole group appear as they are typed in another larger window. Usually, the moderator has additional privileges which might include being able to block certain members from contributing or to send messages to individual members, which are unseen by the rest of the group. An alternative is to set up a private chat room, using any one of the widely available web-based chat sites, and provide participants with permission to access the room. Synchronous systems enable focus groups to take place in a way that encourages the spontaneous generation of ideas, as one would usually wish for, but they can be difficult to manage.

> Regardless of system, real-time focus groups can be fast, furious and highly interactive. You need not wait for others to comment in order to send further messages. The participant who is more proficient in typing is the one with the 'power' to 'say' the most. Important questions which need to be asked here include: who is replying to whom? Is the term 'reply' of relevance at all? In the real-time chat of an online focus group, the distinction between replying and sending becomes blurred as the interactivity defies conversational turn-taking. (Mann and Stewart 2000, p.102)

As technology develops, video-conferencing hardware and software is becoming more widely available, and this would seem like the best way of overcoming problems associated with typing speed and technical difficulties. However, this still requires that participants have the requisite set-up at their end in order for it to work successfully. At present, there appears to be more talk of the future possibilities that video-conferencing might offer than its actual use in qualitative research. There may even be a preference for sticking with text-based communication, since one of the great advantages is that it cuts down on the need to transcribe after the event. There is also a large debate around the additional anonymity afforded by text-based communication, which we shall return to later in this chapter. First, though, we shall turn to a method which raises a number of questions about whether what happens online constitutes 'real' behaviour – that of online observation.

## Observing 'virtual' behaviour

People have been logging on to computer networks and communicating with one another as virtual communities since the mid-1980s (Rheingold 2000). In those early days, virtual communities consisted of a network of people who shared information about themselves with one another through text-based exchanges. Nowadays, with the advent of Web 2.0 technology, virtual communities have become far more interactive, involving a lot of multimedia content. Social networking sites such as *Facebook* and *Myspace* are now two of the most popular Internet sites in the world (Murthy 2008), with millions of users logging on and interacting with each other. Although the technology has changed, one of the core principles of virtual communities has not – they involve a collection of people who come together because of a common interest or connection. This is no different from a 'real' community, whether it be one which is imposed because of geographical proximity, such as a village community, or one which is brought together because of common interests, such as a local camera club. The transition from offline to online represents a change in 'space', from real to virtual, and alongside it a change in the manner in which exchanges are conducted, but not necessarily a reduction in the *range* of communal activities that, for a social researcher, can be extremely informative. Activities can be, very broadly, split into two types: informative and interactive. Informative activities include those which are intended to present a piece of information about the individual to others in the community, whereas interactive activities involve sharing experiences.

Social networking sites, for example, enable people to create online identities. *Myspace* users can customise the look of their pages with a wide range of backgrounds and colours. *Facebook* enables the inclusion of myriad applications which appear in boxes on users' pages, enabling them to show, for example, which books they are currently reading, who their favourite bands are, or where they have travelled in the world. These activities can be seen as replicating the things we do in the real world and are designed to provide a glimpse into our personality, such as choosing the clothes we wear, playing certain songs at a party, or reciting tales of holiday adventures. In the three-dimensional, graphical worlds of online gaming, such as *World of Warcraft*, and online communities, such as *Second Life*, users can go a step further and create 'avatars' (graphical representations of their online selves), which can be customised to their liking.

Interactive activities largely involve textual communication, which can be carried out in private or public spaces, just as real conversations might happen privately or publicly. Other activities involve playing games with others online, or joining particular specialist groups. One particular group on *Facebook* runs a weekly photography competition, in which anyone who joins the group can participate. Each week a different topic is set, and members can post photos on the site. Other members can then vote for their preferred photo and offer feedback. This concept is extended on the specialist site *Flickr*, which is solely dedicated to the sharing of photographs and discussion of photographic issues. It is probably the largest camera club in the world, and it all takes place online, but the basic concept is no different from that which underpins the local camera club which has regular meetings in a town hall.

The graphical communities of online gaming and virtual worlds enable people to arrange meetings in virtual places, perhaps to visit virtual art galleries, go to virtual concerts or simply sit down on the virtual grass and chat.

From an ethnographer's point of view, social networking sites and virtual communities offer us insights into how people shape their identities, how they interact with one another, and importantly, how they shape their environment. Bardzell and Odom (2008) highlight the way in which a virtual space, just like a real space, lacks meaning or connection until people make it their own. A 'space' then becomes a 'place'. The ways in which users can define their place in virtual worlds, by customising layouts or even selecting furniture for a virtual house, tells us something about how people construct meaningful lived experiences.

It would seem that, by logging on to a social networking site, joining a virtual community, or instigating an online discussion or email exchange, we are able to collect a vast amount of qualitative data. One question that must be asked of all online exchanges is: to what extent is a virtual exchange representative of the real self? Another question which might be asked is: does it matter? Some researchers are specifically interested in how people construct online identities, as separate from, or intertwined with, their offline identities. Even if the online component of our research is merely perceived as a data collection tool, rather than a topic of interest in its own right, it is still important to ask whether online communication differs significantly from offline interaction since so often the validity of qualitative research rests on obtaining 'truthful' accounts.

We have already highlighted the importance of observing visual cues such as body language and developing rapport during interviews. When our interviews consist of a text-only exchange, or we are observing a collection of pixels on a screen, to what extent is this possible? Social presence theory, first developed by Short et al. (1976), suggests that during communication, the extent to which we sense an intelligent presence is affected by our physical and psychological relationship with one another during the exchange, which can in turn be affected by the communication medium. In a face-to-face setting, the choice of room layout, proximity to one another, body language and facial expressions can all affect the extent to which we are able to develop rapport. The lack of visual cues in an online, text-based interview can result in little presence being felt, which can then impact upon the development of rapport and trust. However, a lack of cues can also have a liberating effect.

Walther (1996) notes that during communication we seek to create as full a picture of the person with whom we are communicating as possible. Combined with an inherent desire to present the most positive image of ourselves as possible, a two-way process of 'hyperpersonal' communication begins, in which we selectively edit the information about ourselves that we divulge, while at the same time emphasising the importance of particular pieces of information that others have shared with us. The net result of this can be that identities are created which may emphasise certain characteristics while hiding others. For some, who may find it difficult to interact in a face-to-face environment because of low self-esteem, impaired speech or concerns about physical appearance, for example, online communication can therefore provide a valuable alternative for interviewing people who are introverted for whatever reason.

If online communication is affected by a lack of social presence and susceptible to the creation of artificial identities, how does this leave the ethnographer interested in studying relationships? Should we be wary about assuming we can analyse online interactions as substitutes for face-to-face observations? It would seem that there are less tangible qualities to relationships which are not dependent upon face-to-face connection:

> [O]ne of the strongest and most compelling components of social connecting is the perception of a connection in a person's *mind*. Even social connections initiated in face-to-face interaction endure periods of separation – often long periods – in which the connectors are physically apart. (Chayko 2002, p.3)

That the *perception* of a connection is considered more important than the physicality of it might suggest that whether an interaction is played out in the physical world or in the virtual one becomes a redundant issue. For qualitative researchers who are seeking to understand how people interpret their lived experiences, the place in which those experiences occur is arguably less important. Barzell and Odom (2008) conducted a six-month observation of a community in *Second Life*, which specifically set out to recreate a fictional world originally created in a 1970s fantasy novel. The world features dominant-submissive roles and a very clearly defined class structure, and is recreated both visually and structurally in terms of users adopting particular roles. Clearly, such a community marks a departure from the lived experiences of the users outside *Second Life*. Nevertheless, it still constitutes a place, albeit a virtual one, in which meaning is derived from social interaction. As online social places become a larger part of people's lives, they will undoubtedly become a more important topic for investigation for the ethnographer.

In discussing online quantitative research in the previous chapter, we focused on the online medium as a tool for administration. For the qualitative researcher, new technologies offer both useful tools and also intriguing topics for investigation. When using online research techniques, all of the issues that are discussed in the following section apply, but issues of communication, meaning and identity must also be given additional consideration. The practical issues of access to a large pool of data, reduction in transcription time, and increased participation by excluded groups offer very attractive advantages. However, conducting qualitative research online is not merely a matter of transposing conventional techniques to the online world; it requires the exploration of a whole new set of methodological and ontological issues.

## Issues in conducting qualitative research studies

There are a number of issues of central concern to practising qualitative researchers that must be addressed if the findings from such research studies are to be considered credible – and taken seriously – by readers.

### Validity

Perhaps the most critical of these is whether or not the results from a qualitative research study accurately reflect the phenomenon under investigation.

Validity concerns the extent to which observations and/or in-depth interviews achieve a close approximation to the 'truth' of a particular matter, whether that be respondents' views or their actions and whether or not 'the researcher is calling what is measured by the right name' (Kirk and Miller 1986, p.69). Validity can be threatened in a number of ways, including 'reactivity', 'subjectivity' and 'going native'.

### *Reactivity*

People may consciously or unconsciously alter the way they behave or modify what they say if they are aware that they are being researched. This will most likely be the case if the researcher is studying a sensitive area. For instance, in a study of working relationships within an organisation, people observed may adjust their normal method of communicating with their colleagues, as well as their approach to them, if they are conscious that they are being observed. If this issue is not addressed, then it is likely to invalidate the data that you generate. The workplace relations that you record will not therefore be real-world ones; instead, they will be those that the workers want you to witness.

One approach that might be used in an attempt to reduce this effect is to develop a rapport with those whom you are studying and, in so doing, gain their trust. This requires investing considerable time and energy in your research, to develop an understanding with the research participants that they have nothing to fear from revealing their world to you. In her studies of clergymen's wives and of females running and using playgroups, Finch (1993, pp.167–74) discusses the process involved in developing 'an identification' and a 'relationship' with the participants in her in-depth interviews. Punch (1993, pp.188–9) recalls the long and arduous process through which he developed such a rapport with the Dutch police:

> When the chance arose, I showed willingness to help. Sometimes this meant clearing up the canteen, making coffee, helping with English-speaking suspects or 'customers' asking about something at the counter, giving a hand to load a damaged motor-bike into a van, sweeping glass off the road after an accident, searching a house, helping to lift a drunk off the street, and fetching take-away meals.

### *Subjectivity*

Inevitably, the incidents and aspects of behaviour (in participant observation studies) or the views and experiences (in qualitative interviews) focused upon will be determined by what the researcher considers to be significant and worthy of study. The following elements of a qualitative research study are all governed by the choices made by the researcher, and to a great extent are the products of the researcher's preconceptions and existing knowledge:

- the setting selected;
- the people studied;
- what is recorded and what is filtered out;
- the interpretations given to the data.

The researcher should be prepared to justify carefully the decisions taken with respect to all of these features of a qualitative research project. Not to do so would leave the researcher open to criticism from readers, both that the research design is subjective and that the results should not be taken seriously.

### *Going native*

There are obvious dangers with qualitative research (particularly with participant observation, which will often take place over a prolonged period of time) that the researcher will develop too empathetic a view of a group studied through too close an identification with them. In such cases, this is likely to lead to a bias in the observations made and the interviews conducted, particularly in relation to the interpretations given to the data constructed. In such cases, 'going native' will present a distorted picture of the situation researched, or at the very least an uncritical position taken of the individuals (or group or organisation) examined.

## Reliability

When judged by the standards of reliability, qualitative research is often criticised both for lacking structure and system, and for an inability of researchers using this approach to generalise beyond a small number of cases. To respond to such concerns, Silverman (2005) has advocated an approach in which the qualitative research process should be systematised, with all field notes and procedures documented so that other researchers may inspect them and, if necessary, repeat the research to check for accuracy.

Generalisability matters are considered to be problematic in small-scale qualitative research. Some qualitative researchers would claim that generalisability should not be considered a standard against which the credibility of a research study should be assessed:

> For researchers doing (qualitative) work of this sort, the goal is to describe a specific group in detail and to explain the patterns that exist, certainly not to discover general laws of human behaviour. (Ward Schofield 1993, p.201)

However, notwithstanding this defence of qualitative research, Peräkylä (in Silverman 2004) argues that as case studies accumulate in a particular topic area, comparisons may be made to look for similarities and patterns in these varieties of settings. As a body of common trends and insights emerges, it may then be possible to generalise such observations to other settings, situations and cases.

Furthermore, some would argue that the concept of generalisability should be conceptualised differently for qualitative research studies: 'generalisability (for qualitative researchers) is best thought of as a matter of the "fit" between the situation studied and others to which one might be interested in applying the concepts and conclusions of that study' (Ward Schofield 1993, p.221).

## Access

Often the researcher will have to negotiate access to the setting or people to be researched with a number of gatekeepers. For instance, a study of bullying at school may involve the researcher engaging in lengthy discussions and negotiations with a particular local education authority, the school governors, the headteacher, heads of departments, schoolteachers, parents, and the pupils themselves. The likelihood is that the researcher may need to compromise the research questions and/or general methodological approach in order to gain permission from these actors to conduct the research.

However, this issue of political constraint is one that confronts both quantitative and qualitative research studies.

## Ethics

This is a particularly important issue in qualitative research where there is significant potential for misleading people, pretending to be genuinely interested, using contacts to gain confidential information, betraying confidences, and consequentiality. While physical harm may not be intended within a research design, psychological harm may arise at any time through the investigation of sensitive issues that may induce stress or anxiety.

The researcher must take whatever steps necessary to ensure that ethical conventions are not broken, respecting both those who participate in the study as well as new generations of researchers whose tasks may be made all the more arduous if earlier researchers have damaged relationships in the field through insensitive and ethically unsound practice.

## Reflexivity

One way of addressing these issues is to keep a rolling 'critical log' or 'reflexive diary' for all aspects of the research process, including:

- your values and assumptions, and the ways in which you observe that they may be impacting upon the research;
- the choices you make in the research (and your reasons for doing so);
- the strategies you develop in the course of the research;
- the various roles that you adopt;
- the relationships with the people you observe;

- any evidence of reactivity;
- the context of data collection (physical, social and temporal) that you think may affect the data gathered;
- the processes of gaining access to the research field, the negotiations you make along the way, and the impact that this has on your initial research design and plans.

Henwood and Pidgeon (1993, pp.24–5) state that:

> Naturalistic research acknowledges the ways in which research activity *inevitably* shapes and constitutes the objective of inquiry; the researcher and researched are characterised as interdependent in the social process of research.

According to this view, research is not a neutral and impartial activity, and researchers should document their role in the research process: 'In building up such a set of documents the researcher is laying a "paper-trail" open up to external audit' (Henwood and Pidgeon 1993, p.25).

## Summary

In this chapter, we have seen that the logic of qualitative research is to explore the meanings that people have of the world around them. This research approach favours small-scale but detailed and intensive study of the lives of people as they are really lived. As a consequence, the researchers' objective in using this style of research is to construct an understanding of the social world from the point of view of those whom they are examining.

This emphasis on exploration contrasts with the quantitative logic of research that espouses explanation – a scientific approach which aims to identify which social facts are causally connected to the phenomenon under investigation. With the qualitative model of research, a researcher will usually aim to enter the field of inquiry with a relatively open search for meaning; she or he will eschew the use of highly structured a priori research questions in favour of an approach in which the researcher will search for questions, issues and concepts that are important to the people or group being studied.

The methods that qualitative researchers tend to use are varied in character, ranging from in-depth personal or group interviews through to participant observation. The defining characteristic of these and other qualitative research methods is that when compared to quantitative methods they are relatively unstructured. Perhaps just as importantly in understanding what is meant by a qualitative research approach is that it uses methods and sources of data flexibly. So while the methods mentioned above are those that are arguably most commonly used in qualitative research studies, researchers working in this tradition are likely to use whatever other sources of data (such as minutes of meetings) or methods (including highly structured questionnaires) they consider are likely to assist them in their quest for understanding and meaning.

There are a number of issues that researchers must consider when using a broadly qualitative research approach if they are to convince readers and fellow professionals and academics that the findings from their study are credible and plausible. Chiefly, these concern issues to do with validity, access, ethics and reflexivity.

## Chapter research task

### Exercise 1 Qualitative interview task

Design a qualitative, interview-based study on a topic of your choice. Produce an interview guide that focuses on this topic and that is sufficient for an interview of about 30 minutes in length. In addition:

1. Think about how you would identify your target population, justify why you intend to focus on this group, and explain how the thoughts you obtain from them are likely to be especially interesting for your chosen research area.
2. Discuss (and justify) your selection method for including members of this group in your study.
3. Describe how you would go about 'finding' members of this group.
4. Suggest a suitable setting for the interview.
5. Explain any access, logistical or ethical issues for such a study.

#### *How to do this exercise*

1. Write down several questions addressing your intended research for the project, including a standard project explanation (a general statement of the research issues that you can say to the respondent to get things going).
2. Using this guide, conduct an intensive 'pilot' interview with one person from your target group.
3. Make any brief notes during the interview.
4. Check the accuracy of your notes with the 'respondent' – make a separate note of any changes that were suggested to you (perhaps the respondent suggested some inaccuracy in your notes, or perhaps you over- or under-emphasised the respondent's views in some way?).
5. Write the notes up into full notes for a complete record of the interview immediately afterwards.
6. Write up 1–2 sides of reflexive notes about the research process itself. What skills did you manage well and which need improvement? What were your experiences of interviewing, and the accuracy of your original brief notes? How good were you at listening (you should aim for 80–90% of the talk to come from the respondent)?
7. Try some provisional coding (see Chapter 8).
8. Identify any questions that were not particularly relevant as well as new questions that you would like to include in the next interview.

### Exercise 2 Observation task

Do a two-hour observation in a public setting of your choice. Make jottings (short notes). Write up the expanded field notes on 3–4 sides of paper. Write up 1–2 sides of reflexive notes about the research process itself. Try some provisional coding.

Identify 3–4 questions you would take back for the next session of fieldwork. Identify an issue of social research that might be followed up in the research.

### *How to do this exercise*

Observation is all about description – it is a story in a sense. The writing of an observation contains several basic things:

- What was the setting for the observation – the place(s) and buildings which frame the action within?
- How did you gain access?
- What was your role there?
- Who was there?
- What were they doing and/or saying and how did they say it?

But there is also a significant amount of interpretation and analysis of what you observe. You will need to make sense of the data, by asking:

1. What sort of categories can these be placed into (e.g. issues of gender, race, education, anger, love, relations with public figures, humour, etc.)? Here you are involved in coding the action.
2. You may want to search for common themes or patterns in the behaviour you observe.
3. And ultimately you will want to construct some sort of theory to account for the action you have observed.

Issues to consider and questions to ask in conducting a participant observation study

- Outline the focus and context of your study.
- What was your role?
- What did you actually do in the course of your participant observation study? (What was your strategy? How did you gain access? Did you need to develop a relationship with the people that you were studying?)
- How did you record your data? (Do you consider that you were rigorous? Did the field place limitations on your method of data collection?)
- What did you think about the nature of your data? Think about issues of credibility, subjectivity, reliability, validity.
- Consider issues of reactivity, over-identification and ethics.
- Is observation an impartial activity?
- What about using other sources of complementary/alternative data in this research?
- If you made a provisional analysis of your data, what were the coding themes that you used?
- What general area of social research would you investigate further?
- What questions would you focus on in any subsequent research?
- What might you do next time to improve the research (if indeed you think that it could be improved)?

## Recommended Reading

Bryman, A. 1988. *Quantity and Quality in Social Research*. London: Sage.

Burgess, R.G. 1982. *Field Research: A Sourcebook and Field Manual*. London: Allen and Unwin.

Fielding, N. 2008. Ethnography. In: N. Gilbert (ed.), *Researching Social Life*, 3rd edn. London: Sage. pp.266–84.

Fielding, N. and Thomas, R. 2008. Qualitative Interviewing. In: N. Gilbert (ed.), *Researching Social Life*, 3rd edn. London: Sage. pp.245–65.

Hammersley, M. and Atkinson, P. 1995. *Ethnography: Principles in Practice*, 2nd edn. London: Routledge.

Henn, M., Weinstein, M. and Wring, M. 2002. A Generation Apart? Youth and Political Participation in Britain, *The British Journal of Politics and International Relations*, 4 (2), 167–92.

Krueger, R.A. 1994. *Focus Groups: A Practical Guide for Applied Research*. Thousand Oaks, CA: Sage.

Mason, J. 2002. *Qualitative Researching*, 2nd edn. London: Sage.

Silverman, D. 2004. *Qualitative Research: Theory, Method and Practice*, 2nd edn. London: Sage.

Silverman, D. 2005. *Doing Qualitative Research: A Practical Handbook*, 2nd edn. London: Sage.

Ward Schofield, J. 1993. Increasing the Generalisability of Qualitative Research. In: M. Hammersley (ed.), *Social Research: Philosophy, Politics and Practice*. London: Sage. pp.200–25.

# EIGHT

# The Analysis of Data

- To define what is meant by quantitative and qualitative data
- To situate different types of data within the positivist/interpretivist debate
- To provide guidance on ways of effectively organising and managing research data
- To highlight the distinction between the goals of qualitative and quantitative analysis
- To introduce readers to the processes of quantitative data analysis
- To examine fundamental techniques employed in quantitative data analysis
- To introduce readers to a variety of approaches to qualitative data analysis
- To investigate the issues which arise when combining methods at the analysis stage



## Introduction

As we have seen, social research has often been characterised by a number of apparent dichotomies: quantitative and qualitative methods, positivist and anti-positivist epistemologies, objective and subjective accounts. A discussion of data in social research inevitably continues along similarly polarised lines; you will often hear of the distinction between numerical and non-numerical data. This is, however, somewhat misleading. To begin with, a great deal of data that are analysed in a quantitative manner exist in a non-numerical format. A survey questionnaire will occasionally contain questions which are designed to collect raw numerical data: 'How many children do you have?' is just one example. More often than not, however, survey questionnaires make use of questions designed to elicit textual responses: 'To what extent do you agree or disagree with the following statement?' will generate a tick against a phrase such as 'strongly agree'. This data collection method therefore produces non-numerical data, although this kind of survey method is often associated with statistical analysis. On the other hand, non-numerical data are not always analysed using qualitative techniques. We could take a newspaper article which reports on economic downturn and count up the number of references to the global economy. We could then compare this to the frequency with which issues relating to personal finances, such as mortgages, occur. We would be quantifying textual references to global and local economic issues, and this might allow us to say something about the perspective of the newspaper article.

So it would seem that the terms 'quantitative' and 'qualitative' become problematic when applied to data. In truth, very little social science data begin life in a quantitative format, but qualitative data are often treated in such a way as to allow for quantification and the application of statistical techniques. For this reason, when identifying 'types' of data, it is probably more accurate to consider the type of analysis to which they will be subjected:

1. Analysis of data using quantitative techniques.
2. Analysis of data using qualitative techniques.

Treatments of data tend to follow the patterns determined by methodological and epistemological assumptions, although, as we shall see, this does not necessarily fall neatly into a quantitative/qualitative divide. Quantitative data analysis techniques – whether they approximate simple counting exercises or advanced statistical modeling – do, however, tend to rest upon a faith in the ability of structured measures to represent an objective account of social reality. Qualitative analysis techniques, even those which are very structured, tend to accept that data represent an interpretation of meanings which have to be analysed using a more contextual approach. For instance, when coding an interview transcript, a researcher will often read through the entire transcript and interpret various segments of the interview on the basis of what else has been said, the tone of voice, or other notes taken during the interview.

For ease of organisation, we have divided this chapter into separate accounts of quantitative and qualitative analysis. In approaching each, we will begin by exploring important data management considerations, which must be addressed in the collection process, before examining alternative ways of preparing data for analysis. Following on from this, we shall discuss a range of analytical techniques, while addressing some of the broad underlying principles of dealing with different types of data. At this stage, the intention is to introduce you to a variety of what we consider to be the most commonly used analytical techniques in social research. Most of the techniques we have included have an entire body of literature dedicated to them, and in this chapter, our intention is to provide you with a succinct overview of each rather than a comprehensive examination. However, it is hoped that by the end of this chapter, you will be able to:

- differentiate between types of data;
- manage and prepare data in ways that will improve the validity of your analysis;
- have sufficient knowledge to be able to identify appropriate means of analysis;
- have a broad understanding of the processes involved in applying different techniques;
- have a good idea of the key issues you will face in carrying out analysis.

For those who wish to pursue analytical techniques further, a selection of recommended readings are provided at the end of the chapter.

The chapter finishes by tackling the contentious question of how to bring qualitative and quantitative methods together at the stage of analysis. For many, this is an insurmountable task which calls into question one's philosophical perspective as well as a host of practical issues. However, increasingly, researchers are beginning to see the benefits of mixing qualitative and quantitative approaches, and also that using a variety of data sources can be an effective way of increasing the validity of research. We shall conclude by suggesting that the challenges presented by combining qualitative and quantitative data provide a good opportunity for the researcher to reflect upon their own perspectives – and perhaps overcome the divide that is traditionally considered to exist between these data types.

## Preparing data for quantitative analysis

The collection of data in quantitative research will usually require some form of measurement by using indicators. These indicators might be scales or response categories on a research instrument (such as a questionnaire or schedule). The process will usually involve inputting the data into a computer analysis program such as SPSS. More frequently, however, we are seeing the automation of data entry, by using online techniques which involve either the interviewer or respondent entering the data directly into a computer software package or a website. The entries are then sent directly to a computer database. Quite often nowadays, particularly in large research organisations, these steps are combined through a process of computer-assisted personal interviewing (CAPI), whereby the traditional paper questionnaire is replaced by a laptop computer running software which presents an electronic version of the questionnaire on screen for the interviewer to read off. Similarly, in experimental research, computers are often available on site in laboratories, and so data can be entered directly into analysis software. There are also a number of companies who offer online survey services, where a questionnaire or schedule can be constructed as a website, allowing respondents to enter the data directly from anywhere in the world. The increasing availability of online survey services means that even small-scale projects can make use of this technology. The reliability of online surveys, and the validity of the data which they produce, has been discussed in Chapter 6, and you are advised to revisit these points if you are planning to analyse any data collected by these means, since the issues have implications for the methods of analysis that you may employ.

Despite all of these technological advances, it is still likely that, particularly when carrying out a small-scale project, we find ourselves having to rely upon the traditional method of collecting data on a paper research instrument. This inevitably leads to a large collection of paperwork, all of which will have to be managed, while data are transferred to a computer. With this in mind, one point which is often overlooked is the need to be able to trace back responses entered on a computer to the corresponding questionnaire or schedule. So giving each case a unique number and recording this on both the questionnaire and in the computer data set is vital, in the event that checks need to be made or data are lost or damaged.

In addition to the practicalities of managing large quantities of data, there is a lot of work involved in ensuring that the indicators that we are using are compatible with our research questions, and are measured in such a way as to enable quantification. This process begins at the research design and data collection stage.

As we have already seen in Chapter 6, the methods employed in quantitative research seek to gather data using standardised measures. The two most common of these methods, the survey and the experiment, have already been discussed, although Bryman (1988, p.12) notes three further techniques which, while less common, should not be overlooked. The first of these consists of the secondary analysis of official statistics, such as government spending or recorded crime figures. Secondly, there is structured observation, whereby the researcher records observations on a predetermined schedule, thus enabling the occurrence of events or actions to be measured. Such a method might be used to assess the range and types of behaviour exhibited by people in workplace team meetings, and the general meeting dynamics, for example. Finally, a technique often used by media analysts is that of content analysis. This approach involves counting the occurrences of particular words or phrases and, more often, particular subjects or people (actors) involved in media stories. (Refer back to the example above in which we considered how content analysis might be used to assess the amount of content within newspapers given over to the economy as well as the way in which the press present different aspects of this issue.)

All of these methods are linked by a common desire to produce data that can be analysed in a structured way akin to that employed in the natural sciences.

The established link between positivism and quantitative approaches has already been explored in the opening chapters of this book, but it is worth revisiting briefly here, since those factors which help to define data which are suitable for quantitative analysis find their roots in positivism. The assumption that the social world can be observed, recorded and affectively 'measured' pre-determines a format in which data must be produced. This is characterised by the need to operationalise concepts in such a way as to produce indicators which measure things precisely. This therefore suggests:

- the use of closed questions in surveys;
- the use of measurement scales in experimental research;
- the use of counts in structured observations; and
- the use of coding schedules in content analysis.

All of these data collection tools are concerned with measurement, so that variables can be quantified. Quantification can consist of fairly straightforward counting and cataloguing, whereby we assess the number of times certain categories occur, and perhaps group the categories of one variable by those of another. This enables us to describe characteristics of the sample in percentage terms, such as '54% were female' or 'a higher percentage of union members than non-union members vote Democrat'. This may be sufficient for a number of purposes, but there will be times when we wish to conduct more sophisticated analysis, and it is then that we will need to use statistical analysis. For this, it is important that our indicators can be sensibly measured in a numerical format.

We have already mentioned that it is rare to find raw quantitative measures in social research, largely due to the prevalence of the survey method and its associated adoption of categorical responses. If we are measuring something like reaction time in an experiment, we could record the time in milliseconds as numerical information. This provides us with a numerical value for the variable 'reaction time', without the need for any further modification. With the survey method, however, we will often have to transform the raw data into a numerical value.

Limitations on the types of analysis available to us are imposed by earlier stages in the research process. The way in which concepts are operationalised, the ensuing variables which have been defined, and the format the indicators take will all affect our analysis. Linked to all of this is the process of coding, which involves assigning a (usually numeric) value to a category on a variable. We take qualitative data (a word, phrase, or even image, which is based upon an observation) and ascribe a numerical value which is used to represent the category. For example, we might ascribe the numbers 1 and 2 respectively to the categories 'female' and 'male' for the variable 'gender'. For each variable, we therefore end up with a set of values which represent all possible categories into which a case might fit.

By and large, quantitative data are pre-coded, so different responses are listed against their respective codes on a questionnaire, or when a category is selected on an online form from a website, the corresponding code is recorded. For some examples of closed questions which have been pre-coded, see the section on questionnaire design in Chapter 6. The ways in which these codes relate to the categories of the variables will determine what analysis is appropriate. For some variables, coding will be applied using logic (1 for 'low-income', 2 for 'high-income'), whereas for others it will be an arbitrary process (1 for 'urban', 2 for 'rural'). The extent to which we are able to logically assign values has important implications for analysis. To explore this issue in more detail, we need to understand levels of measurement.

The level of measurement of a variable can be determined by examining the relationship between the categories within the variable (De Vaus 1996). There are four levels of measurement: nominal, ordinal, interval and ratio. With each level we see a closer link between categories and associated codes, which in turn enables a greater deal of complexity in the data analysis. This also dictates the extent to which we can say one case is different from another, in relation to the variable in question.

## Nominal variables

Nominal variables contain categories which enable us to say one case is either the same as, or different from, another. An example is that of marital status. This variable might consist of a number of categories ('single', 'married/living as married', 'separated', 'divorced' and 'widowed'). On the basis of these categories we are able to conclude that a case which falls into one category has different marital status from a case that falls into any other category. Beyond this, however, there is little else we can say about how the categories relate to each other since 'it is not meaningful to quantify how much difference there is' (De Vaus 1996, p.130). Would it be possible, for example, to quantify the difference between what it is to be single and married?

If we code the categories using the numerical codes '1' to '5' respectively, the relationship between these codes and the categories they represent is purely arbitrary, and it would be wrong to infer that since the codes have a different numerical value, then there is some implicit difference in the value of each category. The relative difference between the numbers '1' and '2' does not correspond to a relative difference between the value of being single or married. It is for this reason that coding of nominal variables is a purely arbitrary process. There are, however, some exceptions.

Variables which only contain two categories are referred to as dichotomous variables. Quite often, these variables relate to whether a case exhibits a particular quality or not, and are often represented on questionnaires by a single box which the respondent ticks if they are able to demonstrate that quality. Asking someone to indicate which daily newspapers they read at least once a week from a list is one example. Each newspaper is represented by a single variable, and usually this will be coded either '1' if the respondent does read that particular paper, or '0' if they do not. Using '1' or '0' to code the presence or absence of a particular quality is somewhat more logical than arbitrarily assigning any numerical codes, and doing so does mean that such variables can be analysed using more sophisticated techniques than conventional nominal variables, as we shall see later.

### Ordinal variables

Ordinal variables exhibit observable ranking of categories in a hierarchical pattern. As with nominal variables, the categories enable us to say that a case is either the same or different from another case, on this variable. However, unlike nominal variables, the categories of an ordinal variable also indicate to us that one case is of a higher or lower order. An example of an ordinal variable would be that of formal qualifications, with the categories ranging from no formal qualifications, through school and college qualifications, up to university degrees. There is a clear progression through the categories here, so as well as concluding that each category is different, it is also possible to say that some categories indicate a higher level of formal qualifications than others. It is in this progression from 'lower' ordered through to 'higher' ordered categories that a relationship between the categories and the codes begins to form. Put simply, it makes sense when our categories fall into a natural order, for our coding structure to reflect that.

If we were to apply the code '1' to 'no formal qualifications', and a code of '6' to 'higher degree', with four other categories in between being coded accordingly, it would be possible to analyse the codes and conclude that those cases which are represented by a higher code for this variable have a higher level of qualification. This link between the codes and the categories within ordinal variables is an important factor in allowing a higher level of analysis than that obtainable with nominal variables. However, the relationship should not be overplayed. While an order can be found in the coding which reflects an order in the categories, the value of the code does not offer a precise measurement of the concept being observed. Assume that all we knew about this variable was that the coding related to qualifications, in order, from lowest to highest, but that we did not know which qualifications each code related to. By analysing two cases with different codes on this variable, all we could conclude is that one case was better qualified than the other, not by how much.

### Interval and ratio variables

Where we have an indicator which offers a precise measurement of a concept using a numerical scale or raw numbers, we have either an interval or a ratio variable. Both of these variables share many fundamental characteristics, and are often considered together, since they both allow for the same types of analysis. Both types have a natural order, and neither usually require coding, since the types of concept being measured come already quantified. For example, when asked to provide our age in years, annual household income in precise figures, or height in centimetres, we might provide figures such as: 31 years of age; £27,512; 180 cm. The precise correspondence between the values used and the concept being measured is an important factor in understanding the nature of interval and ratio variables. Unlike ordinal variables, interval and ratio variables can be measured in units which increase or decrease in consistent steps for each value. It is possible to say that there is an age difference of two years between a 29 and a 31 year old. It is possible to say the same about the age difference between a 56 and a 58 year old. In other words, as well as being able to say one case is either the same as, or different from, another (as with nominal variables), and that one case is of a higher or lower order than another (as with ordinal variables), we are also able to say by precisely how much one case differs from another.

The single difference between interval and ratio variables is that ratio variables have an absolute zero point, so age is an example of a ratio variable, since someone cannot have an age which is of a negative value. Interval variables, however, allow for negative values. An oft-cited example is that of temperature measured in degrees Fahrenheit. Temperatures can drop to below zero degrees, but the zero point is not an absolute zero (as it is when measured in degrees Kelvin). One crucial implication of this is that ratio variables can be measured in multiples. For example, of someone's age, it could be said that 'at 40 years old, she was twice the age of her 20 year-old son'. This type of statement is not applicable to interval variables because the scales upon which they are based do not have the absolute zero point from which all values are calculated; 40 degrees Fahrenheit is not twice as warm as 20 degrees.

Within the realms of quantitative data, the level of measurement dictates the degree and complexity of analysis that can be carried out, and therefore the questions that can be answered or types of hypotheses that can be tested. Since the indicators you choose to use will affect your analysis, it is important to be clear about the ways in which you wish to interrogate your data, and to build this into the research design from the start. As De Vaus (1996, p.131) suggests:

> The level of measurement of some variables can be determined by the researcher by how the question is asked in the first place, how it is coded and by the purpose for which it is to be used.

For example, it would be possible to create an indicator of performance in a test by either ascribing pass/fail (resulting in a dichotomous variable), or a percentage score (resulting in a 100-point scale ratio variable). It is therefore advisable that when starting out with quantitative research, you consider not only what questions you wish to ask, but the format in which you wish them to be answered. Your indicators then need to be chosen so as to enable the collection of data within categories, or on scales, which suit the level of measurement you wish to achieve.

## Quantitative data analysis

### Using tables to describe single variables

When collecting quantitative data, it can often be difficult to get a 'feel' for what the data are telling us. The qualitative researcher will have made extensive field notes and spent a good deal of time with the participants, and so have a sense of the data as they are being collected. Often, one of the first things a quantitative researcher will want to do is gain a 'snapshot' of the data. This will provide a good basis for further analysis, and may enable skews in the sample to be dealt with (by isolating under-represented groups and boosting the sample with further interviews to collect more data from people in those groups). Descriptive analysis can provide a very basic summary of each variable in our data, by showing a proportionate breakdown of the categories for each variable or an indication of average values. This is most commonly represented in a frequency distribution or by the use of descriptive statistics. An example of a frequency distribution can be seen in Table 8.1 (individual percentages do not add up to 100% due to rounding).

Table 8.1 allows us to see that the most popular mode of transport for travelling to work is as a car driver, with 373 out of 589 cases falling into this category. Importantly, however, it also provides information about how this proportion can be represented as a percentage. When carrying out quantitative research, it is unusual to conduct a census, whereby the entire population being studied is included in the sample. For this reason, when we come to carry out analysis we seek to make inferences from our sample which can be used to form

Table 8.1 Example of a frequency distribution

| *Main mode of travel to work? (q)* | | | |
|---|---|---|---|
| *Code* | *Label* | *Frequency* | *Percentage* |
| 1 | Walk | 50 | 8.5 |
| 2 | Bike | 67 | 11.4 |
| 3 | Rail | 1 | 0.2 |
| 4 | Bus | 63 | 10.7 |
| 5 | Car driver | 373 | 63.3 |
| 6 | Car passenger | 26 | 4.4 |
| 7 | Motorbike driver | 8 | 1.4 |
| 8 | Motorbike passenger | 1 | 0.2 |
| | **TOTAL** | **589** | **100** |

*Source*: Aldridge and Levine (2001, p.139)

generalisations about the population as a whole. If the organisation being looked at actually consisted of 589 workers, then to say 373 workers travelled as car drivers would give us an accurate reflection of the proportion. However, this particular organisation consisted of 4,763 members of staff, and the research only covered a sample of these (Aldridge and Levine 2001, p.79). Now the frequency counts alone become less helpful: to present the information as 373 out of 589 when we are discussing an organisation of 4,763 members of staff does not give us an accurate reflection of how this relates to the population as a whole. A percentage offers a useful solution to this problem because whatever the size of the organisation, a percentage of 63.3 represents the same proportion. There is an additional advantage of referring to percentages because it allows comparison between samples. If we wished to compare the travelling patterns of workers from two differently sized organisations, comparing frequency counts would be pointless, whereas percentages account for the differences in the total number of cases in each sample, and so are more readily comparable.

## Using statistics to describe single variables

Frequency distributions are useful tools for providing an overview of the proportionate breakdown of a variable into its component categories, and will often suffice for basic descriptive analysis. There will be occasions, however, when rather than looking at every category in a variable, it is more useful to get an idea of what is the typical category or average value. In order to do this, we need to make use of measures of central tendency. These provide us with a single value that can be said to typify broadly the way the cases are split between the categories of a variable. For instance, the typical age of the group that we surveyed or the most common leisure pursuit of our sample. There are three measures of central tendency, each associated with a particular level of measurement. These are outlined in Table 8.2.

If data are coded, when using software such as SPSS, measures of central tendency will be returned as the relevant code. The mode, therefore, will be listed not as the most common category, but the code for that category. It may be, for example, that with a nominal variable indicating residential status we

Table 8.2 Measures of central tendency

| *Measure* | *Associated level of measurement* | *Brief description* |
|---|---|---|
| Mode | Nominal | Category with the highest percentage in a frequency distribution |
| Median | Ordinal | The mid-point along a ranked frequency distribution |
| Mean | Scale | The 'mathematical average': the sum of values for all cases divided by the total number of cases |

Table 8.3 Interpreting a median value

The Likert scales below represents a set of responses to a question.
A median value reported as '4' is meaningless without knowing the associated category:

1. Strongly disagree
2. Disagree
3. Neither disagree nor agree
4. Agree
5. Strongly agree

establish a modal value of 3. This is meaningless until we also establish that this value relates to the category 'Home owner' in a questionnaire item. Similarly, an ordinal variable which measures levels of agreement on a Likert scale may present a median value of 4. This only becomes meaningful when we look at the associated category to discover that this value relates to 'agree' (see Table 8.3).

The mean differs from the mode and the median in that it can be a non-integer. If we were looking at age as a ratio variable, it would be perfectly feasible to have a mean age of 36.45. This further emphasises the importance of recognising the level of measurement of a variable and using the appropriate measure. Measures of central tendency and other statistics which we shall cover briefly are all based on working assumptions about the data we are dealing with (in particular the level of measurement) and will be rendered meaningless if these assumptions are incorrect.

Obtaining a single value which provides an indication of typicality is useful in that it provides a concise and precise measure, but it is limited in that by concentrating on what is typical it is possible to lose a sense of how all the values are distributed across the sample. In order to tackle this problem we need to refer to measures of dispersion. Two commonly used measures are the range and the standard deviation. The range simply presents the difference between the maximum and minimum values of a variable. It is therefore useful when stated in conjunction with the median for ordinal variables since it implies a range of values which can be ranked. In Table 8.3 the median value of a Likert scale variable is 4, but some sense can only be made of this because, as well as knowing that the value is related to the category 'agree', we also have a sense of where the value sits within the range of all possible values. Even though a Likert scale contained five categories on the questionnaire, respondents may have only selected some of the categories; only the options agree and strongly agree may have been selected, for instance, and this would tell us that people in general were positive towards the statement. It is therefore important to know something about the dispersion of values as well as the central tendency.

The standard deviation is used in conjunction with the mean, and measures, on average, how far the values for each case deviate from the mean. This is an accurate way of illustrating whether the values are widely dispersed or whether they tend to cluster around the mean. The standard deviation is useful when comparing two or more groups. In a health study, for example, we might discover that the mean values for number of visits to a gym in one week were 3.45 for males and 3.47 for females. On the surface, this might suggest that both males and females, on average, shared similar exercise regimes. However, on further analysis we discover a standard deviation of 2.9 for males compared to a standard deviation of 0.4 for females. This would suggest that, actually, females are far more consistent in their visits to the gym, whereas males varied greatly in their dedication.

## Using tables to describe relationships between two variables

As an initial stage in analysis, describing single variables is very useful. In some cases, such as exploratory research, it may be that this level of description enables us to answer our research questions. Take an example of a research project which sought to establish the prevalence of crime within a particular area. We might devise a series of measures which asked a random sample of respondents from the area whether or not they had been victims of, or witnessed, different types of crime. By looking at frequency tables we could provide an answer to our research question which was perfectly satisfactory.

This example provides us with a description of a phenomenon: it enables us to establish what are the prevalent types of crime within the area. It does not, however, offer any explanation for the existence of these crimes or why certain crimes are more widespread than others. It merely describes the situation: this particular type of crime is more widespread than another. In order to investigate this example further it is necessary to try to establish association between crime and other factors. In other words, we need to look at variables together, through a process of bivariate or multivariate analysis.

The main premise behind bivariate analysis is the identification of association between two variables. To this end, it is necessary to use a variety of tables or statistics which enable us to observe the dispersion of values of one variable in relation to the dispersion of the values of another. In order to establish why these particular crimes took place, we may seek to identify whether certain characteristics of the area, or the victims, had any bearing on the types of crime. Some questions that we might seek to answer by establishing association might include:

- Are males or females more susceptible to different types of crime?
- Do areas with higher unemployment rates have a higher crime rate?
- Is the prevalence of drug use within an area associated with the level of crime?

In order to tackle the first question, which consists of two nominal variables, it is useful to cross-tabulate the frequency distributions of the two

Table 8.4 Example of a cross-tabulation table showing victims of different types of crime by their sex (not real data)

| | *Males* | *Females* |
|---|---|---|
| Violence against the person | 74<br>27.8% | 66<br>28.9% |
| Robbery | 57<br>21.4% | 43<br>18.9% |
| Domestic burglary | 53<br>19.9% | 51<br>22.4% |
| Motor vehicle theft | 82<br>30.9% | 68<br>29.8% |
| TOTAL | 266<br>100% | 228<br>100% |

variables against each other. Cross-tabulation produces a table whereby the frequency distribution of one variable (sex) is set out in columns, and the frequency distribution of the second variable (crime) is set out in rows which intersect the columns of the first. This enables us to look at the distribution of one variable broken down within the different categories of another variable. A cross-tabulation table of these two variables might look something like that shown in Table 8.4 (individual percentages do not add up to 100% due to rounding).

Table 8.4 presents us with a frequency distribution of crimes broken down by the sex of the victim. On the surface, there may appear to be some differences in the frequency counts between males and females. Robbery, and also motor vehicle theft, appear to afflict males more than they do females. However, it is important to look at how these figures translate into proportions because the actual numbers of males to females in the sample are very different. When we observe these figures as percentages, the differences seem to be less apparent. When looking at tables such as this, where the different categories within a variable contain different numbers of cases, it is important to use percentages to enable an accurate comparison of proportions between the two categories.

## Using statistics to describe the relationship between two variables: association

As with univariate analysis, the use of tables to identify patterns is helpful up to a point, but these tables can become particularly unwieldy when cross-tabulating two variables which may both consist of many categories. As an alternative, the use of a variety of statistical tests designed to measure association, or 'correlation', by producing a single value is a more attractive option.

There are many statistical tests for association. The Cross-tabs and Bivariate Correlations menus of SPSS include: Phi; Cramér's V; Lambda; Gamma;

Somers' d; Kendall's tau-b/tau-c; Eta; Pearson's *r*; Spearman's rho. The test you choose will depend on the level of measurement and the number of categories of each of the variables in question. For a useful summary of which correlation to use, see De Vaus (2002, pp.274–8).

The result of a test for association will provide a value between 0 (indicating no relationship) and 1 (a perfect relationship) and, depending on the test, this may or may not be accompanied by a + or – sign to indicate whether the relationship is positive (values of both variables increase together) or negative (values increase in one variable as the values decrease in the other variable). Example 8.1 provides a series of examples to illustrate potential positive and negative relationships between variables. An important point to note is that an identified association between two variables, in which at least one of the variables is nominal, cannot have direction, and so these tests cannot be positive or negative – they just indicate the strength of a relationship. A summary association statistic presents us with a very concise measure of association between two variables (Definition 8.1).

## Definition 8.1 What constitutes a strong level of association?

There is some debate over how large the value for a measure of association should be before it can be considered large enough to warrant commenting upon. However, as a rough guide, the following is a reasonable estimate.

- Between 0 and 0.2: No to weak association
- Between 0.2 and 0.4: Weak to moderate association
- Between 0.4 and 0.6: Moderate to strong association
- Between 0.6 and 0.8: Strong to very strong association
- Between 0.8 and 1.0: Very strong to perfect association

## Example 8.1 Positive and negative association

- The number of cars in a city could have a positive association with levels of pollution.
- Tiredness and concentration can be said to be negatively associated since as we become more tired our ability to concentrate decreases.
- An association between type of industry and average salary could be strong in that certain industrial occupations offer, on average, much greater salaries. However, since different types of industry are not usually ranked in any order of value, this kind of association could not have direction.

## Inference and statistical significance

The whole notion of statistical significance can be rather complicated, but is actually founded on a fairly straightforward question: is the sample representative of the population? This is something that we have also addressed in Chapter 6. When dealing with data that have been collected from a sample rather than from the entire population, we will want to draw inferences from the sample and apply generalisations to the population as a whole. This is fine if we can be relatively confident that the cases we have not been able to observe are likely to behave in a similar way to those that we have. If we know enough about the sample characteristics, and are sure that unobserved cases are not especially unique in any way, we can come to some relatively commonsense conclusions that our findings would apply to the broader population. This is known as theoretical inference. The extent to which we make inferences is based on a theoretical understanding of the population and the sample. This will often provide us with the only way of being confident in our generalisations. However, if we have used a probability sample, such as a systematic random sample, then we can use statistical tests to gauge the confidence in our generalisations.

In social research, particularly when we have only one round of data collection, such as a single survey or one set of experiments, the question of how close our sample characteristics are to those in the population is problematic. The heart of the problem lies in the matter of verification, which we have already encountered in Chapter 1 in the discussion of logical positivism. To take an example from the kind of results we might find in a health survey, assume we collect data from a random sample of smokers and observe that males smoke, on average, three more cigarettes per day than females. There are two possible explanations for the data showing these values. On the one hand, it is because the sample is representative of the population, and if we were to question every smoker in the country, we would also find that, on average, males smoke three cigarettes more each day than do females. On the other hand, it could be that the random sample we have drawn is not representative, and the characteristics of smokers in the population actually look quite different. To try to verify the representativeness of the sample is impossible. This is because we do not have the actual population figures against which to compare the observed data from the sample (after all, if we did, we would not need to conduct a survey in the first place). If we are unable to verify the representativeness, what is the solution? The response to the problem of verification is one of falsification.

There is a rather strange logic behind falsification in statistical inference because it rests on not trying to verify representativeness, but rather on trying to rule out the probability that a sample is unrepresentative.

Hypothesis testing requires two pieces of information: a set of expected values, based on the hypothesis, and the observed values, drawn from our data. By comparing the two, we are able to conclude whether or not the hypothesis should be rejected or accepted. Were we to try to verify the representativeness of the sample, we would want to set up a hypothesis that stated the sample characteristics were the same as the population characteristics (and remember that we can't do this because we don't have the population characteristics – i.e. we don't know the smoking habits of men and women in the wider population). In other words, the values we expect to see are the same as those we actually observe in the data. It follows, then, that if we wish to rule out the probability of an unrepresentative sample, we formulate a hypothesis which states that the sample characteristics are different from the population characteristics, and try to reject this hypothesis. This would result in the observed values being different from those we would expect to see. Hypotheses of this type, which we are seeking to reject, are referred to as null hypotheses, and are essentially statements of what characteristics or values we would expect to see in our data if there were no unusual patterns, or relationship between variables, in the population. The null hypothesis for the smoking example is that males and females, on average, smoke the same number of cigarettes. The original hypothesis, which rests on the sample being representative, and that we would ideally like to verify if we could – that there is a difference in smoking habits between males and females – now becomes known as the alternative hypothesis.

So now we are in a situation where we have developed a null hypothesis consisting of a set of expected values, based upon a pattern of no relationship between gender and smoking in the population. The question at this point is: how different are the expected values of the null hypothesis from the actual observed values in our data? If they are similar, then we must accept that the sample is similar to a population with the expected values from the null hypothesis, i.e. that the population of smokers could actually show no difference between the smoking habits of males and females. On the other hand, if they are significantly different, then we can reject the null hypothesis that there is no relationship, and this gives us more grounds to believe the relationship observed in our data may also be present in the population. The full implications of accepting or rejecting a null hypothesis will be dealt with shortly, but first we need to address the issue of how we decide whether expected and observed values are different enough to support rejection – i.e. whether or not the differences are statistically significant.

Random samples are based upon probability, since every case in the population has an equal probability of being selected. Probability is useful because it enables us to work out the likelihood of something occurring. We are used to the idea of probability in everyday life, and ask ourselves questions which speculate about the probability of something happening. What are the chances of it raining today? How likely is it that my team are going to win the hockey cup? Both of these questions are based on a subjective estimate of the probability that an event will occur. The answers to these questions tend to be similarly subjective: there is a 'good' chance or it will be 'quite' likely. However, in statistics, probability can be calculated more precisely and be given a value ranging from 0 to 1. Events which are sure to happen have a probability of 1, events which will never happen have a probability of 0, and anything in between represents the probability that something might happen. To take a simple example, the probability of rolling a six on a die is one in six: 1/6 = 0.167. When we select cases at random from a population, and each case has an equal probability of being selected, it is possible to calculate how probable it is that different samples with different characteristics will be drawn. Samples with similar characteristics to the population as a whole are more likely to be drawn than samples which look very different. This point can be demonstrated by imagining a population of 100 people of various ages, ranging from 18 to 90 years old and with an average age of 50. The probability of selecting a sample which also has an average age of 50 is fairly high, but the probability of selecting a sample with an average age of 20, for instance, will be very small. The first of these samples is representative of the population, the second not.

If we know which value to expect (in this case, the average age of 50), then it is possible to calculate the probability of selecting different samples with different average ages. This concept can be applied to null hypothesis testing. Using the expected values derived from the null hypothesis as the starting point, the probability of selecting a sample with the observed values from our data can be calculated. If the probability of selecting such a sample is small, then we reject the null hypothesis, but if it is sufficiently high, then we accept it. Beginning, therefore, with expected values which suggest males and females smoke, on average, the same number of cigarettes, the probability of selecting a sample in which the males smoke an average of three more cigarettes per day than the females can be calculated. If there is a high probability of selecting such a sample, then we accept that the null hypothesis could be true, and within the population there might actually be no difference between males and females. In other words, we cannot be sure that the observed differences between males and females in the sample are representative of the population because there is a sufficiently high probability of drawing a sample with these differences apparent, despite there being no difference in the population. If the probability of selecting such a sample would be very low, however, then we can reject the null hypothesis, and be reasonably confident that there are some differences between males and females in the population as a whole. In order to decide whether to accept or reject the null hypothesis, though, we need to decide on what counts as a sufficiently high or low level of probability.

It is important to recognise that no matter how highly improbable it is for certain samples to be selected at random, any sample is possible. Just as winning the lottery is highly improbable, but still possible, so selecting a sample with an average age of 20 from a population with an average age of 50 is unlikely, but still possible. Therefore, seeking to reject a null hypothesis becomes problematic because we cannot conclude that a particular sample in which there appeared to be a relationship would never occur if the null hypothesis were in fact true. Therefore, rather than rule out the null hypothesis on the basis of impossibility, we do so on the basis of improbability. Social scientists are generally agreed that if we cannot completely rule out the null hypothesis, then we should at least be 95% sure. This is known as adopting a confidence level of 95%. By doing so, we accept that even if there were no relationship in the population as a whole, there is still a small chance that we could draw a sample which implied that there was one. However, if we can calculate that the probability of this happening is less than .05, or would happen less than 5% of the time, then we can have sufficient confidence in rejecting the null hypothesis. This probability is written as $p < 0.05$. You may also see 99% confidence levels (where $p < 0.01$) used, in which case the assertion is that were the null hypothesis to be true, the chances of selecting a random sample with these particular observed values are less than 1 in 100. You may even see 99.9% confidence levels ($p < 0.001$), where the chances of drawing the sample given the null hypothesis are less than 1 in 1,000.

Most statistical techniques have associated measures of statistical significance, and will usually be calculated and reported in packages such as SPSS. Where a null hypothesis is rejected, the observations are said to be statistically significant. The conclusions that can be drawn from this are often misinterpreted, so it is important to be clear about what we are saying when we talk of statistically significant results. The use of the word 'significant' is somewhat misleading because it has no bearing on the perceived importance of the results. Put simply, what it means is that the null hypothesis has been rejected. Similarly, this does not mean that the observations in the data are definitely an accurate representation of those which would be found in the population as a whole; the null hypothesis has been tested and rejected, but you have not accepted any alternative hypothesis. Similarly, when talking about confidence levels, it is wrong to suggest that a statistically significant result of $p < 0.05$ means that we are 95% confident that our results are representative. Rather, it means that if the null hypothesis were true, and we were to take 100 random samples, our pattern of observations could still turn up, albeit in less than five of the 100 samples.

To fully explore statistical inference would require more space than we have available here, and it is an area of statistics that does require detailed exploration to fully understand a number of the concepts. The crucial points are that statistical significance provides us with a way of falsifying (or of ruling out) null hypotheses, which in turn gives us a higher degree of confidence that the observations in our sample are unlikely to have occurred by chance. This in turn, is interpreted as supporting (but not proving) the assertion that the sample is representative. For a more thorough account of statistical significance and probability theory, see Warner (2008).

### Example 8.2 Statistical significance in survey analysis

Consider the following quote, which is based on data taken from the 2001 General Household Survey and looks at the association between age and numerous variables concerned with neighbourhood spirit: 'Those in the youngest age group were the least likely to be neighbourly. In comparison, people in the oldest age group (those aged 70 or over) were most likely to speak to, know or trust their neighbours' (Coulthard et al. 2002, p.27). The quote seems to support concerns about 'the youth of today' lacking community spirit. However, when we consider that the survey only covered 8,989 households in Britain, we may start to experience a few doubts. The sample size, while large even by national survey standards, still only represents an extremely small proportion of the population as a whole. We might start to think that the researchers just happened to pick a selection of young people who felt disinclined to talk to their neighbours. Really, we do not want to believe that community spirit is disappearing with the younger generations, but when we read that 'differences mentioned in the text have been found to be statistically significant at the 95% confidence level' (2002, p.ix), then we have to think again. We can see that a null hypothesis – that neighbourliness is not associated with age – has been rejected at the 95% confidence level. If there was actually no association between neighbourliness and age, and a sample of this population was taken 100 times, we would only expect to see these results occur five or fewer times, as a result of chance. It is therefore probable that the null hypothesis is wrong, leaving the possible alternative explanation that the sample could be representative and that there is some potential link between age and neighbourliness. This example demonstrates how important it is to support any inferences made about the population with statistically significant results.

## Independent samples t-tests and ANOVA

A common question in research will be one in which we are trying to establish whether the value of a particular interval variable differs across two or more groups. Consider the example of whether the average number of cigarettes smoked per day differs between males and females. An example in which more than two groups are involved might be whether people living in five different regions earn different salaries. In both of these examples, it is easy to identify what the mean values are for each group (the mean number of cigarettes for males and for females, and the mean salaries in each of the regions). If we notice a difference, we may assume that these groups differ in the population as well. However, as we have just seen, it is possible that this is just a result of the selection of an improbable sample, when really the groups are all very similar. In both circumstances, we need to set up a null hypothesis that all groups have equal means, and then seek to reject it. If we do so, then we can be reasonably confident that the groups are likely to exhibit differences in the wider population. The independent samples *t*-test is used when analysing only two groups, and ANOVA (Analysis of Variance) can be applied to more than two groups. Both tests produce a measure of statistical significance, and both therefore enable questions about group differences to be explored, and for inferences to be drawn on this basis.

## Association and causality

So far we have looked at a number of ways of establishing whether relationships exist between variables and these are all useful tools in seeking out association. However, there is an important difference between association and causality. The notion of causality concerns a relationship between two variables which is based upon cause and effect. That is to say, the values of one variable (an independent variable) will determine the values of another variable (the dependent variable).

Returning to the earlier example of crime, one of our research questions seeks to identify whether the prevalence of drug use in an area affects the level of crime. It may be that by measuring crime rates per capita and numbers of drug users in different areas, we could find an association between these two variables: a higher crime rate exists in areas where there is higher drug usage. While we have managed to identify a pattern, could we conclude from this that the level of drug usage is actually responsible for the level of crime? Or could it be that there is another external factor influencing both variables?

Association and causality should not be confused. Simply identifying a relationship between two variables is not sufficient reason to suggest that one variable affects change in another. Bryman (1990 pp.8–9) highlights three criteria that have to be met in order for causality to be established:

> First, it is necessary to establish that there is an apparent relationship between two variables. This means that it is necessary to demonstrate that the distribution of values of one variable corresponds to the distribution of values of another variable. ...
>
> Second, it is necessary to demonstrate that the relationship is *non-spurious*. A spurious relationship occurs when there is not a 'true' relationship between two variables that appear to be connected. The variation exhibited by each variable is affected by a common variable.
>
> Third, it is also necessary to establish that the cause precedes the effect, i.e. the *time order* of the two related variables. (original emphasis)

Establishing these three criteria is something that experimental research design often strives to achieve. The conditions in which experimental research are carried out allow for close control of external variables, and of the time order of the events being observed.

In survey research, however, these criteria are somewhat more difficult to measure because the researcher collects data relating to many variables at one particular time. The upshot of this is that while association between two variables can be identified relatively easily, the task of ruling out spurious relationships and establishing time order is more difficult to achieve.

Taking these three criteria into consideration, when seeking to establish causality between drug usage and crime rates the first criterion has been met: we have established a relationship. The second criterion is harder to establish. Could it be that both crime and drug usage are affected by a third variable, such as the presence of organised gangs or degrees of poverty? The third criterion is also questionable. Since data were collected at the same time, we have not established whether drug usage increased prior to an increase in crime rates.

In order to establish time order, surveys can be repeated at different points in time using the same sample. This enables us to measure the development of phenomena and to measure patterns. Once again, however, for researchers conducting small-scale projects, this can be an overly time-consuming process.

While time order might be difficult to establish, we have already looked at ways of identifying association, and if we want to rule out the possibility of a non-spurious relationship, we need to turn to a series of techniques designed to help understand the interplay between three or more variables.

## Principles of multivariate analysis

Rarely as social researchers are we presented with a phenomenon that can be illustrated by a simple relationship between two variables. Although we have already highlighted the difficulties of establishing causality, much social research is focused upon identifying the effects of a number of independent variables – or 'predictors' – on a single dependent variable, or outcome. For instance, if we wanted to better understand what makes people recycle their rubbish, we would want to look at a variety of possible reasons: one's awareness of environmental issues; one's own moral sense of civic duty; availability of recycling facilities; the extent to which people's social networks also recycle, for example.

The use of observations collected in a data set to describe relationships between variables is usually referred to as statistical modelling. Models are used to represent something where it is impractical to use the real thing. An architect would test a model of a bridge in a wind tunnel, recreating the effects of high winds as closely as possible in order to evaluate the strength of the bridge's design. If the model collapses, the architect returns to the design, modifies it by creating another model, and tests this. Statistical modelling follows the same process, except rather than building a physical model, we use the building blocks of empirical observations and create a mathematical model where the different components are the variables selected for inclusion. Testing the model is done by using statistical techniques to produce calculations which measure the strength of the model. A strong model is usually one that isolates those independent variables which provide the best explanation of the outcome (the dependent variable). In situations where two or more models provide equally good explanations, it is common to select the one that is based on the fewest independent variables since this provides the most efficient explanation (just as if it were the case that two bridge designs were equally strong, the one which uses the least costly building materials might be chosen). This is referred to as 'parsimony'.

The way multivariate analysis seeks to explain the outcome (as measured by the dependent variable) will often be to explain either (i) the variance in the dependent variable, or (ii) the probability of membership of different groups (as measured by different categories in a dependent variable). Variance is a measure of dispersion, or the extent to which individual cases differ from the average (mean) score. Quite simply, it tells us something about the extent to which cases vary. An example might be the variance of unemployment, measured across different regions and explained by a number of variables, such as educational levels of residents, business investment, number of urban conurbations in the region, and so forth. In such analysis, variance in the dependent variable can only be measured at the interval/ratio level.

Measuring the probability of group membership is useful if the dependent variable is categorical (nominal or ordinal). The recycling example above provides a useful example, where two groups of individuals exist – those who do recycle and those who do not. In this analysis, we would seek to establish the extent to which the various independent variables affect the probability of belonging to one group or another.

There will usually be a number of independent variables that have not been observed, for the purely pragmatic reason that it is impossible to measure everything. In multivariate analysis, we usually seek to measure what we consider to be the most important independent variables, based upon theory in the literature and *a priori* reasoning. Variables that have not been measured, or measured but excluded from our model, contribute to 'error' in the resulting analysis, by which it is meant the analysis lacks an element of precision. The best model, therefore, is one in which error is minimal.

It is clear that a model based upon just one independent and one dependent variable (a bivariate model) would contain a lot of error because we are associating a single independent variable with an outcome that is most likely a result of multiple independent variables. If we want to more accurately assess the extent to which an individual variable affects an outcome, we need to control for other independent variables. Controlling is a process of removing variable effects we do not wish to measure. In experimental research designs this is often done by assigning cases to a control group, in which certain independent variables, such as a particular stimulus, are not present (refer back to Chapter 6 for a further explanation of this). In other research designs, all cases are affected by the variables we wish to control, and so their effect is removed statistically instead. There are a variety of means for controlling statistically, but they generally rely upon using what is known about the variable to be controlled (the 'control variable'), based upon the available data in order to cancel out its effect from the analysis. We must have these data available to us in the first place, of course, so models are usually created in which all independent variables are present, but are in turn controlled for. This enables us to isolate which variables have the greatest effect, and would still have the greatest effect if other independent variables were removed.

To use a simple example, assume we are measuring the association between the independent variables age, income and exercise, and the dependent variable general health. We could establish how much exercise is associated with health, but people of different ages, or with different levels of income might do different amounts of exercise. It may appear, from a bivariate analysis, that exercise is very important for health, but we are not comparing like with like; people of different ages may do more or less exercise, and also generally be more or less healthy. Similarly, people on higher or lower incomes may be able to afford gym membership, or healthier diets, for example, leading to better general health. In order to get a more accurate view of the association between exercise and health, we need to control for the other two variables, thereby keeping their effects constant.

The process of multivariate statistical modelling is one which involves setting up a model, testing it, refining it, re-testing it and settling on one that offers the best explanation for the outcome as measured by the dependent variable. Having achieved this, it is then possible to use the model for prediction. Since we have arrived at a point where we know which independent variables have an effect, and to what extent, we can speculate about outcomes on the basis of hypothetical predictors. We can ask questions such as, 'if we made recycling facilities more widely available and educated people in environmental issues, how much more likely would people be to recycle?' Or, 'if people exercised for two hours per week, what are the likely health benefits?'

In summary, multivariate analysis enables us to ask questions such as:

- What is the combined effect of a number of independent variables on the dependent variable?
- What combination of independent variables offer the best explanation of the outcome, as measured by the dependent variable?
- To what extent can the perceived association between an independent variable and dependent variable actually be explained by the influence of other variables?
- What changes in the value of the dependent variable might occur if we were able to remove the effect of a particular independent variable?
- If we were to set the independent variables at specific values, what would be the value of the dependent variable?

In answering these questions, you will need to adopt one of a large variety of statistical techniques. Which one you choose will depend on the nature of the question you wish to ask, and the levels of measurement of your independent and dependent variables. What follows is a brief overview of some of the most widely used multivariate techniques, explaining when you might wish to use them and what data you will need. It is worth noting that each technique has a number of criteria that the data have to fit. In order to fully understand these criteria, and the application of the techniques, you will need to refer to the list of further reading at the end of the chapter.

## Some common multivariate techniques

### *Partial correlation*

Partial correlation coefficients are a measure of correlation between two variables, when one or more other variables have been statistically controlled. They are based upon a common type of bivariate correlation known as Pearson's *r* and, like that technique, are applicable when both variables are measured at the interval/ratio level. By looking for differences between correlation coefficients and partial correlation coefficients, we are able to identify whether relationships are spurious. If there is no difference, then the control variable is having no effect on the two correlated variables. If the partial correlation is smaller than the correlation, then the control variable has some effect on the correlated variables, and if the partial correlation is 0, then the control variable explains all of the relationship between the two variables. To build on an earlier example, assume we found that a person's general health and the nutritional value of their diet were correlated, with a correlation coefficient of .76. It could be that the nutritional value of a person's diet is largely explained by their income (eating well costs money). By controlling for income, we discover that the partial correlation between health and diet drops to .55, indicating that income partly explains the relationship between diet and health. In other words, the original correlation, based just on two variables, does not take into account the effect of the third variable, until that variable is controlled.

### *Multiple regression*

Multiple regression is one of the most widely used multivariate techniques. It enables us to produce models built around one dependent variable and a number of independent variables. How we choose which variables to include in the model, and in which order to enter them, is dependent upon the nature of our question. If we just want to find out how much variance in the dependent variable can be explained by the independent variables, we can create a model which simply combines all the independent variables at once. A measure of *R* squared ($R^2$) indicates the amount of variance explained as a proportion (i.e. somewhere between 0 and 1). An $R^2$ value of .53 suggests that the independent variables in the model account for 53% of the variance in the dependent variable. Again, returning to an earlier example, if we established that age, exercise and income jointly account for an $R^2$ of .49, or 49% of the variance in general health, then the remaining 51% of the variance is due to error, i.e. variables outside the model that have not been measured (which could include any variables such as diet, gender, family medical history, etc.). An effective model will have a large $R^2$ value, indicating that a lot of the predictors have been isolated in the model.

This model also provides us with a formula that enables us to predict the value of the dependent variable, given known values of the independent variables. The simple regression formula for a model that contains a single independent variable is:

$$Y = a + bX$$

Where:

- $Y$ is the predicted value of the dependent variable, e.g. general health;
- $X$ is the value of the independent variable, which we wish to use as the basis for our prediction, e.g. the weekly exercise routine;
- a is the *constant*. This is the value that we would expect the dependent variable to be at before the independent variables are taken into account, e.g. general health, without any exercise;
- b is the regression coefficient. This is the amount that the value of the dependent variable would increase by for every single unit's increase in the independent variable, e.g. how much health would improve for every additional hour of exercise per week.

When introducing more variables, the regression formula can be extended, with a different regression coefficient for each independent variable. So a formula for a model that includes three independent variables would look like this:

$$Y = a + b_1X_1 + b_2X_2 + b_3X_3$$

This formula is essentially saying, 'the value of the dependent variable will be the value that it would be, given no other effects upon it, plus the values of each independent variable multiplied by their regression coefficients', e.g. general health is equivalent to:

The general health of someone, notwithstanding the effects of age, income or exercise

\+

Age multiplied by the regression coefficient for age

\+

Income multiplied by the regression coefficient for income

\+

Number of hours exercise per week multiplied by the regression coefficient for exercise

The larger the regression coefficient (b), the greater the effect of that particular variable. Regression coefficients can also be negative, indicating that a rise in the value of that particular variable effect a drop in the value of the dependent variable – a rise in alcohol units consumed each week would likely result in a drop in general health. (Such negative coefficients could, of course, be cancelled out by positive regression coefficients for other independent variables.)

Multiple regression can also be used to identify the effects of individual variables. This can be done by creating a series of models in which variables are added and/or removed either using statistical criteria for inclusion or using the researcher's own criteria. Statistical criteria usually add independent variables in order of strength of correlation with the dependent variable. This means that the first model will usually just contain a single variable, with further models becoming more complex. Independent variables are only added if doing so results in a statistically significant increase in the proportion of explained variance of the dependent variable. Variables will also be removed from models if it seems their effect is actually explained by other variables that have since been added. Since partial correlation is used to assess the effects of the independent variables, any variable whose effect drops off when other variables are controlled for is deemed not to be contributing towards a statistically significant change in the variance of the dependent variable.

A researcher can also build models by choosing to add or remove variables in a predetermined order. This is useful if the researcher wishes to test a particular hypothesis that does not necessarily include the independent variable with the highest partial correlation with the dependent variable. For example, if we wish to advise people how they can lead a healthier lifestyle, we cannot alter their ages and their income, but we can perhaps advise on how much exercise they should be doing. Exercise may have the highest partial correlation with health, but we wish to add it last, thereby isolating the change in health that exercise accounts for, after adding in income and age.

Being also based upon the principles of Pearson's *r* correlation, it is usually necessary to ensure that independent and dependent variables are measured at the interval/ratio level, although it is possible to transform categorical independent variables by creating 'dummy' variables. This is a process whereby a number of new variables are created to represent all but one of the categories of the original variable. Each new variable is assigned a value of either 0 or 1. For example, for a nominal variable that indicates which of three different departments a person works in (department A, B or C), we would create two new variables, for departments A and B. A value of 1 for either department A or B indicates a person works in that particular department. If the values are 0 for both A and B, then by a process of elimination, the person must work in department C. Since department C no longer has a particular variable attached to it, it will not actually be entered into the regression equation, but is represented by the constant. Assume we wanted to work out a regression equation which predicted morale scores based on department. The constant would represent the average morale score for people working in department C (the constant without any modifications from the regression coefficients for departments A or B). To predict the morale scores for departments A or B, add or subtract the relevant regression coefficient multiplied by the value for that particular variable – this will always be 1 because the fact that the person works in that particular department is indicated by a value of 1 on that variable.

### *Logistic regression and discriminant analysis*

In situations when the dependent variable is categorical (nominal or ordinal), multiple regression may not be used. Logistic regression and discriminant analysis are two techniques designed for such circumstances, and both share some similarities, although they are based upon entirely different statistical procedures. Both enable the testing of the predictive qualities of a model, in which we want to ask a question about group membership. In situations where the grouping (dependent) variable consists of only two categories, binomial logistic regression may be used. Polynomial logistic regression can be applied when the grouping variable contains three or more categories, but is far more complex and is rarely covered in mainstream statistics textbooks. Discriminant analysis can be applied to any number of groups, which perhaps explains why it remains a popular technique. In the earlier example in which we cited recycling behaviour, we have two groups – those who recycle and those who do not. We may wish to ask the question: 'How well can environmental awareness, availability of facilities and civic duty predict whether or not someone recycles?' In a multiple regression, we can predict the increase or decrease in the value of the outcome variable, whereas here we can predict which group a particular case (or person) falls into. Evaluating the variance in recycling behaviour as it may increase or decrease depending on other variables is a rather different research question from asking whether certain factors make people recycle or not.

There is not enough space to go into the intricacies of both these techniques, other than to say both produce ways of calculating (a) whether the independent variables are generally good predictors of group membership, and (b) if they are, which group a case would fall into, given known values for the independent variables. So we could establish whether the independent variables relating to awareness of environmental issues, a moral sense of civic duty, availability of recycling facilities etc. provide us with sufficient information about an individual to predict whether they recycle or not, and we could also predict whether someone with a particular combination of these qualities recycles.

The way in which group membership is predicted is based on information about the relationship between the independent variables and dependent variables for every single case. The precise relationship will differ from one case to the next, but a single formula is arrived at, which provides the best way of describing, in general terms, how the independent variables combine to determine group membership. When reapplied to every individual case, using the values of the independent variables, this formula will predict the value of the dependent variable to a greater or lesser degree of accuracy. Put crudely, for those cases which follow predictable behaviour, it is probable that the model will accurately predict which group they fall into – recycling or not. Cases in which a connection between the independent variables and group membership is less apparent will be difficult to predict accurately. A good model is one in which the formula accurately predicts the value of the dependent variable for a high proportion of cases. In both discriminant analysis and logistic regression, one of the outcomes is a classification table that compares the predicted group membership with the actual group membership for every case. This enables us to identify the percentage of cases for which the model 'works'. If a high number of cases in our observed data are accurately predicted, then the model is likely to be a useful way of predicting group membership for unobserved data. When applied practically, if a model of recycling behaviour accurately predicted whether people did or did not recycle, we could perhaps use it to determine that particular independent variables were important, and could then seek to address these as a priority in environmental policy.

### *Factor analysis*

Occasionally during the course of our research, we will find we have a number of different indicators, all of which appear to be measuring the same thing. This may be intentional, for example in seeking to increase the validity of a survey questionnaire it is common to ask similar questions that are essentially tapping into the same qualities. If the questions have been designed well, we would expect the responses from each to support the responses from the others for each case. Or it may be that we have recorded a series of measures, and after the event we notice the scores appear to be suggesting that there might be some underlying 'factor' that is causing people to score similarly on particular sets of indicators. Either way, if our data contain a large number of variables that are really only measuring a small number of factors, it can be more efficient to analyse the factors, rather than all of the variables.

Imagine we design a survey questionnaire which consists of a series of questions to investigate a particular phenomenon, such as why people decide to go to university. We might ask questions which measure the degree to which the following aspects play an important role in choosing a particular university to study at: course content; teaching quality; research rating; postgraduate opportunities; the university town's night-life; student union facilities; availability of halls of residence; clubs and societies. (The list would no doubt go on, but for our purposes we will keep this example relatively confined.)

If we look at the eight measures a bit more closely, we can see that some might be related to one another. For example, course content, teaching quality, research rating, and postgraduate opportunities might all be associated with each other because they represent an overall trait which has not been directly measured in our survey, but manifests itself through these measures. That trait might be described as an overall desire to select a university for *academic* reasons. This latent trait is referred to as a *factor*, and is something that is considered to have a causal link to the associated variables (referred to as items). The last four items might also feasibly be caused by a common factor, that of *social* reasons for choosing a university. Factor analysis enables us to identify the presence of these underlying factors, and produce a single new scale for each factor. These scales can then be used in further analysis in the same way that any other variables might be. In this example, rather than having to feed eight individual variables into a statistical model, we can use the two new variables of academic and social reasons for choosing a university.

There are a great many other multivariate techniques, but the ones we have covered here are those that you are likely to come across most often. For some, the prospect of understanding statistical formula can be off-putting, but it is worth bearing in mind that an appreciation of the correct choice and application of appropriate techniques is probably more important than an intricate understanding of the underlying mathematical foundations. Learning which techniques are appropriate for different research questions, and understanding the assumptions about the data that need to be met in order to use them, is crucial. For a more detailed exploration of all of these techniques, see the recommended further reading at the end of this chapter.

## Preparing data for qualitative analysis

Qualitative research is often considered to be a somewhat enigmatic pursuit because it conjures up images of an unwieldy process characterised by lone researchers wallowing in paperwork. This image can largely be attributed to two factors. The first is the fact that qualitative research can generate a large volume of data due to the necessary collection of audio and video tapes, lengthy transcriptions of interviews, field notes, and so on. The second factor is in part due to the relatively recent development of computer software for aiding qualitative analysis, and an apparent reluctance on the part of qualitative researchers to embrace technological advances. Both of these factors are of particular importance when considering how to go about managing qualitative data.

Qualitative data can be found all around us. In the newspapers we read, the television broadcasts we view, memos we receive at work, graffiti we see in the streets, or the text messages we exchange via mobile phones – we come across a wealth of qualitative data every day. These naturally occurring sources of data are initially produced for a purpose other than our research. Nevertheless, they still provide us with rich data to analyse. It is possible to carry out a highly informative research project that is based on the analysis of this type of qualitative data alone, and for some, such as media analysts, this is often the case. However, qualitative researchers often seek to generate their own data, which are gathered in the field. Methods such as interviews and observations enable researchers to collect rich data which are geared towards the research project at hand.

## Naturally occurring sources of qualitative data

Naturally occurring sources of qualitative data can present advantages over primary data because they are formed in the natural setting of the social world, without any influence from the researcher. For example, we may be interested in seeking to understand exploitation and power relations in the workplace. The researcher could interview employees and directors within the organisation and ask about experiences of exploitation or feelings towards relationships with colleagues. However, this approach may only identify agencies at work which the interviewees are aware of and are willing to discuss with the researcher. Observation techniques may result in a more accurate picture of the ways these issues manifest themselves, but there is still the potential for behaviour to be modified in the presence of the researcher (see the section on reactivity in Chapter 7). In instances such as this, existing documentary sources, such as internal memos, job contracts and email correspondence, may provide the researcher with the most valid data.

Some research questions will presuppose the examination of naturally occurring data as the only means of analysis because the processes by which data are produced naturally form part of the process under investigation. This is very much the case with discourse and conversation analysis, both approaches being concerned with what occurs as the spoken or written word is produced. A conversation analyst examining the way a mother talks to her daughter might ask questions about the ways in which control of power is maintained through the choice of particular words or phrases, for example.

When examining naturally occurring documents or texts such as these, the context is often equally as important as the content. Hammersley and Atkinson (1995, p.173) draw attention to the types of question researchers should have in mind when approaching these types of data:

> The presence and significance of documentary products provide the ethnographer with a rich vein of analytic topics, as well as a valuable source of information. Such topics include: How are documents written? How are they read? Who writes them? Who reads them? For what purposes? On what occasions? With what outcomes? What is recorded? What is omitted? What does the writer seem to take for granted about the reader(s)? What do readers need to know in order to make sense of them?

It is evident from the questions that Hammersley and Atkinson pose that the researcher needs to look beyond the meanings portrayed by the words or pictures in naturally occurring sources in order to appreciate the context in which the source is used in its natural setting. This echoes disagreement between positivist approaches and those of naturalism. Positivists strive towards gathering precisely measured data which is uncontaminated by external factors (such as the linguistic ambiguities of open responses). This, they would argue, adds reliability to the data since they are able to use the data to report the observed 'facts'. On the other hand, naturalists would contend that meaning can only be properly derived from data that are collected from within the field.

Data that are collected in this way benefit from being contextually situated. For example, if we were interested in what it was like to be incarcerated in a prison serving a long sentence, we could interview prisoners. These interviews would most likely take place in an interview room especially set up for the purpose: it is unlikely that they would take part in the interviewee's cell. We may acquire a large amount of highly informative interview data, but this will have been provided in a false situation. The interview room is not part of the prisoner's everyday life. However, if we were able to gain access to a prisoner's journal, which had been written in a cell during the long, monotonous days spent serving a sentence, this might tell us a different story. It is such a consideration of the context in which documents are produced, and for what purpose, that enables us to see the advantages of naturally occurring sources of data.

## Activity 8.1

Consider the questions outlined by Hammersley and Atkinson (1995) and how they might be applied to the previous example of exploring power relations and exploitation in the workplace. First, make a list of the different types of naturally occurring sources which may be of use to a researcher seeking to understand this research area. Now ask yourself the following questions, making notes against each source you have identified.

1. The distribution lists on emails might provide us with useful data. What type of data could be derived from the source you have identified?
2. The distribution lists could tell us something about how information is shared with, or withheld from, particular groups via email. How would the data you have identified in the previous question help you to tackle the research question?
3. Are there any limitations to using these sources?
4. Are there any advantages to using these naturally occurring sources?
5. Can you foresee any problems in gaining access to these types of sources?

*(Continued)*

*(Continued)*

6. The ways in which particular people are chosen to be members of certain groups may be hidden in an interview, but the natural context in which emails were sent enables us to identify these groups. How would the natural context of the documents you have identified help to answer the research question?

## Primary data

While qualitative data are fairly abundant in everyday life, researchers often have specific research questions in mind, for which they need to gather specific data. The use of interviews and observation techniques as methods of primary data collection is common in qualitative research and in both cases enables the researcher to exert some degree of control over the data that are collected. While in both the interview situation and the observation setting the researcher is dependent upon the participants providing the data, the setting in which data are collected is identified by the researcher as being most likely to yield data which will coincide with the objectives of the study.

The notable advantage of primary data is precisely this ability of the researcher to be able to determine the context in which the data are collected. Any research that concerns subjects which do not present themselves readily in everyday life lends itself more to the collection of primary data. Since qualitative research is commonly associated with investigating meanings associated with subjects, or the ways in which people interpret their experiences, the researcher will often find she or he simply has to go out and get the data, rather than making use of what already exists. For example, if we were carrying out research which sought to investigate how asylum seekers managed to maintain a sense of their own cultural identity while integrating into a new society, we would be hard pushed to find naturally occurring sources which gave us a true insight. The press coverage around the issue of asylum would possibly provide useful background contextual information for consideration, but to get to the heart of the matter the researcher would have to collect data from the asylum seekers themselves.

When collecting data it is important to be aware of the context in which the data were produced since this will influence the ways in which analysis can be carried out. Much work has been carried out looking at the interview situation, and the effects of power relations between interviewer and participant (see, for example, Oakley 1981). In situations where primary data are being collected, this is of particular importance because artificial settings can be created where inequalities exist between the researcher and participants. For more detail about approaches which have developed in an attempt to tackle this, see Chapter 2, with particular reference to standpoint methodology.

Table 8.5 Examples of qualitative data

| *Type of data* | *Examples* |
|---|---|
| Textual | Field notes; reflective journals; newspaper articles; memos; transcripts; email/text messages |
| Audio | Audio recordings of, for example, interviews, speeches, naturally occurring talk; radio broadcasts; music |
| Visual | Television; cinema; photographs; paintings; sculpture; video recording of, for example, focus groups or observations; video diaries |

Whether data are collected from existing documentary sources or through data collection techniques devised explicitly for the project, qualitative data can be categorised into textual, audio or visual information. Table 8.5 gives just a small selection of the most common examples.

As can be seen:

> qualitative data embraces an enormously rich spectrum of cultural and social artefacts. What do these different kinds of data have in common? They all convey meaningful information in a form other than numbers. (Dey 1993, p.12)

## Interviews as data

A great deal of qualitative research relies upon the analysis of in-depth interview transcripts. The level of detail in the data that are produced by in-depth interviews differs substantially from that obtainable from closed survey questionnaires. For an exploration of these differences, see Example 8.3.

### Example 8.3 The differences between in-depth interview data and questionnaire data

A university department is interested in establishing how new technologies are being implemented by its staff to help with learning and teaching. The project has two main objectives: (1) to find out the extent of the use of new technologies; and (2) to try to understand why the staff are using them, or conversely what the perceived barriers are to introducing them into teaching. The types of learning technology available are already known, and include such things as different word processing, analysis and presentation software packages, email, the Internet and computer-aided testing. To establish the extent of the use of these, a questionnaire is administered to all staff in the department. It consists of questions asking which technologies are used, for what purpose and how often. The data

*(Continued)*

*(Continued)*

provided enables the answers to these research questions to be quantified. The results tell us in fact that 75% of the staff use presentation software as an aid when giving lectures, and that all staff communicate with students via email, whereas only 10% of staff use their own websites as a learning aid. These data are useful in establishing the type and extent of a phenomenon: *What* are people doing? How often? For what purpose? These data therefore suit the first objective of this project. In order to meet the second objective of the project, in-depth interviews are carried out with a selection of participants with a range of experiences of using technology. Questions are far more open than with the questionnaire, and ask such things as 'What made you decide to start using email instead of the notice board?' or 'Are there any elements of your teaching which have been made easier by using new technologies?' The data provided in response to these questions are more detailed and textual in nature. They provide an insight into the experiences of the staff in using new technologies which perhaps could not have been guessed at prior to the interviews. These data are useful in answering such questions as '*Why* do you think you behave in this way?' or '*How* do you feel about this particular subject?' In this sense, the data provided are able to meet the second objective more effectively than data which would be collected through a quantitative survey.

This example highlights the different uses to which quantitative and qualitative data are suited: quantitative data are well suited to explaining what is happening, whereas qualitative data are helpful in understanding how and why something is happening, in terms of a more in-depth exploration of the phenomena. The example also serves to outline some of the characteristics of both data types, which will be explored further in this chapter.

When analysing interviews or focus groups, a decision needs to be made as to whether to rely on notes or to record the dialogue on tape or other electronic device. It is usually preferable to make use of recordings since these offer a more complete representation of what was said. In some instances, however, recording may not be possible. Hammersley and Atkinson (1995, p.185) warn that 'sometimes, interviewees will refuse to allow the discussion to be audio-recorded; sometimes the [researcher] may judge that such recording will dissuade frankness or increase nervousness to an unacceptable level'. Where this is the case, the importance of making full and coherent notes cannot be overemphasised, although in practice this is actually extremely difficult and can have a detrimental effect on the flow of the interview. In such circumstances, it is also important that we recognise that analysis and interpretation are occurring in the field, as we take notes. A process of data selection and interpretation actually takes place during the interview. The researcher has to make quick, sometimes unconscious, decisions about what is to be noted down and how to phrase it. It is therefore necessary to be prepared to be selective in the field, and record notes in such a way that data are collected which respond to the research questions.

Fortunately, if participants are well enough briefed about why recording is important and issues of confidentiality and anonymity are dealt with in full, in most cases recording is possible. This being the case, transcription will need to be carried out to aid analysis. The written word consumes a far greater volume than when spoken, and transcription can take a considerable amount of time. Transcription can be seen as a process which is:

> [N]either neutral nor value-free. What passes from tape to paper is the result of decisions about what ought to go on to paper. Sometimes 'bad' language gets edited out. Sometimes a typist decides to type only words, not pauses and 'er', 'mmm' and 'huh!'. Similarly, there is the notorious problem of how to punctuate speech: where should full stops, semi-colons and commas go? What about paragraph marks? ... Transcriptions are, quite unequivocally, interpretations. For that reason, if no other, it is wise to keep interview tapes as an archive to which reference can be made if transcriptions prove to be inadequate for the level of analysis which becomes necessary. (Arksey and Knight 1999, pp.141–2)

Precise transcription is often used when the nature of interaction is of interest, for example in conversation analysis, but by and large a researcher who is simply interested in what someone has to say about a subject will make do with conventional syntax when transcribing. It is worth noting, though, that hesitation and pauses in speech can be as telling as the actual words since they may form part of the expression of meanings for the participant. Silverman (2001, p.230) warns that 'when people's activities are tape-recorded and transcribed, the reliability of the interpretation of the transcripts may be gravely weakened by a failure to transcribe apparently trivial, but often crucial, pauses and overlaps'. Methods of transcription have been devised to preserve these idiosyncrasies of the spoken word which are not apparent in conventionally written language, but it is advisable to treat transcripts as a tool to aid analysis.

Other unusual characteristics of someone's speech, such as regional accents or use of colloquialisms, may also be of interest, and help in expression. The novelist Irvine Welsh has written many books about working-class youths growing up in the inner-city slums in Scotland. He often writes in a phonetic way in order to convey the unique sound of the characters' accents. This sound helps to contextualise the dialogue and provides cultural reference that would not be apparent if conventional English was used. As a result, a sense of expression is conveyed that would otherwise be lost. While this is a literary example, the same ideas apply to the transcription of interviews, and provide yet another consideration for the qualitative researcher at this point of analysis.

## Managing field notes and journals

Note-taking is a process with which many people are familiar, whether it is from attending lectures, writing up minutes of meetings, writing down telephone messages for others, or any other of the myriad examples in everyday life where we have to commit an idea to paper. In all examples of note-taking, the purpose is the same: to capture the essence of what we are observing and record it for future reference. This purpose applies to field notes when carrying out research. What we are attempting to do is produce a description of the events we are witnessing which will enable us to replay the events in our minds and reflect upon them at a later point in time. In order to do this, a level of accuracy is required, yet a comprehensiveness of coverage is also needed. As we are unable to pause real events while we write our notes, or interrupt the flow of an interview without compromising the dialogue, we need to be creative in the variety of techniques we use for gathering field notes.

Burgess (1984, p.169) provides an informative account of the variety of field notes that he collected, and for what purpose, while carrying out research in a British comprehensive school:

> My notes were predominantly descriptive and aimed to provide a detailed portrait of the various situations in which I became involved. The field notes included physical descriptions of situations and informants, details of conversations, and accounts of events. ... For each day that I was in school my notes comprised: a continuous record of the events in which I was involved and the conversations in which I participated. Here, I focussed on the words and phrases that were used so as to provide an almost literal account of what had been said. My notes also focussed upon details of particular events in each school day and therefore always involved a record of: early morning meetings with the Head of House, morning assembly in the House, break time in the staff room, at the end of the day, as well as detailed observations of lessons in which I participated. In some of these situations I used diagrams to summarise details about particular settings. For example, I used diagrams to show individuals who sat next to each other in meetings and to summarise interactions and conversations between participants. Often these diagrammatic notes were written shortly after the period of observation and provided a summary that could be used later in the day to write up more detailed notes. In particular I kept diagrams of who sat with whom in the early morning meetings, in morning assembly and at break times in the staff common room. The result was that I was able to build up a portrait of the relationships in particular settings and of the structure of particular groups.

Burgess demonstrates here the range of field notes available to the researcher, and it is important to recognise that they act as more than just a series of unrelated observations recorded in shorthand. Field notes should be gathered with the intention of making sense of the subject being researched. They should be looked over as a whole, so relationships and themes can be identified. On occasions, the researcher will have a number of predetermined themes, which may be derived from the research questions, and these will form the basis of a structure for field notes. This thematic organisation, for some, provides an ideal way of managing and analysing field notes, but others may argue that it is too prescriptive and can serve to blinker the researcher, preventing new ideas being generated out of the data. Whether you adopt a thematic approach or a more open approach will largely depend on whether your research is entirely exploratory or revolves around certain focused aims. This notion is explored in more detail later, when we come to discuss different approaches to analysis.

A particular type of field note is the reflective journal. The reflective journal places the researcher and her or his experiences firmly in the research process itself, and so it can bring with it a value-laden emphasis to the research. The reflective journal is a core element of action research whereby:

> It enables you to integrate information and experiences which, when understood, help you to understand your reasoning processes and consequent behaviour and so anticipate experiences before embarking upon them. Keeping a journal regularly imposes a discipline and captures your experiences of key events close to when they happen and before the passage of time changes your perception of them. (Coghlan and Brannick 2001, p.33)

Integrating our own experiences into the research process and reflecting on them enables us to fine-tune our methods and understand our philosophical perspective and therefore make us aware of the ways we are approaching the data. When carrying out qualitative research in particular, our involvement in the process can result in our losing sight of the focus of the research. A journal is a useful way of analysing not just the data, but the whole research process.

## Recording and organising qualitative data

There are a number of fairly straightforward, practical steps you can take in managing your data. When using audio or video tapes, it is important to ensure that these are correctly labelled with the date, location of the recording, the participants, and any other information of particular relevance to your research. It is also advisable to make backup copies – even if the recordings have been transcribed – since you may wish to return to the original recording to establish the existence of certain details that may have not been picked up during the initial transcription. The development of new forms of recordable electronic media, such as DVDs, enables easy transferral of data to a computer for backup. The cost of electronic hard disk recording devices has dropped substantially in recent years, and these are now within the reach of researchers carrying out a small-scale project on a tight budget. Many mobile phones now have recording facilities build in, allowing for reasonable recording of interviews which can then be transferred to a computer quickly and easily.

Storage of data also has to take into consideration elements of data protection, to reflect both general stipulation, such as national legislation, and provision offered by a consent agreement signed by the research participants. It is important that you familiarise yourself with any legislation that governs the way data about individuals is kept. The UK Data Protection Act (1998), for example, lays down specific legislation surrounding the purpose for which data are used as well as the manner in which they are stored. If you have offered your participants confidentiality and anonymity (see Chapter 4), then the data should be kept locked away, or if stored on a computer, then the files should be password protected.

Careful storage of the media in which data are recorded (tapes, transcripts, photographs, electronic files, and so on) will ensure that the data are readily available and not susceptible to damage or loss, but this is only one step towards making the process of analysis easier. In any research project, it is important for each stage of the process to be designed in such a way as to anticipate the next. When it comes to data management and analysis, the task will be made all the more straightforward if the data have first been collected in an organised and structured way. Dey (1993, p.75) poses an interesting question around the organisation of data:

> Data should be recorded in a format which facilitates analysis. Decisions made at this stage can have repercussions later. Suppose we have conducted some interviews and we have to record responses to a large number of open questions. Do we file the data as a complete interview for each case, or as a set of responses for each question? The former allows the interview to be recorded and read as a whole, but inhibits ready comparison between responses; the latter facilitates comparison between responses, but makes it difficult to see the interview as a whole.

The sensible solution to this dilemma is to do both. By making copies of the interview transcript, the original interviews can be preserved, allowing responses to questions to be read in the broader context of the interview as a whole, but in addition segments from excerpts from different interviews which deal with the same topics can be filed together to enable cross-comparison between interviews.

The availability of qualitative analysis software within academic institutions tends to remain overshadowed by that of quantitative software, and many researchers carrying out small-scale qualitative studies will carry out their analysis manually. When doing so, the way in which we file our data needs to be decided from the outset. However, where computer software is available, the ways in which data are stored, organised and accessed remain flexible. Such software can store whole interviews as individual transcripts, but allow the researcher to index and view different sections taken from multiple interviews alongside each other.

Computers have, understandably, become synonymous with 'number crunching'. After all, they process numerical information – even letters have to be turned into numbers before a computer can handle them. So what good is a glorified counting machine to a qualitative researcher? Well, when it comes to carrying out analysis, arguably a computer is not of much use at all, but treat a computer as a tool to help you store, manage and organise qualitative data, and its use begins to become an entirely inviting prospect.

## Qualitative data analysis

Qualitative data analysis is often characterised by its lack of distinct rules. It is possible for quantitative researchers to consult statistics texts and locate the appropriate means of analysis given the type of data they are working with. Qualitative researchers are not afforded this luxury, which helps to explain the bewilderment many face when it comes to analysis. The lack of rules can be liberating – there are no right or wrong approaches. Yet, more often than not to the novice researcher, this can lead to uncertainty about the way to progress with analysis. There do, however, exist general approaches to analysis which can provide a useful framework as well as the valuable knowledge that the approach being adopted has been successfully used by others. Also, as we shall see, the assertion that qualitative analysis is unsystematic can also be countered by the application of approaches such as grounded theory and those developed by Miles and Huberman (1994) in an organised and structured manner.

In considering different approaches to analysis, we have categorised qualitative research into three 'types':

1. Theory-generating, exploratory research.
2. Theory-driven, explanatory research.
3. Research concerned with visual and textual latent meanings.

The first of these represents the type of research with a long tradition in anthropology and ethnography – research which is conducted in circumstances where there are few prior theories, and which seeks to learn about a group or phenomenon through extended study and immersion in the topic. *Grounded theory* research comes under this umbrella, and we shall deal with this first. Then we shall move on to look at both analytic induction and Miles and Huberman's highly structured approach to analysing qualitative data, which seeks to both establish and test theories. Research which begins with a clear conceptual framework based on established theory in the literature might fall into this category. Finally, some researchers are concerned with the processes by which *meaning* is communicated through language and visual signs. Here the focus is less on what is being said, or visualised, but why – for what purpose. Research of this nature can be either theory-generating or theory-driven, but what sets it apart is the focus on latent meaning and communication processes. Semiotics, conversation analysis and discourse analysis are all included in this section.

## Exploratory, theory-generating research

### *Grounded theory*

A popular approach to qualitative data analysis, used particularly in exploratory research where little is known about the phenomenon under investigation, is grounded theory. Grounded theory was originally developed by Barney Glaser and Anselm Strauss and is outlined in its earliest form in their classic text *The Discovery of Grounded Theory: Strategies for Qualitative Research* (Glaser and Strauss 1967). The title of this original text provides us with a vital clue about one of the most important aspects of grounded theory: it is concerned with the *discovery* of theory from the data, which is 'suited to its supposed purpose' (1967, p.3). Since its conception, grounded theory has developed in a number of ways, most notably with the publication in 1990 of *Basics of Qualitative Research: Grounded Theory Procedures and Techniques*, in which Anselm Strauss teamed up with Juliet Corbin. That text is now in its third edition (Corbin and Strauss 2008), and as key proponents of grounded theory, Corbin and Strauss themselves have probably been the most instrumental in refining the approach. Researchers tend to adopt elements of it for their own purposes; on occasions, researchers claim to use grounded theory when really they are just referring to the process of induction. It is important to note that grounded theory concerns a general approach to the entire research process, and not just to analysis alone. It involves the acceptance of an openness to ideas developing and even to the complete rephrasing of research questions as new ideas emerge. Throughout this chapter we have discussed other stages of the research process and how these can determine or shape our analysis. We have tried to emphasise the importance of not treating analysis as a discrete stage of the research process, and this is perhaps no more important than when considering grounded theory.

The process of grounded theory begins with a desire to understand a research area. Research questions may be broad, with no specific objectives or operationalisation of concepts – these will come as the process unfolds. By and large, questions tend to revolve around a simple desire to find out what is going on, either in a particular situation or with a particular group, to make sense of the unknown. The most recent edition of Strauss and Corbin's key text was published some years after Strauss passed away, and much of the revised material was therefore produced by Corbin. She uses a working example throughout the text, based mainly upon the transcript of an extended interview with a Vietnam war veteran. Prior to conducting the analysis, she had not seen the transcript, since it was from an interview conducted by Strauss, and so she was approaching the topic and the data completely afresh. Her intention was 'to explain the Vietnam War from the perspectives of the soldiers who fought in that war' (Corbin and Strauss 2008, p.162). This is the extent of the objectives of the research as it commences. Note that, at the outset, no assumptions are made about which concepts may be of importance, and no hypotheses are stated. She is simply open to discovering what the data tell her about the experiences of the interviewee.

Having isolated a topic, theoretical sampling (see Chapter 7 for a general discussion of this topic) is then employed to identify participants or events from which data can be collected in order to begin to understand the area under investigation. From interviews with participants, observations of events, or documentary sources such as diaries, the first stages of data collection begin.

With the grounded theory approach there is no need to amass a large quantity of data prior to commencing analysis, and, in truth, hesitation in starting analysis can have a detrimental effect on the whole process. As soon as initial data have been collected, a process of *open coding* begins. Open coding involves initially reading the data with the intention of identifying common themes. These themes form the basis for the main *concepts*, which may then be categorised as of a higher or lower level of abstraction. Higher-level concepts may be more general while lower-level concepts are more specific, and help to explain the higher-level concepts. Corbin provides an example of three concepts: the 'war experience', 'psychological survival strategies' and 'blocking', each of which is explained by the following lower-level concept. Part of the war experience can be explained by the ways in which psychological survival strategies become a part of everyday life for the combatants, and of these psychological survival strategies, blocking out of events is one example which explains how such survival is achieved. The linking together of these higher- and lower-level concepts is described as being 'like putting together a series of interlocking blocks to build a pyramid' (Corbin and Strauss 2008, p.198).

As well as identifying higher- and lower-level concepts, it is important to describe the concepts by linking them to the data provided by individual cases, and isolating descriptive *properties* and *dimensions*.

> Under the concept of 'locating' come several minor concepts – **properties** that help define who he was. The first is 'family background', which includes being 'middle-class,' 'religious,' 'God fearing,' 'close,' and above all 'patriotic'. ... The 'path to war' subconcepts include: hearing war stories, being a nurse, volunteering ... becoming a 'six-week wonder', being an officer and being quickly dispatched to the war zone. I must say that his 'path' has the **dimensions** of being 'straight' and 'quick'. (Corbin and Strauss 2008, pp.164–5)

A combination of higher concepts, which are explained by lower concepts, and properties and dimensions which help to specify lower concepts leads to a rich description of the data, and also helps to build a framework within which to organise the concepts. This process is often referred to as 'axial coding' (Strauss and Corbin 1998; Charmaz 2006). Whereas open coding can be seen as a process of breaking the data up into categories, and axial coding as reconnecting data fragments to make sense out of the connections between the fragments, Corbin is keen to de-stress what she says amounts to an 'artificial' distinction between the two, suggesting that '[a]s analysts work with data, their minds automatically make connections because, after all, the connections come from the data' (Corbin and Strauss 2008, p.198).

Initial stages of coding will drive further analysis and help to inform the criteria for further theoretical sampling. By identifying particular concepts, we are able to fine-tune our sampling strategy so the people we interview and situations we observe will be those best placed to enlighten us further about our research area. This cycle of sampling, data collection and coding is driven by the *constant comparative method*. Here the researcher is seeking to identify *categories* which recur throughout the data. Categories enable us to link the concepts to the data, so, for example, references to particular feelings or events made in interviews can be linked to concepts because they fit into a category.

Glaser and Strauss (1967, p.106) offer some useful practical advice on how to approach the data with the constant comparative method, suggesting that:

> Coding need consist only of noting categories on margins, but can be done more elaborately (e.g., on cards). It should keep track of the comparison group in which the incident occurs. To this procedure we add the basic, defining rule for the constant comparative method: while coding an incident for a category, compare it with the previous incidents in the same and different groups coded in the same *category*.

Comparison between incidents in the data enables us to decide whether there are a number of incidents which fall into the same category, or whether incidents suggest different aspects of a category, thereby leading us to create new categories with which to code the data. It is important that we keep track of our thinking behind all of the decisions we make – the creation of categories and how these categories link together conceptually – and this is usually done by creating memos. Memos are short notes written to yourself and attached to categories which 'catch your thoughts, capture the comparisons and connections you make, and crystallize questions and directions for you to pursue' (Charmaz 2006, p.72). Memos are an integral part of the grounded theory process, since they enable you to retrace your analytical steps, but also work through new ideas. They are part of the writing process which, like all the other elements of grounded theory, takes place alongside the other stages.

The process of continual coding, development of categories and recording analytical insights in memos eventually leads to a point of category saturation, whereby further coding of the data becomes no longer feasible nor desirable. At this stage, we begin to look at elaborating the relationships between the categories, and contextualising the data.

Looking to external documents can be useful in adding context. Corbin makes use of memoirs written by survivors of the Vietnam war which provide a detailed description of the culture of war, and which enable a further elaboration of the data. Using these, she is able to identify certain conditions and consequences which all form part of a process. It is these processes which ultimately provide a theory which can help explain what is going on in the situation or group that is being studied. At this stage, all the coding, categorising and theory generation is integrated to form a central, substantive theory, which is solidly grounded in the data. For Corbin, the experience of the Vietnam war for combatants largely comes down to a process of survival – physical and psychological – in which the combatants must go through several transitions. Combatants must grow up quickly. They are forced to face up to a stark reality of war, which contradicts a former glorified vision, for example. She explores various survival strategies in more detail, but crucially, all of the concepts, and the final theories which are developed, have been drawn from the data. Reaching a stage at which a satisfactory theory is arrived at, which explains what is going on, is the stage of *theoretical saturation*. This implies that we have arrived at a theory which is closely linked to (and therefore substantiated by) the data and one which cannot be further developed with the data available – i.e. a *substantive theory*.

The process of grounded theory is, then, a highly involved approach to qualitative research. It should be evident that, while it involves all stages of the research process, the approach to analysis that it advocates is a particularly useful stage. The constant comparative method can be embraced as good practice when it comes to qualitative data analysis, regardless of whether a general grounded theory approach is adopted. It provides a systematic framework in which to develop analysis and generate theory which is firmly embedded in empirical evidence.

## Theory-driven research and causal explanation

### *The analytic induction method*

The analytic induction method represents a response to the challenge that qualitative research cannot be used to investigate causal relationships. The strength of the argument for identifying such relationships rests in the assertion that it is necessary to do so in order to be able to explain and predict social phenomena. The argument continues that, without an understanding of these relationships, social research is limited in its application to an understanding of the specific case being studied. In order to broaden the application of social science, it is necessary to be able to make inferences and develop rules which govern human interaction. The analytic induction method consists of a number of stages where hypothesis refinement is achieved through data analysis, until the hypothesis is borne out by all cases. The researcher begins with a broad research question. In contrast to grounded theory, a hypothesis is also established prior to data collection that attempts to offer a response to the research question. The data from each case are then examined and the hypothesis will be either confirmed or refuted. If there is cause to reject the hypothesis on the basis of data from a particular case, then the hypothesis requires modification.

The aim is to arrive at a situation whereby all cases support the hypothesis. Modifying the hypothesis can be carried out in one of two ways, which involve giving precedence to either the original phenomenon under investigation, or the new data. In the first instance the hypothesis is redefined so as to give a hypothetical explanation which excludes the deviant case. Alternatively, the new data from the deviant case can be taken into consideration and the hypothesis reformulated around these new data. Following on from this, new data are collected against which to examine the reformulated hypothesis further. The process is repeated until no conflicting data are encountered, or the hypothesis is redefined so as to exclude all deviant cases.

Analytic induction does, therefore, offer a way of examining the data with the intention of testing hypotheses. It has, however, come up against criticism, in particular because:

> First, the final explanations that analytic induction arrives at specify the conditions that are *sufficient* for the phenomenon occurring, but rarely specify the *necessary* conditions. ... Secondly, it does not provide useful guidelines (unlike grounded theory) as to how many cases need to be investigated before the absence of negative cases and the validity of the hypothetical explanation (whether reformulated or not) can be confirmed. (Bryman 2004, pp.400–1)

The use of analytic induction has decreased in recent years, perhaps owing to the increased interest in grounded theory, and the growing strength which research carried out by approaches other than those founded in positivism has gained.

### *Miles and Huberman*

Miles and Huberman's *Qualitative Data Analysis: An Expanded Sourcebook* (1994) provides guidelines to techniques designed to move beyond the exploratory approach often adopted in much qualitative analysis, and to take a step towards explaining. Of their orientation towards qualitative data analysis, they say this:

> We aim to account for events, rather than simply to document their sequence. We look for an individual social process, a mechanism, a structure at the core of events that can be captured to provide a causal description of the forces at work. (Miles and Huberman 1994, p.4)

The rigour with which they analyse and visualise the data certainly adds a degree of reliability to analysis, and the firm empirical basis of explanation within their approach stands up well against the standard criticisms levelled at much qualitative research. The approach is one which many students looking for structured guidelines will gladly turn to; the use of causal models and displays helps to make their methods 'orderly ones, with a good degree of formalization' (Miles and Huberman 1994, p.5).

The formal structure and order can be found from the outset, prior to data collection, with the development of a very carefully considered conceptual framework. Whereas grounded theorists might look to start with a completely open, exploratory question, Miles and Huberman suggest that we tackle research questions which have an identified purpose, and that usually we will have a predetermined set of concepts we wish to investigate. Therefore, it is recommended that we begin with all the knowledge available to us on the subject, which is then used to point towards the general concepts or variables we should look at, and the sample required to do so. The conceptual framework might include people, organisations, behaviours, interactions – in short, almost anything that is relevant to our research question. Although they will be explored and explained in a lot more depth as the analysis unfolds, identifying the components of the framework, and the ways we believe they might be connected, provides a good degree of focus to start with. For instance, in a study of the introduction of a ban on smoking in public places, we might assume that we will want to include smokers and their attitudes, changes in behaviours, owners of licensed establishments and the impact on their trade, policy-makers, and the various processes involved in a consultation exercise, to name a few. Using a diagram to illustrate how concepts are arranged together is encouraged, but the precise format this takes is entirely down to the researcher; it is a tool for visualising the concepts that the research is intended to tackle, so whatever works for the researcher is good.

Having developed a conceptual framework, sampling and collection of data can take place. Data are coded and categorised according to the concepts identified within the conceptual framework, alongside any new concepts which arise during analysis. Initial coding is usually descriptive, and will be used to categorise people, events, types of behaviour, and so on. Later coding, described as *pattern coding,* involves linking the categories together in ways which seek to explain why things occur. The development of a conceptual framework, identifying a sample, and coding of data are all part of the first stage of analysis – data reduction. Data reduction is a practical way of limiting the amount of data we have to deal with when it comes to interpretation, but it is also a way of taking initial steps towards theory development. In this sense, data reduction shares much in common with many other approaches to qualitative analysis. It relies heavily upon theoretical sampling and open coding according to certain categories (both of which are informed by the conceptual framework). Where Miles and Huberman's approach begins to deviate from other techniques is the strong reliance upon data display in the form of matrices and diagrams.

Data displays enable the visual organisation of data. They 'fall into two major families: matrices, with defined rows and columns, and networks, with a series of "nodes" with links between them' (Miles and Huberman 1994, p.93). Matrices enable the researcher to organise the data in a way that cross-tabulates the concepts or variables that have been coded. Returning to the smoking ban example, it may be that a matrix is developed which details the various stages of the consultation process in rows, and the people involved in the process in columns. Where each row and cell intersects, we might include a brief description of how that particular person is involved in that particular stage of the process, with an illustration from a quote from an interview or other document.

Networks are less prescribed in their format, consisting of diagrammatic illustrations of how ideas are connected. This may be in the form of a simple, linear diagram connecting one stage of a process with the next by an arrow, or they may be much more complex. For example, networks can be used to display how the different units within an organisation work together, or how management structures operate. They can also show decision-making processes or communication patterns. Once again, flexibility is a key characteristic of data displays, both in terms of the format they take and their function. They can be used to *describe* something (such as how departments in an organisation are structured) or *explain* something (such as why certain departments perform much better than others).

The coding and display of data should evolve alongside continuous rounds of data collection, and as it does, theories will also evolve. Whereas much qualitative research results in the development of a theory that fits the case(s) in question, but leaves it there, Miles and Huberman are extremely keen to be able to verify conclusions. This is the final stage of the research, which also sets it apart from a lot of exploratory qualitative research. They provide a lot of helpful advice on how to draw strong conclusions, but also how to verify them. Tactics revolve around important methodological considerations that should be taken on board when assessing the reliability or validity of any research, but they also provide some useful practical guidance. Checking the data for cases which apparently contradict conclusions (as with analytic induction) is one way to try to validate and make more sense of findings. Questions over the generalisability of the conclusions can be partially answered by testing the theories against other cases, and one such example is by performing 'if-then' tests. These enable us to test causal explanatory theories by inquiring of other cases, '*if this cause is present, does this outcome occur?*'. If we repeatedly see the predicted outcome in other cases, we have stronger evidence for the generalisability of the conclusions we have drawn.

It must be said that a number of the techniques Miles and Huberman ascribe to will appear to many qualitative researchers as if they are too close to the variable-oriented, causal-explanatory approaches adopted in much quantitative work, and this may be enough to deter some. They talk of spurious relationships between variables, tabulating, counting and outliers, all of which are at home in the vocabulary of statistical modelling. However, as a defence against the oft-cited criticism of qualitative research – that it lacks generalisability – Miles and Huberman's approach does offer a transparent, structured, empirically-based analytical framework which many will find helpful and reassuring. It also offers a useful solution to the problem of how to present qualitative data in a way that does not simply read as a narrative compiled of lengthy quotes.

## Research concerned with visual and textual latent meanings

### *Conversation analysis*

Conversation analysis (CA) was pioneered by Harvey Sacks, in the 1960s, as the result of an attempt to study naturally occurring talk by analysing its structure. This was quite a departure from the widely held belief among many linguists at the time that naturally occurring talk was too complex and unwieldy to be deconstructed and analysed in this systematic way. Sacks was not, however, a linguist. He was a sociologist, and saw conversations not just as tools of communication, but as social activities which have a purpose. He also saw them as sequential, involving turn-taking and recognised patterns – such as something referred to as the *adjacency pair*. Adjacency pairs consist of two parts to a conversation which naturally complement one another – if one is present, the other is expected to follow. Perhaps the most obvious of these is the question–answer pairing, whereby if a question is presented during the course of a conversation, we would expect an answer to follow.

Fundamental to CA is the premise that participants in spoken interchanges have a tacit understanding of these patterns and structures. If someone asks us a question, we understand that we are supposed to give an answer. This performs the task of giving and receiving information. There are other rules which are less obvious, but which nonetheless appear to be universally understood. If, for example, someone were to say 'I'm really worried about the test I have tomorrow', there is an expectation that the response would offer reassurance: 'I'm sure you'll be fine, don't worry'. The first speaker *expects* the second to offer words of comfort. If the response was 'I'm not surprised – it's going to be really tough', this would mark a deviation from the anticipated response, and a break in the anticipated structure of the conversation. These anticipated structures underline a 'normative character of paired actions' (Wooffitt 2001, p.53), so conversations can be seen as unfolding along an expected path. By analysing adherence to, and deviation from, these paths, we are able to understand how the speakers perform social actions through conversation.

CA pays very close attention to all elements of conversation; utterances, pauses and hesitations are all considered to be important in understanding structure. In conducting CA, there are few hard-and-fast rules, although the analyst will scrutinise transcripts in minute detail and seek to identify the structures that exist. The aim of CA is to describe how the social activity of spoken interactions works, and to identify the rules and patterns which appear to be universally understood. It is important to note that CA is interested less in specifically what people *mean* by their choice of phrases, but in *how* things are said, and in what order. CA sees 'talk-in-interaction as a domain of social activity that is inherently ordered and not reducible to the personality, character, mood, and so on, of the people doing the talking' (Wooffitt 2001, p.52). To this end, CA focuses very much on content, and is absolutely grounded in the data. Speculation about what *may* be intended, given what is known about the identity of the speakers, is not considered appropriate in CA. However, there may be times when broader context may be important. It is recognised that spoken interactions may have different purposes in different settings. A conversation between friends will perform different actions, with different objectives, from a job interview, for example. By studying talk in different settings, CA can help to understand how people organise their activities when confronted with different situations. Example 8.4 provides an illustration of how a short exchange between two people in an everyday situation might be analysed to reveal the social performative actions of conversation.

## Example 8.4 Analysis of a brief conversation using CA

Take the following exchange between a couple getting ready to go out for an evening.

W: Which dress shall I wear, the red one or the black one?
M: The red one.
W: Oh, err, right, ok. You don't like me in the black one?
M: No – the black one suits you too. They're both nice. You look great in both.

The first adjacency pair is in the form of an apparently simple question, 'Which dress shall I wear', which appears to be performing an apparently straightforward action of asking for an opinion. This opinion is promptly given by the man in the form of the response 'the red one'. If the original question was really intended just as a request for an informative response, that request would have been satisfied, and the conversation would end at that point. It becomes clear from the next question that this is not a satisfactory response, however, since she returns seeking clarification. That she suggests the man does not like her in the black dress implies that her original question in some way was seeking confirmation that she looked good in any dress. In other words, it was a veiled request for a compliment. Since compliments lose their honesty if they are asked for outright, they have to be sought covertly. The man then realises that he has not performed the expected role of compliment-giver and so responds positively. He also recognises an earlier mistake in his actions, that of singling out one particular dress, and so his response is an attempt to reconcile this and avoid a repeat of that mistake. His final remark, 'You look great in both', is a way of steering the focus away from the dress and on to the woman, thus finally providing the compliment that was sought initially.

This short example illustrates how certain actions are performed during the course of a conversation, and how the course of a conversation can be altered if the unexpected occurs. It also shows how much happens in a very short space of time, and how many actions, therefore, are likely to be performed on an unconscious level.

### *Discourse analysis*

It is impossible to define discourse analysis (DA) as a singular 'technique' with a set of identifiable procedures because it is something that has taken on many different forms across a variety of disciplines, including linguistics, psychology, sociology and politics. Even the idea of what constitutes 'discourse' is disputed in its specifics. However, what is generally agreed upon is that discourse concerns the way in that language is used to construct meanings and make sense of the social world. Gee (2005, p.1) describes language as being something that is used to 'support the performance of social activities and social identities and to support human affiliation within cultures, social groups and activities'. Here, language is seen as having a purpose beyond the merely informative, and as something that helps to legitimise the actions of individuals and institutions. Discourse therefore combines both language and the function and effects of language. It is here where discourse analysis begins to deviate from the concerns of conversation analysis. Although discourse analysts do examine naturally occurring exchanges, they are also interested in other forms of spoken language (speeches, addresses and broadcasts, for example) and the language of written documents. Their interest also tends to lie in understanding the psychological and political function of language.

Much qualitative research makes use of written or spoken texts purely for informative reasons. Research participants might even be referred to as 'informants'. Discourse analysis marks quite a departure from this approach, however, recognising that any two people informing us about the same event might do so in different ways and for very different reasons. Imagine two people went to visit an exhibition of modern art, which included Damien Hurst's piece *The Physical Impossibility of Death in the Mind of Someone Living*, probably more recognisable as a shark preserved in a tank of formaldehyde. One visitor describes how the piece brought to mind reflections on the human lifecycle, our mortality and the eventual, inevitable path to certain death. The other states 'it's a shark in a box – I could have done that'. These two versions of the same event both provide a description of something (one through metaphor, the other literally), but what else do these descriptions tell us about the actions of the individuals and their belonging to a group?

First, they tap into different discourses about the art world. On the one hand, there is an 'intellectual' discourse which says art should be thought-provoking and, as such, anything that achieves that aim can be considered to be art. It also suggests that since a degree of intellectual engagement is required, in order to 'get' modern art, one needs to be part of an intellectual elite. This discourse is referenced by the first person in our example, through their citing of the emotional connection and thought processes that the piece evoked. It is also, however, the practices around the art world which support this discourse: for example, private viewings of exhibitions by invitation only, or the prohibitively expensive auction prices, or perhaps the late night, post-prime time slots in which art programmes are broadcast on television.

The second discourse is a 'popular' discourse, which views art as consisting only of things that are both aesthetically pleasing and an accurate representation of the object they seek to portray. The language which is used to describe modern art within this discourse is used to distinguish it from 'proper art'. This is why we often see modern art described in negative terms which are intended to legitimise the stance of those referencing this discourse. The suggestion that 'I could do that' by the second person is a way of legitimising the position that has been adopted. They are saying that if it were truly a piece of art, it would require talent outside the reach of the layperson. There is a logic to this argument, but a logic which only makes sense within the popular discourse.

These different versions of events point to what Potter and Wetherell describe as 'the notion of variability in accounts along with the idea that accounts are constructed to have specific consequences' (1987, p.43). For both people in our example, the consequences are that each constructs a particular identity and aligns themselves with a particular group.

It is important to realise that these constructions, and the consequences of them, may well occur on an unconscious level. Although we may sometimes choose our words carefully so as to give the right impression, some of the most powerful discourses operate on such a deep level that we don't regard them as discourses, but just experience them as reality – we believe them to be true. In the example above, we have seen how two brief comments might be analysed to isolate discourses and understand meaning construction on a personal level. This is similar to the approach adopted by social psychologists. For some, though, discourse is something that must be studied on a broader societal level.

Michel Foucault (1926–84) has had a significant influence in the study of discourse. For Foucault, discourses create and reinforce forms of knowledge, and knowledge can be used to maintain control of power. At the heart of Foucault's notion of power is hegemony, the achievement of power by consent, rather than force. In order to obtain consent, it is important that the people we wish to control subscribe to the particular version of reality we want them to, one which they perceive to be 'truthful'. For example, if society wished to exert power over women in order to justify lower pay than men for equivalent work, one way to do it would be to convince women that they were worth less than men. Discourses around femininity and masculinity have for a very long time served to reinforce this. Terms such as 'breadwinner' and 'housewife', and practices such as inflexible working hours for mothers, all contribute to a gender discourse designed to justify gender inequality at the same time as reinforcing it.

Foucault was particularly interested in the discourses of large institutions, such as the criminal justice system and those involved in the treatment of mental illness. In *Madness and Civilisation*, Foucault describes 'those called, without exact semantic distinction, insane, alienated, deranged, demented, extravagant' (Foucault 2001, p.62). The use of language here clearly marks out those individuals in society with mental health conditions as somehow different – as not normal. The treatment of these individuals through the practices of the institutions is also highlighted:

> There was a certain image of animality that haunted the hospitals of the period. Madness borrowed its face from the mark of the beast. Those chained to the cell walls were no longer men whose minds had wandered, but beasts preyed upon by a natural frenzy. ... This model of animality prevailed in the asylums and gave them their cagelike aspect, their look of the menagerie. (Foucault 2001, p.68)

These practices and the language that Foucault described were from the eighteenth century and earlier. They reflected what was generally held to be a truth about madness, that it was a possessive force that made individuals in some way inhuman. This is convenient for a society that wishes to preserve a particular notion of what is right and wrong, and provides a good example of how the analysis of discourses through language and practice can help us to understand how knowledge is produced, and power maintained. This example also helps us to understand a further important aspect of Foucauldian discourse – what is held to be the truth changes over time. Mass reforms in Mental Health Acts, driven by a new understanding of mental health problems, have led to a change in practices and the ways in which we talk about mental 'illness'. Practices such as care in the community and the inclusion of children with learning difficulties in mainstream schools generally reflect a move away from the notion of 'difference' or 'abnormality'. What this discourse reflects is a new reality, and highlights the fact that what is real, or held to be true, can change over time. The dominant discourses operating at any one time contribute not to an absolute truth, but to regimes of truth. The fact that what is held to be true can change over time crucially illustrates the point that dominant discourses reflect the interests of those wishing to exert power at the time. Challenges to dominant discourses or changes in the interests of those in power can bring about a new regime of truth. A recent example was the signing of an executive order to shut down Guantánamo Bay Prison by Barack Obama upon his presidential inauguration in 2009.

The Bush administration used attacks on freedom to justify the treatment of terror suspects and legitimise the invasion of Iraq. Speaking in an interview with Trevor McDonald on *The Tonight Show* in 2005, George Bush had the following to say:

> See, these folks represent an ideology that is based upon hate and kind of a narrow vision of mankind – women don't have rights. And I believe this is an ideological movement. And I know that they want to use suicide bombers and assassinations and attacks on the World Trade Center, and the attacks in Madrid, to try to shake our will and to achieve an objective, which is to topple governments. And the best way to defeat an ideology is with a better ideology.

What we see here is continual reference to a discourse of freedom, but one that is represented as a unilateral freedom which is under attack. Contrast this with Obama's inauguration speech, in which he proclaimed:

> [A]s for our common defense, we reject as false the choice between our safety and our ideals. Our Founding Fathers, faced with perils that we can scarcely imagine, drafted a charter to assure the rule of law and the rights of man – a charter expanded by the blood of generations. Those ideals still light the world, and we will not give them up for expedience sake.

Obama references the discourse of freedom, but as a universal right for everyone. The 'rule of law and the rights of man' should apply to everyone, and these principles do not have to be sacrificed in order to ensure safety ('we reject as false the choice between our safety and our ideals'). The previous administration constantly used the discourse of freedom to suggest that there was in fact *no choice* other than to torture and imprison.

By now it should be evident that discourse provides us with a rich vein of subject matter for investigation. But what is actually involved in a discourse analysis? The procedures adopted by different analysts in different disciplines vary, as does the precise focus of investigation. What is important to bear in mind, however, is not so much how you go about your analysis, but what you are looking for, remembering that 'the research questions discourses analysts … focus on are broadly related … to construction and function: how is discourse put together, and what is gained by this construction' (Potter and Wetherell 1987, p.160).

For research problems in which we are interested in analysing the function of language and practice, we must look to the artefacts of discourse. These can be found in verbal exchanges, speeches, policy documents, public addresses, codes of practice, manifestos, legislation, court proceedings, video and audio recordings of events – anything, in fact, that provides data relating to discourse. The process of analysis requires that when we look at *what* is being said and done, we consider *why* it is being said or done. We need to take each piece of data and place it within the context of discourses, asking questions such as:

- How do certain words or phrases reference ideas from particular discourses?
- How are references to discourses used to justify actions?
- How do the functions of language and institutional practices affiliate individuals with certain groups?

- How are regimes of truth created?
- How are regimes of truth perpetuated, and what actions are legitimised as a consequence?

For a detailed investigation of the mechanics of analysis, see Wetherell et al. (2001a), which offers a number of very useful examples of discourse analysis in practice, and across different disciplines.

### *Visual data: semiotic analysis*

Semiotic analysis was originally developed by the Swiss linguist Ferdinand de Saussure and is often referred to as the 'science of signs' (De Saussure 1983). In its early form, the approach was geared towards the study of written text, but has since been expanded, particularly through the work of Barthes (1967), so it is now often used in analysing a wide range of material, including visual data such as photographs and magazine advertisements. The main premise of the approach is that a sign consists of two elements: the signifier, which might relate to a word or particular image, and the signified, which relates to how the signifier is interpreted, or the meaning that is derived by the observer of the signifier. The signified consists of a surface (denotative) meaning and a deeper (connotative) meaning. An important aspect of semiotic understanding is that signs only make sense when considered in relation to other signs within the same 'code'. When analysing written text, the code within which signs operate is language. However, the range of codes to which the approach can be applied are many and varied.

Fashion provides a good example of a code. Within the code of fashion, signs exist which consist of an item of clothing (the signifier) and the expression of meaning which the wearing of that particular item conveys (the signified). The signs which exist in the clothing worn by punks have particular connotative meanings: 'anarchy', 'rebellion', 'non-conformity'. However, these meanings can only be understood in relation to other signs in the code of fashion. In isolation, punk clothing is simply clothing, but when compared to other fashions (jeans and T-shirt, plain skirts, suits) the signs become apparent. Semiotic analysis relies on identifying codes such as these within which signs work, and then breaking the signs down into their constituent parts.

## Combining quantitative and qualitative data analysis

We have already explored some of the questions thrown up by combining methods and the justification for wishing to do so. When it comes to data analysis, there are essentially two broad ways in which we might want to handle the data. First, methods can be used sequentially. An initial stage of qualitative inquiry can facilitate an ensuing quantitative stage (Bryman 1988), and vice versa. It is relatively common to begin the research process with an inductive, exploratory stage, out of which we generate theory that is then to be tested in a deductive, explanatory stage.

As an example, imagine a community organisation was seeking to tackle delinquency by better tailoring community facilities available for young people to meet their needs. It might be useful to carry out an initial focus group with a small group of young people to try to understand their interests, what facilities they would like to see provided, their frustrations, and why they felt they engaged in delinquent behaviour.

We would hope to generate an understanding of the issues that were important to young people, and develop some ideas of how facilities could be improved. In order to see whether these were universally held beliefs, we could then carry out a survey of young people in the area. In this example, the data collected in the initial exploratory stage is analysed and coded, and this then forms the basis for the design of the questionnaire. Data are analysed sequentially, in order to develop and then test theory.

As Bryman (1988, p.136) suggests, 'examples of investigation in which quantitative research precedes and provides an aid to the collection of qualitative data, are less numerous', although he does draw attention to the possibility of using quantitative data to help with drawing a sample for qualitative work. When wishing to draw a theoretical sample, it is important that the cases in our sample match certain criteria which will enable us to strive towards theoretical saturation. It has already been suggested that theoretical saturation is achieved in the process of grounded theory by continually refining our research instruments and sample. Carrying out a large-scale survey which collects data based on variables which match the criteria of our sample can be an effective way of accessing such a sample.

When using methods sequentially in this way, the analysis of data, while focusing on the research question, has a dual purpose of aiding research design and refinement. It is therefore necessary to look at the data with these outcomes in mind. Analysis of the data does not represent a final stage in the research process, but a stepping-stone between stages. In this respect, combining methods sequentially shares many characteristics of the process of grounded theory.

Another common reason for combining methods is that of *data triangulation*. The idea of triangulation stems from the geographical term whereby, if the distances between two known points and a third point are taken, the exact position of the third point can be located. This is a useful analogy to keep in mind when carrying out data triangulation, since both methods of analysis must remain focused on the same point, which in this case is the research question.

Brewer and Hunter (1989, p.83) explain the rationale behind this approach:

> Multimethod research tests the validity of measurements, hypothesis and theories by means of triangulated cross-method comparisons. Triangulation requires multiple sets of data speaking to the same research question from different viewpoints. The researcher infers validity from agreement between the data-sets, and invalidity from disagreement. To support these inferences, the data must be collected with truly different methods that are employed independently of one another but that are focused as tightly as possible upon the particular question being investigated.

An often-used method of data triangulation is that of the survey questionnaire supported by in-depth interviews or focus groups. Questions over the validity of the survey method tend to centre around the limitations of a closed response in providing enough scope to explore meaning fully. De Vaus (1996, p.57) uses the example of church attendance to explore the problem of validity. A survey provides a useful tool for quantifying church attendance, but as an indicator of religiosity this alone is problematic. We may find from analysing survey data that we discover a prevalence of church attendance. While it is possible to explore the rationale behind this behaviour with a survey, the possibilities are somewhat limited. Through data triangulation we could carry out some in-depth interviews to see what attending church meant to different people. It may transpire that attendance at church was considered a moral and social responsibility, rather than a religious practice.

On a practical level, combining data has obvious implications for the time and resources involved. We have already dealt with the issues concerned with managing large quantities of both qualitative and quantitative data, and so when bringing the two together the magnitude of these issues increases. However, once the practical barriers are overcome, there are many benefits to combining methods. Many of these benefits involve overcoming the problem of forced choices. When using single methods, we might be confronted with decisions about whether to use a deductive or inductive approach, whether to maximise the reliability or validity of our data, or whether one process of analysis is more desirable than another. By combining methods we seek to eliminate these choices and tackle the flaws of either approach.

It is useful to look at the possibilities offered by combining methods and tackle the question from a practical as well as a theoretical point of view. Using different methods sequentially can overcome the problem of choice between an inductive or deductive approach, while aiding research design. The use of data triangulation can offer increased validity. Combining methods would, therefore, appear to offer a variety of ways of improving the research design, which should arguably be the pursuit of all researchers regardless of their theoretical standpoint.

## Summary

This chapter has situated data analysis as a component of the research process which needs to be considered throughout every stage of the design. We have noted how early design decisions can shape the types of data that will be collected and therefore influence the analysis that will be possible. It is important to recognise this and make sure that the types of data collected are suited to responding to our research questions. In this sense, it is useful to work backwards through our research design. Once research questions have been formulated, it should be apparent what types of data will be required in order to meet the objectives of the research. This will then form the basis of the choice of methods, selection of sample, and design of research instrument.

We have considered the different formats in which both quantitative and qualitative data can present themselves, and how to manage the data. Issues of data collection need to take into consideration data analysis because data are often organised in the field, whether this be through the writing of field notes or recording of survey responses.

Statistical analysis techniques can be complicated. We have chosen to concentrate on introducing just some of the techniques that researchers use in order to explore the data and seek out associations. Owing to the widespread use of computers in analysing quantitative data nowadays, the emphasis has shifted from an understanding of how to calculate statistical tests to understanding where it is appropriate to use one test or another and how to interpret the results. There are many texts which offer an in-depth exploration of the techniques we have discussed and many more (see Bryman 1990; Fielding and Gilbert 2000; Salkind 2003).

While the wealth of tools available to the quantitative researcher can be bewildering, it does at least offer comfort to the analyst in the form of strict guidance and established practice. Qualitative data analysis does not benefit from such strict guidelines, but models and approaches such as grounded theory can be used to gain assurance and confidence in our treatment of the data. Without the luxury of having a specific test that applies to identifiable types of data, it is important to remain focused on the research questions and to select data for analysis that are best able to answer these questions.

The debate over combining methods is one that can perhaps be best tackled by focusing on data analysis, since it is from analysis that the benefits can best be gained. Using analysis of data to inform the research design, or to validate our research, are both useful ways of strengthening our research in the face of criticism. The seemingly eternal question of epistemological concerns will remain, but it is worth considering combining methods for the fresh challenges it presents and for the possible practical advantages to be had.

Analysis is an element of research that is often perceived as the most problematic stage. This can often lead to a reluctance to begin analysis and time spent collecting more and more data instead, which simply exacerbates the problem. Getting started with data analysis is perhaps the most difficult part of the research process, but by seeing the analysis stage as part of the whole process, and not just something that happens at the end of your research, is a good way of overcoming this barrier. It is, after all, only through the analysis of our data that we begin to see our research questions finally illuminated.

## Chapter research task

Select an example of a research project which has been reported using extensive reference to the data. (Journal articles are a good source for this exercise.) Read through the methods and presentation of the results and answer the following questions.

1. What type(s) of data have been used in the research (quantitative/qualitative)?
2. How were the data collected?
3. Consider the research questions/hypotheses. How do the data help to address these? How does the researcher justify her or his choice of data? Do you think the data are the most appropriate given the nature of the research?
4. What do you think of the reliability/validity of the data?
5. Are there any gaps in the data (e.g. unanswered questions, incomplete samples)?
6. What techniques have been used to analyse the data? Has a particular approach (e.g. grounded theory) been used? Do you think that the choices taken here were appropriate?

## Recommended Reading

Barthes, R. 1967. *Elements of Semiology*, trans. Annette Lavers and Colin Smith. London: Jonathan Cape.

Corbin, J. and Strauss, A. 2008. *Basics of Qualitative Research: Techniques and Procedures for Developing Grounded Theory*, 3rd edn. London: Sage.

De Vaus, D.A. 2002. *Analyzing Social Science Data: 50 Key Problems in Data Analysis*. London: Sage.

Miles, M.B. and Huberman, A.M. 1994. *Qualitative Data Analysis: An Expanded Sourcebook*, 2nd edn. London: Sage.

Warner, R.M. 2008. *Applied Statistics: From Bivariate through Multivariate Techniques*. London: Sage.

Wetherell, M., Taylor, S. and Yates, S. (eds) 2001. *Discourse as Data: A Guide for Analysis.* London: Sage.

# NINE

# Writing Up and Presenting Research Results

- To highlight the ways in which research writing links theory with practice
- To alert readers to the aims of research writing
- To sensitise readers to the need to communicate their research with their audience
- To provide readers with a framework within which they can write up research reports
- To provide practical guidance on the management of the writing process
- To enable good referencing and citation practice



## Introduction

The culmination of a research project arrives when all the hard work is put to paper and the fruits of our labours are shared with a wider audience. This means writing up our research in a way that presents not just our findings, but the process through which we arrived at these findings. It demands an honesty about our research design and our perspectives, so that others can understand not just the research we have produced, but something about the way in which we have produced it. The foundation for this approach to writing is that research projects do not exist in isolation, but contribute to a wider body of knowledge that is constantly developing.

When carrying out research it is all too easy to become embroiled in our own research questions and objectives, so that when it comes to presenting our research we forget about situating it within the wider body of knowledge. Tackling this tendency is one of the core themes to run through this chapter. We shall emphasise the need to enter into dialogue with our writing. This requires contextualising our research within a theoretical framework and demonstrating an awareness of our audience. Who we write for will largely depend on the objectives (and sponsors) of the research, and our audience can determine writing style and linguistic choices, but whatever the audience, much of the purpose of writing up research remains the same. It is about sharing knowledge – knowledge that can help us to understand phenomena, open up other areas for future research, and enlighten the methodological debate.

As well as offering a consideration of the theoretical context in which writing up research takes place, we shall also look at some of the more practical steps towards constructing a research report. This will involve approaches to writing, knowing our audience and structuring reports.

In exploring the writing up process, it is useful to consider Denscombe's (2003, p.286) suggestion that:

> There are some common themes and shared concerns that underlie formal reports of research across the spectrum of approaches within the social sciences. There is some general consensus that when writing up research, the aim is to:
>
> 1. Explain the purpose of the research
> 2. Describe how the research was done
> 3. Present the findings from the research
> 4. Discuss and analyse the findings
> 5. Reach conclusions

These five aims form a useful basis upon which to approach the writing of a research report. As Denscombe suggests, this appears to be one area, at least, where there is a degree of consensus among researchers. Qualitative and quantitative researchers may disagree on the precise layout or presentation of reports, and we shall acknowledge this, but for our purposes, the mutual aims of writing up provide a useful focus for our discussion.

We shall finish by considering the process of writing up and review. Particular consideration is given to situating our writing with the audience in mind, and review and reflection. We recognise the difficulties that novice writers can face when receiving criticism, but look at ways in which peer review as well as self-reflection can help with the writing process.

## Addressing the research question with your data

When presenting the outcomes of our research it is important to return to the very beginning and ask ourselves 'what was the purpose of this research?' The research process can be lengthy, and time spent in the field, or mulling over reams of data, can make the point of origin of our research seem like a dim and distant memory. So, when it comes to writing up, the temptation can be to see the light at the end of the tunnel and simply focus on bringing the research to a close, but it is important to remind ourselves of the aims and objectives of our research, since it is these that we need to address in our writing.

Research, by its nature, can generate lots of interesting observations. As we journey through the process, our perceptions of, and ideas about, our research area may change, leading us to consider new possibilities (for future research, perhaps?). It is easy to see how, by becoming distracted by alternative ideas presented by our data, we may forget what our original stance was. These new ideas are every bit as important as our original ideas, as they represent an advancement in knowledge, but we must remember that at some point, some time ago, we came up with a research question that we set out to address.

Enforcing the research question upon our write-up may appear to be a restrictive measure. What if the data present issues outside the research question? Well, what we are suggesting is not that these issues are ignored, but that the research question should be used to guide the *primary* focus of our writing. One of the greatest barriers researchers face when it comes to writing up is tackling the problem of what to write about, and how to organise it. The research question can be used as guidance here since it provides us with a framework within which we can organise the data.

In order to explore this issue further, we shall consider an example of a research project that produces rich data (see Example 9.1).

### Example 9.1 Addressing the research question with your data

The following research question is from a fictitious example of a research project which asks: *What effects, if any, has the increase in the use of email and text messages had on the ways people write English?* The broad aim of the research is to see whether the acceptance of 'shorthand' formats for computer-mediated communication (such as using 'l8r' instead of the word 'later') has permeated into other areas of written English. For our research design, we may decide to use a mixed method approach, comprising the following methods:

- Analysis of a range of documentary sources: saved emails and text messages as well as handwritten documents (letters, diaries, student assignments) from two different points in time: prior to email and text usage, and from now.

- A series of focus groups in which participants are asked to discuss how they write emails and text messages, and whether they think this style has crossed over into other forms of written language.
- A series of questionnaires asking about frequency of use of email and text usage, and for what purpose. Additionally, the questionnaire comprises a 'quiz', which asks respondents whether they thought examples taken from both 'text' language and conventional written English were suitable for a number of different situations.

As a mixed method research project, this produces a very large quantity of data. Some of the issues that are uncovered are as follows:

The documentary sources show that younger people use shorthand freely when communicating via email or text message, and there are some examples of student assignments where this language is also used. In addition, we discover that grammatical differences, characterised by a lack of punctuation, or use of new forms of punctuation (enclosing words in asterisks to denote strongly felt emotion) are creeping into writing. Older people tend to use some shorthand in text messages, but write emails in the format of a traditional letter, complete with full salutations. These data are relevant to our research question and so provide a useful structure for our writing. We can begin to write something about the finding that new technology-based language formats do seem to be affecting the way people are using written English, but that this appears to be a generational phenomenon. These data have provided information that we can use in direct response to our research question.

Our focus groups may provide us with similar findings, as people discuss among peers how they use language. The discussion may also lead to a discovery that some of the younger participants are not aware that the shorthand language they use has come out of technological communication, and have accepted it as the conventional way to write English. These data are also relevant to our research question since they suggest something not only of the nature of the effect we are investigating, but also of its extent.

During our focus group, as is common with the method, discussion also turns to other related topics and we discover that, because of email, some of our participants are keeping in touch with friends and relatives who are living abroad a lot more frequently. This is interesting and poses the question: *Does email have the potential for improving communication and preventing people from losing touch with each other?* However, while it does relate to communication, it does not answer our research question since it does not relate to changes in the linguistic nature of written English. We also discover that people make use of text message information services to keep up to date with developments in the news and sport. This also presents us with some interesting thoughts about the nature of the need to access information while on the move. It does not, however, answer our research question.

*(Continued)*

*(Continued)*

Finally, the questionnaires provide us with data that suggest that text language is only considered acceptable in certain situations, for example leaving notes for people, but that it would not be used in a formal essay. This is useful in isolating part of the nature of the effect we are investigating and the degree to which it has infiltrated written English – some situations are still considered too 'formal' for the use of shorthand. The questionnaires also present us with data that suggest that some people are now frequently using emails to communicate with people with whom they share an office in the workplace. We may think 'now this is interesting – is the art of conversation being lost to email?' Yet this, once again, is a different matter from the main focus of our research question.

In looking at the types of issue that are presented by our analysis of the data in this example, it appears that the data can be split into two categories. First, data that provide a response to the initial research question(s) and, secondly, data that enable us to formulate new questions about related issues. It is important when writing up to be able to distinguish between these two categories of data and to structure much of our writing around the first. Research often ends up posing more questions than it answers. Sometimes, new questions will be fully pursued as part of an expanded remit of the project, but often the limitations of resources and time mean these matters are left for future research, and can be included as secondary points for consideration. The research community relies on such suggestions for future research in order to maintain a momentum in the development of knowledge.

## Inductive and deductive approaches to the research question

Responding to the research question in the fashion we have outlined so far is arguably more straightforward when using a deductive approach. (Refer back to Chapter 3 for an explanation of deduction.) When we wish to test a theory, the theory will provide us with a hypothesis. A hypothesis for the example we have discussed may posit that the increased use of shorthand when sending text messages is leading to a normalisation of such use in conventional written language. A hypothesis such as this is a very useful device in framing our writing, since it tells us precisely which data we require in order to be able to test the hypothesis. We need to discover whether there is any correlation between two variables: increased use of shorthand in text messages, and increased use of shorthand in conventional written English. (Using a content analysis of the documentary sources, we are able to allow for the timeliness of both variables and see whether the first precedes the second.)

When it comes to writing, the hypothesis enables us to keep focused on the research question because of the direct relationship between the two, and it also tells us exactly which variables in the data we need to be writing about in order to answer our research question.

When writing about inductive research, we have to make more choices about which issues to include. Since our research question is likely to be open and exploratory, we must make a judgement call as to what data enable us to respond to the research question in such a way as to produce useful and valid knowledge. In other words, what do we need to write about in order to provide an answer to our research question? The inductive process invariably produces a large amount of data which in turn generates theories. From the focus groups carried out in our example, we might generate a number of theories about how people's use of email has changed the way they communicate, but we still need to relate these back to the specific effects this has had on their use of conventional written English.

The development of conceptual frameworks can help with making links between the data, research questions and emerging theories, which will help structure your writing. Much deductive research begins with a conceptual framework which identifies variables for investigation and hypothesised relationships between those variables. At the outset of inductive research, having a conceptual framework that is so clearly defined is unlikely, but we will usually have some idea of which concepts we are seeking to investigate. As Miles and Huberman (1994, p.18) put it:

> Theory building relies on a few general constructs that subsume a mountain of particulars. Categories such as 'social climate', 'cultural scene', and 'role conflict' are the labels we put on intellectual 'bins' containing many discrete events and behaviours. Any researcher, no matter how inductive in approach, knows which bins are likely to be in play in the study and what is likely to be in them. Bins come from theory and experience and (often) from the general objectives of the study envisioned. Setting out bins, naming them, and getting clearer about their interrelationships lead you to a conceptual framework.

Addressing the research question through the application of a conceptual framework is, then, a primary concern of the write-up. However, while it is important to remain focused on our own research questions, we must not lose sight of the fact that our research forms part of a wider body of knowledge. It is therefore also necessary to be aware of the need to situate our research within the context of theory and the literature.

## Relating your findings to existing literature and theories

The carrying out of research is not an isolated act. It may feel like it is at times, particularly if we are working as a lone researcher on a thesis. We may think that while we are carrying out our research we are looking into a topic which is of great interest to us, but of little relevance to others. It is easy to become caught up in our own research project, with its specific aims and outcomes, and its research design which enables us to answer our research questions. However, the impact of social research is far more wide-reaching than this, and it is worthwhile returning to the question 'what is social research?' that was posed in the first chapter to see why. Social research is about generating a body of knowledge that will enable us to understand better the world around us. In order to build up such a body of knowledge we must continually expand what we know by scrutinising our research in relation to established theory.

Situating research within theory elevates the application of our research to a new level because, as May (2001, p.29) points out:

> The idea of theory, or the ability to explain and understand the findings of research within a conceptual framework that makes 'sense' of the data, is the mark of a mature discipline whose aim is the systematic study of particular phenomena.

As we shall see, the interrelation between theory and research can be a complex one, but before we can attempt to understand this relationship, it is necessary to identify the theories that will be relevant, and for this we need to turn to the literature.

When we talk about 'the literature' in research we are referring to anything that provides us with background information relevant to our research area, whether this be definitions of terminology, results of previous research or methodological guidance. Examples of a variety of literature sources are given in Example 9.2.

## Example 9.2 Different sources of literature

### General guides to the literature/databases

Because of the enormous wealth of academic literature, it is impossible to trawl through everything in order to find what we are looking for. A first port of call should be databases of literature available in libraries and on the Internet. University libraries (as well as other reference libraries) have their own electronic databases which enable us to search for keywords, authors and titles. Alternative resources are online databases, available via the Internet, and CD-ROM databases of abstracts. Use of these general guides will help to locate the further sources of literature outlined below.

### Encyclopaedias/dictionaries

Encyclopaedias and dictionaries are particularly useful for defining terms and isolating key ideas and arguments within our chosen topic. Specialist subject encyclopaedias, dealing exclusively with concepts in, for example, sociology or philosophy, are increasingly available through the Internet. Making use of these helps us to become conversant with the subject terms and build up a general picture of the field we are going to research. Certain online resources, such as Wikipedia, should, however, be treated with caution; the ability for content to be openly authored by members of the public leaves information susceptible to being unreliably sourced.

**Books**

Books can provide a good deal of methodological literature, and are valuable resources for informing research design, but other than major research studies, many research findings never make it to a full-length book publication. Another point worth noting is that the time lapse between research being conducted and publication in a book can often be several years, so books are not always the best source for up-to-the-minute information.

**Journal articles**

Journal articles can provide some of the most recent research findings and debate in our chosen field. There are a substantial number of academic journals available. Many of these are available electronically, via websites. While subscription is often required to access electronic journals through websites, universities often have institutional subscriptions and can provide a password to enable access. There are an increasing number of journals that are only published online via the Internet, and some of them are extremely valuable resources which have the kind of editorial control associated with printed media. When making use of online journals, always check the editorial criteria by which articles are selected for inclusion and, if possible, get information about the publishers. It is likely that journal articles will help provide a large proportion of the material relating to theory in our research area, but there are other sources that may provide even more up-to-date theory.

**Conference papers**

Conference papers can be useful in that quite often research in progress is presented at conferences, allowing an insight into current research in practice, and into contemporary theory. It is important to be aware that what is presented may well differ from the end product and so any results or findings will need to be treated with caution. Conference papers are particularly useful for gauging the current climate of a research area and getting a feel for the most up-to-the-minute methodological developments.

**Statistics/official publications**

Official statistics can be extremely useful in providing evidence of the existence of a phenomenon (e.g. regional unemployment figures, housing figures, educational

*(Continued)*

*(Continued)*

attainment). University libraries will generally have statistics collections, and the websites of public agencies are a good place to locate statistics in electronic format. Official publications such as government White Papers can provide useful guidance on national or regional policy. See Chapter 5 for further discussion about the methodological issues to be aware of when making use of statistics and official publications.

**Websites**

Websites provide many different types of literature, including most of the above. It is important to note that some will be far more useful than others. With the proliferation of Internet technology, web design tools and the resulting fall in the cost of setting up and maintaining a website, researchers must be able to evaluate the quality of a website. It is also important to recognise that, while the Internet provides us with a wealth of information, it cannot provide us with everything, and we do still need to make use of other, traditional formats of literature.

**News groups and mailing lists**

News groups and discussion forums can provide a useful place to access up-to-date debate around given subjects. While they are often informal and will not really provide much concrete literature themselves, they may well provide access to other researchers in the field who will be willing to point us in the direction of useful literature. Most of the large search engines, including Google and Yahoo!, provide access to groups, categorised into subject headings, and are a good starting point for locating news groups and discussion forums.

Hart (2001) distinguishes between two different sources of literature: 'topic literature' and 'methodological literature'.

## Topic literature

Topic literature refers to sources which relate to the subject area we have chosen to investigate. It can tell us what theories and debates currently exist about the phenomenon we are investigating. These theories will be based on prior research, but of equal importance is the identification of gaps in knowledge – areas which are as yet unexplored, or at least are yet to be explored using a particular perspective or method. By discussing our research in the context of theory from the literature:

> New research provides a link with the past, while at the same time pointing to new directions for the future. This is achieved by seeking answers to questions that have

yet to be asked, and challenging answers that form the basis of current, conventional wisdom. (Cuba and Cocking 1997, p.54)

In order to do this, we need to have approached the literature with a number of questions in mind:

- What research has been carried out which is relevant to our own research?
- What were the main conclusions to be drawn from previous research?
- What were the methods employed by previous research?
- In which ways (conclusions and methods) are previous studies similar?
- In which ways (conclusions and methods) are previous studies different?
- Where are there gaps in knowledge?

Approaching the literature in this inquisitive way helps us to be critical of what we are reading, a vital skill in evaluating the literature. We should not take what we read at face value. When reading about previous research we must question the relevance of theory to given situations as well as scrutinising the methods that have been employed by others to reach conclusions. As Example 9.3 indicates, relevance of theory needs to be considered in geographical, political, historical and cultural terms.

## Example 9.3 The relevance of theory to specific situations

If we were carrying out research into the effectiveness of different teaching methods used in English inner-city state schools, we would have to be very careful to ensure that the theory in the literature was relevant to our particular topic. Research carried out in the USA relates to a different culture of schooling, as would research carried out in Japan. Research carried out in 1940s' England would relate to a different point in history, when many aspects of the English schooling system were different from today's. Studies carried out in China would be set against a very different political backdrop. Any theory that has been derived from these studies needs to be considered in terms of these topics. Theories may be radically different when applied to different situations in different parts of the world or at different points in history. Even when the geographical, political and historical points of reference become closer to those of our own research, there can still exist fundamental differences. For example, contemporary research into teaching methods employed in private schools in England will be based on theory that is informed by the cultural peculiarities of the private school system, and may not be relevant to inner-city state schools.

The literature review provides us with a theoretical framework for our research as well as a justification for carrying it out. While, by its very nature, it has to be carried out prior to starting our own research, reference to the literature should not be considered as something that is only done when designing our research. When it comes to writing up the results of our research, we must continue to consider theory in the literature, and discuss our results in relation to this theory. This helps us to contextualise our results as well as confirming or challenging existing theory. Without this discussion, our results become isolated and have no relevance to the body of knowledge to which we are seeking to add.

The following extracts are from a discussion of results in an article by Strange et al. (2003). Their study concerned whether young people would prefer to receive sex education in single- or mixed-sex classes.

> Those advocating the inclusion of work discussing 'gender' in the sex education curriculum argue that, by exploring these issues, young people can move away from unconstructive 'gender wars' and begin to change their ways of interacting with each other (Prendergast, 1996). Our analysis of discussions between groups of girls demonstrates how single-sex work with young women has the potential to enable girls to understand these gendered discourses and structures (see also Kreuse, 1992). (Strange et al. 2003, p.212)

The authors relate the discussion of their own results to the work of others that has preceded theirs. In doing so, they are able to add strength to the theories posited previously, but also they are able to make sense of their own data, by relating it to theory. Here we see a two-way relationship between theory and research. On the one hand, our research supports (or refutes) theory, and on the other, theory helps us to make sense of our data. Theory can be useful when we find ourselves asking of our data 'what does it mean?'

> Some of the data drawn on in this article also indicate the ways in which girls are willing to compromise their own needs in order to create classroom conditions that will be of benefit to boys (see, for example, girls' views that a male teacher would be beneficial because boys will respond better). The belief from girls that they can and perhaps should act to 'civilise' boys reflects wider social norms about gender (Prendergast, 1996) which may well have an impact on their views about the appropriateness of mixed-sex versus single-sex sex education. (Strange et al. 2003, pp.211–12)

Here, the authors are able to build on broader social theories, in this case about gendered roles in society as a whole, and apply them to a specific situation. This link between more general theories and specific situations is important as it adds strength to the argument that a given theory is relevant to, and can permeate, a number of different situations.

> The pressures on boys to conform to particular forms of (heterosexual) masculinity may well make expressing a difference in opinion on sexual matters risky, and involve the possibility of being victimised or labelled as sexually inadequate (Salisbury &

> Jackson, 1996). This might explain why the views of boys who reported a preference in the questionnaire survey for single-sex education are not represented in the focus group data. (Strange et al. 2003, p.211)

In this last extract, the authors are making an important observation, not about the interpretation of the results, but about the validity of the methods. They point out an apparent conflict between two sets of data, but offer a plausible explanation for why this may be the case, based on theory. This demonstrates a need to consider our methods in relation to theory as well as our results.

## Methodological literature

Methodological literature is often mistakenly perceived as reference material which helps us to justify our research design on merely practical grounds. (For example, survey methods have these limitations; this is how an interview schedule is structured; organising a focus group can be problematic in these ways.) If we adopt this stance, methodological literature is not seen to offer us anything in the way of a theoretical framework in which to situate our research, but this assumption denies any epistemological context. Throughout this book we have sought to emphasise the place that theories of knowledge have in thinking about research, and methodology must be considered in its own theoretical framework in much the same way that sociology, political science or psychology should.

Whether we are explaining or critiquing our methods, our writing must make reference to the methodological literature and key methodological debates. First, we need to demonstrate that our design has been considered in light of the lessons learned, and advice given, by others. For instance, we might write the following passage:

> For our research, we wanted to access participants from other countries so we could make cross-cultural comparisons. In order to do this, we made use of Internet chat rooms in which we held online focus groups. Mann and Stewart (2000, p.17) suggest that this method is 'a practical way to interview, or collect narratives from, individuals or groups who are geographically distant'.

By supporting our research design with reference to the methodological literature in this way, we are able to defend against criticism. Our research will also add to the series of examples which help to justify this method, so once again we see a two-way relationship between research and the literature.

Secondly, we must demonstrate in our writing that we are aware of current debates around methodology, for instance by writing:

> While some commentators still maintain that combining methods only amounts to a compromise of one's theoretical perspective, we are increasingly seeing the use of both qualitative and quantitative approaches alongside each other accepted as a means to increasing the validity of data.

By engaging in methodological debates we make our own position known. Our research can then be read with a clear understanding of the theoretical reasoning as well as the practical reasoning behind our methodology.

## Writing strategies

Of all the stages of the research process, the one that arguably plagues researchers the most is writing up, yet writing is arguably a skill which most of us acquire before becoming researchers. It makes use of our experiences of expressing our ideas by putting pen to paper – something that we start to learn from a very early age. Perhaps this explains why it is an activity that is regarded as undeserving of the same degree of attention as, say, statistical analysis. There certainly appears to be a lack of attention to the process of writing in the literature:

> Social scientists write about the methods they use to collect and analyse social data, and about the results these methods yield. They rarely examine the process of writing itself. (Cuba and Cocking 1997, p.1)

A possible reason for this, as Bingham (2003) suggests, is that writing has become viewed as a process which is 'unproblematic and transparent', and that this stems from the early emphasis placed on realism in the social sciences. In attempting to emulate the scientific community, the writing up of research was seen as an objective process, whereby the researcher simply presented the results in an uncomplicated, straightforward fashion. However:

> The consequences of adopting this way of writing in pursuit of an easy and error-free knowledge of the truth … continue to be felt today, and will affect you when you come to write up as they do everyone else. For, over time, what we might think of as an envy of those early social scientists has become sedimented in our ways of thinking to such an extent that we could now call the unproblematic and transparent model the standard discourse of writing up in the social sciences. (Bingham 2003, p.148)

So what we have is a lack of guidance on how to approach writing, combined with an expectation that writing is straightforward, so we should all just be able to get on with it. In the previous section we saw that writing is plainly *not* simply about reporting results, but about situating our writing within a broader theoretical context. Writing is also not just a skill we have that can be applied to any situation that requires putting words down on paper. Research writing has different objectives, style and audiences from other forms of writing, such as essays, letters and stories, and so the very idea of embarking upon writing up research can be a daunting task to the uninitiated. We cannot simply launch into writing; we need a strategy.

Having a writing strategy requires discipline. The process of writing can be quite an organic one – our writing grows as we explore and express ideas.

When we are feeling creative, our arguments and discussion might flow freely and this is when the writing process can be at its most rewarding. A word of caution, though: in getting carried away by these moments, we may forget to stop and reflect. Similarly, in the moments when we face blocks in our writing, it is all too easy to get frustrated because we just want the writing to keep moving. It is at times like these when we need the discipline to say 'stop, it's time to take a break and reflect on what we have done so far'. A strategy helps us to plan how to approach our writing, and work out how to deal with barriers when we inevitably face them.

Before we look at strategies for the actual process of writing, there are a few practical things that we can do in advance that will make the process easier. Cuba and Cocking (1997, p.11) suggest that appraising the environment in which we do our writing can be beneficial. They suggest that a number of questions relating to where, when and how we write need to be addressed before we actually sit down to write. Some of these questions are outlined below.

### Is there a dedicated environment in which we can write?

If we are fortunate enough to have an office or study in which we can work, then this may prove to be the ideal environment. If we are going to be using a shared environment (a shared office, university computer rooms, a family room, the library), then we need to assess at what times the space will be exclusively available to us. Being interrupted during a particularly productive writing session can be extremely frustrating, so it is important to plan to write at times when interruptions are least likely.

### When is the best time of day to write?

If we are fitting in writing around other commitments, then we shall have to try to maximise our use of the time available, but if we know that we work better at certain times of the day, and are able to, trying to plan to write at these times can help. This may involve reorganising other aspects of our lives, but if it improves productivity it will be worth it.

### How are we going to store our writing?

Most formal writing nowadays is carried out on a word processor. This means thinking about electronic storage and peripherals such as printers. Saving work regularly is a habit most definitely worth getting into. Most word-processing software packages have auto-save features. By enabling these and making regular backup copies on other disks and storage devices we can avoid any of the heartache of losing a day's worth of work. Emailing files to oneself is also a good way of producing a backup copy which is stored on the server of our email client, which in turn will be regularly backed up.

### How familiar are we with the software?

Word-processing skills are common features of school curricula and are often taught at universities nowadays, but it is worth investigating the software we are using for additional features which may make the process of writing easier. Word-processing packages come with a variety of automated features which make the organisation and production of complex documents a lot more manageable. Features such as Word's 'auto-correct' function enable abbreviations or short-hand to be used in place of words that are going to be used frequently. The software is told which characters to replace with other words, so as the abbreviations are entered, they are over-written by the corresponding full-length words or phrases. In the writing of this book, setting up the software to automatically change 'qul' to 'qualitative' and 'qun' to quantitative has probably saved quite a bit of time! It is worth becoming familiar with these features prior to starting our writing, and also investigating additional software that can be used to manage and organise references. Such packages can be particularly helpful if we are producing a lengthy, heavily referenced text.

Having thought about the environment in which our writing is going to take place, we need to turn to planning. Day (1996) suggests that an academic paper can be written in under a week. This seems rather optimistic, but then she points out that this is just the actual writing, which can be done briskly, and this is dependent on a great deal of consideration and planning taking place before the writing even begins. She argues that with proper planning carried out in advance, the writing can be an enjoyable and relatively quick task. This seems like an attractive prospect, and certainly adds strength to the argument that planning needs to be taken seriously.

The first stage of planning requires producing a broad outline. We offer advice on the structure and style of research reports later in this chapter, and the structure of a research report will most likely relate to some, or all, of the section headings we mention. Using these section headings as an outline is a useful signposting mechanism since it helps us keep focused on the relevant section during our writing, and it tells our readers how the report is organised.

Within each section we need to consider what is to be dealt with, how and for what purpose. Cuba and Cocking (1997, p.94) inform us that the different sections have:

> different functions. For example, the introduction section is largely descriptive; it aims to identify the research problem, and provide a clear statement about the purpose of the report. Detailed discussion and lengthy, critical analysis are unnecessary at this stage. These aspects are dealt with later, in the review of the literature for example, where you will need to put your work into context by considering the background reading you have undertaken for your project. Recognising the difference of purpose should help you to break down the writing task into manageable proportions.

This advice is useful for planning our approach. The organisation of our writing is governed by different sections which require distinctive styles. As Cuba and Cocking suggest, our literature review requires that we have appraised the key arguments in our research area, and this requires a critical style. The introduction, however, requires a descriptive style since the aim is to give a summary of the purpose of the research. Similarly, if we decide to deal with the description and evaluation of methods in separate sections, then the former will have a very different style from the latter.

With these different styles in mind, we can begin to plan an outline structure of the report, accompanied by a series of objectives for each section, and the necessary style required in order to meet these objectives. Broadly speaking, our sections will require either a descriptive or a critical style of writing, depending on the objectives, although some commentators, such as Bingham (2003), advocate a critical approach to all of our writing. This argument is informed by epistemology, and rests on the notion that the social world cannot merely be described if it is to be truly understood. It follows that even with a seemingly straightforward section of our report, such as where we are stating the objectives of our research, we should take a reflexive approach to our writing. In other words, we must not make assumptions about how our writing will be interpreted or understood. Even descriptive writing is subjective, and will reflect our own perspectives through our choice of language. The lesson to learn from this is that we should not underestimate the importance of reflection in our writing.

Reflection involves having the time to be able to return to our writing, reread and rewrite. It requires writing several drafts. Gilbert (2001, p.367) advises that at least three will be required: the first as a personal starting point; the second for criticism from peers; the third a further refinement based on this criticism. He also points out that we may not write the sections in the order they are to appear in our report. Some of our writing may happen at different stages of the research process: our literature review, for example, may be written early on in order to help us situate and operationalise our research. The first draft should be seen as a way of getting something down on paper, even if the different sections have been written in a different order and appear disjointed. Something that we must keep in mind at all times is that our first draft does not have to be perfect.

The first draft should therefore be seen as a tool – a process for making sense of the ideas in our head. Putting these ideas down on paper is a good way of organising our thoughts, as writing forces us to communicate our ideas. In many senses, the process of writing a first draft serves as a way to operationalise the abstract thoughts about our research that are in our heads. Once this first draft is written, the next thing to do is take a break. There is no point in typing the final full stop of our draft and then returning to the beginning and rereading it straight away. If we do, we shall be reading it from a privileged position, in which the thought processes that shaped the writing will still be fresh in our mind. This enables us subconsciously to fill in gaps in the writing with our own thoughts. By returning to our draft a few days later, we shall be reading from a fresh perspective, much more akin to that of our readers, and so the writing will have to speak for itself. We are far more likely to spot flaws in our arguments, structure and grammar from this perspective. This will enable us to write the second draft, which deals with these flaws. Then we are ready to show our writing to someone else.

This can be a nerve-wracking experience due to the prospect of receiving criticism and having our confidence knocked. Often the person whom we ask to review our work at this stage will be a supervisor or colleague, and so it is easy to feel that we are exposing our flaws to someone of an equal or superior academic standing. However, it is important that we do not hold back. The temptation might be to seek to gain perfection in our writing before showing anyone else, but this is simply counter-productive. If there are any fundamental flaws which run through our writing, it is far more beneficial to have these pointed out to us as early as possible. We also need to remember that criticism is not a solely negative act. Having someone read our work can be a very positive experience. It can give us renewed confidence and motivation, and this should carry through to further refinements for the following draft.

## Writing for your audience

Aldridge and Levine (2001, p.161) highlight the importance of recognising your audience when writing a research report:

> In 1995, the Economic and Social Research Council published a booklet entitled *Writing for Business*. It contained the following extract from a research team's summary of their work:
>
> 'The research will present a structuralist informed challenge to both positivistic and humanistic/post-structuralist approaches to the study of the environmental crisis, and in particular to the neo-classical environmental economics paradigm.' (ESRC 1995, p.13)

This excerpt demonstrates how easy it is to become entangled in the language of social science when reporting to a lay audience. The passage would work with an academic audience, but to a business audience most of the excerpt may be lost. It is important when writing a research report (of any nature) to ensure that we remain informative while providing information in an easily digestible manner.

As we have seen, though, writing up research is not just about presenting our findings objectively to the reader. The problem of writing becoming viewed as a straightforward process of communicating our findings discredits our readers. All of the critical skills which we have thus far attempted to imbue in our own approaches to other stages of the research process apply as much at the writing stage as anywhere else.

Writing styles are many and varied, and very much depend on the individual. A writing style suggests something of the way in which we use the tools of language to communicate ideas. Such tools might include our choice of words, punctuation and sentence structure. All of these elements combine to create a style which will, in part, be a reflection of our own personality, and also a reflection of the audience for whom we are writing. When considering our audience, we need to be aware of two factors: who is in the audience, and how best to communicate to them? The above excerpt has demonstrated how important it is to consider both of these points. Research is read by a variety of people, and these will not always be fellow researchers or people with a specialist interest in, and knowledge of, our field. Our research is also competing with a wealth of other research, and readers do not have the time to read everything. With this in mind, Day (1996) suggests that a reader will approach research with three questions in mind: Is it interesting? Can I understand it? And can I use it? In order to write for our audience, we need to be sure to address these questions.

Ensuring that our research is interesting places a lot of emphasis on the part that a reader will read first: the introduction. The introduction needs to draw our readers in and make them want to continue, even if it is not their specialist field of interest. Making the research interesting will largely depend on our style of writing, but this point is also strongly linked to the other two questions. In order to understand our research the reader will need to be comfortable with the terminology and sentence structure. The use of unnecessarily complex language when something a lot simpler will do is, unfortunately, a rather common practice among some academics. In an attempt to present themselves as experts through their grasp of technical terms and ornate words, they actually end up alienating many readers. We should seek to avoid this. Writing up is first and foremost about communicating our research to others, and not seeking attention for the extent of our vocabulary.

Clarity will therefore help our readers to understand our writing, and if it is easy to follow what we are saying, we are more likely to maintain an interest. Interest cannot be assured through the use of simple language alone, however. Research must be seen to have implications, to be doing something worthwhile, in order for it to be interesting. The way we write in relation to theory can help in this matter. Are we challenging established theory? If so, then this is very interesting as it offers something new. Even if we are confirming what is already known, this can be done with a strong sense of affirmation. Are we being critical of a situation? Writing critically can also add interest. Interest should not stop at theory either: we should talk about our methods in an interesting way. Methods should not simply be seen as a tool with which we eventually generate data; they should be seen as part of an interesting process. With the range of methods available to us, and the range of subject matter out there to be researched, writing up research will inevitably involve writing about something new. This is a tremendous advantage and we should make the most of it. The most important thing is to believe in our research. If we think it is worthwhile, and has something to add to the debate, and are truly passionate about it, then this should come out in our writing.

The final question of whether the reader can use it will often be the only question that is ever asked. Recalling our earlier discussion of situating our own research within the context of theory in the literature, we suggested that research we use should be relevant, and that abstracts can be useful devices for deciding this. Other researchers will be looking at our research and asking the same questions of us as we have already asked of others. Is this relevant to what I am doing and can I use it? This applies not only to researchers, but to policy-makers, students, businesses, voluntary sector organisations, the list goes on. Our research is likely to be read by a range of audiences, but they will all be asking whether they can make use of the findings of our research for their own purposes. To achieve this, we need to make sure we have addressed the research questions with our data, as previously discussed.

### Activity 9.1 Thinking as a reader (adapted from Day 1996)

This activity will enable you to develop a critical eye for a good research write-up and empathise with the reader. Select a piece of research that you have not read before. This should ideally be a short piece, such as a journal article. Read the article considering the three questions below, and note down examples in each case.

1. Is it interesting? If so, what makes it interesting? Is it just the subject matter, or the way it is written? Does it challenge theory? Is it written in a critical manner?
2. Can I understand it? Is the language simple or complicated? Is it well organised? Do paragraphs and sections flow from one to another? Or is it disjointed? Is it clear which part of the article deals with which element of the research?
3. Can I use it? Are the outcomes and implications of the research clear? Are any relevant cultural, historical, political, economic and geographical frames of reference made clear?

## The structure and style of research reports

Up to now we have tried to avoid being too prescriptive when discussing the process of writing up. We have to recognise that different approaches to writing work better with some authors than others, and that our audience will partially dictate the way in which we write. However, upon reading a variety of research reports, we may notice something encouraging about the way different authors organise their reports. This is one area where there does appear to be some consensus. Whether our research is quantitative or qualitative in nature, the research report needs to consist of a number of sections which deal with the different stages of, and rationale behind, the research process. The sections we outline here are offered as a guide to structure, and should not be taken as the final word on the matter. Journal articles or theses may have a predetermined list of headings which have to be adhered to, but regardless of the precise wording of the headings, the same elements will need to be included. What follows can be used as a checklist when writing up a research report.

## Title

Sometimes the most obvious elements are overlooked. The title of the research should be made to be concise but also give a flavour of the purpose of the research. The title does not have to be the same as the research question – this can be appended as a subtitle – but sometimes when we have a whole series of research questions, even this may not be appropriate. Eileen Barker's *The Making of a Moonie* (1984) is a good example of a study which sought to answer a large number of questions that helped to provide an insight into a group, something which is common in ethnographic studies. To try to frame all of the objectives and research questions in the title would have been futile, so instead she chose the far shorter version that appears in print. This title gives a sense of what the research is about, but leaves the precise nature of the goals of the research to research questions found within the text.

In addition to the title, the front page should contain the name of the author, date and names of any sponsors of the report.

## Abstract

The abstract, while appearing at the front of the report, should be written last of all. In order to understand the purpose of an abstract, it is useful to consider where we might come across them. Earlier in the chapter we mentioned using databases to aid with literature searches. These often consist of a collection of abstracts which enable the searcher to decide upon the relevance of the source. With this in mind, consider what someone might be looking for in an abstract. They would want to know the aim of the research, the methods employed, the outcomes of the research, and any theoretical implications. These, then, are the points which need to be covered in the abstract, but it must remain brief; 200 words is normally more than sufficient, and often abstracts appear as single paragraphs.

## Acknowledgements

There may be occasions where the success of a research project has been in part dependent on the services or guidance of certain individuals or organisations. In these instances, it is appropriate to acknowledge the ways in which your research has been helped. It may be that, if we were carrying out a study which involved observing class activities in schools, we may wish to acknowledge the teachers who agreed to let us sit in on their class. Acknowledgements should not be given at the expense of anonymity, if this has been offered though, since in doing so we would compromise ethical safeguards offered to participants.

## Introduction

The introduction and conclusion to any form of writing can be the most difficult elements to get right. The introduction serves a dual purpose of providing an idea as to the content of the report and convincing the reader that it is worth reading.

Gilbert (2001, p.370) says the introduction should:

> Indicate the topic of the paper, demonstrate why this topic is interesting and important, and show how the approach taken in the paper is an advance on previous work. In brief, the purpose of the Introduction is to get the reader hooked. This means starting from the reader's present knowledge and leading him or her on to seeing that the topic is worth spending some time investigating.

The importance of captivating the reader cannot be overstated. It is a misconception to assume that research will be read simply because it is inherently valuable. We must convince the readers that our addition to the body of knowledge is going to further their understanding of the topic as well as providing an interesting read along the way.

## Literature review

The introduction sets the scene for the literature review, in that it states the objectives and any hypotheses that are to be tested. It also provides an overview of the theoretical framework and context (social, historical, political, cultural, economic, geographical). The literature review then expands on this. It provides a justification for the research as well as a critical appraisal of the theoretical backdrop against which the data will be analysed.

The literature review helps to make sense of the research. It should silence any doubts about why the research has been carried out, and it should demonstrate that we are conversant with the terminology and theory which relate to the phenomenon under investigation.

## Research design: methods

When describing our methods it is necessary to provide sufficient detail so that the reader could replicate our research design (if not our results). This enables the reader to affirm the reliability of the study. In pursuing this aim, relevant elements from the following list should be included:

- Who is involved in the research: participants/organisations, and how these have been selected.
- How data have been collected.
- How data have been analysed (choice of statistical tests or analytical models).
- Any practical barriers which had to be overcome, such as access to sample or potential gaps in the data.
- Ethical considerations arising from the research.

One of the commitments we have as researchers is to share not just what we have learned from what our results tell us, but our experiences of using our chosen methods. In order for a reader to have confidence in our study and our interpretations of the data she or he must be told about how the research progressed. Once again, this requires reflection on the research process and demands that we question our methods. No matter how carefully we design our research in advance, it is only upon completion, when we look back over it, that we can truly scrutinise our methods. We need to ask whether the methods we applied were appropriate to our study. Key issues that have been addressed throughout this book can be used to shape our methodological evaluation. These include:

- validity;
- reflexivity;
- objectivity; and
- ethics.

In offering an evaluation it is important to admit to any subsequent shortcomings in the design. If our research is being read in a critical manner by our readers, these will become evident and we shall be expected either to defend them or to accept them and take them into account with our discussion of the data. Possible issues to be aware of are:

1. Limitations of the sample in terms of its size, response rate and representativeness, e.g. when reliance has been placed upon the success of a snowballing approach to sampling which has resulted in fewer participants being found than had been hoped, or low returns from a postal survey resulting in difficulties when analysing small subsections of data.
2. Reliability of measures, e.g. ambiguous questions in a survey or timing of events in an experiment by hand with a stopwatch.
3. Validity of indicators, e.g. where secondary data have been used and variables which relate to perceived levels of crime have been analysed as a representation of actual crime.
4. Ethical implications, e.g. where data collected in an in-depth interview could potentially reveal the identity of the interviewee, so very few quotes have been included in the analysis and discussion of results.

5. Inappropriate analytical models, e.g. where a causal relationship has been identified between two variables without using multivariate analysis to exclude the possible influence of third variables. If textual data are quantified, this would also require justification, for example.

## Statement of results

When writing about our data we need to decide whether to present the data first, and then discuss them in the ensuing section, or combine our discussion with the presentation of results. The former option has the advantage of allowing the readers to interpret the data by themselves and draw their own conclusions about the implications of the results. This can be favourable, as it enables us to defend our report against criticisms of overly subjective interpretation. If we assume this approach, data should be presented in such a way as to describe the results. With quantitative data, this can be achieved with tables and graphs, and reference to figures. Indeed, quantitative data lend themselves more readily to complete summaries since large quantities of data can be summarised relatively easily in tables. Qualitative data present a rather different challenge, though. Results can be described with reference to selected parts of the data which reflect our research questions. However, it is extremely unlikely, because of the expanse of data that qualitative research produces, that we will be able to offer a complete picture of all of it. In deciding what to include and what not to, we must accept that we are introducing a degree of subjectivity. There is no easy way around this; all we can do is try to ensure that a balanced picture of the data is provided, by selecting data from different participants which provide an account of the competing perspectives found in the data.

## Discussion

Assuming that we have opted to provide a separate descriptive overview of the data, the discussion provides an opportunity to reflect on the data, address our research questions, and contextualise the findings within theory from the literature. This section should be the most enlightening. In some respects, it is the reason for carrying out the research in the first place, since it is here where the way in which our research enhances knowledge comes to light. The purpose of our research is addressed through our interpretations of the data and how we see this fitting in with what else is already known. The discussion relies heavily on the ability to link our research with theory, as discussed earlier in this chapter. We should make our position clear in relation to any debates or schools of thought in the field. If we are using a particular model or philosophical perspective with which to interpret our data, this should be stated.

### Conclusion

Apart from the introduction, the conclusion is often the most difficult part of the report to write. It signifies the end of a lot of hard work, so we shall want to get it right. It is also, along with the introduction and abstract, often the only part of the report that will get read. The conclusion should draw the report to a close, by reiterating the main points, which might seek to address some, or all, of the following questions:

- What were the main findings of the research?
- How do these findings sit within the context of theory?
- What are the implications of the research?
- What lessons can be learned from the experience of carrying out the research?
- What can be learned from the way methods were employed?
- What areas are open for future research?

### References/bibliography

Throughout the write-up, we will have made reference to a number of sources. These all need to be included in a list of references. (See the next section for details of how and when to cite references.) This is the minimum requirement, although there will inevitably be more sources that you have used throughout the research process, but to which you have not cited a reference in the text. These can still be included as a bibliography, as it provides the reader with a useful list of relevant material.

### Appendices

It is easy to perceive appendices as a repository for all the bits of a report that do not seem to fit anywhere else. However, appendices need to be carefully thought out and relevant. Items such as a copy of a questionnaire, interview schedule or observation plan are useful elements of an appendix. Statistical tables can be gathered together in an appendix, with only a selection relevant to the discussion dealt with in the main body of the text. The important thing to remember is that appendices should be cross-referenced in the text. The readers should be made aware at what point during the report they need to turn to the appendix and make use of the information. Without such clear signposting, the appendices will just take on the form of some additional information that has been included at the end to pad out the report.

## Referencing and citation

We have placed a good deal of emphasis on the importance of situating our research in the context of theory in the literature, in terms of both our topic and methods. With this in mind, it is important to understand how and when these references to others' work should be included within our writing. Moreover, it is important to have an idea of *why* they should be included, and we will turn our attention to this now.

When considering why references are important, it is useful to consider who the practice of citation affects and benefits. There are three interested parties with regards to referencing:

1. The reader – citing references directs the reader to the original source, therefore enabling a more thorough understanding of our research and development of ideas. Our writing may contain assumptions based on established theory. It is not sufficient, however, merely to assume that the reader is familiar with a particular theory and so it is necessary to provide readers with enough information to understand the topic. This can be done through the literature review, and by offering clues as to where they can pursue the topic in more depth through our references.
2. The cited author – we are showing our recognition of another individual's work, whether we are supporting it or criticising it. This can enable constructive dialogue between writers. In addition, sometimes an idea may have already been voiced so fluently that it would seem pointless to try to phrase it differently. In these instances it is useful to quote an author directly.
3. Ourselves – not only does citing references add credibility to our work, but it can also help to avoid legal complications brought about by wrongfully passing off another's work as our own.

## When should you cite references?

There are two important factors to be considered when deciding when we should cite a reference. First, we need to decide at what stages in our writing it is suitable to cite others' work. This is something that will depend very much on our own style. Some writers have a persuasive, articulate style which can stand up on its own extremely well and can rely less on others' work to relate arguments. Others may find that they need to include quotations more often to add conviction to their argument. This will also depend on the nature of the subject matter – some topics can be backed up by real examples from historical or contemporary events, rather than taking them from texts.

In addition to deciding when it is *suitable* to cite a reference we have to decide when it is *necessary*. Often this is fairly self-evident, when we are using a direct quote, for example. However, there are more ambiguous occasions which can be overlooked. Take the following example:

> Jones has argued that social research is a futile task, characterised by an endless desire to provide answers to questions which are essentially unanswerable.

In this passage an idea has been credited to the author. There is no direct quote from a certain text and so why cite a reference? The passage seems only to paraphrase a theme running through the text, but this still requires proper citation.

The reader may want to read Jones' original piece which deals with this idea, so it is essential that a reference is provided, particularly when, as in this example, an entire argument has been reduced to a few lines of description.

The reworked passage below is far more informative in that it provides the reader with the exact source from which the author is drawing her or his information. The reader will now be able to read this and conclude that the passage is, indeed, a rather poor summary of the idea it is attempting to describe.

> It has been argued that social research is a futile task, characterised by an endless desire to provide answers to questions which are essentially unanswerable (Jones 1999, pp.119–28).

It becomes evident from this example that great care must be taken when introducing other scholars' ideas into our own work. As a general rule, if we are referring to another person's work whether directly or indirectly, then we should cite a reference.

There are situations when it is unnecessary to cite a reference. When relating our research to established theory we should cite the source of this theory. Theoretical development is not always this straightforward, though. Theories are more often than not the result of the culmination of years of work by a great many theorists and become more a school of thought. (Paradigms are good examples of this: positivism and interpretivism are difficult to attach to any one singular source.) In these cases, some licence may be granted and the ideas can be seen as 'public domain information' (Moxley 1992, p.129). So, for example, we might say:

> Feminist methodology places much importance on equity between researcher and participant.

We do not have to cite a reference for feminist methodology, since while it may be possible to trace its origins back to a handful of particular individuals, it has now developed into a widely used approach to research.

## Placing references in context

Giving a point of reference to the reader is helpful in aiding further exploration of the topic, but it would be very unusual if a reader stopped at each citation to find the relevant reference and read the relevant work. It is therefore our responsibility to introduce citations and place them in a context that will make sense to the reader. Politicians are often found to be complaining about being misquoted by the press, often as a result of journalists placing a phrase in the wrong context and providing an entirely different interpretation. Likewise, statistics are particularly open to manipulation and misrepresentation. As academic writers, not journalists, it is in our interest to ensure that we do not do this.

When introducing a quote, no matter how comprehensive the quote is in conveying its meaning, we need to inform the reader of any similarities to, or differences between, the contexts in which the author cited and ourselves are writing. When writing about contemporary popular culture we may wish to include a quote from the nineteenth century which is relevant to the argument, but it is important to recognise the different social, political, economic and cultural environments in which the author was writing.

When citing research findings, it is vitally important to include a summary of the methods used to draw the conclusions to which we are making reference. Take the following example:

> Ninety percent of Britain consider the economy to be in a healthy state.

While on the surface the information seems useful, there is no way of being sure of the quality of the source. There is no indication of sample size (it could have been as few as 10 people) or sampling methods, no indication of how the survey responsible was administered, no definition of 'economy' (British or world economy?) and no comparative responses (e.g. very unhealthy, unhealthy, neither, healthy, very healthy).

The above example is an extreme one, but helps to illustrate the importance of providing the reader with the necessary information to make an accurate reading of the meaning of our references.

## Systems for referencing

Having established when we should cite references and why it is necessary, it is important that we do so in a manner that is consistent with an established approach. There are two forms of citation which are most commonly used in the social sciences: the numerical system and the Harvard system.

The system we have used in this book is the Harvard system, and involves placing the surname of the author and date of the publication immediately after the relevant part of the text. In addition, if the citation refers to a particular section or quotation from a specific page, then the relevant page numbers should be included. This is perhaps the most widely used and accessible system, so it is this one we shall concentrate on here, by offering a summary of some of its key conventions.

The list of references is arranged alphabetically, by author, then chronologically by date. If references are made to publications by the same author in the same year, then each publication is identified by a letter following the year (a, b, c, …) in order (see Example 9.4).

### Example 9.4 Referencing multiple works by the same author

Hammersley, M. 1992a. On Feminist Methodology, *Sociology*, 26 (2), pp.187–206.
Hammersley, M. 1992b. *What's Wrong with Ethnography?* London: Routledge.

Hammersley, M. and Atkinson, P. 1995. *Ethnography: Principles in Practice*, 2nd edition. London: Routledge.
Hammersley, M. and Gomm, R. 1997. Bias in Social Research, *Sociological Research Online*, [online], 2 (1). Available at: http://www.socresonline.org.uk/2/1/2.html [Accessed 20 June 2001].

There are a couple of things to note about the order of this list. First, the sources for which Hammersley is the sole author come before those for which he was joint author. Secondly, the two sources published in 1992 are identified by the letters 'a' and 'b' to distinguish them. This list also shows how books, journal articles and online references should be formatted. Common to all is the fundamental information relating to the author's name and year of publication. The first reference is to a journal article and includes the name of the article as well as the name of the journal. Then it states the volume and the issue, followed by the pages on which the article can be found. The second and third references are books, for which the title and the location and name of the publishing company are included. Finally, the last reference is to an online article. This follows the same principles as a printed article, with the addition of [online] after the titles, the web address at which the article can be found and the date accessed. This final point is important since the Internet is an inconsistent medium and pages can be made available or discontinued at short notice. Notice that there are strict conventions as to where punctuation goes in the list of references. Titles should also be highlighted, by either underlining them, or marking them in italics.

The references shown in Example 9.4 are perhaps the most common sources we need to reference in our writing, but the Harvard system addresses a far wider range than this, including conference proceedings, television broadcasts, email correspondence and other commonly referenced sources. Most university and reference libraries will have their own guides to the full use of the Harvard system, and it is useful to have one of these to hand when writing up. For a full and detailed exploration of referencing, see Cuba and Cocking (1997, pp.113–25).

## Polishing up and finishing off

Having planned, organised, structured, drafted, reread and rewritten our research, we are now finally nearing the end of the writing-up process. By this stage in our writing we should have something that could almost be called a finished product. The structure and content will have been established through redrafting, so at this point we can turn our attentions to the finer points, such as presentation, formatting and small refinements in our use of language.

The final read over our research should be with a different aim in mind from the previous cycles of the redrafting process. Here, we are not looking for major flaws or alterations to structure, but for finer improvements to the way we are expressing our ideas. With this in mind, as we read through our writing, we should be asking whether there are any words, phrases or sentences that do not add anything to what we are trying to say, or could be better expressed. Grammatical details should be checked to make sure sentences flow. There remains much debate over the use of certain punctuation in the English language; the comma seemingly defied regulation, and so to try to edit writing in such a way as to make it grammatically 'correct' is a more or less pointless task. While we would not want to advocate flagrant disregard of common grammatical rules, we must recognise that in some instances it is possible to interpret the use of grammar differently, and so the best we can seek to achieve is writing which reads in the way we intend it to sound.

Spelling, on the other hand, is something we must be extra vigilant about. With the widespread use of word-processing software, spell-checking has become automated. This is something of a double-edged sword; it is a great labour-saving device, but it is also responsible for harbouring bad habits in so much as there can be a tendency not to check our spelling ourselves. Computer spell-checking will not flag up instances where a correctly spelled but inappropriate word has been included. This can lead to potentially embarrassing situations:

> The wedding ceremony features a number of acts of symbolism, not least of which is the moment at which a father 'gives away' his daughter as the bribe.

A computer spell-checker would not be able to inform us that the word at the end of this sentence should be 'bride', so it should be apparent that we cannot rely solely on technology to check our writing for us.

While checking for spelling and grammar we can also assess whether our writing manages to communicate what it is we are trying to say in the most coherent way possible. Given the time, it is useful to leave as long as possible between writing the final draft and checking for these last revisions. This enables us to come to our writing with a freshness, but still be aware of the points we are trying to make. In doing so, we shall be better placed to spot words or phrases which seem out of place, or suggest something other than the intended meaning. Once we have fine-tuned the details of grammar, spelling and comprehension, we can move on to the presentation.

It is easy to overlook the importance of good presentation, as we spend most of our time worrying about what is going into the report, rather than how it looks. However, good presentation of a report can make our research more accessible to the reader, so we must ensure that we leave enough time prior to any deadlines to work on this aspect. Depending on how our research is going to be disseminated, we may have to adhere to a house-style with regards to formatting. Whether it is a journal article, book chapter or thesis, there will be certain impositions of style, and we will be expected to submit our writing in a format that is within certain guidelines.

Presentation needs to ensure that the structure of the writing is clear. The use of different heading styles can help with this. Tables and graphs/illustrations should be presented in a consistent format. This applies to the numbering of these as well. Numbering will usually be linked in to the different sections/chapters. The font used should be chosen for clarity, but a specified font is easy to overlook. It is worth checking any requirements for font, as well as other layout aspects such as margin size, line spacing and paragraph numbering. Finally, it is important to check the format in which the writing needs to be submitted. In some instances we will be required to provide an electronic copy in a certain file format. Other occasions may demand that we submit a printed and bound copy (e.g. when submitting a thesis). All of these finer points may seem trivial individually, but together they have a significant effect on the overall product of our writing, so they should be given sufficient time and attention to be dealt with properly.

## Summary

The writing-up process should be an enjoyable one since it enables us to bring together all the other stages of the research process into an end product. It should not be seen as an easy process, though. It requires planning, motivation, organisation and reflection. If handled poorly, it can prove to be the undoing of a lot of hard work. The writing-up process needs to be treated with respect: to view writing as 'unproblematic and transparent', as merely a simple way of reporting our research, is a terrible mistake. It is necessary to remember the objectives of writing up research that we have discussed. These are:

- to address our research questions;
- to discuss our findings;
- to conceptualise our research within a broader theoretical framework;
- to reflect on the research process;
- to share our experiences; and
- to contribute to methodological debates.

Writing up research should be viewed as a means of connecting with knowledge and other researchers. We can view research as a cyclical process of gathering knowledge, establishing theories, gathering more knowledge to test theories, developing new theories, then challenging those theories, and so forth. Writing is the part of the process that links all the cycles together. It is something akin to the baton in a relay race, which is passed on from one teammate to another so that the whole team can benefit.

We have seen the importance of linking our research to theory in the literature and to addressing our research questions with our data. We have also emphasised the need to understand that our writing is for others, not just ourselves. To this end, it is necessary to consider our audience and try to comprehend our writing from the point of view of the reader. This is not an easy task, but if due consideration is given to the audience, our writing will improve as a result.

*(Continued)*

*(Continued)*

Finally, we have seen the importance of some of the conventions of academic writing: references, presentation, structure and format. Writing up research is a different process from that involved in other forms of writing. We must recognise this, and not assume that because we have spent our whole lives writing in other forms that writing up research will come easily to us. As with many skills, the key to successful and enjoyable writing is practice.

## Chapter research task

Think back to the project outline you devised for a research project in the chapter research task from Chapter 3 and imagine you are to write up the research into a report. You should draw up an outline plan of the different sections you would include in the report, and then break these down into sections which are specific to your research topic. First, think of a title for your research, and then try writing a few brief paragraphs summarising the following:

1. What sources of literature you would refer to.
2. The theories that inform the research.
3. The aims and objectives of the research.
4. The main aspects of the methods chosen for your design, with justification. As you do this ask yourself, 'For each of the aims and objectives of my proposed project, have I set out the method(s) necessary to capture the data?'
5. Any ethical implications you foresee arising.
6. How you would approach your data so you are able to tackle your research question.

Having done this, ask a friend or colleague to read your plan and provide feedback. Particular questions you might want to ask them are:

1. Does the title effectively convey a sense of what the research is about?
2. Are there any particular phrases or terms that are not clearly defined?
3. Is the writing style accessible?
4. Does the research seem to be important?
5. Is it clear how the research is to be carried out, and why?

## Recommended Reading

Cuba, L. and Cocking, J. 1997. *How to Write about the Social Sciences*. Harlow: Longman.

Day, A. 1996. *How to Get Work Published in Journals*. Aldershot: Gower.

Gilbert, N. 2001. Writing about Social Research. In: N. Gilbert (ed.), *Researching Social Life*, 2nd edn. London: Sage. pp.361–77.

Hart, C. 2001. *Doing a Literature Search: A Comprehensive Guide for the Social Sciences*. London: Sage.

Moxley, J. 1992. *Publish, Don't Perish: The Scholar's Guide to Academic Writing and Publishing*. London: Greenwood Press.

Pryke, M., Rose, G. and Whatmore, S. (eds) 2003. *Using Social Theory: Thinking through Research*. London: Sage.

# TEN

# Designing a Research Proposal

- To examine the role of the proposal within research
- To inform readers of the criteria by which successful proposals are judged
- To examine an example of a successful research proposal
- To identify distinctions between quantitative and qualitative proposals
- To provide a framework structure for a research proposal

- **Introduction**
- **What is a research proposal?**
- **The reviewers' assessment criteria**
- **Quantitative and qualitative research proposals**
- **Is there a formula for writing successful research proposals?**
- **Outline of the proposed research**
- **Summary**
- **Recommended reading**

## Introduction

In order to address the major questions and issues of everyday social life, the researcher may well need to conduct empirical work of some description. However, such research work is not an isolated activity. It is a social activity that has potential repercussions for others – whether that be the people or the organisation or the culture that we are studying, or the people that we work with as students or employees or community group members. For instance, a project idea that aims to investigate workplace harassment needs to consider all sorts of matters that one might not initially consider to be part of the research process. Such matters might include the potentially traumatising impact on respondents who might themselves have been victims of bullying but have lived with this in enforced silence. Or perhaps as a consequence of the research revealing endemic yet hidden workplace bullying, the employing organisation may find itself the target of a law suit, by failing to provide adequate duty of care for employees.

Whether you are a student intending to commence with a Masters or doctoral research programme, or a project leader applying for funding support, your research idea will need to be assessed by others, and you will need to present a convincing case in the form of a research proposal.

All researchers should therefore be able to prepare a proposal for a research topic to a professional standard. Being able to produce such a proposal is an important skill. Intending doctoral students are required to prepare such a proposal when applying for studentships and seeking formal registration for their project. Such requirements are also common on many university Masters courses. Outside the academic arena, there are also many organisations that provide funding for social research. Where this is the case, how do you convince a funding body that may be assessing a large number of competing proposals that your research is worthy of support in preference to the others that it will look at? You may have a great idea that immediately captures the imagination, but are you capable of transforming this idea into a feasible project?

The research proposal is the means by which we are able to demonstrate that we are able to do this. As such, it allows us to spell out what exactly is the research problem that we are intending to investigate, why this is worthy of investigation, and how we intend to carry out the research. In putting such a proposal together we shall not only need to demonstrate our knowledge of the area in which we are interested, but also be required to show that we have the necessary methodological competence and sensitivity to carry out the research.

This chapter covers the essential ground in constructing a high-quality research proposal. Specifically, it considers:

- What is a research proposal?
- What is the value of a research proposal?
- By what standards are research proposals assessed?
- What should be included in a good research proposal?
- How should a research proposal be structured?

## What is a research proposal?

The research proposal is an application that is prepared by a student, university academic or professional researcher for support prior to embarking upon a research study.

At one level, the objectives of a research proposal may be seen as providing a statement about the purposes of the research, how it is to be carried out, the resource implications of the proposed investigation, as well as the timescale for completion. At another level, however, the research proposal is an argument. Through the document, you are presenting a case, in which the intention is to convince others of the general merits and feasibility of the proposed study. The research proposal should therefore aim to convey three key aspects of an intended research project:

1. Its objectives and scholarly significance.
2. Your technical qualifications.
3. The level of funding required.

## The objectives and scholarly significance of the proposed study

The general research issues to be examined, together with the methodological strategy to be pursued, need to be carefully explained to the reviewer. Each must also be fully justified.

The proposal, then, should communicate your specific intentions. This involves a clear overview of the purpose of the proposed study and of its importance, together with a step-by-step plan for conducting it. The research problem(s) needs to be identified, questions or hypotheses should be stated, and key terms defined. You must specify and justify which target group is to be included in the sample, together with the research design to be adopted, the research instrument(s) to be used, the procedures to be followed, and the methods of analysis to be used.

All of these aspects of the project should be covered and at least a partial review of previous related literature must be included. This will enable you to 'ground' your project theoretically – to make explicit links between this and existing ideas and debates that are taking place within the wider academic or policy community. The literature review will also enable you to demonstrate the suitability of your proposed research strategy. Your case will be strengthened if you: (a) reference the types of method used by other authors in the past to conduct similar studies; (b) are then able to demonstrate from this that you have appraised the effectiveness of these approaches in generating data to examine the issues at hand, and therefore justified your own choice of research strategy.

## The technical qualifications of the researcher

This will need to be stated, whether you are a student intending to commence with a Masters or doctoral research programme, or a project leader applying for funding support. Your experience and level of expertise should be carefully set out, in terms of both your knowledge of the subject area and your methodological 'qualifications' and skills. (Note that when applying for funding, it should not be assumed that by 'experience', precedence is inevitably given to those who are well published with a long history of research in the field, over new and aspiring researchers. As we shall see, an application is judged on the basis of the applicant's track record to date, which will be measured against the particular stage reached in her or his academic career.)

### The level of funding required

It goes without saying that all review committees will need to be convinced that the intended project provides 'value for money'. This, as we shall see, does not necessarily mean that cheapest is always best. Instead, it requires that the researcher provides evidence that she or he has carefully costed the proposed project, and that the level of funding sought is warranted, given both the aims and objectives of the study and the methods to be used to implement it.

If yours is a proposed Masters dissertation or doctoral thesis, and you are not applying directly for financial support, you will nonetheless need to convince the course team that you have access to sufficient resources to complete your study.

## The reviewers' assessment criteria

The essential criteria for assessment of the research proposal will be broadly the same, regardless of which body the prospective researcher is targeting. This will be the case whether or not you are applying for funding from an external agency or a university research committee, or to a postgraduate course team in order to receive its approval to proceed with a postgraduate dissertation. The proposal should contain sufficient information to persuade both specialist and non-specialist members of the review committee that the proposed activity is sound and worthy of support under their criteria for the selection of projects.

### Activity 10.1 Review committee's judgement of a research proposal

What do you think the research review committee will consider most important in assessing a research proposal? Make a list of the areas that you think members of such a committee would focus upon when considering a research proposal.

### What are the key criteria that such bodies use to assess a research proposal?

The criteria most typically used by review committees to measure the potential of your research proposal can be listed as:

- track record;
- originality;
- feasibility;
- clarity;
- outputs.

### Activity 10.2 Review committee assessment criteria

Consider the assessment criteria listed above. Which do you think the research review committee will consider most important in assessing a research proposal? How would you rank them in terms of their priority for such a committee? For each, write short notes explaining why you think it is a low- or high-level criterion for review committees.

## Clarity

The assessors will be scrutinising a research proposal to ensure that there is an internal coherence to the project:

- Is it clearly thought through in terms of what you have set out to do?
- Is there a clear identification of the research problem that you intend to investigate?

It will be anticipated – indeed expected – by the review committee that the research proposal will not be deficient in these areas. Therefore, clarity is a low-level criterion. Very few research proposals would be expected to fail because they lacked internal coherence.

## Feasibility

Can you achieve what you initially set out to do in your proposal (within your budget and your estimated timescale, and using your initial research strategy)?

You should think through your research plans carefully, and try to anticipate all possible issues and detours that you may encounter during your study. But the review committee will be sufficiently experienced in these matters to appreciate that research programmes cannot be precisely mapped out, particularly for emergent qualitative research studies. Certainly, the notion of 'delivery within budget' is a red herring.

And there will be issues that arise during the course of your study which may impact upon your initial methodological strategy – issues that you could not realistically have predicted at the outset. Perhaps these will be in terms of access difficulties encountered, or sickness of a key 'gatekeeper', or ethical matters that arise in addition to those discussed in your research design.

Feasibility is an important issue, and the review committee will use this as one of the criteria upon which they will assess your research proposal. However, risk will take precedence over predictability. Producing a book on time is of course important, but the review committee will ask the question, 'will the book be read by 5, 500 or 5,000 people?' before they ask, 'will the applicant meet her/his deadline?' Similarly, if you can demonstrate that your research is innovative, then your proposal is likely to be considered very seriously by the review committee. The exciting, yet expensive, research idea has a greater likelihood of approval than a proposal that is considerably cheaper, but is nonetheless not as inspiring.

Feasibility is an important criterion therefore – more so than clarity – but it is nonetheless a relatively low-level one.

## Track record

Understandably, if your research proposal is to be assessed competitively against those submitted by other candidates, the review committee will take into account the track records of each applicant. But an established track record by itself is certainly no guarantee of success. And review committees will be realistic enough to appreciate that a 'new' researcher can only develop a good track record if bodies like their own provide the researcher with the support to embark upon a research career.

Furthermore, such committees will have different expectations of 'new' and more 'long-standing' applicants. Indeed, a good track record can be achieved even at a relatively early stage for researchers. The expectations held by assessors of what counts as a good track record is relative to the stage of a research career achieved by a particular applicant. New and aspiring researchers should therefore pitch their application for research support appropriately. Typically, the route to be taken is a 'staged' one. It involves the aspiring student applying initially for a university postgraduate course. Paid academic research posts, or practitioner research posts, are likely to follow only after qualification. Such a trajectory may be a long and arduous one, but achieving a good track record comes only with talent and hard work.

## Outputs

This is a very important criterion, more so than those already mentioned. The review committee will be particularly interested in supporting project proposals that have the potential for achieving publication, or that may have 'utility' for the wider policy community.

Extract 10.1 provides an example taken from a (successful) research proposal – the Youth and Politics project (Henn and Weinstein 2000) – that was awarded a research grant from an external research-funding agency (the UK Economic and Social Research Council). Here, the applicants were required to demonstrate the relevance of the research for different user groups.

Notice that there are very explicit statements from the funding agency concerning its expectations about the following:

- the usefulness of the proposed research for this community;
- that there is evidence that such organisations and individuals have had some input into the design of the research;

- that the research is of sufficient interest to practitioners that they may have provided tangible support to the project (perhaps in terms of part-funding or a letter of support).

## Extract 10.1 Youth and Politics project (Henn and Weinstein 2000)

**Relevance to 'user' groups**

Please explain below the likely contribution to policy or practice; details of consultation with user groups (such as public, private and voluntary sector practitioners and policy-makers) in the development of the research and proposed collaboration/communication with such groups during the research should be included. Details of any potential co-funding or support in kind should also be included here. Do not *exceed one side.*

1. The proposed research will be of value to policy users and to the wider political community. In previous research, we have dealt with a number of agencies and organisations that have links to youth, including amongst others, the Institute for Citizenship, the Citizenship Team at the Department for Education and Employment, the National Union of Students, various trades unions (notably the GMB), and the party youth sections. Meetings will be held to further progress these links through the research, in terms of: the design of the research and the survey questionnaire; testing out the plausibility and utility of the research findings; the dissemination of the findings through presentations at the end of the research. Together, these organisations will be able to provide invaluable advice and support to the project.
2. Non-technical summaries and briefing papers shall be disseminated to various policy users and other interested groups, including those mentioned in 1. above, but also others such as the British Youth Council, the Young Fabians, as well as all members of the Crick Commission, and think-tanks.
3. Academics will be consulted during the design stage of the research – particularly in terms of discussion of theoretical issues in the development of the questionnaire.
4. Research results will be communicated to the academic community via conferences (the annual meetings of the UK Political Studies Association and the British Sociological Association) and academic journals (papers will be submitted to the 'British Journal of Political Science', and 'Sociology' in the first instance).
5. Earlier research that we have conducted has already been widely disseminated through the national and local media. It is anticipated that the proposed research will lead to similar levels of media exposure, and press releases will be produced for this purpose.

You may not have been able to achieve this level of external support, but it will significantly add to the robustness and credibility of your research proposal if you can demonstrate that it has importance to the wider practitioner or policy-making communities. This will be the case regardless of whether or not you are applying for external funding for research, or you are preparing a research proposal for a Masters dissertation or a doctoral thesis. With respect to the latter, a letter offering support for the applicant's project plans, or even a possible collaboration, would be considered to be a positive feature of a student's research proposal.

## Originality

Members of a review committee who are charged with the task of reviewing your research proposal will recognise that the project's perceived contribution to the external users, or its potential for publication in an academic journal, or to gain a good pass on a Masters course will be largely dependent upon its originality. The potential to generate new knowledge is the key to a good research proposal. If you can convince the review committee that you have met this criterion, then and only then will they assess your proposal on the basis of the other criteria mentioned above. By the same token, if you fail to convince these assessors that you have an original idea that you intend to investigate through your proposed project, then the reviewers are unlikely to consider your application further.

But different types of reviewer will have different yardsticks against which to measure 'originality':

1. External funding agencies (higher education funding councils like the ESRC, charitable funding bodies like the Nuffield Foundation) – will assess originality in terms of an expected significant contribution to knowledge likely to follow from the proposed research.
2. PhD review committees – will look for indications that the intended study programme has a significant potential for publication.
3. Masters supervisors – will be concerned that the dissertation proposal will lead to an authentic and independent research project.

So, how will you discover your 'big idea'?

It is likely to develop organically from your own research interests. Most importantly, you must read widely – adopting too narrow a focus in your reading may limit your ability to discover your research question. You must look consciously for it. This will, by necessity, involve you in one or more of the following:

- Developing an awareness (through reviewing the literature and/or attending conferences) of the research which is currently being developed in your field.

As you do so, search for an idea that you consider to be significant by its omission from your field. Try to identify what is conventionally referred to as a research gap in your chosen area.
- Challenging current thinking in your field (to do this requires you to be aware of the key issues and debates in your subject area first of all).
- Applying an existing idea to a new field or a different academic or policy context. This may not involve you in developing a 'new' idea as such, but the way in which you use that existing idea will be innovative. It therefore has the potential to make an original contribution to knowledge. An example might involve you examining a marketing technique that is used widely within the general field of business studies, and researching the extent of its usage by political parties in their campaigning. Through your research, you may gain a greater understanding of the development of modern electioneering methods.

The research proposal is therefore an important document. As such, it will take significant time, effort and patience to get it right. It will also likely involve the preparation of several drafts, as well as feedback from colleagues in the field, before it is ready for submission. But such preparation has some important potential benefits for the final project itself. Submitting the research proposal enables an expert review committee to evaluate the merits of your research plans, and in so doing – especially where they may offer suggestions for revision – provides important 'expert' insight into how to improve the study.

## Quantitative and qualitative research proposals

Prior to the drafting of a research proposal, the nature of the research design to be selected should be set out. Whether one is intending to adopt a broadly qualitative research design, or a strategy that is largely quantitative in nature, is likely to affect the shape and format of the research proposal. Of course, those charged with reviewing proposals would have very clear expectations that certain content will be included in the proposal, regardless of the intended research strategy. However, some elements of a quantitative research proposal will not be included in a qualitative research proposal, and vice versa. Furthermore, quantitative research proposals are likely to be more uniform than those designed for broadly qualitative-based studies. As Punch (2005, p.264) notes:

> It is easier in many respects to suggest proposal guidelines for a quantitative study, since there is greater variety in qualitative studies, and many qualitative studies will be unfolding rather than prestructured. An emerging study cannot be as specific in the proposal about its research questions, or about details of the design. When this is the case, the point needs to be made in the proposal.

In the remainder of this chapter, the core elements of a research proposal will be reviewed. Where appropriate, the specific aspects that are necessary for drafting either a qualitative or a quantitative proposal will be noted.

## Is there a formula for writing successful research proposals?

A research proposal, then, is a written plan for a study. It spells out in detail what the researcher intends to do. It permits others to learn about the intended research, and to offer suggestions for improving the study. It helps the researcher to clarify what needs to be done, and aims to avoid unintentional pitfalls or unknown problems.

Before examining what a research proposal might look like, it is important to be aware that what will be suggested in the remainder of this chapter is intended to serve as a general framework, not a definitive set of instructions. The only general rule that must always be adhered to is that the research proposal should be both succinct and complete. Other than that, each university research committee or external funding agency will have its own expectations about the actual format of the research proposal, and some will be more explicit than others in this respect. Research proposals often vary significantly in terms of length. In some cases, application forms that prescribe precisely what is wanted will need to be completed. In others, the researcher will have more latitude to decide upon the format of the proposal.

However, the onus will be on the researcher to 'bend' to meet the requirements of the university review committee or external funding agency.

Finally, it's important to avoid using a discursive, essay-like style; instead, you should make plentiful use of headings and bullet points. If it is necessary to use references (in any *Background* or *Literature Review* sections, for instance), the Harvard style is to be preferred. Pay full attention to appearance and to user-friendliness.

## Outline of the proposed research

In the absence of any forms or guidelines, there are general themes that you might use to structure your own research proposal, whether this is for a postgraduate dissertation or an application for external research funding. However, what follows are 'elements' of a proposal – you do not need to have each as a particular heading.

### Title page

This should include each of the following: your name, the title of the proposed project, any collaborating agencies that have been involved in the preparation of the proposal, the date of submission, and, if applicable, the funding agency to which you are applying for support.

### Abstract

The abstract is a brief synopsis of the planned research investigation. It appears at the front of the proposal, but it is usually the last element to be written. It should include two key areas – the major objectives of the proposed study, and the procedures and general methodological strategy that are to be used in order to meet these objectives. The abstract should be approximately one page or less in length.

The abstract is an important strategic element of the proposal, and therefore should be afforded considerable attention in the drafting of your proposal. It serves three key interlinked purposes:

- The reviewer usually reads it before the full proposal to gain a perspective of the study and of its expected significance.
- The reviewer uses it as a reference to the nature of the study if the project comes up for discussion.
- It will sometimes be the only part of the proposal that is read when making preliminary selections of applicant proposals.

Read through Extract 10.2. As you do so, look carefully at the two aspects of an abstract outlined above, and note how they are covered.

#### Extract 10.2 Abstract: Youth and Politics project (Henn and Weinstein 2000)

Conventional wisdom holds that young people in Britain are alienated from the political process. Moreover, some have suggested that there is an 'historic political disconnection' of youth from formal party politics, with this group more likely to participate in new politics formations. Paradoxically, there is a recognition that formalised youth activities are a potentially significant aspect of party development. They serve the purposes of recruiting the future political elite, raising political awareness among young people, and widening the pool of party activists. The aim of this project is to reveal the level of engagement that young people have with party politics in Britain. Specifically, the research will examine whether there is a crisis of democratic legitimacy in terms of the attitudes of young people towards party politics. It will also investigate differences in this respect, along socio-demographic and spatial lines. Importantly, regional analysis will enable an examination of the efficacy of new political institutions in Wales, Scotland and London for strengthening levels of young people's political engagement. Quantitative data will be collected by means of a national postal survey of young people. This will be the first British nation-wide study to focus exclusively on first-time voters with only limited experience of formal politics.

## Activity 10.3

Think about a research project that you intend to conduct. Write an abstract of between 200 and 250 words, setting out (a) the general issues and debates/or policy field that you intend to engage with through your study, (b) your specific aims and objectives, and (c) the research strategy that you propose to follow to meet these objectives.

## Research problem to be investigated

There are usually four areas to be addressed in this section of the research proposal: the purpose of the proposed study, a justification for the project, the specific research questions that you intend to explore, and a definition of any key terms and concepts that you will examine. However, you will write only one section. This must contain all of these four aspects; you will not deal with each under a separate heading.

### *Purpose of the study*

You will need to state succinctly what the research proposes to investigate. The purpose should be a concise statement, providing a framework to which details are added later. Generally speaking, any study should seek to clarify some aspect of the field of interest that is considered important, thereby contributing both to the overall knowledge in the field and to current practice.

### *Justification for the study*

The researcher must make clear why this particular study is important to investigate. You must present an argument for the work of the study. This will usually form a substantial section of your research proposal, and will require you to provide evidence that you have conducted a detailed literature review in the area, in order to:

- demonstrate to the reader that you have studied the field with insight and are therefore well qualified to undertake the research;
- identify what is already known, and by implication what is as yet unknown – and therefore worthy of empirical study.

The literature review forms a crucial element in any research proposal. It has already been discussed in the previous chapter, and will be returned to at a later stage in this particular chapter (see *Review of the literature*, below).

As an example, you might be interested in the general field of organisation studies. If you intend to study a particular method through which a local authority deals with harassment at work, you need to make a case that such a study is important, and that people are or should be concerned with it. You might indicate through your literature review that previous studies have identified a pattern of harassment that is linked to poor morale within the workplace, increased incidences of people suffering from occupational stress, and high levels of absenteeism. Or perhaps, where the issue is not checked, it may lead to poor industrial relations. The net result either way may lead to an erosion of quality within the particular department and a decline in public confidence in the service.

Alternatively, you may be interested in conducting a research study which aims to evaluate the effectiveness of 'care in the community' solutions for mental health patients. Existing research may indicate that since the introduction of the current arrangements, there has been a marked increase in the general suicide rate among this group, or perhaps an expansion in the rate of homelessness among people with severe learning difficulties.

You must also make clear why you have chosen to investigate the particular method adopted by organisations to tackle such problems. In many such proposals, there is the implication that current methods are not adequate to tackle the problem seriously.

Coley and Scheinberg (1990, p.41) have developed a useful framework for conceptualising issues for research that helps to justify how research may reveal interesting new insights into the problem. The framework may not, in its entirety, be appropriate for all styles of research, but the general method they adopt is a useful way of beginning to think about how you may structure the 'case' for your proposed study:

> People with 'A' characteristics and background live in 'B' conditions/environments and have 'C' problems/needs that are caused by 'D'.
>
> People are blocked from solving these problems because of 'E'. This problem is related to other problems 'F', and have 'G' short- and long-term impact if not addressed.
>
> The impact of their needs/problems on the community is 'H'. Others have addressed their needs/problems by doing 'I', the result of their interventions have been 'J'.
>
> The most promising strategy for intervention now is 'K'.

Key questions to ask yourself at this point are:

- Have I identified the specific research problem that I wish to investigate?
- Have I indicated what I intend to do about this problem?
- Have I put forward an argument as to why this problem is worthy of investigation?
- Have I based this argument on a review and examination of key literature in the area?

### *The research questions*

The particular research questions that you intend to examine should be stated next. These are usually, but not always, a more specific form of the problem in question form. For quantitative researchers, research hypotheses will be set out at this stage for reasons of clarity and as a research strategy. If a researcher has a hypothesis in mind, it should be stated as clearly and as concisely as possible. It is unnecessarily frustrating for a reader to have to infer what a study's hypothesis or hypotheses might be. Examples of the research questions that were to be pursued in the Youth and Politics project noted in Extracts 10.1 and 10.2 are included in Extract 10.3.

## Extract 10.3 Key research questions: Youth and Politics project (Henn and Weinstein 2000)

- What is the popular understanding of parties?
- Are young people indifferent, or even hostile to political parties?
- What, if anything, do they like about them?
- Do their attitudes towards parties significantly differ from those of other sections of the population (such as their parents' generation)?
- Is there evidence to suggest that young people are now more disaffected from parties than at any time since the introduction of universal suffrage?
- And is there a case for arguing that young people, given their particular socialisation and formal educational experiences, might actually be more predisposed to party appeals?

For qualitative researchers, especially those adopting an emergent research design, the actual research questions and hypotheses will not become clear until the research has begun. Typically, these begin to take shape in the course of data collection and analysis. As Punch (2005, p.265) notes:

> If a tightly structured qualitative study is planned, the proposal can proceed along similar lines to the quantitative proposal. If a more emergent study is planned, where focus and structure will develop as the study proceeds, this point should be made clearly (in the research proposal). In the former case, there will be general and specific questions. In the latter case, there will only be general orienting and guiding research questions.

The research questions are often drafted as *Aims and Objectives*. These are the means by which what is to be attempted and what is to be accomplished are specified (Anderson, 1998; Verma and Mallick, 1999). The aims and objectives should immediately follow your review of the existing literature, serving as a bridge between what has previously been investigated and what still needs to be studied through your proposed research. They therefore serve as a crucial part of the justification for your research proposal, and we suggest that you consider setting them out as a series of bullet points in order to give them emphasis, and to direct the reviewer's attention to them.

## Aim(s)

The aim is a statement of intent. It indicates the overall purpose and thrust of the research. It is also a statement of the main associations and relationships that you seek to discover or establish. In any proposed project, the aims should be small in number – setting yourself too many aims indicates that you are probably embarking on more than one project. Examples might include:

1. To determine whether or not lecturing is the most beneficial and preferred teaching strategy in higher education.
2. To explore how health and safety legislation is applied in hospitals, and to evaluate which values tend to dominate management practice.
3. To investigate the effects of alcoholism on the family.

Notice how none of these aims is directly answerable. The aims will be 'answered' by accumulating and integrating answers to a series of *objectives* that you set.

## Objectives

The objectives are specific action statements. They can be perceived as 'stepping stones' that eventually direct the study towards the more comprehensively stated aim(s). They express in detail, and in a more technical way than the aim(s), what the research is intended to achieve. It may be to 'explore', 'identify', 'describe', 'explain', 'understand', 'discover', 'predict', 'measure', 'evaluate', 'establish', 'assess', 'ascertain', 'determine', or simply to 'find out'. A key question to ask yourself when drafting your objectives is: Is it clear which data are required to address each objective?

An example taken from Kumar (1999) provides objectives for the aim listed above concerning the study of alcoholism in the family. The project objectives are:

1. To ascertain the impact of alcoholism on marital relations.
2. To determine the ways in which alcoholism affects the different aspects of children's lives.
3. To find out the effects of alcoholism on the financial situation of the family.

Such objectives help to define the scope of the study. As Kumar (1999, p.40) asserts:

> They should be worded in such a way that the wording clearly, completely and specifically communicates your intention. There is no place for ambiguity, non-specificity, or incompleteness, either in the wording of your objectives or the ideas they communicate.

Key questions to ask yourself at this point are:

- Do the aim(s) and objectives adequately encapsulate the full scope of the proposed project? Does/do the aim(s) clearly indicate the overarching thrust of the intended study? Are the objectives sufficiently precise so that they indicate clearly what is to be done in order to collect the data necessary to address the research aim(s)? Are there logical connections between the aim(s) and the objectives?

- Do I have any hypotheses in mind? If so, have I expressed them clearly and appropriately?
- Do I intend to investigate a relationship between different phenomena or variables? If so, have I indicated the variables that I think may be related?

> ## Activity 10.4
>
> Write down a list of five key questions that you aim to research in your project. As you do, make brief notes to remind yourself why you are asking these questions – what do you aim to achieve in doing so?

### *Definitions of key terms and concepts*

All key terms should be defined, although you should be selective in those that you consider to be 'key', and you should be succinct with your definition of each that you decide to include. In a quantitative hypothesis-testing study, these are primarily the terms that describe the key variables of the study. Your task is to make your definitions as clear as possible. If previous definitions found in the literature are clear to all, that is well and good. Often, however, they need to be modified to fit your proposed study. It is often helpful to formulate operational definitions as a way of clarifying terms or phrases. While it is probably impossible to eliminate all ambiguity from definitions, the clearer the terms used in a study are – to both you and others – the fewer difficulties will be encountered in the subsequent planning and conducting of the study.

For instance, if you are conducting a study which involves researching harassment at work, you will want to examine different aspects and dimensions of this key concept. One of these may be violence, and you should carefully define this by taking account of the different forms of violence – physical, verbal and emotional. Now review the section on operationalising concepts in Chapter 3.

In an emergent qualitative-based research study, however, the key concepts that you intend to engage with in your research will not all be clear to you at the outset of your research. The key issues, their dimensions, and how you intend to define them will only become clear in the course of the actual empirical investigation. Where this is so, you should state this clearly within your proposal.

A key question to ask yourself at this point is:

- Have I defined all key terms clearly and (if possible) operationally?
- Have I been succinct in my definition of key terms?

## Review of the literature

It was noted earlier (in the section headed, *Justification for the study*) that in order to gain support for a proposed project, the researcher will need to conduct a review of the literature. In a research proposal, the literature review is a partial summary of previous work related to the focus of the study. You will need to demonstrate to a review committee that you are familiar with the major trends in previous research as well as opinions on the topic, and that you understand their relevance to your planned study.

The major weakness of many literature reviews is that people cite references without indicating either their relevance or their implications for the planned study. Within any research proposal, a literature review is designed to serve the twin purposes of 'explain[ing] and justify[ing] the decisions made' (Locke et al. 2000, p.59) about the nature of the research question and also the methodological strategy to be adopted:

> The writer's task is to employ the literature review artfully to support and explain the choices made for this study, not to educate the reader concerning the state of science in the problem area. (Locke et al. 2000, p.59)

This is a very important point. Many people are tempted to reference every study, every article and every book that they have read, for the purpose of setting out to impress the proposal reviewer that they are experts in the field, with a comprehensive knowledge and understanding of everything written in the area. And of course, you need to review the literature related to your research question in order, for instance, to identify a research gap that will serve as a stimulus for your study. However, the space available for you to develop this in your research proposal will be limited. You will therefore need to be concise and succinct in your review, and reference only that work that is of direct relevance to your research question. The writer should set out the major concepts in an organised and logical order, and then support these references from the literature. Remember – the literature review for a research proposal is somewhat different from that which you would use in a dissertation or a thesis. It is (quite obviously) more modest in scale and breadth, and it is:

> not the place to review the [entire] body of literature that bears on a problematic area, or even the place to examine all the research that relates to the specific question raised in the proposal. (Locke et al. 2000, p.58)

Cormack (1984) provides a useful overview of the three key uses of a literature review. It will:

- provide you with a wide range of documentary information on facts, opinions and comments concerning the topic to be investigated;
- help you to discover whether the topic has already been studied, and, if so, to what extent your work will be affected;
- help you to decide which research techniques will be most appropriate for your study.

In the early stages, the literature review will consume much of your time and energy. However, it should be regarded as a continuous process, with new information added as the project proceeds.

You should take a structured approach to your literature search. Ask yourself what information are you after? If you are going to use word searches of electronic bibliographic sources or the Internet, you should list all the possible keywords and synonyms that you consider to be relevant to your research question(s). You should also be clear about which timescale you intend to cover in your project (only articles since 1991?), and what the geographic boundaries are that you intend to work within (Australian but not Canadian studies?). Finally, you should be flexible about the range of material that you consider for your literature review – especially if your initial searching fails to uncover a sufficient body of literature for your study. For instance, you may consider studies that investigate the sources and impact of occupational stress in the teaching and nursing professions, and how these experiences apply to the fire service in terms of the implications for safety. Or perhaps in a project focusing on youth engagement with politics, you might find it valuable to consider studies that examine the political participation of ethnic minority groups. For more information about consulting the literature, see Chapter 9.

Key questions to ask yourself at this point are:

- Have I surveyed and described relevant studies that are related to my research problem?
- Have I surveyed existing expert opinion on the problem?
- Have I summarised the existing state of opinion and research on the problem?

## Methodology to be used for conducting the research

The methodology section should include a discussion of your intended research design, the sample you will examine, the instruments to be used to conduct the investigation, procedural detail for collecting your empirical evidence, and the data analysis technique(s) to be used. This section should be carefully justified by linking it to the aims and objectives of the proposed study:

> In empirical research, it is necessary that data be linked to concepts and concepts be linked to data, and that the links between concepts and data be tight, logical and consistent. … [A] well-developed and well-stated research question indicates what data will be necessary to answer it. … If the research questions do not give clear indications of the data needed to answer them, we will not know how to proceed in the research when it comes to the data collection and analysis stages. … [A]s you develop your research questions, ask for each question 'What data are needed to answer this question?' (Punch 2006, pp.25–6)

With these words, Punch lucidly summarises one of the decisive aspects upon which a research proposal will be judged – the *Empirical Criterion*. When deciding on the research design for your proposed project, you must ensure that it carefully addresses all of your aims and objectives, as reviewers will need to be reassured that you will be able to answer all of the research questions that you have set yourself in your proposed research investigation. A useful way of establishing this is to link your aims and objectives with the proposed approach and methods as set out in Example 10.1.

### Example 10.1 The Empirical Criterion

*Phase 3: Fieldwork (months 4–28)* – In order to meet key objectives (3) and (4) and as part of the case study, a series of semi-structured reflective interviews will be conducted with professionals working with young people at risk of social exclusion and offending behaviour, and a further collection of data through work shadowing and observation will be conducted in the two case study areas. It is expected that these interviews will aid access to young people. It is anticipated that four practitioners per geographical location will be interviewed. The practitioners will be key personnel in agencies that work with the stated young people. The early part of this phase will be focused on securing access to practitioners and young people.

Notice that the particular methods to be used have been determined by two of the objectives that the researcher has obviously already stated within the research proposal. Several other matters are also covered, and we will consider these in the following sections. They are as follow:

- the range of methods to be deployed;
- the scale of the research phase – in terms of the number of case study areas to be investigated, and the numbers of practitioners to be studied in each agency;
- the type of practitioners to be included in the sample;
- how the chosen methods will assist access to the young people;
- that this particular phase of the proposed study is time-bound.

## Research design

The particular research design to be used should be identified, as well as how it applies to the present study. You therefore need to ensure that your choice of approach is justified in this section (see Extract 10.4). Typically, the basic design is fairly clear-cut, and fits one of the following models (see Chapter 3):

- comparative design;
- experimental research design;
- cross-sectional design;
- longitudinal design;

- case study design;
- action research design;
- evaluation research design.

## Extract 10.4 Youth and Politics research proposal (Henn and Weinstein 2000)

As you read through this extract, notice how the two methods are justified with respect to the project aims and objectives.

**Focus on attainers**

As a methodological innovation, we will focus exclusively on 'attainers' – young people eligible to vote for the first time when the 2001 electoral register comes into force. As far as we are aware, the proposed study would be the first of its kind to focus solely on attainers. Our intention in limiting our study to this age group is twofold. First, in research terms, attainers are a relatively unique target group. Most social and political surveys that examine the views of young people tend to combine their views with older youths. Hence, attainers will typically be analysed as part of an 18–24 (or 18–25) year-old group (see, for instance, Parry et al. 1992) or included in studies of students (e.g., Denver and Hands 1990), often alongside respondents with an increasingly mature age profile as Higher Education is opened up to new entrants. Secondly, they will have had minimal formal experience of participating in politics in terms of voting, with the possible exception of the 2001 local elections. They are, therefore, relatively inexperienced politically in comparison to older people and are therefore less likely than their older contemporaries to have formed deep-seated views about politics, parties and politicians. As a consequence, attainers provide a fascinating target group for study in terms of their perceptions of political institutions and actors in Britain. The study will form the baseline for understanding future developments in youth attitudes of, and orientation towards, British political parties as these attainers gain experience of engaging with politics. There is potential therefore to track attitudes over time for comparative purposes.

However, you may want to use a variety of approaches. Combining methods and strategies may help to add depth to your study as well as enable you to identify whether your approach is valid and reliable. See Chapter 3 for a discussion of this mixed-method research design.

Emergent qualitative research designs may involve you in approaching your methods more flexibly during the course of the study. As Punch (2005, p.268) explains, when opting for such a research design: 'There is a need to explain the flexibility the study requires and why, and how decisions will be made as the study unfolds.'

Nonetheless, you should be as explicit as you can be in your proposal about the general research design that you intend to use, and provide as much material about your plans as you are able.

### Activity 10.5

Decide what is to be the research design for your intended study. State clearly why you have chosen that particular approach in terms of the aims and objectives you set out for your project in Activity 10.4.

## Sample

In your proposal, you should indicate in considerable detail how you will include participants – the sample – for investigation in your study. You should indicate what the size of the sample will be, how members will be selected, and what claims you may legitimately make about the representativeness of your sample. For a quantitative research study, you should aim, if at all possible, to adopt a random sampling technique, or, if this is unrealistic, a quota sampling method should be used in an attempt to maximise representativeness.

However, for small-scale projects of the type likely to be undertaken by postgraduate students where your study will be subject to various resource constraints, it may be legitimate to use other less rigorous sampling methods, such as the convenience sample. It is more important to complete a project with an unrepresentative sample than abandon the study because it fails to achieve a sample that is representative of your target group. If a convenience sample must be used, relevant demographics (gender, ethnicity, occupation, age, housing, and any other relevant characteristics) of the sample should be described. The legitimate population to which the results of the study may be generalised should be indicated.

For emergent qualitative research designs, you are likely to use theoretical sampling to select your research participants. Where this is the case, you are much more likely to include respondents whose presence is designed to maximise theoretical development than to achieve representativeness. Your reasons for choosing this sampling strategy should be indicated (and justified) within this section of the research proposal, together with an acknowledgement that: (a) the sample has been chosen to generate insights (as opposed to definitive conclusions) about your research area; and (b) the results will be indicative, rather than representative, of the views of the wider population. For a further discussion of this point, see the section on case selection from Chapter 3.

Key questions to ask yourself at this point are:

- Have I described my sampling plan?
- Have I described the relevant characteristics of my sample in detail?
- If you are using a predominantly quantitative research design, have I identified the population to which the results of the study may legitimately be generalised?
- If you are using a predominantly qualitative research design, have I demonstrated that my selection of cases is reasonably typical of what might be expected if I had conducted my research elsewhere?

## Instruments to be used

Whenever possible, existing research instruments should be used in your study, since construction of even the most straightforward test or questionnaire (or selection of questions) is often very time-consuming and difficult. Furthermore, doing so will enable you to make comparisons between your findings and the results from the earlier study from which the research instrument was borrowed.

However, you cannot justify using an existing research instrument if it is not appropriate for your purpose, even though it may be more convenient. You will therefore need to assess whether existing instruments are suited to your needs.

In the event that appropriate instruments are not available, the procedures to be followed in developing your own research instruments to be used in the study should be described with attention to how validity and reliability will be enhanced. It will be important to indicate within your proposal that you intend to build a *pilot stage* (Extract 10.5) into your project, or, if the research instrument has already been tested for these purposes, include a version within the appendices. For example, if you are conducting a survey, you should include a specimen questionnaire or some questions that you consider to be good illustrations of what you will ask. For a more qualitative research design, you might include an observation schedule, or a topic guide for in-depth interviews.

### Extract 10.5 Pilot stage: Youth and Politics research proposal (Henn and Weinstein 2000)

As you read through the following extract, you will notice how a pilot study has already been conducted to examine both what sorts of question areas will likely need to be explored for the qualitative part of the project, and how the quantitative aspect will take advantage of an existing research instrument.

**Pilot research**

A qualitative-based pilot study, using focus groups, has already been completed by the research team in preparation for this full project (Henn, Weinstein and Wring 1999). This preliminary research was designed to help establish which questions should be asked, as well as their structure. We will also hold meetings with various party youth activists and youth organisers, interested user groups, and academics in order to further our understanding of which questions to include in the questionnaire. In addition, the proposed survey will include questions that appear on other national political opinion studies to enable comparative work with other age groups (including among others, the British Social Attitudes surveys, the British Election Studies surveys, and the British Election Panel surveys). Considerable attention will be paid to the design and layout of the questionnaire to ensure an attractive presentation of the postal survey. This will draw on previous experience of conducting postal surveys of this particular target group (Wring, Henn and Weinstein 1999; Henn, Weinstein and Wring 2000). A pilot study will be conducted in the Nottingham area in order to test the efficacy of the questions to be used in the postal survey.

Key questions to ask yourself at this point are:

- Is the research design fit for purpose, and does it meet the Empirical Criterion? That is, will it yield all the data necessary to answer each of the aim(s) and objectives?
- Have I described the instrument(s) to be used?
- Have I indicated their relevance to the present study?
- Have I stated how I will check the reliability and validity of my data collection instruments?
- Have I built a 'piloting the instrument' stage into the research design?

## Procedures and data collection

Outline your proposed method(s) of research. This should be presented in sufficient detail for the reader to know whether the project is realistic, feasible and worthwhile. You will need to describe how you intend to access your target group and contact your research participants. Is your target group one that is typically difficult to involve in research studies of your kind? If so, what steps will you take to maximise your response rate and minimise bias? What method of data collection will you use? For instance, if your proposed study involves the use of a questionnaire, you should indicate whether you intend to use a self-completion version, or implement it in a face-to-face situation, or via the telephone.

It is important to make your procedures of data collection clear so that if another researcher wants to repeat the study in exactly the same way as the original, they are able to replicate your procedures. Certain procedures may change from those previewed in the proposal as the study is carried out, but a proposal should always aim to have this level of clarity as its goal. Explain why you think this is the best method for investigating the research problem.

A key question to ask yourself at this point is:

- Have I fully described the procedures to be followed in the study – what will be done, where, when and how?

## Data analysis

The researcher should indicate how the data to be collected will be organised, interpreted and analysed. You need to show how and why the proposed research will yield the information and insights that will enable you to address your research questions. You therefore need to justify your choice of methods of data analysis. For a quantitative-based study, explain which statistical procedures and tests you intend to use, and why you are choosing to do so. Similarly, if you intend to conduct a qualitative research study, then you should indicate the methods of analysis you will use to analyse the data. Perhaps you intend to quantify the results obtained from your unstructured interviews? If your project is more emergent in nature, you may be proposing to adopt a grounded theory approach. See Example 10.2 for an example of how to approach the drafting of the data analysis section of a research proposal.

### Example 10.2 Data analysis

One of the elements of the research proposal that students seem to have some difficulty in writing is the section on data analysis. You must not just state that you will 'analyse your data with SPSS' or some other such statement. SPSS is a tool for analysis, not a method or analytical strategy. Instead, state what sort of approach you will use to manage your data, as below. (Please note that it is perfectly acceptable to mention that SPSS will be used as a tool for carrying out your data analysis strategy, but only in that context).

*Phase 5: Data analysis (months 19–30)* – The questionnaire will provide data on variables such as pay, hours, job satisfaction and the nature of work (managerial, professional, etc.) which will be analysed using SPSS. Following Hardill and Watson (2004) I will use multivariate analysis to explain hours of work or pay (as dependent variables) in terms of gender, the nature of the household and work. These data can then be used to explain the relationship between work satisfaction and working hours. By comparing the results of the 1994–5 study with the proposed 2007–8 study, I will be able to offer an assessment of whether the statistical relationships identified as significant by Hardill and Watson (2004) are stable at these two reference points.

## Ethical considerations

The review committee will have been alerted to any potential or any actual ethical problems likely to arise from your proposed study while reading the methodology section. The proposal may be reviewed by a committee whose primary objective is to assess the scientific methods of a study, but they will also be aware of ethical issues.

It is important that you anticipate gaining written consent from adults or parents or guardians when members of your target group cannot themselves give approval. Ethical matters may also be relevant to protecting these research participants from any negative consequences of your study. However, you will also need to demonstrate to the review committee that you have taken adequate steps to ensure that both yourself and others associated with your intended project are protected from harm, particularly if the research situation is one that has the potential to place people in positions of danger. For data protection purposes, you will also need to give due regard to how you intend to store your data securely.

At some point in the proposal it is necessary to indicate clearly what you regard as the major ethical issues of the project, and to state clearly how these will be handled. Alternatively, you may state that the proposal raises no ethical issues. In order to complete this section effectively and convincingly, you should pay close attention to the ethical guidelines that are set out in the codes of conduct that many academic and professional organisations have developed. For a full discussion of ethics, see Chapter 4.

## Timescale

The amount of time you need to devote to the study should be set out in the proposal. It may be that this is a proposal for a full-time commitment, or perhaps for only a few hours in a week. But whichever is the case, the research proposal must specify the amount of time involved (Extract 10.6). The review committee will need to know how long the project will take when considering whether to fund it, or, if yours is a proposal for a Masters dissertation, whether the project can be finished within your deadline.

### Extract 10.6 Timetable for the Youth and Politics project

Completion of all preparation and design work (3 months); commencement of survey data collection phase of study (3 months); completion of survey data collection phase of study (6 months); commencement of analysis phase of study (6 months); completion of analysis phase of study (14 months); commencement of writing up of the research (12 months); completion of preparation of any new data sets for archiving (14 months); completion of writing up (18 months).

## Facilities and resources

Describing particular forms of expertise or back-up facilities can strengthen a proposal. Good computer and library facilities fall into this category. Where established networks are integral to a project, or cooperation has been obtained from particular agencies or institutions, some indication of this, like a letter of agreement, may be included as a helpful appendix.

## Budget

Preparing a research budget is as much a skill as preparing other parts of the proposal. Part of the skill lies in locating other people who know the price of all appropriate commodities: staff time, tape-recorders, photocopying, travel costs, and so on. Preparing a budget means translating the timescale and plan of work into financial terms.

In preparing a budget, use a checklist to include main headings such as:

- research salaries;
- data collection costs (purchase of equipment and other materials, printing, travelling expenses);
- stationery and postage;
- data analysis expenses.

## Pre-submission

It is likely that a research proposal will go through many drafts. Indeed, there would be major cause for concern if it did not. There are a number of things to be achieved in reviewing a proposal – not least considering its physical presentation. Legibility, lucidity and clarity of presentation are all important. While readers of a proposal will not be evaluating its presentation, the relatively small amount of time it takes to ensure a layout that is easily followed will be time well spent.

Check carefully that the proposal meets all of the criteria set by the review committee.

Perhaps most importantly, ask colleagues to read and comment upon your proposal, and take any criticisms that they may have of it seriously. As Hessler (1992, p.287) states:

> We assume too much, taking for granted the nuances and assumptions of our research, which is tough on readers who do not share this knowledge ... take nothing for granted. If in doubt, spell it out, even to the point of repeating yourself. Redundancy is not the worst sin in grant writing.

## Summary

This chapter has reviewed the process of constructing a research proposal, setting out the main points that need to be considered in producing a professional and convincing document. As we have seen, in any proposal it is of paramount importance that the research that is envisaged is clearly articulated and is of value to the body looking to support the research.

In assessing your proposal, a reviewer will also be looking to see that your proposed study is a feasible one. As well as capturing a reviewer's imagination with the subject of your research, you will have to satisfy the reviewer that you are in a position to carry the research out to a high standard. Having a bright idea is the starting point from which you have to construct a compelling case that your research is not only interesting, but also capable of execution.

In this respect the reviewer will be looking for you to demonstrate your methodological proficiency and sensitivity. For example, have you adequately addressed the complexities of the sampling strategy that will need to be adopted and are you fully aware of any potential issues that may preclude you obtaining access to your intended research participants?

As we have seen, there are different audiences for different sorts of research proposals. If your research is intended to be carried out as part of a Masters course at a university, you may be primarily focused on persuading your tutors that you have located your research in a particular body of specialist literature. On the other hand, if you are applying for funding from an external agency that places a high premium on policy-oriented research, then you will need to convince the reviewing panel that your research not only is of academic interest, but also has wider societal value.

Of course, all reviewers will have their own set of criteria by which they will judge the proposals that come before them. Unfortunately, there is no easily applied formula that can be applied to all research proposals that can guarantee success. However, the more consideration that you have been able to give to the research you plan to carry out, reflecting on the outline elements that have been covered in this chapter, the more likely it is that you will have produced a proposal that stands up to keen scrutiny.

## Recommended Reading

Blaikie, N. 2000. *Designing Social Research*. Cambridge: Polity Press.

Brewer, E.W., Achilles, C.M. and Fuhriman, J.R. 1993. *Finding Funding: Grant Writing for the Financially Challenged Educator*. London: Sage.

Bryman, A. 2004. *Social Research Methods*, 2nd edn. Oxford: Oxford University Press.

Coley, S.M. and Scheinberg, C.A. 1990. *Proposal Writing*. London: Sage.

Hart, C. 2001. *Doing a Literature Search: A Comprehensive Guide for the Social Sciences*. London: Sage.

Henn, M. and Weinstein, M. 2000. *First-time Voters' Attitudes towards Party Politics in Britain* [online]. Economic and Social Research Council. Available at: www.statistics.gov.uk/downloads/theme_social/Peoples_perceptions_social_capital.pdf (Accessed 9 January 2004).

Punch, K.P. 2005. *Introduction to Social Research: Quantitative and Qualitative Approaches*, 2nd edn. London: Sage.

Punch, K.P. 2006. *Developing Effective Research Proposals*, 2nd edn. London: Sage.

# GLOSSARY

**Action research** – a research design employed to improve practice by evaluating change. Action research works in a cycle of stages: identification of a problem; introduction of change intended to solve the problem; evaluation of the impact of change. It is common for action research to repeat these cycles as practice is gradually refined through ongoing change.

**Analysis of variance (ANOVA)** – a statistical technique for establishing whether groups differ from one another on a particular variable and whether these differences are statistically significant.

**Analytic induction** – a process of analysis which emphasises hypothesis verification and modification through repeated observations. Data which refute the hypothesis are usually accounted for by either reformulating the hypothesis or establishing the deviant characteristics of the case which differentiate it from other cases. This leads to refined hypotheses which are supported by large numbers of observations.

**Androcentrism** – reflecting and reinforcing male perspectives through one's choice of research topic and methodology.

**Anonymity** – non-disclosure of identity by name or other identifiable characteristics; anonymity of cases is often assured in qualitative research by using pseudonyms in place of real names and not reporting behaviour or characteristics that are particularly unique to a case, and therefore identifiable. Quantitative researchers usually only report aggregated statistics rather than values for individual cases in order to maintain anonymity. Anonymity should apply to organisations as well as individuals.

**Bivariate analysis** – a collection of statistical analysis techniques applied to quantitative research designs in which the relationship between two variables is of interest.

**Case study** – a research design which focuses on a single case, or very small number of cases, in detail, usually employing mixed methods in order to generate a holistic picture of the case(s) from multiple data sources.

**Causality** – the notion that social phenomena can be explained by identifying causes and effects, and ascertaining directional relationships between variables.

**Census** – a study in which data are collected from every case within a population (*cf.* sample).

**Code of ethics** – a set of guiding principles, usually administered by a professional body or institution, which are used to guide researchers in the design and conduct of ethically sensitive research.

**Coding** – the process of categorising data into either different response groups or values (quantitative), or concepts (qualitative). Much quantitative coding is applied prior to data collection, for example in the selection of answer categories to a survey question, whereas qualitative analysis employs coding after data collection, by identifying core themes and concepts within the data.

**Comparative design** – a research design which is specifically concerned with identifying similarities and differences between cases; comparative research is commonly conducted in the field of politics and international relations, where comparisons between countries and their political systems are of interest.

**Conceptual framework** – a description of the concepts and/or variables to be investigated, and the theorised relationships between these. The conceptual framework may consist of, or be supplemented by, a diagram.

**Confidentiality** – safeguarding of data to ensure information relating to participants is undisclosed, other than for the purposes of the research, and as agreed by the participants.

**Construct validity** – an assessment of the effectiveness of a measure, dependent on whether the measure produces results which are in line with those to be expected given existing theory.

**Content analysis** – a research technique which utilises coding to analyse documents and describe the manifest content found within.

**Context of discovery** – the exploratory chain of events and processes through which new ideas come into being.

**Context of justification** – scientific approach used by researchers to logically and empirically verify claims for knowledge.

**Convenience sample** – a non-probability sampling method in which the researcher selects cases that are conveniently available.

**Covert research** – research that is conducted without informed consent, and in which the purposes of the study, and the identity and the role of the researcher, remain hidden from view.

**Cross-sectional design** – the examination of variation across cases, usually in terms of a range of variables of interest to the researcher. The cross-sectional design will aim to take quantitative measures on the topic of interest from a relatively large number of cases, and at a single point in time.

**Data** – information that forms the focus of a research study, that may either be numerical (quantitative) or textual or visual (qualitative).

**Deduction** – an approach to research in which data collection, analysis and interpretation are guided by existing theory (*cf.* induction).

**Dependent variable** – in a causal relationship, a variable which is said to be influenced or explained by the independent variable.

**Discourse analysis** – concerns the way in which language is used to construct meanings and make sense of the social world.

**Empirical criterion** – the extent to which the research design of an intended study will yield all the data necessary to answer each of its aims and objectives.

**Empiricism** – a position which claims that only evidence which is directly observable should be considered in a research investigation.

**Epistemology** – considers questions to do with the nature of social reality, what is acceptable knowledge concerning that reality, and what are the appropriate methods for studying that reality.

**Ethnography** – the systematic study of institutions, cultures and customs that seeks to see the world in a new way, and from the point of view of the people under investigation. It involves participating in the everyday activities and life of those who are being studied, primarily through observation and for a prolonged period of time.

**Evaluation research** – a research design used for the purposes of examining the effectiveness of policies, initiatives, services and social programmes, and for determining whether or not these are achieving their stated aims.

**Experiment** – considered to be the archetypal scientific research design, used by social researchers for the purpose of making inferences about the predictive effect of an independent variable on a dependent variable. Cases (usually people) will be randomly assigned to either an experimental group (which is exposed to a stimulus/the independent variable), and a control group (which is not).

**External validity** – the extent to which the findings from a research study faithfully represent, and can be applied to, the wider population.

**Face validity** – a subjective measure of validity; the extent to which an indicator appears to measure the concept it is intended to.

**Factor analysis** – a statistical technique for reducing a number of variables to a smaller number of latent factors which can be shown to account for some of the variance in the variables.

**Focus group** – a qualitative research technique involving a group discussion on the topic of interest. Focus groups often take on the form of a lively discussion, rather than individual responses by everyone in the group to the same questions, and therefore focus groups are particularly useful in understanding the ways in which opinion is formulated through consensus, and the dynamics of group interaction.

**Frequency distribution** – a total of the counts for each category or value of a variable, usually displayed in a table or chart.

**Generalisability** – the extent to which the findings of research based on a sample can be applied to the wider population (*see also* external validity).

**Grounded theory** – an inductive approach to qualitative research which begins with a highly exploratory, open question. Through several rounds of data collection, analysis and interpretation, substantive theory is generated which is said to be wholly grounded in the data.

**Hypothesis** – a statement about the suspected relationship between two or more variables, based upon existing theory or a priori reasoning.

**Hypothetico-deduction** – a process of research in which the testing of hypotheses is given precedence.

**Idealism** – a philosophical claim that social reality only exists within the ideas of individuals, and that physical objects can only be known by the concepts with which they are associated by individuals. The implications for research are that an objective study of a fixed social reality, shared by people is impossible, so we must seek to understand individual ideas about the world in order to make sense of it.

**Independent variable** – in a causal relationship, a variable which is said to be the cause; also referred to as a 'predictor'.

**Induction** – an approach to research in which data collection, analysis and interpretation leads to the development of theory (*cf.* deduction).

**Inference** – applying the conclusions from research based upon a sample to the wider population, either through a process of *theoretical* inference, in which there are strong theoretical grounds to believe the observations of the sample would match observations of the population, or by *statistical* inference, in which statistical tests are used to support inferential claims (*see* inferential statistics).

**Inferential statistics** – a group of statistical tests specifically designed to calculate a level of confidence that a random probability sample is representative of a population; such tests result in a measure of statistical significance.

**Informed consent** – confirmation from a research participant that they wish to take part in a study having had the aims, outcomes and nature of their involvement fully explained; informed consent should usually be gained in writing.

**Internal validity** – the extent to which a claim about causal relationships between variables can be said to be accurate; this type of validity most widely applies in experimental designs.

**Interpretivism** – an approach to research which suggests that people have individual interpretations of the social world, and therefore cannot be studied in the same way that objects in the natural world can. Interpretivism tends to emphasise interpretation and understanding of specific instances, rather than seeking to apply general laws (*cf.* positivism).

**Interval variable** – a variable which is measured on a precise numerical scale of consistent, precise units.

**Interview schedule** – a flexible list of open questions and accompanying probes used to guide the interviewer during a semi-structured, in-depth interview.

**Level of measurement** – a means of categorising the extent to which a variable can be measured precisely using numerical coding; the level of measurement increases through nominal, ordinal, interval and ratio as numerical coding becomes less arbitrary and the possibility of precise, consistent measurement increases.

**Likert scale** – a way of measuring attitudes in survey research; commonly used to measure levels of agreement with a series of given statements relating to a single issue.

**Longitudinal research** – research which makes use of repeated rounds of data collection, usually at regular intervals in order that changes over time may be measured.

**Mean** – a measure of central tendency applied to interval- or ratio-level variables; the mathematical average, calculated by dividing the sum of values for each case by the number of cases.

**Measurement** – the process of understanding a concept by gathering data using numerical indicators.

**Measures of central tendency** – statistical measures which provide an indicator of a typical or average value in a frequency distribution.

**Measures of dispersion** – statistical measures which provide an indication of the distribution, or spread, of values on a variable.

**Median** – a measure of central tendency applied to ordinal variables; the value at the midpoint of a ranked frequency distribution.

**Methodology** – the overall research strategy which takes into consideration the ethical, philosophical and political rationale for adopting particular methods. The adoption of a particular methodology might be influenced by a number of factors, including one's own epistemological position, discipline-based precedents or the theoretical dimensions of the research question.

**Mixed-method research** – the adoption of more than one research technique, either simultaneously or consecutively, to study a particular phenomenon. Different methods may be employed to achieve different objectives within the research, for example to first develop and then test a theory, or to increase the validity of conclusions through triangulation.

**Mode** – a measure of central tendency applied to nominal variables; the category with the highest frequency of occurrence.

**Multiple regression** – a statistical technique used to measure the variance in a single dependent variable that can be attributed to two or more independent variables. Multiple regression also enables the testing of statistical models which can be used to predict the value in the dependent variable, given known values of the independent variables.

**Multivariate analysis** – a collection of statistical analysis techniques applied to quantitative research designs in which the relationship between three or more variables is of interest.

**Naturalism** – an approach to research which emphasises the need to observe social phenomena within the natural setting in which they occur. The approach is mostly associated with observation since it minimises researcher intervention and therefore removes the influence of artificial forces not usually found to be at work in the setting being studied.

**Nominal variable** – a variable which consists of mutually exclusive categories or groups that have no natural order.

**Non-probability sample** – a sample which has been produced using techniques other than those which are employed to create a random probability sample. These techniques include theoretical sampling, convenience sampling, snowball sampling and quota sampling. Non-probability samples cannot be used to make statistical inferences because some cases within the population will have a stronger likelihood of being selected than others.

**Null hypothesis** – a hypothesis about a pattern in the data, or relationship between variables which one is usually seeking to reject. Often the null hypothesis will state that two or more variables are unrelated. Rejecting the null hypothesis results in statistically significant conclusions derived from the data, and support for – but not confirmation of – the alternative hypothesis.

**Ontology** – a set of assumptions about what constitutes the social world and how it is experienced.

**Operational definition** – a means of enabling a concept to be measured using empirical techniques. An operational definition sets out the ways in which concepts are manifested in human behaviour. By isolating such manifestations, we are able to study otherwise abstract concepts in an empirical manner.

**Ordinal variable** – a variable consisting of categories which are both mutually exclusive and ranked, often used in survey research when a subjective measure of an attitude, behaviour or belief is required.

**Panel** – a sample from which observations are taken repeatedly throughout a research study, usually over a period of time. Panels are most commonly found in longitudinal survey research, and are often used in consumer market research where changes in behaviour or attitudes over time constitute an important focus of the research.

**Paradigm** – a collection of beliefs and assumptions about what should be studied, and how. Researchers often operate within a particular paradigm which will influence the topic of interest, the methods that are considered appropriate for research and the nature of social reality. Paradigms concern methodology, epistemology and ontology. See *positivism* and *interpretivism* for examples of competing paradigms.

**Partial correlation** – a means of measuring the relationship between two variables while statistically controlling for the influence of a third variable.

**Participant observation** – a form of observation in which the researcher takes part in the activities being observed. This may be carried out overtly, when the members of the group being observed are aware of the researcher's identity, or covertly, when the researcher achieves membership of the group without her or his true identity being known to the group. Covert participant observation can remove the problem of reactivity, but is widely considered as an ethically problematic technique.

**Personal interview** – a data collection technique in which the researcher asks a participant a series of questions and records the answers in a face-to-face setting.

**Population** – all cases that are of interest in a research study. It is theoretically possible to select any member of the population for inclusion in the research by sampling, although practical limitations, such as access to a complete sampling frame, may make this impossible. The population will therefore include cases which have not been observed as well as some which have. Researchers usually wish to draw inferences from a sample, and generalise these to the population.

**Positivism** – an approach to research most often associated with the adoption of the scientific method to develop general laws in order to explain social phenomena (*cf.* interpretivism).

**Postmodernism** – represents a reaction to the search for general laws and grand narratives which seek to offer all-encompassing explanations for human behaviour. Rather, postmodernism encapsulates a recognition of the diverse and highly individualised experiences that constitute social life, and that all experience is subjective, therefore denying the possibility of a singular, objective explanation.

**Probability sample** – a sample in which every case within the population (or, more accurately, within the sampling frame from which the sample is selected) has an equal chance of being chosen. Types of probability sample include simple random, systematic random, multi-stage cluster and stratified samples (*cf.* non-probability sample).

**Qualitative research** – typically associated with interpretive perspectives in social research, in which the logic of research is to develop an appreciation of the underlying motivations that people have for doing what they do, which involves an examination of their perspectives, ideas, attitudes, motives and intentions. Data will usually be semi-structured and textual in nature, and collected from a small number of cases using a range of methods.

**Quantitative research** – typically associated with positivist perspectives in social research, the logic of which is to (i) collect structured and quantifiable data using standardised approaches on a range of variables, (ii) search for patterns of causal relationships between these variables, and (iii) test given theory by confirming or refuting hypotheses.

**Questionnaire** – a data collection form that includes a series of pre-specified (mostly structured) questions, the answers to which will address the objectives of the research.

**Quota sample** – a non-probability sampling method in which cases are selected according to set criteria. The researcher sets quotas for the sample, based on the known characteristics of the population, such as age, sex and occupation, to ensure that the correct number of certain types of person is included in the sample.

**Random sample** – probability sampling methods involve randomised selection, in which all members of the population have an equal chance of being selected for inclusion in the research study.

**Reactivity** – occurs in situations where people may consciously or unconsciously alter the way that they behave or modify what they say if they are aware that they are being researched. Reactivity represents a threat to validity.

**Realism** – an approach to research which is based on the claim that the social world exists outside our ideas and beliefs, and can therefore be assessed by carefully crafted research instruments.

**Reflexivity** – concerns the place that researchers occupy within the research process, and their impact upon the social world that they are investigating (through, for instance, their values and assumptions, as well as the choices that they make about the research study in terms of sampling strategy, research role, data collection methods, and so on). Assuming that there can be no objective separation of researchers from the social world that they are investigating, researchers will reflect on their personal impact on the research situation.

**Relativism** – an approach which suggests that there is no single standard measure of reality. Instead, the researcher who aims to understand and make sense of human actions must seek to appreciate these from the cultural perspectives of those that they observe.

**Reliability** – the effectiveness of data collection instruments for taking accurate and consistent measurements of a concept.

**Representative sample** – the outcome from a sampling strategy in which the profile of the cases selected closely matches the profile of the broader population.

**Research design** – a programme of research that involves initial specification of the research problem to be investigated, and the plan for collecting and analysing data.

**Research hypothesis** – a specific statement that relates to the research problem, the answers to which are likely to be 'yes' or 'no', depending on what is uncovered from the research. The hypothesis is usually derived from, and aims to test, an existing theory.

**Research problem** – the matter to be investigated through the research study.

**Research-then-theory approach** – an emergent or exploratory research approach in which the researcher starts with a relatively broad research question and, in the course of collecting and analysing the data, gradually develops an understanding of the research problem (*cf.* theory-then-research approach).

**Response rate** – the proportion of respondents from the original sample who participated in the research.

**Sample** – a carefully selected group of cases that is intended to reflect the broader population from which it has been drawn.

**Sampling frame** – a list of potential cases (often people) for inclusion in the research project.

**Secondary analysis** – the analysis of existing data that was previously collected by others and in which the current researcher is likely not to have been involved.

**Semiotics** – referred to as the science of signs, semiotics is used in the study of *meanings* as conveyed in different types of document and visual data, such as photographs and magazine advertisements.

**Semi-structured interview** – an interview in which the researcher will use a relatively flexible questioning approach, using a topic guide. The range and types of question will be predetermined by the researcher, but the way in which they are framed, and the order in which they are asked, will vary according to the context of the interview. Additional questions may be asked if the research situation calls for it (*cf.* structured interview and unstructured interview).

**Snowball sample** – a method for selecting cases where no obvious lists of such cases exists. It relies on the researcher obtaining a strategically important contact who can recommend other possible participants who might be approached to take part in the study.

**Social constructionism** – the extent to which the phenomenon under investigation (whether that be people's actions or their ideas) is the product of the interaction of social forces, of individuals, of institutions and/or of other agencies.

**Social facts** – phenomena that are directly observable, which are considered to have an independent existence, and which guide and influence our ideas and our actions.

**Statistical significance** – a statistical measure of the extent to which the conclusions derived from a random probability sample are generalisable to the wider population from which that sample has been drawn.

**Structured interview** – an interview in which the questions and the range of possible answers are pre-specified by the researcher, often in the form of a questionnaire. All respondents will be asked the exact same questions and *in the same order* (*cf.* semi-structured interview and unstructured interview).

**Survey research** – a research design for the examination of variation across cases (whether they be people, households or organisations), usually in terms of a range of variables of interest to the researcher. This cross-sectional design will aim to take quantitative measures on the topic of interest from a relatively large number of cases, and at a single point in time.

**Theoretical sampling** – a subjective approach for selecting cases that are critical for the development of an aspect of theory that is of interest to the researcher. Unlike conventional probability and non-probability sampling methods, this sampling approach is not concerned with demonstrating either typicality or representativeness, but instead with maximising theoretical development.

**Theoretical saturation** – used in qualitative research, it is the point within the process of data analysis at which no new insights are gained from a given situation.

**Theory-then-research approach** – a research approach in which the initial research question/s and the research strategy is guided by an a priori theoretical proposition (*cf.* research-then-theory approach).

**Triangulation** – the combination of multiple methods (and/or empirical materials, and/or perspectives, and/or observers) in a research project, with the intention of developing a more valid and holistic picture of society than would be possible using a single method.

**Univariate analysis** – a collection of statistical techniques and data display methods used for analysing individual variables in quantitative research designs.

**Unstructured interview** – an informal interview in which the researcher will have a broad list of topics to address in the interview, using a topic guide. Unlike semi-structured interviews, the questions will be deliberately open-ended and the line of questioning will be partly determined by the respondent's answers, and therefore vary from interview to interview (*cf.* structured interview and semi-structured interviews).

**Validity** – the extent to which the conclusions derived from the research activity approximate the truth, and the degree to which the phenomenon under investigation has therefore been faithfully examined.

**Variable** – an item or a quality that is to be measured or assessed (such as the social class or the beliefs of individuals). These items will vary from case to case and will therefore have two or more values (thus, some people will be middle class and others working class).

**Verstehen** – empathetic understanding of the ideas, motives and behaviour of others. It is an approach to the study of the social world that has its roots in the writings of Max Weber (1864–1930), who argued that, in order to increase our knowledge of the social world, we must seek to understand it from the points of view of the people we are observing, rather than by explaining human action by means of cause and effect.

# BIBLIOGRAPHY


Adler, P. 1985. *Wheeling and Dealing*. New York: Columbia University Press.

Aldridge, A. and Levine, K. 2001. *Surveying the Social World: Principles and Practice in Survey Research*. Buckingham: Open University Press.

Ali, S. and Kelly, M. 2004. Ethics and Social Research. In: C. Seale (ed.), *Researching Society and Culture*, 2nd edn. London: Sage. pp.115–27.

Allport, G. 1942. *The Use of Documents in Psychological Science*. New York: Social Science Council.

Anderson, G. 1998. *Fundamentals of Educational Research*. London: Falmer Press.

Arber, S. 1993. Designing Samples. In: N. Gilbert (ed.), *Researching Social Life*. London: Sage. pp.68–92.

Arber, S. 2001. Secondary Analysis of Survey Data. In: Gilbert, N. (ed.), *Researching Social Life*, 2nd edn. London: Sage. pp.269–86.

Arksey, H. and Knight, P. 1999. *Interviewing for Social Scientists*. London: Sage.

Asch, S.E. 1965. Effects of Group Pressure upon the Modification and Distortion of Judgments. In: H. Proshansky and B. Seidenberg (eds), *Basic Studies in Social Psychology*. New York: Holt, Rinehart and Winston. pp.393–410.

Atkinson, J.M. 1978. *Discovering Suicide: Studies in the Soc Organisation of Sudden Death*. London: Macmillan.

Babbie, E. 2004. Laud Humphreys and Research Ethics. *International Journal of Sociology and Social Policy*, 24 (3/4/5), 12–19.

Bardzell, S. and Odom, W. 2008. The Experience of Embodied Space in Virtual Worlds: An Ethnography of a Second Life Community, *Space and Culture*, 11, pp.239–59.

Barker, E. 1984. *The Making of a Moonie: Brainwashing or Choice*. Oxford: Blackwell.

Barnes, C. 1996. Disability and the Myth of the Independent Researcher, *Disability and Society*, 11, 107–10.

Barnes, C. 2003. What a Difference a decade Makes: Reflections on Doing 'Emancipatory' Disability Research, *Disability and Society*, 18 (1), 3–17.

Barnes, C. and Mercer, G. (eds) 1997. *Doing Disability Research*. University of Leeds: Disability Press.

Barnes, J. 1979. *Who Should Know What? Social Science, Privacy and Ethics*. Harmondsworth: Penguin.

Barthes, R. 1967. *Elements of Semiology*, trans. Annette Lavers and Colin Smith. London: Jonathan Cape.

Bechhofer, F. 1974. Current Approaches to Empirical Research: Some Central Ideas. In: R.G. Burgess (ed.), *Field Research: A Sourcebook and Field Manual*. London: Allen and Unwin. p.211.

Becker, H. 1967. Whose Side Are We on?, *Social Problems*, 14, 239–47.

Becker, H. 1974. Photography and Sociology. *Studies in the Anthropology of Visual Communication*, 1, 3–26.

Becker, H.S. and Geer, B. 1960. Participant Observation: The Analysis of Qualitative Field Data. In: R.G. Burgess (ed.), *Field Research: A Sourcebook and Field Manual*. London: Allen and Unwin. p.239.

Behling, J.H. 1984. *Guidelines for Preparing the Research Proposal*. Lanham, MD: University of Maryland Press.

Ben-Tovim, G., Gabriel, J., Law, I. and Stredder, K. 1986. *The Local Politics of Race*. London: Macmillan.

Benn, T. 1988. *Out of the Wilderness: Diaries 1963–67*. London: Arrow Books.

Beresford, D. 2002. User Involvement in Research and Evaluation: Liberation or Regulation?, *Social Policy and Society*, 1 (2), 95–105.

Berg, B. 2001. *Qualitative Research Methods for the Social Sciences*, 4th edn. Needham Heights, MA: Allyn and Bacon.

Berger, A.A.S. 1993. *Improving Writing Skills: Memos, Letters, Reports and Proposals*. London: Sage.

Berger, R. 1990. Nazi Science: The Dachau Hypothermia Experiments, *New England Journal of Medicine*, 332 (20), 1435–40.

Bernard, B. 1999. *Century*. London: Phaidon Press.

Bernard, H.R. 1994. *Research Methods in Anthropology: Qualitative and Quantitative Approaches*. London: Sage.

Bilton, T. et al., 1987. *Introductory Sociology*. London: Macmillan.

Bingham, N. 2003. Writing Reflexively. In: M. Pryke, G. Rose and S. Whatmore (eds), *Using Social Theory: Thinking through Research.* London: Sage. pp.145–62.

Bhavnani, K-K. 1994. *Talking Politics: A Psychological Framing of Views from Youth in Britain*. Cambridge: Cambridge University Press.

Blaikie, N. 2000. *Designing Social Research*. Cambridge: Polity Press.

Bogdan, R. 1974. *Being Different: The Autobiography of Jane Fry*. New York: Wiley.

Bolling, K., Grant, C. and Donovan, J-L. 2008. *2007–08 British Crime Survey (England and Wales) Technical Report, Volume I*. London: Home Office [online]. Available at: www.data-archive.ac.uk/doc/6066/mrdoc/pdf/6066techreport1.pdf (Accessed 9 March 2009).

Brewer, E.W., Achilles, C.M. and Fuhriman, J.R. (eds) 1993. *Finding Funding: Grant Writing for the Financially Challenged Educator*. London: Sage.

Brewer, J. and Hunter, A. 1989. *Multimethod Research: A Synthesis of Styles*. Newbury Park, CA: Sage.

Brooks, N. 1989. Writing a Grant Application. In: G. Perry and F.N. Watts (eds), *Behavioural and Mental Health Research: A Handbook of Skills and Methods*. Hove, Sussex: Lawrence Erlbaum Associates.

Brunskell, H. 1998. Feminist Methodology. In: C. Seale (ed.), *Researching Society and Culture*. London: Sage. pp.37–47.

Bryman, A. 1988. *Quantity and Quality in Social Research*. London: Unwin Hyman.

Bryman, A. 1989. *Research Methods and Organisation Studies*. London: Unwin Hyman.

Bryman, A. 1990. *Analysing Quantitative Data for Social Scientists*. London: Routledge.

Bryman, A. 2004. *Social Research Methods*, 2nd edn. Oxford: Oxford University Press.

Bulmer, M. (ed.) 1982. *Social Research Ethics*. London: Macmillan.

Bulmer, M. 1984. Why Don't Sociologists Make More Use of Official Statistics? In: M. Bulmer (ed.), *Sociological Research Methods*. London: Macmillan. pp.131–52.

Bulmer, M. 2008. The Ethics of Social Research. In: N. Gilbert (ed.), *Researching Social Life*, 3rd edn. London: Sage. pp.145–61.

Burgess, R.G. 1982. *Field Research: A Sourcebook and Field Manual*. London: Allen and Unwin.

Burgess, R.G. 1984. *In the Field: An Introduction to Field Research*. London: Routledge.

Butler, D. 1994. *The Opinion Polls and the 1992 General Election*. London: Market Research Society.

Cain, M. 1990. Realist Philosophy and Standpoint Epistemologies or Feminist Criminology as a Successor Science. In: L. Gelsthorpe and A. Morris (eds), *Feminist Perspectives in Criminology*. Milton Keynes: Open University Press. pp.124–40.

Campbell, D. 1995. PC Condon Fuels Race-Crime Furore, *The Guardian*, 8 July, p.5.

Carr, W. and Kemmis, S. 1986. *Becoming Critical*. London: Falmer.

Cassell, J. 1982. Harms, Benefits, Wrongs, and Rights in Fieldwork. In: J. Sieber (ed.), *The Ethics of Social Research: Fieldwork, Regulation, and Publication*. New York: Springer. pp.7–31.

Cavendish, R. 1982. Women on the Line. London: Routledge.

Chadwick, A. 2006. *Internet Politics: States, Citizens, and New Communication Technologies*. Oxford: Oxford University Press.

Charmaz, K. 2006. Constructing Grounded Theory: A Practical Guide Through Qualitative Analysis. London: Sage.

Chayko, M. 2002. Connecting: How we Form Social Bonds and Communities in the Internet Age. New York: State University of New York Press.

Coghlan, D. and Brannick, T. 2001. *Doing Action Research in Your Own Organisation*. London: Sage.

Coley, S.M. and Scheinberg, C.A. 1990. *Proposal Writing*. London: Sage.

Collins, P. 1991. Learning from the Outsider Within: The Sociological Significance of Black Feminist Thought. In: M. Fonow and J. Cook (eds), *Beyond Methodology: Feminist Scholarship as Lived Research*. Bloomington, IN: Indiana University Press. pp.35–59.

Collins, P. 1998. Negotiating Selves: Reflections on 'Unstructured' Interviewing [online]. *Sociological Research Online*, 3(3). Available at: www.socresonline.org.uk/socresonline/3/3/2.html (Accessed 7 April 2009).

Comte, A. 1974. The Essential Comte: Selected from 'Cours de philosophie positive' by Auguste Comte (ed.), introduction by Stanislav Andreski, trans. and annot. Margaret Clarke. London: Croom Helm.

Corbin, J. and Strauss, A. 2008. *Basics of Qualitative Research: Techniques and Procedures for Developing Grounded Theory*, 3rd edn. London: Sage.

Cormack, D.F.S. 1984. *The Research Process in Nursing*. Oxford: Blackwell Scientific.

Corrigan, P. 1979. *Schooling the Smash Street Kids*. London: Macmillan.

Cotterill, P. 1992. Interviewing Women: Issues of Friendship, Vulnerability, and Power. *Women's Studies International Forum*, 15 (5/6), 593–606.

Coulthard, M., Walker, A. and Morgan, A. 2002. People's Perceptions of Their Neighbourhood and Community Involvement [online]. London: HMSO. Available at: www.gsr.ntu.ac.uk/esrcyouth.htm (Accessed 28 February 2005).

Coxon, A. 1988. Towards a Sociology of AIDS, *Social Studies Review*, January, 84–7.

Crewe, I. 1983. *Surveys of British Elections: Problems of Design, Response and Bias*. Colchester: University of Essex.

Crossman, R. 1975. *The Diaries of a Cabinet Minister, Vol. 1: Minister of Housing 1964–1966*. London: Hamilton.

Crotty, M. 1998. *The Foundations of Social Research: Meaning and Perspective in the Research Process*. London: Sage.

Crow, I. 2000. The Power of Research. In: D. Burton (ed.), *Research Training for Social Scientists*. London: Sage. pp.68–80.

Cuba, L. and Cocking, J. 1997. *How to Write about the Social Sciences*. Harlow: Longman.

Danieli, A. and Woodhams, C. 2005. Emancipatory Research Methodology and Disability: a Critique, *International Journal of Social Research Methodology*, 8 (4), 281–96.

Davis, M., Bolding, G., Hart, G., Sherr, L. and Elford, J. 2004. Reflecting on the experience of interviewing online: perspectives from the Internet and HIV study in London, *AIDS Care*, 16 (8), 944–52.

Day, A. 1996. *How to Get Work Published in Journals*. Aldershot: Gower.

De Saussure, F. 1983. *Course in General Linguistics*, trans. and annot. Roy Harris. London: Duckworth.

De Vaus, D.A. 1996. *Surveys in Social Research*, 2nd edn. London: UCL Press.

De Vaus, D.A. 2002. *Analyzing Social Science Data: 50 Key Problems in Data Analysis*. London: Sage.

Denscombe, M. 2003. *The Good Research Guide for Small-Scale Research Projects*. Buckingham: Open University Press.

Denscombe, M. and Aubrook, L. 1992. It's Just Another Piece of Schoolwork: The Ethics of Questionnaire Research on Pupils in Schools. *British Educational Research Journal*, 18, pp.113–31.

Denzin, N. 2009. *The Research Act: A Theoretical Introduction to Sociological Methods*. New Brunswick, NJ: Transaction.

Denzin, N.K. and Lincoln, Y.S. 1998a. *Collecting and Interpreting Qualitative Materials*. Thousand Oaks, CA: Sage.

Denzin, N.K. and Lincoln, Y.S. 1998b. *Strategies of Qualitative Enquiry*. Thousand Oaks, CA: Sage.

Denzin, N.K. and Lincoln, Y.S. 1998c. *The Landscape of Qualitative Research: Theories and Issues*. Thousand Oaks, CA: Sage.

Dey, I. 1993. *Qualitative Data Analysis: A User-Friendly Guide for Social Scientists*. London: Routledge.

Diener, E. and Crandall, R. 1978. *Ethics in Social and Behavioural Research*. Chicago: University of Chicago Press.

Dolnicar, S., Laesser, C. and Matus, K. 2009. Online Versus Paper: Format Effects in Tourism Surveys, *Journal of Travel Research*, 47, pp.295–316.

Dolowitz, D., Buckler, S. and Sweeney, F. 2008. *Researching On-line*. Basingstoke: Palgrave Macmillan.

Douglas, J. 1967. *The Social Meanings of Suicide*. Princeton, New Jersey: Princeton University Press.

Douglas, J. 1976. *Investigative Social Research: Individual and Team Research*. London: Sage.

Drew, C.J. 1980. *Introduction to Designing and Conducting Research*. St Louis, MO: C.B. Mosby.

Durand, J.D. 1960. Mortality Estimates from Roman Tombstone Inscriptions, *American Journal of Sociology*, 65(4), 365–73.

Durkheim, E. 1952. *Suicide*. New York: Free Press.

Engel, D. and Munger, F. 2003. *Rights of Inclusion: Law and Identity in the Life Story of Americans with Disabilities*. Chicago: University of Chicago Press.

Erikson, K. 1967. A Comment on Disguised Observation in Sociology, *Social Problems*, 12, 336–73.

ESRC (Economic and Social Research Council). 1995. *Writing for Business*. Swindon: ESRC.

ESRC, 2005. *Research Ethics Framework* [online]. Available at: www.esrc.ac.uk/ESRC InfoCentre/Images/ESRC_Re_Ethics_Frame_tcm6-11291.pdf (Accessed 7 April 2009).

Ess, C. and the AoIR ethics working committee, 2002. *Ethical decision-making and Internet research: Recommendations from the AoIR ethics working committee*. Approved by AoIR, *November 27, 2002* [online]. Available at: www.aoir.org/reports/ethics.pdf (Accessed 26 March 2009).

Eysenck, H. 1971. *Race, Intelligence and Education*. London: MT Smith.

Fay, B. 1993. The Elements of Critical Social Science. In: M. Hammersley (ed.), *Social Research: Philosophy, Politics and Practice*. London: Sage. pp.33–6.

Festinger, L., Riecken, H. and Schachter, S. 1956. *When Prophecy Fails*. New York: Harper and Row.

Fetterman, D. 1989. *Ethnography: Step by Step*. London: Sage.

Fielding, J. and Gilbert, N. 2000. *Understanding Social Statistics*. London: Sage.

Fielding, N. 1981. *The National Front*. London: Routledge.

Fielding, N. 2008. Ethnography. In: N. Gilbert (ed.), *Researching Social Life*, 3rd edn. London: Sage. pp.266–84.

Fielding, N. and Thomas, R. 2008. Qualitative Interviewing. In: N. Gilbert (ed.), *Researching Social Life*, 3rd edn. London: Sage. pp.245–65.

Finch, J. 1993. It's Great to Have Someone to Talk to: Ethics and Politics of Interviewing Women. In: M. Hammersley (ed.), *Social Research: Philosophy, Politics and Practice*. London: Sage. pp.166–80.

Finkelstein, V. 1996. The Disability Movement has Run out of Steam, *Disability Now*, 11 February.

Fletcher, D.E. 1997. Organisational Networking and Strategic Change in a Small Family Business. Unpublished doctoral thesis, Nottingham Polytechnic.

Fonow, M. and Cook, J. (eds), 1991. *Beyond Methodology: Feminist Scholarship as Lived Research*. Bloomington, IN: Indiana University Press.

Fonow, M. and Cook, J. 2005. Feminist Methodology: New Applications in the Academy and Public Policy, *Signs*, 30 (4), 2211–36.

Foucault, M. (ed.), 1980. *Power/Knowledge: Selected Interviews and Other Writings 1972–1977*. New York: Pantheon.

Foucault, M, 2001. *Madness and Civilization: A History of Insanity in the Age of Reason*. London: Routledge.

Fowler, F. 2002. *Survey Research Methods*, 3rd edn. London: Sage.

Frankfort-Nachmias, C. and Nachmias, D. 1996. *Research Methods in the Social Sciences*, 5th edn. New York: St Martin's Press.

French S. and Swain, J. 1997. Changing Disabled Research: Participatory and Emancipatory Research with Disabled People, *Physiotherapy*, 83 (1), 26–32.

Gee, J.P. 2005. *An Introduction to Discourse Analysis: Theory and Method*, 2nd edn. London: Routledge.

Gelsthorpe, L. 1992. Response to Martyn Hammersley's Paper 'On Feminist Methodology', *Sociology*, 26 (2), 213–18.

Gilbert, N. 2001. Writing about Social Research. In: N. Gilbert (ed.), *Researching Social Life*, 2nd edn. London: Sage. pp.361–77.

Gill, J. and Johnson, P. 1997. *Research Methods for Managers*. London: Paul Chapman.

Gillespie, T. 1994. Feminist Research: Reclaiming Objectivity, *Research, Policy and Planning*, 12 (2), 23–5.

Glaser, B. and Strauss, A. 1967. *The Discovery of Grounded Theory: Strategies for Qualitative Research*. New York: Aldine.

Goldthorpe, J., Lockwood, D., Bechhofer, F. and Platt, J. 1969. *The Affluent Worker in the Class Structure*. London: Cambridge University Press.

Gomm, R. 2008. *Social Research Methods: A Critical Introduction*, 2nd edn. Basingstoke: Palgrave Macmillan.

Goodley, D. and Moore, M. 2000. Disability Research: Activist Lives and the Academy, *Disability and Society*, 15 (6), 861–82.

Gorden, R. 1980. *Interviewing: Strategy, Techniques and Practice*. Homewood, IL: Dorsey.

Government Statisticians' Collective, 1993. How Official Statistics are Produced: Views from the Inside. In: M. Hammersley (ed.), *Social Research: Philosophy, Politics and Practice*. London: Sage. pp.146–65.

Graziano, A. and Raulin, M. 1997. *Research Methods: A Process of Inquiry*, 3rd edn. New York: Addison-Wesley.

Guba, E. and Lincoln, Y. (eds), 1989. *Fourth Generation Evaluation*. Newbury Park, CA: Sage.

Hakim, C. 1982. *Secondary Analysis in Social Research: A Guide to Data Sources and Methods with Examples*. London: Allen and Unwin.

Hakim, C. 1987. *Research Design: Strategies and Choices in the Design of Social Research*. London: Routledge.

Hakim, C. 1993. Research Analysis of Administrative Records. In: M. Hammersley (ed.), *Social Research: Philosophy, Politics and Practice*. London: Sage. pp.131–45.

Hammersley, M. 1992a. On Feminist Methodology, *Sociology*, 26 (2), 187–206.

Hammersley, M. 1992b. *What's Wrong with Ethnography?* London: Routledge.

Hammersley, M. 1993a. What is Social Research? In: M. Hammersley (ed.), *Principles of Social and Educational Research: Block 1*. Milton Keynes: The Open University.

Hammersley, M. (ed.), 1993b. *Social Research: Philosophy, Politics and Practice*. London: Sage.

Hammersley, M. 1995. *The Politics of Social Research*. London: Sage.

Hammersley, M. 1997. A Reply to Humphries [online]. *Sociological Research Online*, 2 (4). Available at: www.socresonline.org.uk/2/4/6.html (Accessed 20 June 2001).

Hammersley, M. and Atkinson, P. 1995. *Ethnography: Principles in Practice*, 2nd edn. London: Routledge.

Hammersley, M. and Gomm, R. 1997. Bias in Social Research, *Sociological Research Online* [online]. 2 (1). Available at: www.socresonline.org.uk/2/1/2.html (Accessed 20 June 2001).

Hamner, J. and Hearn, J. 1993. Gendered Research and Researching Gender: Women, Men and Violence. British Sociological Association Annual Conference, 'Research Imaginations'. University of Sussex, 5–8 April.

Hanfling, O. 1981. *Logical Positivism*. Oxford: Blackwell.

Harari, H., Harari, O. and White, R.V. 1985. The Reaction to Rape by American Bystanders, *Journal of Social Psychology*, 125, 653–8.

Haraway, D. 1991. *Simians, Cyborgs and Women: The Reinvention of Nature*. London: Free Association.

Harding, S. 1987. Is there a Feminist Methodology? In: S. Harding (ed.), *Feminism and Methodology*. Milton Keynes: Open University Press. pp.1–14.

Harding, S. (ed.) 2003. *The Feminist Standpoint Theory Reader: Intellectual and Political Controversies*. London: Routledge.

Harding, S. and Norberg, K. 2005. New Feminist Approaches to Social Science Methodologies: An Introduction, *Signs*, 30 (4), 2009–15.

Hart, C. 2001. *Doing a Literature Search: A Comprehensive Guide for the Social Sciences*. London: Sage.

HC Deb 1 Sep 2008 c1532W

Hekman, S. 1997. Truth and Method: Feminist Standpoint Theory Revisited, *Signs*, 22, 341–65.

Henn, M. 1998. *Opinion Polls and Volatile Electorates: Problems and Issues in Polling Volatile Electorates*. Aldershot: Ashgate.

Henn, M. and Weinstein, M. 2000. *First-time Voters' Attitudes towards Party Politics in Britain* [online]. Economic and Social Research Council. Available at: www.esrcsocietytoday.ac.uk/ESRCInfoCentre/AdvancedSearchPage1.aspx (Accessed 11 February 2009).

Henn, M., Weinstein, M. and Wring, D. 1999. *Young People and Citizenship: A Study of Opinion in Nottinghamshire*. Nottingham: Nottinghamshire County Council.

Henn, M., Weinstein, M. and Wring, M. 2002. A Generation Apart? Youth and Political Participation in Britain, *The British Journal of Politics and International Relations*, 4 (2), 167–92.

Henn, M., Young, M. and Hill, N. 1997. Labour Renewal under Blair? A Local Membership Study. In: J. Stanyer and G. Stoker (eds), *Contemporary Political Studies*. Belfast: Political Studies Association. pp.495–509.

Henwood, K. and Pidgeon, N. 1993. Qualitative Research and Psychological Theorizing. In: M. Hammersley (ed.), *Social Research: Philosophy, Politics and Practice*. London: Sage. pp.14–32.

Henwood, K. and Pidgeon, N. 1995. Remaking the Link: Qualitative Research and Feminist Standpoint Theory, *Feminism and Psychology*, 5 (1), 7–30.

Hessler, R.M. 1992. *Social Research Methods*. St Paul, MN: West.

Hewson, C., Yule, P., Laurent, D. and Vogel, C. 2003. *Internet Research methods: a Practical Guide for the Social and Behavioural Science*. London: Sage.

Hoinville, G. and Jowell, R. 1978. *Survey Research Practice*. London: Heinemann.

Holdaway, S. 1982. 'An Inside Job': A Case Study of Covert Research on the Police. In: M. Bulmer (ed.), *Social Research Ethics*. London: Macmillan. pp.59–79.

Homan, R. 1991. *The Ethics of Social Research.* London: Longman. pp.41–68.

Hood, S., Mayall, B. and Oliver, S. (eds), 1999. *Critical Issues in Social Research: Power and Prejudice.* Buckingham: Open University Press.

Howard, K. and Sharpe, J.A. 1983. *The Management of a Student Project*. Aldershot: Gower.

Humphreys, L. 1970. *Tearoom Trade: Impersonal Sex in Public Places*. Chicago: Aldine.

Humphries, B. 1997. From Critical Thought to Emancipatory Action: Contradictory Research Goals? [online]. *Sociological Research Online,* [online], 2 (1). Available at: www.socresonline.org.uk/2/1/3. html (Accessed 20 June 2001).

Humphries, B. 1998. The Baby and the Bath Water: Hammersely, Cealey Harrison and Hood-Williams and the Emancipatory Research Debate [online]. *Sociological Research Online*, 3 (1). Available at: www.socresonline.org.uk/3/1/9.html (Accessed 20 June 2001).

Inglehart, R. 1971. The Silent Revolution in Europe: Intergenerational Change in Post-Industrial Societies, *American Political Science Review*, 65, 991–1017.

Irvine, J., Miles, I. and Evans, J. (eds), 1979. *Demystifying Social Statistics*. London: Pluto Press.

Jayaratne, T. 1993. The Value of Quantitative Methodology for Feminist Research. In: M. Hammersley (ed.), *Social Research: Philosophy, Politics and Practice*. London: Sage. pp.109–23.

Jayaratne, T. and Stewart, A. 1991. Quantitative and Qualitative Methods in the Social Sciences: Current Feminist Issues and Practical Strategies. In: M. Fonow and J. Cook (eds), *Beyond Methodology: Feminist Scholarship as Lived Research*. Bloomington, IN: Indiana University Press. pp.85–106.

Jones, J. 1995. *Understanding Psychological Science*. New York: HarperCollins.

Jones, P. 1993. *Studying Society: Sociological Theories and Research Practices*. London: Collins Educational.

Jupp, V. and Norris, C. 1993. Traditions in Documentary Analysis. In: M. Hammersley (ed.), *Social Research: Philosophy, Politics and Practice*. London: Sage. pp.37–51.

Kane, E. 1990. *Doing Your Own Research: Basic Descriptive Research in the Social Sciences and Humanities*. London: Boyars.

Katz, J. 1972. *Experimentation with Human Beings*. New York: Russell Sage.

Kelly, L., Burton, S. and Regal, L. 1994. Researching Women's Lives or Studying Women's Oppression? Reflections on what Constitutes Feminist Research. In: M. Maynard and J. Purvis (eds), *Researching Women's Lives from a Feminist Perspective*. London: Taylor & Francis. pp.27–48.

Kelman, H. 1972. The Rights of the Subjects in Social Research: An Analysis in Terms of Relative Power and Legitimacy, *American Sociologist*, 27, 989–1015.

Kershaw, C., Nichoas, S. and Walker, A. (eds). 2008. *Crime in England and Wales 2007/08: Findings from the British Crime Survey and police recorded crime. Home Office Statistical Bulletin 07/08*. London: Home Office [online]. Available at: www.homeoffice.gov.uk/rds/pdfs08/hosb0708.pdf (Accessed 27 March 2009).

Kesby, M. 2005. Retheorising Empowerment-through-Participation as a Performance in Space: Beyond Tyranny to Transformation, *Signs*, 30 (4), 2037–76.

Kibby, M. 2005. Email Forwardables: Folklore in the Age of the Internet, *New Media Society,* 2005 (7) pp.770–90.

Kincheloe, J. and McLaren, P. Rethinking Critical Theory and Qualitative Research. In: N. Denzin and Y. Lincoln, (eds), *The Landscape of Qualitative Research: Theories and Issues*. Thousand Oaks, CA: Sage. pp.260–99.

Kirk, J. and Miller, M.L. 1986. *Reliability and Validity in Qualitative Research*. London: Sage.

Kirsch, G. 2005. Friendship, Friendliness, and Feminist Fieldwork, *Signs*, 30 (4), 2163–72.

Kitchen, R. 2000. The Researched Opinions on Research: Disabled People and Disability Research, *Disability and Society*, 15, 25–47.

Kitzinger, C. 2007. Feminist Approaches. In: C. Seale, G. Gobo, J. Gubrium and D. Silverman (eds), *Qualitative Research Practice*. London: Sage. pp.113–28.

Kolakowski, L. 1993. An Overview of Positivism. In: M. Hammersley (ed.), *Social Research: Philosophy, Politics and Practice*. London: Sage. pp.1–8.

Krathwohl, D.R. 1988. *How to Prepare a Research Project: Guidelines for Funding and Dissertations in the Social and Behavioural Sciences*. New York: Syracuse University Press.

Krueger, R.A. 1994. *Focus Groups: A Practical Guide for Applied Research*. Thousand Oaks, CA: Sage.

Kuhn, T. 1970. *The Structure of Scientific Revolutions*. Chicago: University of Chicago Press.

Kumar, R. 1999. *Research Methodology: A Step-by-Step Guide for Beginners*. London: Sage.

Kuzwayo, E. 1985. *Call Me Woman*. London: Women's Press.

Lasswell, H. 1942. Communications Research and Politics. In: D. Waples (ed.), *Print, Radio and Film in a Democracy*. Chicago: University of Chicago Press.

Laurie, H. and Sullivan, O. 1990. Combining Qualitative and Quantitative Data in the Longitudinal Study of Household Allocations, *Sociological Review*, 1 (39), pp.113–30.

Leedy, P.D. 1989. *Practical Research: Planning and Design*. London: Macmillan.

Letherby, G. 2004. Quoting and Counting: An Autobiographical Response to Oakley, *Sociology*, 38, 175–89.

Levitas, R. and Guy, W. 1996. *Interpreting Official Statistics*. London: Routledge.

Lewin, K. 1946. Action Research and Minority Problems, *Journal of Social Issues*, 2, 34–6.

Locke, L.F., Spirduso, W.W. and Silverman, S.J. 2000. Proposals That Work: A Guide for Planning *Dissertations and Grant Proposals*. London: Sage.

Lofland, J. and Lofland, L. 1995. *Analyzing Social Settings: A Guide to Qualitative Observation and Analysis*, 3rd edn. Belmont, CA: Wadsworth.

Macdonald, K. and Tipton, C. 2001. Using Documents. In: N. Gilbert (ed.), *Researching Social Life*, 2nd edn. London: Sage. pp.194–210.

Mann, C. and Stewart, F. 2000. *Internet Communication and Qualitative Research: A Handbook for Researching Online*. London: Sage.

Market Research Society, 1992. *Report of The Market Research Society Inquiry Into the 1992 General Election*. London: Market Research Society.

Marsh, C. 1979. Problems With Surveys: Method or Epistemology?, *Sociology*, 13 (2), 293–305.

Marsh, C. 1982. *The Survey Method: The Contribution of Surveys to Sociological Explanation*. London: George Allen and Unwin.

Martinson, R. 1974. What Works? Questions and Answers About Prison Reform, *Public Interest*, 35, 22–45.

Mason, J. 1996. *Qualitative Interviewing*. London: Sage.

May, T. 2001. *Social Research: Issues, Methods and Process*, 3rd edn. Buckingham: Open University Press.

Mayhew, H. 1861–2. *London Labour and the London Poor: A Cyclopaedia of the Conditions and Earnings of those that will work, those that cannot work, and those that will not work*, 4 vols. London: Griffin Bohn.

Maynard, M. 1994. Methods, Practice and Epistemology: The Debate about Feminism and Research. In: M. Maynard and J. Purvis (eds), *Researching Women's Lives from a Feminist Perspective*. London: Taylor & Francis. pp.10–26.

Maynard, M. 1998. Feminists' Knowledge and Knowledge of Feminisms: Epistemology, Theory, Methodology and Method. In: T. May and M. Williams (eds), *Knowing the Social World*. Buckingham: Open University Press. pp.120–37.

McRobbie, A. 1991. *Feminism and Youth Culture: From Jackie to Just Seventeen*. London: Macmillan.

Mies, M. 1993. Towards a Methodology for Feminist Research. In: M. Hammersley (ed.), *Social Research: Philosophy, Politics and Practice*. London. pp.64–82.

Miles, M.B. and Huberman, A.M. 1994. *Qualitative Data Analysis: An Expanded Sourcebook*, 2nd edn. London: Sage.

Miles, I. and Irvine, J. 1979. The Critique of Official Statistics. In: J. Irvine, I. Miles and J. Evans (eds), *Demystifying Social Statistics*. London: Pluto Press. pp.113–29.

Milgram, S. 1963. Behavioural Study of Obedience, *Journal of Abnormal and Social Psychology*, 6, 371–8.

Millen, D. 1997. Some Methodological and Epistemological Issues Raised by Doing Feminist Research on Non-Feminists. *Sociological Research Online* [online]. 2 (3). Available at: www.socresonline.org.uk/socresonline/2/3/3/html (Accessed 18 May 1999).

Miller, D.C. 1991. *Handbook of Research Design and Social Measurement*. London: Sage.

Mishler, E. 1986. *Research Interviewing*. Cambridge, MA: Harvard University Press.

McKay, G. 1998. ed., *DiY Culture: Party and Protest in Nineties Britain*. London: Verso.

Moon, N. 1997. The Opinion Polls Since 1992 – Lessons Learned and Changes Made, *Social Research Association News*, May, 5–6.

Morgan, D.L. and Kreuger, R.A. 1998. *The Focus Group Kit Vols 1–6*. Thousand Oaks, CA: Sage.

Moser, C. and Kalton, G. 1971. *Survey Methods in Social Investigation*. London: Heinemann.

Moxley, J. 1992. *Publish, Don't Perish: The Scholar's Guide to Academic Writing and Publishing*. London: Greenwood Press.

Murthy, D., 2008. Digital Ethnography: An Examination of the Use of New Technologies for Social Research, *Sociology*, 42, 837–55.

Myhill, A. and Allen, J. 2002. *Rape and Sexual Assault of Women: Findings from the British Crime Survey. Findings 159*. London: Home Office [online]. Available at: www.homeoffice.gov.uk/rds/pdfs2/r159.pdf (Accessed 27 March 2009).

Neuman, W. 2006. *Social Research Methods: Qualitative and Quantitative Approaches*, 6th edn. Boston: Allyn and Bacon.

Newell, R. 1993. Questionnaires. In: N. Gilbert (ed.), *Researching Social Life*. London: Sage. pp.94–115.

Oakley, A. 1981. Interviewing Women: A Contradiction in Terms. In: H. Roberts (ed.), *Doing Feminist Research*. London: Routledge & Kegan Paul. pp.30–61.

Oakley, A. 1999. People's Ways of Knowing: Gender and Methodology. In: S. Hood, B. Mayall and S. Oliver (eds), *Critical issues in Social Research: Power and Prejudice*. Buckingham: Open University Press, pp.154–70.

Oakley, A. 2000. *Experiments in Knowing: Gender and Methods in the Social Sciences*. Cambridge: Polity Press.

Oakley, A. and Oakley, R. 1979. Sexism in Official Statistics. In: J. Irvine, I. Miles and J. Evans (eds), *Demystifying Social Statistics*. London: Pluto Press. pp.172–89.

Obama, B.H. 2009. Presidential Inauguration Speech delivered in Washington DC, USA, Jan 21.

O'Connell Davidson, J. and Layder, D. 1994. *Methods: Sex and Madness*. London: Routledge.

Ó Dochartaigh, N. 2007. *Internet Research Skills*. London: Sage.

Office for National Statistics, 2008. Internet Access 2008: Households and Individuals: First Release [online]. Available at: www.statistics.gov.uk/pdfdir/iahi0808.pdf (Accessed 20 March 2009).

Olesen, V. 1998. Feminisms and Models of Qualitative Research. In: N. Denzin and Y. Lincoln (eds), *The Landscape of Qualitative Research: Theories and Issues*. Thousand Oaks, CA: Sage. pp.300–32.

Oliver, M. 1996. *Understanding Disability: From Theory to Practice*. Basingstoke: Macmillan.

Oliver, M. 2002a. Changing the Social Relations of Research Production, *Disability, Handicap and Society*, 7 (2), 101–15.

Oliver, M. 2002b. *Emancipatory Research: A Vehicle for Social Transformation or Policy Development*. First Annual Disability Research Seminar, Centre for Disability Studies, University College, Dublin, 3 December.

O'Muircheartaigh, C. 1997. Election 97: A Triumph for the Pollsters?, *Research, Market Research Society*, June, 14–22.

O'Toole, T., Lister, M., Marsh, D., Jones, S. and McDonagh, A. 2003. Tuning out or Left out? Participation and Non-Participation among Young People, *Contemporary Politics*, 9 (1), 45–61.

Oppenheim, A. 1993. *Questionnaire Design, Interviewing and Attitude Measurement*, 2nd edn. Aldershot: Gower.

Parry, G., Moyser, G. and Day, N. 1992. *Political Participation and Democracy in Britain*. Cambridge: Cambridge University Press.

Patrick, J. 1973. *A Glasgow Gang Observed*. London: Eyre-Methuen.

Patton, M. 1987. *How to Use Qualitative Methods in Evaluation*. London: Sage.

Pawson, R. 1989. *A Measure for Measures: A Manifesto for Empirical Sociology*. London: Routledge.

Pawson, R. and Tilley, N. 1997. *Realistic Evaluation*. London: Sage.

Peräkylä, A. 1997. Reliability and Validity in Research Based on Tapes and Transcripts. In: D. Silverman (ed.), *Qualitative Research: Theory, Method and Practice*. London: Sage. pp.201–20.

Piliavin, I.M., Rodin, J. and Piliavin, A. 1969. Good Samaritanism: An Underground Phenomenon, *Journal of Personality and Social Psychology*, 13, 289–99.

Platt, J. 1981. Evidence and Proof in Documentary Research and Some Specific Problems of Documentary Research, *Sociological Review*, 29 (1), 31–52.

Platt, S. and Kreitman, N. 1985. Parasuicide and Unemployment Among Men in Edinburgh 1968–1982, *Psychological Medicine*, 15, 113–23.

Popper, K. 1959. *The Logic of Scientific Discovery*. London: Hutchinson.

Popper, K. 1972. *Objective Knowledge*. Oxford: Clarendon.

Potter, J. and Wetherell, M. 1987. *Discourse and Social Psychology: Beyond Attitudes and Behaviour*. London: Sage.

Powdermaker, H. 1966. *Stranger and Friend: The Way of an Anthropologist*. New York: W. W. Norton.

Priestly, M. 1997. Who's Research? A Personal Audit. In: C. Barnes and G. Mercer, (eds) *Doing Disability Research*. University of Leeds: Disability Press. pp.88–107.

Pryke, M., Rose, G. and Whatmore, S. (eds) 2003. *Using Social Theory: Thinking Through Research*. London: Sage.

Punch, K.P. 2005. *Introduction to Social Research: Quantitative and Qualitative Approaches*, 2nd edn. London: Sage.

Punch, K.P. 2006. *Developing Effective Research Proposals*, 2nd edn. London: Sage.

Punch, M. 1993. Observation and the Police: The Research Experience. In: M. Hammersley (ed.), *Social Research: Philosophy, Politics and Practice*. London: Sage. pp.181–99.

Punch, M. 1986. *The Politics and Ethics of Fieldwork*. Beverly Hills, CA: Sage.

Punch, M. 1998. Politics and Ethics in Qualitative Research. In: N. Denzin and Y. Lincoln (eds), *The Landscape of Qualitative Research: Theories and Issues*. London: Sage. pp.156–84.

Rabinowitz, V. and Martin, D. 2001. Choices and Consequences: Methodological Issues in the Study of Gender. In: R. Unger, (ed.), *Handbook of the Psychology of Women and Gender*. New York: Wiley. pp.29–52.

Ramazanoglu, C. 1992. On Feminist Methodology: Male Reason Versus Female Empowerment, *Sociology*, 26 (2), 213–18.

Ramazanoglu, C. 2002. *Feminist Methodology: Challenges and Choices*. London: Sage.

Reinharz, S. 1983. Experiential Analysis: A Contribution to Feminist Research. In G. Bowles and R. Duelli Klein (eds), *Theories of Women's Studies*. London: Routledge & Kegan Paul. pp.162–92.

Reinharz, S. 1992. *Feminist Methods in Social Research*. Oxford: Oxford University Press.

Reiss, A. 1971. *The Police and Public*. New Haven, CT: Yale University Press.

Rheingold, H. 2000. *The Virtual Community: Homesteading on the Electronic Frontier.* Massachusetts: MIT Press.

Roberts, H. (ed.), 1990. *Doing Feminist Research*. London: Routledge & Kegan Paul.

Rodgers, J. 1999. Trying to get it Right: Undertaking Research involving People with Learning Difficulties, *Disability and Society*, 11, 317–32.

Roethlisberger, F.J. and Dickson, W.J. 1939. *Management and the Worker*. Cambridge, MA: Harvard University Press.

Roker, D. and Eden, K. 2002. *'...Doing Something': Young People as Social Actors*. Leicester: National Youth Agency.

Romm, N. 1997. Becoming More Accountable: A Comment on Hammersley and Gomm [online], *Sociological Research Online*, 2 (1), 2 (3). Available at: www.socresonline.org.uk/socresonline/2/3/2/html (Accessed 18 May 1999).

Roy, D. 1952. Quota Restriction and Goldbricking in a Machine Shop, *American Journal of Sociology*, 67 (2), 427–42.

Ruebhausen, M. and Brim, O. 1966. Privacy and Behaviour in Research, *American Psychologist*, 21, 432.

Ryen, A. 2007. Ethical Issues. In: C. Seale, G. Gobo, J. Gubrium and D. Silverman (eds), *Qualitative Research Practice*. London: Sage. pp.218–35.

Sacks, H. 1995. *Lectures on Conversation* (ed.). E.A. Schegloff with an introduction by G. Jefferson. Oxford: Blackwell.

Salkind, N. 2003. *Statistics for People Who (Think They) Hate Statistics*. London: Sage.

Sapsford, R. 1993. Problems, Cases and the Logic of Research Studies. In: M. Hammersley (ed.), *Principles of Social and Educational Research*. Milton Keynes: The Open University.

Sapsford, R. 1999. *Survey Research*. London: Sage.

Sarantakos, S. 2005. *Social Research*, 3rd edn. Basingstoke: Macmillan.

Schofield, W. 1993. Sample Surveys. In: M. Hammersley (ed.), *Principles of Social and Educational Research: Block 2*. Milton Keynes: The Open University. pp.75–108.

Schostak, J. and Schostak, J. 2008. *Radical Research: Designing, Developing and Writing Research to Make a Difference*. London: Routledge.

Schumacher, D. 1992. *Get Funded!: A Practical Guide for Scholars Seeking Research Support from Business*. London: Sage.

Schutt, R. 1999. *Investigating the Social World*. London: Sage.

Schwartz, M. 1964. The Mental Hospital: The Researched Person in the Disturbed World. In: A. Vidich, J. Benson and M. Stein (eds), *Reflections on Community Studies*. New York: Harper and Row. pp.85–117.

Seale, C. 1998. *Researching Society and Culture*. London: Sage.

Seeman, M. 1972. On the Meaning of Alienation. Reprinted in: C. Frankfort-Nachmias and D. Nachmias (eds) 1996. *Research Methods in the Social Sciences*, 5th edn. New York: St Martin's Press. pp.32–3.

Seymour, W.S. 2001. In the Flesh or Online? Exploring Qualitative Research Methodologies, *Qualitative Research*, 2001 (1), 147–68.

Short, J., Williams, E. and Christie, B. 1976. *The Social Psychology of Telecommunications*. London: Wiley.

Sieber, J. 1992. *Planning Ethically Responsible Research*. Newbury Park, CA: Sage.

Silver, C. 2008. Participatory Approaches to Social Research. In N. Gilbert (ed.), *Researching Social Life*, 3rd edn. London: Sage. pp.101–24.

Silverman, D. 1998. *Harvey Sacks: Social Science and Conversation Analysis*. Oxford: Oxford University Press.

Silverman, D. 2001. *Interpreting Qualitative Data: Methods for Analysing Talk, Text and Interaction*, 2nd edn. London: Sage.

Silverman, D. 2004. *Qualitative Research: Theory, Method and Practice*, 2nd edn. London: Sage.

Silverman, D. 2005. *Doing Qualitative Research: A Practical Handbook*, 2nd edn. London: Sage.

Simpson, G. 1952. Editor's Preface. In: E. Durkheim, *Suicide*. New York: Free Press. pp.9–12.

Slattery, M. 1986. *Official Statistics*. London: Tavistock.

Smart, C. 1984. *The Ties That Bind: Law, Marriage, and the Reproduction of Patriarchal Relations*. London: Routledge & Kegan Paul.

SRA (Social Research Association) 2003. *Ethical Guidelines* [online]. Available at: www.the-sra.org.uk/documents/pdfs/ethics03.pdf (Accessed 7 April 2009).

Stanley, L. and Wise, S. 1983. *Breaking Out: Feminist Consciousness and Feminist Research*. London: Routledge & Kegan Paul.

Stavenhagen, R. 1993. Decolonializing Applied Social Sciences. In: M. Hammersley (ed.), *Social Research: Philosophy, Politics and Practice*. London: Sage. pp.52–63.

Stern, S.R. 2003. Encountering Distressing Information in Online Research: A Consideration of Legal and Ethical Responsibilities, *New Media Society*, 5 (2), 249–66.

Stone, E. and Priestly, M. 1996. Parasites, Pawns and Partners: Disability Research and the Role of Non-Disabled Researchers, *British Journal of Sociology*, 47, 699–716.

Strange, V., Oakley, A. and Forrest, S. 2003. Mixed-sex or Single-sex Sex Education: How Would Young People Like Their Sex Education and Why?, *Gender & Education*, 15 (2), 201–14.

Strauss, A. and Corbin, J. 1990. *Basics of Qualitative Research: Grounded Theory Procedures and Techniques*. London: Sage.

Strauss, A. and Corbin, J. 1998. *Basics of Qualitative Research: Techniques and Procedures for Developing Grounded Theory*, 2nd edn. London: Sage.

Swain, J., French, S., Barnes, C. and Thomas, C. (eds) 2004. *Disabling Barriers – Enabling Environments*, 2nd edn. London: Sage.

Thatcher, M. 1993. *The Downing Street Years*. London: HarperCollins.

Thomas, R. 1996. Statistics as Organizational Products [online], *Sociological Research Online*. 1 (3). Available at: www.socresonline.org.uk/1/3/5.html (Accessed: 30 March 2009).

Thomas, W. and Znaniecki, F. 1918–20. *The Polish Peasant in Europe and America*. Chicago: University of Chicago Press.

Thompson, H. 1967. *Hell's Angels*. Harmondsworth: Penguin.

*Tonight with Trevor McDonald*, 2005. TV, ITV1, Jul 5.

Todd, M. and Taylor, G. (eds) 2003. *Democracy and Participation: Popular Protest and New Social Movements*. London: Merlin Press.

Tonkiss, F. 1998. The History of the Social Survey. In: C. Seale (ed.), *Researching Society and Culture*. London: Sage. pp.58–71.

Townend, D. 2000. How Does Substantive Law Currently Regulate Social Science Research? In: D. Burton (ed.), *Research Training for Social Scientists*. London: Sage. pp.113–21.

Trotsky, L. 1975. *My Life: An Attempt at an Autobiography*. Harmondsworth: Penguin.

US Census Bureau 2007. Current Population Survey (October 2007) [online]. Available at: www.ntia.doc.gov/reports/2008/Table_HouseholdInternet2007.pdf (Accessed 20 March 2009).

Van Maanen, J. 1979. On Watching the Watchers. In: P. Manning and J. Van Maanen (eds), *Policing: A View from the Street*. Santa Monica, CA: Goodyear. pp.309–49.

Verba, S. and Nie, N. 1972. *Participation in America: Political Democracy and Social Equality*. New York: Harper and Row.

Verma, G.K. and Mallick, K. 1999. *Researching Education*. London: Falmer Press.

Von Wright, G.H. 1993. Two Traditions. In: M. Hammersley (ed.), *Social Research: Philosophy, Politics and Practice*. London: Sage. pp.9–13.

Walklate, S. 2007. *Understanding Criminology: Current Theoretical Debates*, 3rd edn. Maidenhead: McGraw Hill International.

Wall, D. 1999. *Earth First! and the Anti-Roads Movement: Radical Environmentalism and Comparative Social Movements*. London: Routledge.

Walmsley, J. and Johnson, K. 2003. *Inclusive Research with People with Learning Disabilities – Past, Present and Future*. London: Jessica Kingsley Publishers.

Walther, J. 1996. Computer-Mediated Communication: Impersonal, Interpersonal, and Hyperpersonal Interaction. *Communication Research,* 23 (3).

Ward Schofield, J. 1993. Increasing the Generalisability of Qualitative Research. In: M. Hammersley (ed.), *Social Research: Philosophy, Politics and Practice*. London: Sage. pp.200–25.

Warner, R.M. 2008. *Applied Statistics: From Bivariate Through Multivariate Techniques*. London: Sage.

Warren, C. 1981. *Gender Issues in Field Research*. London: Sage.

Warwick, D. 1983. The Politics and Ethics of Field Research. In: M. Bulmer and D. Warwick (eds), *Social Research in Developing Countries: Surveys and Censuses in the Third World*. Chichester: Wiley. pp.315–30.

Waterhouse, R. 1994. Census Figures are Abandoned after Two Million are Missed, *The Guardian*, 23 December, p.1.

Webb, E.J., Campbell, D.T., Schwartz, R.D. and Sechrest, L. 1984. The Use of Archival Sources in Social Research. In: M. Bulmer (ed.), *Sociological Research Methods*. London: Macmillan. pp.113–30.

Weber, M. 1949. *The Methodology of the Social Sciences*. New York: Free Press.

Weinstein, M. 2005. A Comparative Analysis of Youth Activism in Mainstream Political Parties and New Social Movements in Britain. Unpublished PhD thesis, Nottingham Trent University.

Weisberg, H., Krosnick, J. and Bowen, B. 1996. An Introduction to Survey Research, Polling and Data Analysis, 3rd edn. London: Sage.

Wetherell, M., Taylor, S. and Yates, S. (eds) 2001. *Discourse as Data: A Guide for Analysis.* London: Sage.

White, C., Bruce, S. and Ritchie, J. 2000. *Young People's Politics: Political Interest and Engagement Amongst 14–24 year-olds.* York: Joseph Rowntree Foundation.

Willis, P. 1977. *Learning to Labour*. Farnborough: Saxon House.

Winter, R. and Munn-Giddings, C. 2001. *A Handbook for Action Research in Health and Social Care.* London: Routledge.

Wolhuter, L., Olley, N. and Denham, D. 2008. *Victimology: Victimisation and Victims' Rights*. London: Taylor & Francis.

Woofitt, R. 2001. Researching Psychic Practitioners. In: Wetherell, M., Taylor, S. and Yates, S.J. (ed.), *Discourse as Data: A Guide for Analysis*. London: Sage.

Wright Mills, C. 1959. The Sociological Imagination. In: R.G. Burgess, *Field Research: A Sourcebook and Field Manual*. London: Allen and Unwin. p. 209.

Yablonsky, L. 1968. *The Hippy Trip.* Harmondsworth: Penguin.

Zarb, G. 2002. On the Road to Damascus: First Steps Towards Changing the Relations of Disability Research Production, *Disability, Handicap and Society*, 7 (2), 125–38.

Zimbardo, P. 1973. On the Ethics of Intervention in Human Psychological Research, *Cognition*, 2, 243–56.

Zuckerberg, M. 2009. *On Facebook, People Own and Control Their Information* [Online]. 16 February. Available at: blog.facebook.com/blog.php?post=54434097130 (Accessed 26 March 2009).

# INDEX